Praise for John Feinstein's

A MARCH TO MADNESS

"Fascinating. . . . There's a tension in *A March to Madness* that keeps the pages turning." — Charles Hirshberg, *Sports Illustrated*

"A meticulously detailed account of a season of college basketball. . . . Full of insider's jargon, the drama of personal rivalries, the melodrama of hard-fought contests. . . . Fans will find everything in this book: the games, the locker-room pep talks, the coaches' sleepless nights, their philosophies about attitude and heart, their personal rivalries. . . . Even those of us not fascinated by college basketball are likely to be gripped by some passages in Mr. Feinstein's book about the intense striving involved in these games and the capriciousness of fate." — Richard Bernstein, *New York Times*

"John Feinstein didn't invent the literary construct of following subjects intimately through a chronological series of events. . . . But Feinstein has become the modern master of the formula. A sport hasn't really arrived until Feinstein has spent a season with it." — Bob Ford, *Philadelphia Inquirer*

"If you were to ask for a guide on your in-depth tour of college basketball, you could not do better than John Feinstein. . . . A worthy successor to *A Season on the Brink* — and maybe a little better than that. . . . Reading *A March to Madness* is a high-energy experience. Just like watching the game that it so ably explores and describes." — Geoffrey Norman, *American Way*

"John Feinstein has written his best basketball book. . . . The talent that separates Mr. Feinstein from so many others is an unparalleled knack among sportswriters for recognizing a good story."

— Mike DeCourcy, *Cincinnati Enquirer*

"What keeps the reader involved are the anecdotes, insights, and unguarded moments that Feinstein liberally sprinkles amid the play-by-play."

— Jim Shear, *Hartford Courant*

"Like the ACC, the nation's most competitive college league, *A March to Madness* is a winner. You won't be able to put it down. . . . Feinstein explores the minds, hearts, and souls of the league's coaches in a way that makes you feel like you're standing beside them in the locker room. . . . In the end, you'll wish Feinstein would spend all of his time around the ACC. That way you'd know the *real* story behind the league's annual march to madness."

— Jim Ducibella, *Virginian-Pilot*

"Readers know how this book turns out and they won't care. *A March to Madness* is an excellent look at coaching at the sport's highest level."

— Budd Bailey, *Bookpage*

Feinstein's access to all nine coaches yields some rich, dramatic stories. . . . Feinstein's beat, it turns out, isn't sports; it's human nature."

— Alex Tresniowski, *People*

"*A March to Madness* is 464 pages of excitement in the guise of multiple biography, as the coaches' lives and methods are described in the course of an exciting and heart-straining season. The book, which must have been a bear of a job to undertake, is Feinstein's finest achievement."

— Clark Cox, *The Pilot*

"As he has proven repeatedly, this writer knows how to use his access to great advantage, finding the telling moment or detail, reading the mindset of participating athletes and coaches with uncommon astuteness. This volume is no exception. Moreover, he pulls off the difficult feat of keeping nine narratives moving relatively seamlessly. . . . Feinstein has a great shooting touch, and this one is a three-pointer from downtown. Swish!" — *Kirkus Reviews*

"Another winner. . . . Almost everything Feinstein writes turns into a bestseller; he's that good." — *Richmond Times-Dispatch*

"A . . . tour de force full of anecdotes, loaded with background information, and fun to read." —*The Sporting News*

"Feinstein returns to his true passion — basketball. . . . He displays a gift of storytelling about college basketball that is unparalleled." — Everett J. Merrill, *Newark Star-Ledger*

"If you're an ACC basketball fan, this book is for you. If there are ACC basketball fans in your family, you need to read this to understand why they act the way they do. John Feinstein has written seven other sports books, but I think this one is his best. Feinstein writes well; that's been shown in each of his books. But, more than that, he knows what interests the reader. . . . Reading Feinstein's report is like sitting down with a bunch of old friends and talking about last year." — Mary Garber, *Winston Salem-Journal*

Also by John Feinstein

John Feinstein

A MARCH
TO MADNESS

The View from the Floor in the Atlantic Coast Conference

LITTLE, BROWN AND COMPANY

Boston   New York   London

Originally published in hardcover by Little, Brown and Company, 1998
First Back Bay paperback edition, 1999

Library of Congress Cataloging-in-Publication Data

A march to madness : the view from the floor in the Atlantic Coast
    Conference / John Feinstein — 1st ed.
            p.   cm.
      Includes index.
      ISBN 0-316-27740-1(hc)   0-316-27712-6 (pb)
      1. Atlantic Coast Conference.   2. Basketball — United States.
    GV885.415.A85M37   1997
    796.323′63′0975 — dc21   97-31060

10   9   8   7   6   5   4   3   2   1

MV-NY

Printed in the United States of America

For the three people who first taught me about newspapers and about ACC basketball . . .

Susan Carol Robinson

David Arneke

Steve Garland

Contents

Introduction

ON THE MORNING of the 1997 national championship game, I was sitting in an Indianapolis coffee shop with a couple of friends when I heard someone calling my name. I looked over and saw a couple, probably in their late sixties, sitting at a table diagonally across from where we were seated.

"John, who do you like tonight?" the man said once I looked in his direction.

I was prepared for the question. Since I appear on ESPN during the basketball season, it's not unusual for basketball fans to recognize me. Most are either polite or friendly. Some are neither. These folks fell into the polite and friendly category. So, I smiled and gave them the answer I had been giving everyone since late Saturday night.

"I like the Wildcats," I said firmly.

This was my kind of pick, since the final matched the Kentucky Wildcats and the Arizona Wildcats. The couple looked at me blankly for a moment, figured out that I was firmly entrenched on a comfortable fence, and laughed. The man walked over to our table and introduced himself.

"If you don't want to answer that one," he said, check in hand, his wife now standing next to him, "answer a serious question for me."

I'm not big on serious questions, especially when I don't know the motivation behind them. Then again, if the serious question was something like, "How do you like Indy?" I could handle it. (I love Indy.)

"What's the question?" I asked, cautiously.

"You've been around," the man said. So far no argument. "Didn't you think Dean got outcoached on Saturday?"

I burst out laughing. Dean Smith has won more college basketball games (879) than anyone who has ever lived. He is a role model for almost anyone who has ever coached at any level. In 1,132 games as a head coach, I would guess he's been outcoached a half dozen times. Maybe. Of course, since I am a 1977 graduate of Duke and since Smith has coached all of those 1,132 games eleven miles down the road at the University of North Carolina, many people assume that my relationship with Smith is a hostile one. That's just not true. We agree often and disagree often. He is as stubborn and competitive as anyone I have ever met, intensely shy and difficult to interview because he literally begins squirming when you ask any question that is even a little bit personal. But I have tremendous respect for him and the program he has created over these many years in Chapel Hill.

"Let me ask you a question," I said in reply to the query about Dean being outcoached. "Was it Dean's fault that his best shooter was one for thirteen? Was it his fault that his team couldn't make a jump shot all day? Is that coaching?"

The man shook his head. "It's just that Dean's sixty-six. Maybe the game is passing him by."

This had to be a setup. "Yeah, I guess you're right," I said. "After all, he only won twenty-eight games this year and got to the Final Four. And he'd only won sixteen straight games before Saturday."

Now the man looked surprised. "I'm not saying he hasn't been a wonderful coach," he said. "You see, we're Carolina fans and we just want what's best for the Tar Heels."

Of course. What's best for the Tar Heels. "Sir, with all due respect, if you think that Dean Smith not coaching Carolina is what's best for the Tar Heels, then you don't know anything at all about basketball."

Now, he was put out. "I've been watching basketball since before you were born."

"I don't doubt it. I guess we'll just have to agree to disagree."

His wife was tugging on his arm. "Seriously," he said one more time, "who do you really like tonight?"

"I really like the Wildcats."

The conversation reminded me why coaching is never as easy or glamorous as it appears to be, especially in the Atlantic Coast Conference. After all, if the winningest coach ever can be a target for disgruntled fans — his own fans — after losing a Final Four game, who isn't a target? My guess is the couple in Indy do not represent a majority of Carolina fans, but I would also guess they aren't unique either.

And it isn't as if Carolina fans are any different from fans at other schools. Here is a small sampling of comments I have heard from ACC fans — season-ticket-holder types who follow the game closely — in the last twelve months:

"He's lost interest. He isn't working at recruiting, that's why we aren't getting any players. He ought to just go coach in the NBA and we'll get someone in here who cares" (longtime Maryland fan and booster talking about Gary Williams after the Terrapins had reached the NCAA tournament for a third straight year in 1996 but lost in the first round).

"I can't believe we're paying him that kind of money. We could get a dozen guys in there to do what he's done" (Wake Forest alumnus and self-proclaimed basketball expert talking about Dave Odom, who has taken a program that had missed the NCAAs for five straight years before he arrived to seven straight tournaments and back-to-back ACC titles in '95 and '96 after Wake had gone thirty-three years without winning one).

"He owes us all an explanation for not playing Newton. If he had played Newton, we might have gone to the Final Four" (Duke fan angered by the benching of senior center Greg Newton, insisting that he knows more basketball than Mike Krzyzewski, who has only won two national titles and been to seven Final Fours and who won the ACC regular season title in 1997 after sitting Newton down).

This is just a sampling. Trust me, I could go on. Every coach alive is second-guessed by his fans, no matter how much he has won or how long he has been a consistent winner. Coaches understand intellectually that it comes with the territory. But they are all sensitive to it and are often angered by it. They make a lot of money because the public cares about what they do. This is the price they pay.

That's true, to some degree, at every level of coaching, including Little League or peewee, where there's always some parent whose kid isn't playing enough. Big-time college basketball is a coach's game. The players, no matter how brilliant, come and go — faster all the time these days — so the constant is the coaches. Inevitably, they become the stars, even someone spotlight-shy like Smith. They become rich and famous, and in some cases become raving, raging egomaniacs.

There's nothing wrong with criticizing coaches. They make mistakes like the rest of us, and, for the money they are paid, they should answer to the public to some degree. It is the rush to judgment that I find amazing. Dean Smith loses one game and he's over the hill? And this sort of hysteria isn't limited to fans. Read some of the newspaper clippings from last January when Carolina was 0–3 in the ACC. When it comes to hysteria, there's no place like the ACC during basketball season.

My first memories of ACC basketball date back to the 1960s, when the ACC game of the week was televised in New York City on WPIX on tape delay. I would always check the newspaper in the morning to find out what the ACC TV game was and then try to make a point not to know the final score before the game came on. I remember the 1966 Duke team with Bob Verga and Jeff Mullins that lost to Kentucky in the national semifinals and the Larry Miller Carolina team that lost to Dayton in the same round a year later. I also remember that the TV announcers seemed to think that Charles Scott's full name was actually "Charles Scott the first black player in the history of the University of North Carolina."

It had never occurred to me that there were teams that didn't have black players, so I really didn't understand what all the hoo-ha was about until I was much older. After all, the greatest basketball player alive as far as I was concerned was Willis Reed, and Walt Frazier and Cazzie Russell weren't far behind.

As a teenager, I used to go to every game of the National Invitation Tournament. Back then, the entire tournament was played in Madison

Square Garden. I remember going to a Saturday triple-header in 1971 that began at 11 A.M. and seeing North Carolina beat Massachusetts in the opener, 90–49. That was Julius Erving's last college game. Years later, when Erving made the mistake of teasing Dean Smith about a game the Tar Heels had lost, Smith smiled sweetly at him and said, "And what was the final score of your last college game, Julius?"

Later in that tournament, I saw my first Duke–North Carolina game. Both schools made the semifinals. Carolina won, 73–67. I was torn watching the game. I was a big fan of Dick DeVenzio, the clever little Duke guard, but my friends and I had adopted a Carolina benchwarmer named Don Eggleston as our hero. The Egg, as we called him, never got into games, but he was up on every play leading cheers from the Carolina bench. Initially, we assumed he was a freshman whose time would come in later years. It wasn't until Carolina won the championship game and the Egg went out to accept the trophy as one of the senior captains that we understood that we would never see his like again.

I was thrilled for the Egg, disappointed for DeVenzio, especially when Duke blew a big lead in the consolation game and lost to St. Bonaventure in overtime.

My decision on where to go to college was made on a Saturday afternoon in Cameron Indoor Stadium. That afternoon, a Duke team that would finish 12–14 beat number two–ranked Maryland, 83–79. The students mockingly sang "Amen" to the Terrapins and Lefty Driesell, since that was the song the Maryland pep band played when victories in Cole Field House had been wrapped up. I had never been in a basketball atmosphere like Cameron. It was also sixty degrees outside on a January afternoon. My mind was made up.

Duke was awful during my four years as an undergraduate, finishing last or tied for last in the ACC every year. But I had a great time learning my way around the ACC as a reporter at the Duke student paper, *The Chronicle*. I could always get Dean Smith or Lefty Driesell to return my phone calls by saying, "I just want to give Coach Smith/Driesell a chance to respond to what Coach Driesell/Smith said about him." Amazingly, they always called back. I found out that if you wanted to talk to Norman Sloan at NC State, you called during lunch hour because he often answered the phone himself.

I learned how to do passable imitations of Dean and Lefty, a requirement if you were going to cover the ACC. Years later, I was talking to Smith one day along with his sports information director, Rick Brewer. I believe Rick first went to work at Carolina at the age of six. He does Dean about as well as anyone. Dean was saying that he had been told that Phil Ford did him almost perfectly, but whenever he asked Phil to do the imitation, Phil claimed he had no idea what he was talking about.

"I hear you do me pretty well," Dean said.

"Well, actually, Dean, Rick does you a lot better than I do," I said.

Smith looked at Brewer. "Rick," he said, "do *you* do me?"

Brewer turned beet red. He hemmed and hawed for a couple of minutes, then said, "Coach, *everybody* does you."

He was right. Everyone did Dean. Everyone still does.

The ACC was different in the seventies than it is now. It was smaller (seven schools as opposed to nine) and less corporate, and it seemed, to me anyway, that everyone knew everyone. Even in the nineties, there is still a certain intimacy about the league, even though virtually every basketball game is on TV now and millions of dollars pour through the coffers. Many of the same people who covered the ACC when I was in college still cover it. Some could easily have moved on to other jobs and bigger markets but chose not to because they loved what they were doing.

The coaches are more collegial now than they were then, perhaps because they're all rich or perhaps because, as Gary Williams points out, they don't necessarily have to beat one another to win a national championship. For a long time, that wasn't the case because to play for the national championship you had to win the ACC tournament. My freshman year at Duke was the last year that each league got only one bid to the NCAA tournament, and, probably not coincidentally, it produced the greatest ACC final ever, the 103–100 NC State over Maryland overtime epic. I still remember John Lucas sitting down on the press table practically in my lap during the awards ceremony, crying so hard the table shook. After that, the league decided that only the winners had to remain on the floor after the final.

What hasn't changed are the rivalries. Fans are emotional about their teams everywhere, but because of the ACC's geographic makeup, there is more intermingling of fans from the various schools than in any other league. Duke and North Carolina are the prime example, but in varying degrees ACC alumni encounter one another constantly. Teasing about the ups and downs of each other's teams is a constant part of life in the league. And because the media covers ACC basketball so intently and so constantly fans feel as if they know the coaches, especially those who stay a long time.

As the 1997–98 season begins, Dean Smith has just retired after thirty-six years at Carolina; Mike Krzyzewski is in his eighteenth at Duke; Bobby Cremins is in his seventeenth at Georgia Tech; Dave Odom and Gary Williams are in their ninth years at Wake Forest and Maryland; and Jeff Jones, who many ACC fans still remember vividly as a player, is in his eighth year at Virginia. The new kids on the block are Rick Barnes, fourth year at Clemson; Herb Sendek, second at NC State; and the rookie, Steve Robinson, of Florida State. For the most part, ACC coaches stick around. After all, where would they want to go? They make very good money, have huge recruiting budgets, and — if they win — they are treated like royalty.

This book is about coaching and coaches in the ACC. Who are these guys? What makes them the coaches and the men that they are? How are they similar, how different? How do they deal with the pressures of the job and with one another? Because I have been around the league and college basketball for so many years, I have had the chance to know eight of the nine '96–97 league coaches for a long time. In some cases I knew them long before they were coaching in the ACC. The exception is Herb Sendek, whom I had only met briefly before he arrived at NC State in the spring of 1996.

Seven of them were willing to give me what amounted to complete access to them and their teams during the 1996–97 season. That included entrée to practices and coaches' meetings; being in the locker room before games, at halftime, and immediately after games; and sitting close enough to the benches so I could listen in on huddles during the game. In each case, when I asked for this access, I told the coach that anytime he felt uncomfortable because of my presence, all he had to do was ask me to leave and I would, no questions asked. To the credit of those seven men, none of them ever asked me to do that.

The two coaches who did not grant me complete access were Herb Sendek and Dean Smith. Sendek said he simply didn't feel comfortable with a stranger in his locker room when he was talking to his players. I understood completely. What Herb did do was give me all the time I asked for with him and, in a number of cases, re-create for me things he had said in the locker room during games.

I knew when I first conceived this project that Dean Smith wasn't going to let me into his locker room. When I wrote my first book in 1986 and had complete access to Bob Knight's locker room at Indiana, I remember Dean expressing amazement. "You mean he lets you hear *everything?*" he asked me.

"Everything," I said.

"I wouldn't let my mother do that," Smith said.

And, it should be remembered, unlike most coaches, Smith doesn't use profanity, so his mother probably would not have been offended by anything he said.

In the spring of 1996, he had rephrased his answer. "I wouldn't let the President of the United States in my locker room," he said.

I knew that, but I figured I had to give it a shot. "Dean," I said, "the President's not writing a book on ACC basketball."

In the end, he gave me all the cooperation I could possibly have hoped for: four lengthy interviews (one preseason, two in-season, one postseason), none of which he could possibly have enjoyed, and a willingness to walk me through many of his routines: when he arrived for a game; when he spoke to the players; what he did at halftime and after games. The only time he balked was when I asked him what prayers, if any, he and his team said in the locker room before and after a game.

"That's none of your business," he said. "That's private."

A couple of weeks later, he waved me over prior to a game at Clemson and said quietly, "We say the Lord's Prayer before the game and a prayer to a general creator after the game. [Frank] McGuire did the Lord's Prayer, so I just kept doing it when I took over. I do the other after the game because I don't want any of the players thinking that they have to participate in a Christian prayer if they don't want to."

I thanked him for changing his mind. "I figured if you really wanted to find out you could," he said. "This way, at least, you'll understand my thought process."

Of course understanding the thought processes of all nine coaches was what I was trying to do all winter. It was never easy, but I think all nine of them went out of their way to help me make the attempt. I can honestly say I like and respect each of them and I hope every one of them makes the Final Four someday — or again, someday. Wouldn't it be great if some year, the ACC did what former Duke player Gene Banks once predicted. "If the ACC got six teams into the NCAAs," Banks said, "They'd all make the Final Four."

OK, maybe that can't happen. But if the ACC ever sent four teams to the finals, no doubt, the three coaches who didn't win would be second-guessed all summer by their fans.

A MARCH TO MADNESS

One Shining Moment

IN COLLEGE BASKETBALL, when you say the words "Monday Night," they mean only one thing: the national championship game. Every coach dreams of seeing his team play on Monday Night. Throughout each season coaches tell their players over and over what it will take to play on Monday Night. To those who follow the college game, Monday Night has every bit as much meaning as Super Sunday does to fans of pro football.

The great Al McGuire, who twice reached Monday Night when he was the coach at Marquette, always tells coaches to remember to pause and take a look around when they walk on the floor on Monday Night. "There is nothing like that feeling," McGuire tells them. "You are at the absolute top of your profession. You are coaching in the one game that every coach dreams of coaching in."

Each year, only two coaches get their teams to Monday Night. The rest watch. Although every Division I college basketball coach in America has a ticket for Monday Night, very few of them actually come to the arena. Most have been in town earlier in the week for the annual coaches' convention that is part of the Final Four, but few stay for Monday Night. They all say it is because there is work to be done back home, and all are telling the truth. Or part of the truth. For most, being that close to the grand stage but not being on it is simply too painful.

So, they leave. But they all watch the game. Everyone in basketball watches Monday Night.

Technically, there are 306 schools competing to play on Monday Night. Most of them have no real chance to get there. But because it only takes thirteen players (or less) to field a college basketball team, and because the potential for riches is great, almost every university with a gym either plays in Division I or aspires to play there. By contrast, only 112 schools play Division I-A football.

Even among the sixty-four who make the NCAA tournament field, only a handful have a serious chance of playing on Monday Night. For Coppin State and Navy, Valparaiso and Boston University, Fairfield and Jackson State (among others), just being in the field is a thrill and a financial windfall. Winning a game — as Coppin did in 1997 — is gravy. Anything beyond that is basketball nirvana. For a majority of the 306, Monday Night is nothing more than a fantasy.

For a chosen few — fifty, perhaps sixty schools — Monday Night is *the* goal. In the major conferences, the ones whose games are on TV throughout the season, it is the benchmark of success for every coach.

Nowhere is that more true than in the Atlantic Coast Conference. The ACC may not be the most powerful basketball conference in the country every single year, but year in and year out it is the most consistent. It is the deepest in talent and the most competitive. There are few off nights in the ACC. Every other league in the country has a team or two or three that the top teams know they will beat every time they play unless they make an absolute pratfall. That's just not true in the ACC. In 1997, Georgia Tech finished last in the ACC. A year earlier, the Yellow Jackets had finished *first*. Seven years earlier, they came within one game of playing on Monday Night. That's how quickly fortunes can change in the ACC. Let down just the slightest bit and you become instant roadkill.

The eighth-place team in the league in 1997 was North Carolina State.

During the '96–97 season, the Wolfpack beat the team that finished first, one of the teams that tied for second, and both teams that tied for fourth. It lost to the other second-place team by one point in one game and blew a nine-point lead in the last two minutes in another.

No off nights.

On this Monday Night, a cold windy last day of March 1997 in Indianapolis, none of the nine ACC teams were in the building. There were seats reserved for the players from North Carolina because they had reached the Final Four, coming within one victory of Monday Night. But the Tar Heels were nowhere to be found. They had flown home to Chapel Hill — devastated, even after a remarkable 28–7 season that had included a sixteen-victory, two-month winning streak — twenty-four hours before the championship game began.

Their coach, Dean Smith, had walked out of the RCA Dome on Saturday evening after the loss to Arizona looking crushed. Two weeks earlier, he had become the winningest coach in the history of college basketball. The look on his face as he walked to his car showed a man who wasn't thinking about the 879 games he had won, but of the one that had just gotten away. That's the way coaches are. They remember the losses much longer than the wins.

But that's part of the job. Almost all successful coaches — at least the ones good enough to get into the NCAA tournament field — end their season with a loss. When it is all said and done, only two coaches get to Monday Night. And only one wins.

The only ACC coach in the building for 1997's Monday Night was Duke coach Mike Krzyzewski. As Arizona and Kentucky dueled on the floor of the RCA Dome, Krzyzewski sat about one hundred feet away on a raised CBS-TV platform that had been built directly above the tunnel Kentucky was using to get to and from the court. Krzyzewski had a perfect view of the other tunnel, on the far side of the arena, the one Arizona would use — the same tunnel his Duke team had used six years earlier on Monday Night.

It was in this building — then known as the Hoosier Dome, before RCA paid millions to rename it — that Krzyzewski's coaching career and his life had changed forever. On a magic final weekend, he and his players had pulled off one of the most monumental upsets in NCAA tournament history, beating the defending national champion, Nevada–Las Vegas, in the semifinals. UNLV was 34–0 going into the Final Four and had already been anointed as one of the greatest teams of all time. A year earlier, UNLV and Duke had met in the national championship game and the final score had been 103–73, the most lopsided final in the tournament's fifty-two-year history. Given virtually no chance the next year to keep the game close, much less win it, the Blue Devils had won.

In 1995, after taking Duke to four championship games in five years, Krzyzewski had missed the last two months of a disastrous Duke season because of back problems and exhaustion. He had, for all intents and purposes, crashed — physically, mentally, and emotionally. He wondered then if he would ever coach again, if he even wanted to coach again.

He had come back in the 1996 season, but continued to wonder if coaching was what he wanted to do. Six weeks before Arizona and Kentucky met, Krzyzewski had turned fifty. Watching the season's final game, Krzyzewski knew there was only one thing he wanted to do with his life right now: get his team back to Monday Night.

Back in Chapel Hill, Dean Smith watched the game in his living room along with his wife, Linnea. Like his archrival, Krzyzewski, Smith had taken teams to the final game five times and, like Krzyzewski, had won twice. Six years, including this year, he had taken teams to the Final Four, only to lose in the semifinals.

At sixty-six, Smith was one of the coaching icons in the game's history. He had coached at North Carolina for thirty-six years, winning every one of those record-setting 879 games there. He had been at Carolina so long that he had coached in three different arenas, the most recent a 21,444-seat palace that bore his name.

All winter, there had been rumors circulating in the ACC that Smith was going to retire at season's end. He would break Adolph Rupp's record of 876 victories and he might also have a fairy-tale national championship. The possibility of the latter had ended against Arizona when Smith's team made seven of 11 shots to start the game and then missed 47 of its next 63. The Tar Heels had been rattled by Arizona's speed and, after a jackrabbit start, had played the next ten minutes about as poorly and carelessly as a Smith-coached team could possibly play. That bothered Smith almost as much as losing the game did — perhaps more. His team had played so well during February and March and then arrived at the Final Four and fallen to pieces.

In the aftermath of the loss to Arizona, Smith had been asked about Arizona's quickness. A stream-of-consciousness talker — the previous day he had turned a question about Adolph Rupp into a lengthy monologue about his former player and assistant Larry Brown becoming a father again at the age of fifty-seven — he had somehow finished his answer by predicting that Arizona and Duke would be in the Final Four next year. Smith did that often — predicting success for Duke. It was a defense mechanism, but also a reflection of the rivalry between Carolina and Duke and between their two hugely successful coaches. Neither was ever far from the other's thoughts.

Now, as he watched Arizona and Kentucky, Smith was again struck by Arizona's speed and poise. He felt better understanding that his team's loss hadn't been a fluke. Arizona *was* good. It had beaten Kansas, the pretournament favorite, in the round of sixteen, a devastating loss for Smith's ex-assistant, Roy Williams. Now, it had beaten North Carolina and Kentucky. The best team had won.

But Smith knew his team wasn't far from being that good. He believed his team had been worthy of this Monday Night. He knew that if his best player, sophomore Antawn Jamison, returned to play another year of college ball, his team would have a chance to be very good again in 1998. Still, even though it had been a good season, it had been a long, tiring winter. Again.

And even though he had a contract to coach four more years, he had no idea how much longer he would want to coach. This year had been fun. Some of the previous ones hadn't been. He hoped he would be as eager next October as he had been for the thirty-six previous ones.

Wake Forest coach Dave Odom also watched the final with his wife that night. Lynn Odom had driven to their brand-new beach house on North Carolina's eastern shore on the same day that Odom had flown to Indianapolis for the Final Four. Odom had a number of meetings to go to there and he always looked forward to seeing his friends in the coaching fraternity. Few men in coaching had more friends than Odom.

Most years, Lynn would have gone too. She enjoyed Dave's friends and was close to a number of the wives she had met through the years. This year, though, with the new house finally ready after more than two years of planning, she decided to go to the beach. What's more, this was the Final Four that Dave and Lynn Odom had planned on attending as participants rather than spectators. The reality — that Wake Forest's season had ended three wins shy of that goal — was a painful one. Lynn didn't have to go; Dave did.

Seeing other coaches was good for him. It reminded him of how much he enjoyed being in the business. The toughest part came on Thursday night at the NCAA's annual "Salute Dinner," which was really a snooty NCAA way of throwing a party for its various corporate sponsors. Odom found himself sitting at a table with Clemson's Rick Barnes, Virginia's Jeff Jones, and Georgia Tech's Bobby Cremins.

"You know what we ought to do," he said as they were taking their seats. "We ought to go over and congratulate Dean on the record and getting to the Final Four."

The others nodded. There had always been an unseen barrier between Smith and the other ACC coaches. Part of it came from Smith being the target in the league for so many years. Part of it came from his shyness, which some coaches saw as aloofness. Years before, when Smith had been the same age as most of the other top coaches in the league, they constantly sniped at him, convinced that he was always sniping at them. When Lefty Driesell was the coach at Maryland, he often said that he was convinced that the name of the coach at North Carolina was "that goddamn Dean," because North Carolina State coach Norman Sloan would call him almost every morning screaming, "Do you know what that goddamn Dean just did!"

Now, Smith was twelve years older than Odom, the league's second-oldest coach. Jones and NC State coach Herb Sendek weren't even born when Smith arrived at North Carolina. He is respected now as the elder statesman, but that doesn't mean there isn't antipathy. Smith and Krzyzewski haven't gotten along since 1984, when Krzyzewski insisted there was a "double standard" in the way ACC referees worked — one for North Carolina, another for the rest of the league. Smith still bridles at that claim, and the two men have exchanged brickbats — publicly and privately — ever since. In 1995, Rick Barnes's first year in the league, he and Smith nearly fought during an ACC tournament game. A year later, they were called to Commissioner Gene Corrigan's home and told in no uncertain terms to quit calling each other names in public. Now, they just do it in private.

But time is a healer. After Smith broke the record for most career wins by a college coach, the first ACC coach to write him was Barnes. And so, when Odom suggested crossing the room to offer congratulations, Jones, Barnes, and Cremins followed him to Smith's table. But Smith hadn't arrived yet. As organized as he is when it comes to basketball, Smith can be a mess when it comes to matters that aren't that important to him — like a dinner where he knows he has to speak and doesn't really want to. "He'll be here in eleven minutes," said Woody Durham, who has been North Carolina's play-by-play man on radio for almost as long as Smith has been the basketball coach.

Odom and company returned to the table. When Odom saw Smith walk in, he suggested another pilgrimage. By now, the others were eating their salads. Later, they said. Odom didn't want to wait. He walked back to Smith's table — no small feat since he had had surgery on a toe six days earlier — and put a hand on Smith's shoulder.

"Coach" — Odom has never been comfortable calling Smith "Dean" — "I just wanted to congratulate you for everything," he said. "No one's more deserving."

Odom meant it. He was awed by the very fact that someone could coach at the ACC's level of intensity and pressure for thirty-six years, much less win at that level every single year. Smith stood up to shake hands. "Thanks," he said. Then, awkwardly, not quite sure what to say, he added, "I really thought you" — Wake Forest — "would be here too."

That thought had been with Odom almost nonstop ever since the clock had hit zero twelve days earlier in Tucson and the Deacons had five fewer points on the scoreboard than Stanford. "Our guards," he said for about the five hundredth time. "Somewhere, they just lost confidence in their shot and —"

"I never thought they were that good to begin with," Smith interjected.

Odom couldn't help himself. He started to laugh. He knew Smith wasn't putting down his guards; he was trying to say, "It wasn't your fault." He also knew that come next January, when North Carolina and Wake Forest were getting ready to play again, Smith would talk about those guards as if they were Oscar Robertson and Jerry West. Nonetheless, he appreciated the gesture.

Later that night, each of the four coaches whose teams would be playing Saturday had to get up and speak briefly. "Someday," Odom thought, "I want to speak at this dinner."

That was why watching Monday Night from his living room was difficult. In eight years as the head coach at Wake Forest, he had rebuilt a sagging program into a national power. But the closest Odom had come to Monday Night had been in 1984, when he had been an assistant coach at Virginia and the Cavaliers had lost to Houston in overtime on semifinal Saturday.

The Deacons had played almost flawlessly for fourteen games, looking like a team that might not lose all season. But then chinks had appeared in the armor. They went from a preseason Final Four certainty to a team that shocked no one by losing in the second round to Stanford.

Intellectually, Odom knew he had done everything a coach could do to try and shake his team loose from its malaise. Still, the pain was palpable. Odom had gotten into college coaching later than the other ACC coaches and hadn't settled in at Wake Forest until he was already forty-six. The only other coach who had been forty when he arrived in the ACC was Maryland's Gary Williams, who was forty-four when he was hired to coach at his alma mater. But Williams had already been a successful head coach for eleven years by then. Odom's head coaching résumé when he got to Wake had consisted of a three-year stint at East Carolina that had produced a 38–42 record.

The Wake job had come at a time when Odom wondered if he would ever get the chance to run his own program in the ACC. He had steadily built it, first to respectability, then to this point, this year. It was difficult to look back on a 24–7 season and wonder what had gone wrong, but that was what Odom was doing. As he watched Kentucky and Arizona go at one another, he was struck by the quality of the game. The two teams had speed and quickness. They were both tough. Their coaches seemed to understand them perfectly. Odom had known Rick Pitino since they had worked together at the Five-Star Camp when both were climbing the coaching ladder. He was genuinely happy that his friend had become such a star in the coaching pantheon because he knew how much Pitino craved that sort of recognition.

Odom has never needed the spotlight. But he still felt a craving as he watched the game wind down. "Our basketball team could not have played with Kentucky or Arizona in March," he said later. "But we could have played with them in December or January. The trouble is, they don't play the Final Four then. The question I will always ask myself is why we didn't get better as the season went on. I can speculate, but I'll never really know. Because if I had known, I would have done something about it."

The entire Barnes family of Clemson, South Carolina, watched the championship game together. Rick and Candy, Nick and Carly. Nick was twelve, Carly nine. Nick made it to the finish, just before midnight. Carly was sound asleep long before the final buzzer.

Rick Barnes had no regrets about his third season at Clemson. He had looked at the tape of his team's double-overtime loss to Minnesota in the round of sixteen and had discovered something he hadn't known in the immediate aftermath of the game. "When we were up 80–74 in the first overtime and they caught us, I thought we'd blown it," he said. "But when I looked at the tape, I saw that they made some hellacious plays. I mean, hellacious plays. Sometimes, you've got to give the other guy credit. As coaches, we don't always do that. Either our kids messed up or the refs made a bad call — something. Not this game. They just went out and won it."

The Tigers had come agonizingly close. And yet, Barnes felt no agony, just pride. He knew where the program had been in the spring of 1994 when he had fled Providence after six difficult years to take over the ACC's worst program. His athletic director, Bobby Robinson, had told him during the interviewing process that Clemson might be the worst team in ACC history the next winter. Instead, the Tigers finished sixth in the league and went down fighting — literally — in the ACC tournament against North Carolina. That game had made it clear to people who Barnes was. He could be both funny and charming and no one liked a practical joke more than he did. But if you missed the competitive side of him, you missed *him*.

Exactly a year later, again facing North Carolina in the ACC tournament, the Tigers came from behind to win the game. The victory put them in the NCAA tournament. There wasn't a senior on the team. Suddenly, they had gone from the league's worst team to a team many thought would finish second to Wake Forest in 1997. The turnaround was breathtaking.

Barnes was now a hot young coach. At forty-two, his name seemed to come up every time a major school was looking for a coach. He had no interest in leaving Clemson. Candy loved living there. Both had grown up in western North Carolina, and they were a lot more comfortable living in a small town in the South than they had been living in the Northeast.

Time and again throughout the 1996–97 season, Barnes had told his players, "This is your time; this is what you've worked so hard for." They had responded with twenty-one victories in the regular season, then had come back in the NCAA tournament to beat both Miami of Ohio and Tulsa to reach the Sweet Sixteen. It was the school's first appearance there since 1990 and only the third in Clemson history. And then they had played and lost a classic against Minnesota.

Only one senior had started for Clemson in the Minnesota game — shooting guard Merl Code. Everyone else would be back. A strong recruiting class was on the way. Clemson would probably begin the '97–98 season as no worse than a cofavorite to win the ACC. It would be ranked in everyone's top ten and in a lot of top fives.

All of that, Barnes knew, guaranteed nothing.

"As soon as the championship game was over, I wanted to go to work," he said. "We were only two games from the Final Four. Hell, we were one shot from the final eight. But I knew how hard we had worked to get that far. I knew how hard Kentucky and Arizona had worked to get where they were. It's such a fine line. All I wanted to do was remind my players that every drop of sweat they produce this summer will pay off next winter. That last game, that last night is what it's all about. It has to be your goal. If it isn't, why bother doing all this?"

*   *   *

Gary Williams, who had once been Barnes's boss back at Ohio State, felt the same way. In a sense, Williams had done exactly what he had set out to do when he graduated from Maryland thirty years earlier. He had won as a high school coach and been a successful assistant coach at the college level. He had dreamed about being a head coach and had become one at the age of thirty-four. He had built the program at American University into a consistent winner and then moved on to Boston College and Ohio State. He had won at both those places. Finally, in 1989, his dream had come true: Maryland had called and asked him to come back.

He couldn't say no to Maryland. And so he left a program at Ohio State that was loaded with players to take over one that was loaded with problems. He knew that the NCAA was investigating deposed coach Bob Wade for rules violations and he knew the cocaine-induced death of Len Bias still hung over the campus even three years after it had happened. It wouldn't be easy, but Williams could handle it. He *knew* he could handle it because he had always handled coaching challenges. All you did was outwork people. It wasn't that hard if you wanted it bad enough.

Outworking people couldn't overcome two years of NCAA sanctions, though, and that was what Maryland got hit with at the end of Williams's first season. As if to twist the knife a little deeper, the Tournament Committee then left the Terrapins out of the NCAA field even though they had won eighteen games during the regular season.

That was the least of Williams's troubles. Recruiting got hammered. His private life was in disarray. He was recently divorced and, shortly after his first season at Maryland ended, his fiancée called off their planned wedding and skipped town. That summer, he was stopped on his way home from a golf outing and hit with a DUI charge.

"There were times those first couple of years," he said, "when I really thought my career was over." It wasn't. Williams recruited brilliantly, rebuilt the team, and made it into a fourth straight NCAA tournament in March 1997 before losing in the first round to the College of Charleston. The Terrapins weren't awful that night, but they weren't nearly good enough to win the game. And so, on a rainy night in Memphis, what had been a dream season crashed. Williams woke up wondering if he really cared if the plane home — which rocked and rolled all over the sky in awful weather — landed safely or not.

Sixteen days later he sat in his living room on Monday Night and watched Arizona and Kentucky, feeling calmer but nonetheless frustrated. He was fifty-two. Tim Ryan of CBS had called him one of the game's "best young coaches" in the waning seconds of the College of Charleston loss. Williams had been called that often during his career. He knew it wasn't true anymore. He was the third-oldest coach in the ACC. He was two years older than Mike Krzyzewski, who had been to seven Final Fours. He was a year older than Dean Smith had been when he won his first national title in his seventh Final Four. He was eight years older than Rick Pitino.

But he was also ten years younger than Arizona coach Lute Olson, who had waited more than forty years for this night. He still had plenty of energy and he knew he had a good team returning for next season. It was much too soon to give up hope. He never had before, why should he start now?

Jeff Jones was still young enough to be accurately called a hot young coach. He wouldn't be thirty-seven until June and, after seven seasons at Virginia, he had already won 135 games (Smith had won 120 in his first seven seasons) and taken the Cavaliers into the NCAA tournament five times. Two years earlier, they had upset top-seeded Kansas in the Sweet Sixteen before losing in the round of eight to defending national champion Arkansas.

But things were hardly sanguine in Jones's life. He spent the first half of the championship game on the phone to a recruit, in part because that's what coaches do but also because he knew his team needed reinforcements. The Cavaliers had pieced together a difficult, though solid, season, winning eighteen games and making it into the NCAA tournament. That was a far cry from the 12–15 of the previous year. What's more, there hadn't been any arrests — as opposed to four in 1996, including one for aggravated assault in which a UVA recruit had slashed someone with a knife after an argument during a pickup basketball game. The other good news was that Jones's personal life, which had been the subject of constant gossip in Charlottesville after he had split from his wife, Lisa, had also become little more than a back-burner item.

Still, Jones couldn't get the memory of the season finale, an embarrassing one-sided loss to Iowa in the first round of the NCAAs, out of his mind. He had yet to figure out why his team had failed to show up for that game after working so hard to get there. Five days earlier, he had made the most difficult decision of his coaching career, firing his top assistant, Tom Perrin.

The coaching change was symbolic of the uncertain waters Virginia basketball was in. Jones had only one year left on his contract, and UVA's athletic director, Terry Holland, who had coached him at UVA and then hired him as an assistant coach, had been hemming and hawing about an extension. Jones knew that going into the final year of a contract without an extension was a recruiting nightmare. Holland knew that too. And yet, Jones was still waiting for a definitive talk about his future.

His divorce would be final in a matter of weeks. He still saw his three children often because he had moved into a townhouse that was only ten minutes from where they lived. As long as he coached at Virginia, it was likely he would get to see his children frequently. He and Lisa were having an amicable divorce. But he didn't know if he would be the coach at Virginia for one more year or thirty more years.

Jones is not, by nature, a confrontational person. That was why he had been unable to make eye contact with Perrin during their last conversation. That was why he hadn't pushed Holland harder about an extension. That was why, as he watched the championship game, he chose not to think about the uncertainty of his future. When forty minutes of regulation didn't produce a winner, Jones turned off the TV and went upstairs to his bedroom. He climbed into bed and turned the television on to watch the overtime. When the game was over, he watched all the post-game celebrating and the interviews. He stayed awake right through CBS's annual signoff, a montage of pictures from the tournament that flashed on the screen while the sappy song "One Shining Moment" played over them. Jones knew how corny it all was, and yet, there was that lump in his throat again.

Still there after all these years. He had watched Monday Night as a kid with his dad, who had been a coach; then he had watched it with friends as a player and with Lisa as a young husband and father. Now, he watched it alone, a successful coach with an uncertain future. So much had changed. But the lump hadn't changed. "Being in that game has always been my dream," he said. "I've been close" — semifinals as a player in 1981; semifinals as an assistant coach in 1984 — "but never been there. I just feel until I get there, I won't have done what I set out to do in basketball."

As soon as the final notes of the song faded, Jones turned the TV off. The season was over. It was time to start thinking about the next one.

Three of the nine ACC coaches had not taken their teams into the NCAA tournament. Pat Kennedy's Florida State team had missed the tournament for a fourth straight year, coming up one victory short. It had played in the National Invitation Tournament as a consolation prize and pieced together a successful four-game run, reaching the final in Madison Square Garden before losing to Michigan.

Kennedy had been at Florida State for eleven years. A year earlier, after a third straight losing season, his boss, Dave Hart, had told him that the school would not roll over his five-year contract as it had done in the past. That meant he had four years left. He had then talked to St. John's about its coaching vacancy and had been sharply criticized back home in Tallahasee for doing so. Now, Kennedy wanted to know if Hart was going to give him an extension after a 20–12 season in which four of those victories had come in the consolation tournament rather than in the Big Show of the NCAAs.

He had been called the previous week by several Rutgers alumni. Would Kennedy, who had grown up on the Jersey Shore, be interested in their job? Only if the job is offered to me without an interview, Kennedy answered. He simply didn't think he could afford to go through another situation like St. John's, where he showed interest, didn't get the job, and had to crawl back to Florida State looking like he had been willing to desert.

But hours before the championship game, Kennedy had gotten a call from Rutgers athletic director Fred Grunninger. What if you were offered a ten-year contract, Grunninger asked. Would you be willing to interview then? Kennedy didn't think he could afford to say no to that possibility. So he agreed to fly to Newark the morning after the final to meet with Grunninger.

He and his wife, Jeannie, made it as far as Cincinnati. There, they were snowed in. They checked into the Radisson Hotel right there at the airport and ordered room service while they watched the final. Kennedy remembered attending the Final Four as Florida State's new coach — 1986 — when he had sat in the stands on Monday Night surrounded by Louisville fans and it occurred to him that he was now coaching in the same conference as Louisville. "It was the first time I ever thought of myself as a coach who could compete on that level," he said.

Florida State had left Louisville's conference in 1991 to join the ACC, and the stakes had gotten even higher. Kennedy never thought the day would come when he would walk away from the chance to compete in the ACC. But three years was a lot less security than ten years. That was why he had to listen to Grunninger.

It turned out to be a mistake. Kennedy talked to both Grunninger and the school president the next day. The contract wasn't for ten years, it was for six — with possible rollovers. Kennedy had been the rollover route before. Still, six years was more than three. He would listen if they called back. They didn't. Grunninger offered the job to Rider College's Kevin Bannon the next day. Kennedy was still at Florida State. He had three years left on his contract. And there was no extension in sight.

Herb Sendek had no such problems. In this, his first year at North Carolina State, he had thrilled his new fans by taking his eighth-seeded team to the ACC tournament championship game — beating Georgia Tech, Duke, and Maryland — before losing the final to North Carolina. A win over Carolina would have put the Wolfpack into the NCAAs for the first time since 1991. Instead, it too went to the NIT, winning one game before losing to West Virginia. Even so, Reynolds Coliseum was packed for the West Virginia game and the atmosphere in the building brought back memories of the seventies and eighties, when State had been a national power and won national championships. State fans were thrilled with the late run, the 17–15 record, and the hope for the future built around a thirty-four-year-old coach and a recruiting class that was already being touted nationally. Sendek had given a speech to an NC State booster club in Charlotte on Monday night. He pulled off the road en route home and found a restaurant with a TV. He sat riveted, watching Pitino — his old boss — and pulling for him to win. And dreaming of the night he would be there with his own team.

The only ACC coach who didn't seem to have a single thing to grab on to as the season ended was Georgia Tech's Bobby Cremins. It hadn't been that long ago that Cremins had been one of the game's hot coaches. He had taken over a Georgia Tech program that had been in tatters in 1981 and quickly built it into a power. The Yellow Jackets won the ACC tournament in 1985 and reached the Elite Eight. A year later, they were ranked number one in preseason. That was the first time Cremins dealt with failed expectations. His team was upset by Louisiana State in the Sweet Sixteen and didn't get that far again until 1990. But that year, fueled by the brilliance of freshman point guard Kenny Anderson, Tech made it to the Final Four. There, it lost a superb game to eventual champion UNLV.

Three years later, Cremins went through what he called his midlife crisis. "I had an affair," he said. "Only it wasn't with a woman, it was with South Carolina."

His alma mater, which had fallen on hard times, had come calling. Cremins said no. Then he said maybe. Then he said no again. Finally, he said yes. He went to Columbia and was introduced as the new coach at a press conference. Forty-eight hours later, he backed out. "I couldn't go through with it," he said. "I felt like Judas."

His wife, Carolyn, drove from Atlanta to Columbia to pick him up. Several times during the drive back, Cremins told her to turn around and go back. Once he told her to pull over so he could hitchhike back. She kept driving. Cremins went through months of therapy after it was all over, then came back declaring himself a new man. But Tech missed the NCAA tournament the next two years and some people wondered if Cremins had lost the magic. But in 1995, he convinced Stephon Marbury, like Anderson a prodigy from Brooklyn, to come to Tech. Marbury led a revival. The Yellow Jackets won the ACC regular season and made it back to the Sweet Sixteen.

And then Marbury said "so long," heading for the promised land of big bucks and shoe contracts after just one year of college ball. Cremins had known that Anderson was going to leave after his sophomore year and had prepared accordingly, recruiting a point guard that fall to replace him. But he hadn't really believed Marbury would leave after one year, and he had only recruited a replacement halfheartedly. He was caught off-guard — or more important, *without* a guard — when Marbury left.

In 1996–97, Tech struggled through its first losing season since Cremins's first year, going 9–18, finishing a dismal 3–13 in the ACC. There were some close calls — including a blown 11-point lead at home against Duke and a 19-point lead lost in the last ten minutes against North Carolina — but when it was all over, it had been an awful year.

Cremins was going to turn fifty on the Fourth of July. He insisted he would not have another midlife crisis. He made radical decisions. As soon as the season ended, Cremins was on the road, looking for players — especially guards. Deep down, Cremins knew the mistakes were his and so was the responsibility. He also knew that next year might not be a lot better than 1997 had been. He had one great player — Matt Harpring — and a lot of question marks.

After the final loss to NC State, he uncharacteristically kicked over a garbage can in the locker room, then walked out without saying a word to the players. He knew he had hit rock bottom. He absolutely believed he would be back. He had been "this close" to Monday Night once; he knew he could get there.

And, like everyone else who coaches in the ACC, he knew he couldn't feel completely fulfilled until he made that walk that Al McGuire talked about. Like every coach in the ACC he had plenty of money and people around him who would tell him he was great no matter what happened. And, like the rest of them, he knew that money and fame weren't what it was all about.

Monday Night was what it was all about. Another had come and gone. They had all been through another grueling season, one that began in September with recruiting visits and didn't end until the last net came down in Indianapolis. As Arizona celebrated, each of the nine ACC coaches knew only one thing for certain. They all had a lot of work to do between now and the next Monday Night.

2

Starting Over

ONCE UPON A TIME, October 15 was a special date for everyone in college basketball. It was the first official day of practice for teams all around the country. It didn't really matter that players had been playing pickup games all fall that were only technically voluntary. It didn't matter that most coaches had sneaked into the gym, or sent assistants in their stead, to check on the progress of their players. October 15 meant rebirth. It meant everyone was 0–0 and all was still right with everyone's sweaty world.

Then, the NCAA began to tinker. First, it decreed that practice could not start until November 1. That way, it reasoned, players could have more time for their studies before practice got under way. Of course they were playing every day anyway and all the change meant was that they played for an extra sixteen days without anyone there to monitor them or check them in case someone got hurt. Having figured out that November 1 wasn't a solution, the NCAA went the other way. It decided to allow coaches to work with their players for up to twenty hours a week before practice began as long as there were no more than three players present if a ball was being used. That meant, for all intents and purposes, that practice began on the first day of school.

In October of 1997, the rule changed again. Because of the popularity of "Midnight Madness," the newly minted tradition of starting practice at 12:01 A.M. on opening day, the NCAA decided that the first day of practice should henceforth be the first Saturday after October 15 so Midnight Madness would not take place on a school night. After all, aren't most college students tucked into bed by midnight on school nights?

Dave Odom didn't really care when the NCAA mandated the start of practice. He had been working with his players all fall and he knew how eager they were for this season to begin. None of them could possibly be more eager than he was. This was the season Dave Odom had waited for his entire life.

"Most people go to a liberal arts college to figure out what they want to do with their lives," he said. "I went to a liberal arts college, but I already knew what I was going to do."

George David Odom was going to be a coach. He didn't know what kind of coach, but he knew he was going to coach. Or at the very least be around athletics in some way. From the time he could ride a bicycle the three blocks from his house to the Wayne County Boys Club, sports had dominated his life. Sports and his family.

To his family, Dave Odom has always been David. That's what Lynn calls him now. But as a star athlete growing up in Goldsboro, North Carolina, he was, "Little Davey Odom," a nickname first hung on him by a local sportswriter. To this day, when Dick Vitale calls him "Little Davey," the entire Odom clan bristles. In the business world, no one who is five foot ten would be called "little." In Dave Odom's world, he has always been described that way.

The Odoms were a close family. Every summer, they would make two long trips. One would always be to New York to see the Yankees play. Dave's father, Bill Odom, wasn't a big sports fan, but he loved baseball and the Yankees. Dave inherited the love of baseball, but was always a fan of the Dodgers. If the Dodgers were playing at Ebbets Field while the family was in New York, they would go and see the Dodgers play too. The other summer trip could be anywhere: Chicago (so Dave's mom, Janie, could see the Don McNeil Breakfast Club radio show in person), Houston, New Orleans. Long, happy trips.

When the family wasn't traveling, Dave worked at least half of every summer day at his father's Pontiac-Cadillac dealership. Bill Odom was a man of habit. He left the house every morning at 5:30 and drove to Central Lunch for coffee. After an hour there, he would make his way to Howard's Billiard Parlor. Each morning, Dave would run inside to find Mr. Howard standing there with five Muriel Senator cigars, his father's brand. "Only time in my life I've ever been in a pool hall." He would hand them to his father, who would immediately light the first one of the day. They would arrive at the dealership at 7:30. His father would open, make sure everything was running smoothly, and then he and Dave would drive home for breakfast. Then back to work. At noon, they would come home for lunch. Most days, Dave was off after that and he would ride his bike to the boys club and spend the afternoon playing ball.

It was, for the most part, a happy way to grow up. The only sadness came on those nights when Bill Odom came home late. "If his car wasn't in the driveway by five-thirty, my stomach would twist into a knot," Dave remembered. "I knew, just knew, where he was. Never in my life, not ever, have I felt fear like I felt when he was late."

Bill Odom was an alcoholic. If he was late, Dave knew it was because he was drinking Seagram's Seven, and he knew he would be almost falling down drunk by the time he got home. His dinner, cold, would be waiting for him. Some nights Bill Odom ate a few bites. Most nights, helped out of the car by Dave, he went straight to bed. He was still ready to leave the house at 5:30 the next morning, but when he came back for breakfast and went into the bathroom by the front door for his morning shower, he would shut the door. Dave and his sister, Janie Margaret, knew what was coming next. Their mother would follow him in. Then the shouting would start.

"She never said a word when he came home at night," Dave said. "She knew that was a waste of time. But the next morning was her time."

On more than one occasion, Bill stopped drinking for a while. Then he would start again. Treatment wasn't nearly as sophisticated then as it is now. In fact, he was never actually diagnosed as an alcoholic. But Dave knew. During Dave's senior year in high school, his father stopped drinking. He never started again. "The last five years of his life he was completely dry," Dave said. "I choose to remember him that way."

Bill Odom was never extroverted. The warmth in the family came from Dave's mother, who was very open with her emotions. She was also the person Dave talked to most of the time about his hopes and dreams. "Our relationship went beyond mother-son," he said. "We were best friends."

It is easy to see how his parents left their mark on Odom. He has never smoked and never had a drink in his life. He is a man of habit. To this day he cannot leave to coach a basketball game unless he has personally ironed his game shirt. If Lynn gives him one that is ironed, he either re-irons it or finds one that needs ironing. On the road, one of the first tasks he attends to after pregame meal is making certain he has an iron in his room. His pregame routine in the locker room, from the moment he walks in and finds a towel and a soft drink to the moment he puts on his jacket as he walks out the door, is always the same. All of that comes from his dad.

His warmth, his closeness to family, friends, and his players, comes from his mom. In the locker room and in the huddles, he almost always talks to each player directly and personally — he almost never uses a blackboard or a clipboard to draw a play. After a loss, he will frequently insist that his players form a tight circle around him as he speaks to them. "Let me feel you," he will say. Often, when he is talking to a player he will put his arms around him, or lean down and put his hands on his head.

He is that way in his personal relationships too. He has stayed close to many of his childhood friends and seems to know more coaches than anyone alive. It is the rare Wake Forest road trip that does not include some old friend of Odom's — a pal from Goldsboro, a coach he met at a clinic in France, a former teammate — who comes along just to spend some time with their old friend Dave, who has made the big time but still has to iron his own shirt on game day.

Odom is convinced to this day that he became a coach not so much because of his love for sports but because of the men who coached him. "I never had a bad coach," he said. "From my days at the Wayne County Boys Club, through high school and college, right up through the men I worked for when I became a coach, they were always people I admired and looked up to. That's why I knew when I went to college that I wanted to coach."

He did not, however, know *what* he wanted to coach. He played everything in high school — quarterback on the football team, point guard on the basketball team, second base on the baseball team. He set all sorts of passing records as a quarterback, largely because Goldsboro High School was the smallest school in the state's largest high school division, and spent most games trying to come from behind. He probably could have gone to one of the state's big schools on the basis of his academic record, but he wanted to go someplace where he would have a chance to play ball. That place turned out to be Guilford College, in Greensboro. He played varsity football as a freshman and freshman basketball. That spring, Guilford hired Jerry Steele to coach basketball and he asked Odom if he wanted to try out for the team after watching him play in an intramural game. Odom said sure and, in his words, "a love affair began."

Steele was the kind of coach Odom wanted to be: smart, tough, and fair, close to his players, and able to bring the best out in them. Since he hadn't played as a freshman, he was able to come back for a fifth year (he had to drop several courses in order not to graduate in the spring of his fourth year), something he decided to do largely because it meant spending another season learning from Steele.

Odom's "first" senior year turned out to be a critical time in his life. In December of that year, his parents came to see him play one night. Dave thought he had never seen his dad look better. Two days later, on a Saturday afternoon, Bill Odom went to take his Saturday bath and had a heart attack sitting in the tub. He was sixty-nine. As a boy, Dave had always been struck by how much older his father was than the other kids' dads. Losing him relatively early in his life wasn't a shock, but it was traumatic anyway. He still talks with great emotion about his father, memories of the morning trips to Central Lunch and Howard's Billiards Parlor making him smile. And, as is always the case for children, his parents will pop into his mind at moments when he least expects it.

In the spring of 1996, Odom was making his annual swing through North Carolina, speaking to Wake Forest alumni groups, when he found himself driving through the farms of Sampson County. He knew he was very close to where his dad grew up and he remembered a Sunday afternoon years before when his father had surprised him after church by telling him to be back home from playing ball at two o'clock so they could go for a drive. Bill Odom — naturally — had a Sunday ritual: drop his family off at church (he only attended at Easter and Christmas) and go to Central Lunch for coffee, pick the family up, come home for Sunday dinner, then nap in the afternoon.

On this day he skipped the nap and he and Dave drove about forty miles from Goldsboro into Sampson County. Finally, Bill Odom pulled the car to a halt in an open field. It was filled with the white sand of eastern North Carolina and was bare, except for a few trees. Dave remembers it was spring, the leaves were starting to come back, and a cold wind was blowing. Bill Odom stood in the middle of the field and pointed to an empty spot. "Son, right there is where I was born," he said. "And over there is the barn where we kept our horses, cows, and livestock." He pointed to a huge oak tree. "That's where we had all our family reunions. We'd set up big buffet tables under the tree and eat all day long." He pointed in another direction. "Used to be a baseball field there. That's where I learned to play."

Father and son stood there for a while in silence. Finally, Dave said, "Daddy, doesn't it make you sad that everything's gone except for the tree?"

Bill Odom looked at him for a moment, then smiled. "Son, it's not gone," he said. He pointed to his head. "It's right here, clear as can be. I've got everything that matters right in here."

Years later, when his teams began to win championships, Dave Odom could still see his father standing in the middle of that field on that windy Sunday. "In the end, championships are nothing more than memories that you store away and revisit whenever you can or want to," he said. "Because in this business, nothing is ever enough. If you win one, you're going to want two. Get two, you want three. That's just the way life is. Nothing is ever enough.

"The point is, you better lock into something that's real and will always be there. In the end, enjoying the chase is more important than the catch because you can't guarantee the catch. A championship is like food — eventually, it leaves you. But the memories don't."

Thinking about his dad that spring day alone in the car and about the importance of the chase and of memories gave Dave Odom a theme he would return to often with his players as they made their way through the long winter ahead.

The other seminal event of Odom's first senior year didn't take place until the summer. He had noticed a freshman named Lynn Atkins almost from the moment she stepped on campus that fall. "It was a small campus," he said, smiling. "There wasn't much chance I was going to miss her." Lynn Atkins had Mediterranean blue eyes — "there has never been another set of eyes like that," her husband says thirty-three years later — an easy smile, and a friendly manner. That summer, she was dating a friend of Odom's named Johnny Coble. They double-dated one night and Dave ended up driving Lynn home. They pulled into her mother's driveway shortly after midnight and were still there about three hours later when her mother turned the lights on. By then, Johnny Coble was history. The next day when Dave showed up at a fashion show Lynn was in, her mother pointed a finger at Dave and said, "Don't you ever bring my daughter home late!"

Dave got the message. "Never did it again," he said. "Fortunately, she warmed up to me as time went on."

So did Lynn. They were married the next summer, after Dave had graduated, and immediately headed for Goldsboro, where they had a week to honeymoon before Dave started work as a teacher and basketball coach at his old high school. Dave had promised Lynn a week at the beach, but when they arrived, all the hotels were booked. They ended up at Whitey's Motel in Wilmington. "I'm not sure," Dave admitted, "that she's ever forgiven me."

They stayed in Goldsboro for four years before Dave was offered the job at Durham High School, one of the better high school programs in the state. It was during his days in Durham that Odom began to make some of the key contacts in his coaching life. None was more important than Chuck Daly, then an assistant coach at Duke. Odom worked at the Duke camp each summer and it was there that he met Daly, who suggested to him that he should try to get work at a place up north called Five-Star. Back then, Five-Star was a new concept: an all-star camp for top high school players launched by a slick, wisecracking New Yorker named Howard Garfinkel. Daly gave Odom Garfinkel's number, and a year later Garfinkel offered him a spot at his camp as a coach.

The camp Odom attended in the summer of 1973 was in Wheeling, West Virginia. His first assignment was to run the offensive pick-and-roll station. Then, as now, station drills were a huge part of the Five-Star experience. One morning, working his station, Odom overhead Garfinkel whispering (a Garfinkel whisper is like a normal person's bellow) to a coach that "this kid's going to be a great coach and I discovered him."

Five-Star was full of young coaches in those days. Hubie Brown, who would go on to coach the Knicks, was the master clinician at the time. One of the coaches Odom found himself working with — and coaching against in games — was a fast-talking New York kid named Rick Pitino. In the semifinals of the first week's tournament, Odom's team was matched against Pitino's team. "They were the first camp team in history to employ a full-court press," Odom remembered with a laugh.

Pitino's team won that game, but Odom won his share of camp games against Pitino over the years. Twenty years after first meeting at Five-Star, they would face each other again in the NCAA tournament.

Although Odom was influenced by the coaches he played for, it was at Five-Star that his coaching philosophy began to take shape. Many of the practice drills he runs today come directly from Five-Star and his belief that going over things — especially fundamentals — over and over and over again, comes straight from the Garfinkel manual, which holds that "station work" (drills) is a lot more important in the development of a player than scrimmaging, no matter how much players might prefer scrimmaging. If a Five-Star session is wiped out by rain, the first thing canceled are the games. The last thing canceled is station work. With Odom it is no different. If his team can't get a drill right in practice, he will lengthen the time scheduled for that drill, even if it means shortening something else.

At Five-Star, Odom spent countless hours listening to the older coaches at clinics, then watching them sit around the dinner table arguing about motion offenses and matchup zones. He came away convinced of one thing: there was no one right way to coach. The only right way was the way that fit you. If Rick Pitino felt that ninety-four-feet of defensive pressure was the best way to coach, that was fine. It worked for him. But it didn't work for Odom. So, he didn't try to be Rick Pitino. He just tried to be Dave Odom.

Odom made numerous coaching contacts at Five-Star, on both the high school and college level. In 1976, Carl Tacy, then the coach at Wake Forest, offered him the chance to move to the college level. Odom had made his mark as a high school coach. He was ready. He went to Wake Forest and stayed three years. In 1979 East Carolina was looking for a coach and came looking for Odom. It was a chance to go home and a chance to run his own program. Odom jumped at the chance.

But East Carolina wasn't a basketball school. Its priority was football, and putting together a basketball program at a small school that had no conference affiliation in a state that was dominated by four ACC schools was virtually impossible. ECU went from 16–11 to 12–14 to 10–17 in three seasons. Not a positive trend. When Terry Holland, another North Carolinian from a small town, called and asked Odom if he'd like to come to Virginia as his top assistant, Odom decided to go even though it was, in some ways, a step down.

"I missed the ACC," he said. "I missed that kind of basketball atmosphere. I'd gotten spoiled. And we were struggling at ECU. I didn't honestly know if we could turn it around or not. Terry was someone I felt comfortable with and I knew I would be going into a very exciting situation right from the first day."

The situation was both exciting and tense: Ralph Sampson, the seven-foot-four-inch center who had been the most significant recruit in the history of Virginia basketball, was entering his senior year. Although the Cavaliers had reached the Final Four in his sophomore season, there had been no national championship. Holland had been blasted for not winning more games with Sampson, and Sampson had been criticized for not wanting to win enough.

Odom's first season in Charlottesville was a roller coaster. There were several great wins — most notably over Georgetown in the ballyhooed meeting between Sampson and Patrick Ewing — and one humiliating loss, to tiny Chaminade in a game still considered the greatest upset in college basketball history. The season ended with a stunning loss in the West Regional final to Jim Valvano's Cinderella North Carolina State team that would go on to win the national title nine days later. One year later, with Sampson in the NBA and former walk-on Kenton Edelin starting at center, the Cavaliers made it to the Final Four with a Cinderella run of their own. Suddenly, Holland was a genius again and all was well in UVA hoops land. The Odoms — sons Lane and Ryan were now teenagers — moved into a house two doors down from the Hollands and a close friendship and working relationship bloomed.

When Holland was hospitalized with stomach problems in 1989, Odom took over the team and went 6–2, including a dramatic victory over North Carolina. By then, Holland was thinking about retiring. He was frustrated by the fact that Virginia seemed to be putting all of its efforts — not to mention dollars — into building a football program when it was basketball that had made the most money and had the most success. When the school decided to build a multimillion-dollar building adjacent to University Hall that would be strictly for offices and weight rooms for the football team, Holland decided it was time to think about his next step. It was that same spring — 1989 — that Wake Forest was looking for a coach to replace Bob Staak. Having been there as an assistant coach, and having proven himself as a head coach during Holland's illness, Odom was high on athletic director Gene Hooks's list of possible replacements. When Hooks called him, Odom went to see Holland. He told him he thought it possible that Hooks would offer him the job.

"Don't do anything until I can talk to [Virginia athletic director] Jim Copeland," Holland told him. "If Gene calls, don't take the call. Stall him. Don't give him an answer."

The next day Holland went to see Copeland. He was ready to step down as coach, he told him. He wanted to coach one more year, but if Copeland wanted, he would retire immediately if Copeland would give the job to Odom. Ideally, Holland wanted to announce his retirement that summer, have Odom named as his successor, and then coach one more season.

Copeland said he couldn't do it. He believed the job was too good and too important not to conduct a national search. Odom would certainly be a candidate, but he couldn't make any promises.

Holland walked back across the bridge that led from University Hall to the block where he and Odom lived. "Take the Wake Forest job," he said. "I can't guarantee you anything here."

And so when Hooks called and told Odom he wanted to hire him, Odom accepted. He took over a program that had gone through four straight losing seasons during which it had compiled an ACC record of

8–48. His first season there was more of the same: 12–16 overall, 3–11 in the league, but Odom had some young talent on the way, most notably Rodney Rogers, a six-foot-eight power forward who had grown up in Durham but was not recruited heavily by either Duke or North Carolina. He also signed a guard named Randolph Childress, who might have gone to Maryland if the Terrapins hadn't been on probation. Those two were the foundation Odom was looking for. In his second season, 1991, the Deacons were 19–11 and made it back to the NCAA tournament for the first time since 1984. That began a run in which the Demon Deacons went to seven straight NCAA tournaments.

Two years later, Odom recruited a skinny kid from the Virgin Islands named Tim Duncan. When he first saw Duncan, he saw potential in him. Maybe, he thought, he could redshirt him a year to put some weight on him. Maybe, by his third year at Wake, he could be an effective player.

Little did Odom know that the day he signed Duncan his coaching life would be changed forever. In 1994, Duncan's first season, they had lost in the second round to Kansas. In 1995, with Duncan becoming a force in the middle, they had reached the Sweet Sixteen before losing to Oklahoma State. A year later, with Duncan clearly established as the best player in the country, they had made the Elite Eight before losing to Kentucky.

Most people had figured Duncan would follow every other college star's example and turn pro that spring. He was an absolute lock to be the first player chosen in the NBA draft. But Duncan wasn't like a lot of college athletes. He decided he enjoyed college too much to give it up before he had to and wanted to come back for his senior year. He wanted to play in the Final Four. He wanted to take Wake to Monday Night.

Wake Forest hadn't been to the Final Four since 1962. As practice began in October, there wasn't anyone connected with the program who did not believe that the drought would end in March. The Deacons had been ranked number two nationwide in preseason polls and were favored to win the ACC.

Odom was very conscious of the expectations surrounding his team and of the notion that most people would be focusing on the catch rather than the chase. He was hoping — somehow — to avoid that. And so, on the night before practice for the 1997 season was scheduled to begin, he showed up for a team meeting carrying a book. It was called *The Precious*

Present. He had heard his pal Pitino make reference to it during the summer at a clinic and had found a copy. The book is about a little boy who grows into a man looking for a present that is supposed to be hidden somewhere. He searches for it for years until he finally realizes that the present isn't anything tangible, that it is today; and it is as precious as any present can be.

Odom spent twenty minutes reading the book aloud to his players that night. He didn't want them to think about March in October or November or December. He wanted them to enjoy the precious present. They sat and listened. Whether they heard, Odom knew, was another question entirely.

Although most of the national attention was focused on Wake Forest, there was no place in the ACC more wound up about the start of basketball season than Clemson.

That fact, all by itself, was a measure of the miraculous work Rick Barnes had done in two years. Until 1991, when the powers that be had decided to try to make the ACC into a football conference by admitting Florida State, Clemson had been the one school in the league where football was unquestionably the sport that mattered. The school had won a national championship in football in 1981 and if you happened to mention to a Clemson person that it had been put on NCAA probation the next season for violations that involved the 1981 team and coaching staff, you were apt to find yourself ducking quickly.

Of course Clemson had a basketball past too. In the mid-1970s, Tates Locke (the man who had been Bob Knight's first and last coaching boss at West Point in the 1960s) had gone out and recruited a number of top players, including seven-foot star Wayne "Tree" Rollins. The problem was, he had cheated to get many of those players and, shortly after Clemson reached postseason play for the first time ever, in 1975, Locke resigned in the middle of an NCAA investigation that would lead to two years of probation. His successor, Bill Foster, did what Locke couldn't do: build a winner without cheating. Clemson made the NCAA tournament for the first time in 1980 and went all the way to the round of eight before losing to UCLA. Foster left for Miami in 1984 and was followed by Cliff

Ellis, who managed three more NCAA trips and one ACC regular season title in 1990. But the wins came less often after that season and, with yet another NCAA investigation in progress, Ellis resigned early in 1994.

That was when Athletic Director Bobby Robinson put in a call to Big East commissioner Mike Tranghese. Like everyone else in basketball, he had heard that Barnes wasn't terribly happy at Providence. He also knew that Barnes and his wife, Candy, had both grown up in the South — Hickory, North Carolina — and might be eager to be closer to their roots and their families. Tranghese put in a call to Barnes. "I think you should talk to this guy" was all he said.

Barnes was in his sixth year at Providence. He had been successful there, with an 88–66 record in five years, but not wildly successful. The Friars had reached the NCAA tournament his first two seasons, but hadn't been back since. Providence is one of those schools with enough past glory — including Final Four appearances in 1973 and 1987 — that its fans and alumni expect great things most years. But it is also a small city school with an off-campus playing facility in a place that gets very cold during the winter months. Winning is always possible but never easy.

Barnes hadn't won enough to be a beloved figure at Providence, certainly not the kind of beloved figure that Rick Pitino had become during his two-year tenure there in 1986 and 1987. Pitino had turned a foundering program around and taken the Friars to an unlikely Final Four in his second year. Then he had promised not to leave Providence and, about fifteen minutes later, had left to become coach of the New York Knicks. Most Providence people had forgiven him for that. They weren't as willing to forgive Barnes — who was dubbed Rick II when he was hired a year after Pitino's exit — for not winning as often as Pitino.

"Rick had to be the least happy coach with a winning record in America," said Larry Shyatt, Barnes's longtime assistant and close friend. "Those people up there just tortured him."

It didn't help that Barnes had a North Carolina twang in his voice as opposed to Pitino's strident New York accent. It didn't help that he had graduated from Lenoir-Rhyne, a school most people in New England had never heard of.

Barnes had almost left Providence in the spring of 1990 to replace Terry Holland at Virginia, but had been talked out of the move at the last instant by Dave Gavitt, Tranghese's predecessor as Big East commissioner. Gavitt had coached Providence to the Final Four in 1973, had been the athletic director there, and remained the godfather to Providence athletics even while he was running the Big East. Gavitt convinced Barnes that leaving Providence after just two years would be a mistake for him and for the school.

The next two seasons were miserable for Barnes. Providence just missed the NCAA tournament in 1991, but fell apart the next year, going 14–17. That was Barnes's first — and to date only — losing season as a head coach. "I did a lousy job that year," he said. "A horrible job. I let everything get to me. I was short-tempered with everyone, most of all my players. I blamed them when I should have been blaming myself."

Things got better the next season as a group of young players began to mature. The team was still improving in 1994 when Robinson and Barnes talked. Robinson wanted to meet as soon as possible. On Monday, January 25, forty-eight hours after a dramatic victory at Syracuse, Barnes flew to Baltimore-Washington International Airport and met with Robinson in an airport hotel room. "I'm not going to lie to you," Robinson said. "We could have the worst team in the history of the ACC next year. It may take three years just to get decent."

Barnes knew all about Clemson and all about the ACC. He had grown up on the league in western North Carolina and had never stopped following it as an adult. In 1978, when he was a year out of college, he had driven to Greensboro to see the ACC tournament for the first time in his life. He had walked out of the Greensboro Coliseum that night with one thought. *Someday I'm going to coach in that tournament.* He had turned down the chance once already, in part because he would have had to walk away from a group of freshmen he had just recruited; in part because he felt he owed Providence more than two years. It had broken his heart to say no in 1990 and he knew it had broken his wife's heart.

That didn't mean he was going to jump the minute Robinson put the carrot in front of him. He knew Clemson's history, or as he put it, "lack of history." He knew what he would be up against in the ACC, competing both in recruiting and on the court with North Carolina and Dean Smith, Duke and Mike Krzyzewski, not to mention his old boss Gary Williams, who was now at Maryland.

"Do you believe Clemson can win the national championship?" he asked Robinson.

"More important," Robinson answered, "do you?"

Barnes thought about it for a moment. The ACC was the best and best-known conference in America. He had seen the Clemson campus years before when he had interviewed for an assistant's job under Bill Foster. It was certainly scenic enough to attract players. The football-school reputation didn't bother him because he had worked at Ohio State, another so-called football school, and had seen that you could win big in basketball.

"Yes, I do," Barnes answered.

"Then come do it," Robinson said.

Barnes had certain conditions. Given that Robinson thought it likely the school would spend at least two years at the bottom of the ACC, he wanted at least a seven-year contract. And if he was going to make a commitment now, in midseason, there could be no leaks. He would not be a lame-duck coach with a senior-dominated team. Robinson agreed. Barnes still had to consult with Candy. He flew home that night and laid the offer out to her.

Candy Barnes is always straightforward. She shrugged her shoulders and said, "I don't know what you're planning to do, but I'm going to Clemson."

The deal was made, a handshake between Barnes and Robinson. Concerned that Barnes might be talked out of his decision the way he had been when Virginia approached him four years earlier, Robinson called every night. But that wasn't going to happen this time. Barnes hadn't told Gavitt or anyone else except his assistant coaches. Amazingly, rumors that he was leaving didn't become heated until the week of the Big East tournament. By then, it was too late to bother the players. The Friars won the Big East tournament to get back into the NCAAs. Three days after the Friars lost in the first round of the tournament to Alabama, Barnes was introduced as Clemson's new coach.

The Tigers had finished eighth in the ACC in '94, but Barnes quickly understood why Robinson had been so pessimistic. As expected, Clemson's best player, junior center Sharone Wright, announced that he would not be back for his senior year. That left the team with one experienced player, Devin Gray. Less than a month after Barnes arrived, Gray had a heart attack. Doctors said he might be able to play again, but it was uncertain. So were his grades.

"I never for one second thought that Devin Gray would play for us," Barnes said. "I made all my plans as if he was gone."

That left Barnes with a team that would be small, slow, and woefully inexperienced in '94–95. Barnes knew that if he tried to play the up-tempo style that his Providence teams had played, he would be looking at a lot of blowouts. The only way to play was slowly — walk the ball up the floor, milk the thirty-five-second clock for as long as possible, and hope that enough three-point shots fell during the course of an evening to keep things competitive.

Knowing that and convincing the players to buy into it were two different things. College basketball in the nineties is all about speed and glitz and dazzle. No one wants to play slow. And no one wants to spend the summer going through the most grueling conditioning program of their lives. But that's what Barnes insisted his players do. By the time the summer of '94 was over, he had five players left — and Gray, who remained a question mark. He also had one outstanding freshman, Greg Buckner, who he was convinced could step in and play right away in the ACC. "Actually there wasn't any choice in the matter," Barnes said. "He had to play right away."

The leading returning scorer (other than Gray) was sophomore Merl Code, who had averaged 4.1 points per game as a freshman. The other four returnees — seniors Andy Kelly, Rayfield Ragland, and Bruce Martin and sophomore Bill Harder — had all played very limited roles in the past. But Barnes decided they were going to be the foundation of his program. He nicknamed them the "Slab Five" — "I told them I couldn't call them the Fab Five because there was nothing fabulous about them" — threw in Buckner and another freshman, Iker Iturbe, and prepared to go to battle in the ACC. He told them over and over again that the world expected them to be awful, that people were picking them to be the worst team in ACC history. "If you do what we tell you," he said, "you will surprise a lot of people."

The players hated the summer, hated all the work, but they bought into it. Clemson had traditionally played the ACC's weakest December schedule, loading up with easy home games to pad the record, so few people took much notice when the newly minted Barnes Tigers finished the month with an 8–0 record, even though one of the victories was a twenty-four-point road rout of archrival South Carolina and another was a twenty-point win over a respectable Miami of Florida team. But the players noticed. The slowdown system worked. Barnes had told them that the worst team in ACC history had won only five games. When they went to 6–0 with a win over Citadel, they celebrated. More important than that, their confidence in the new way of playing was growing.

By the time the Tigers rolled into Cameron Indoor Stadium to start ACC play on January 4, Barnes actually had them convinced that they could beat Duke. Which was, of course, a ridiculous notion. Good Clemson teams — very good Clemson teams — had lost in Cameron, often by embarrassing scores. In fact, Clemson had won exactly three times in the storied old place, in forty-five tries. Two years earlier another undefeated Clemson team had come to Cameron to open ACC play — and had been beaten 110–67.

Before the game, Barnes told his team repeatedly that the Blue Devils wouldn't take them seriously. After all, they had arrived home from Hawaii the previous Saturday and had played a game Monday even though their conference opener was on Wednesday. "They think we're so easy to beat, they can travel five thousand miles and play a game forty-eight hours before they play us," he said. "I think we're tougher than that. I think we're tougher than they are. And the tougher team will win this game."

His last words were direct. Among coaches, Barnes probably ranks somewhere in the middle of the ACC when it comes to using profanity. When he does use it, more often than not, it is to make a specific point — although at times it is simply because he's angry. On this night, he was making a point. "Be motherfuckers," he told his team. "That's what it is all about."

In the Bible Belt South there are many people who object to such language. Mike Krzyzewski was criticized by some of those people in 1991 when he said during Duke's victory rally after winning the national championship, "We finally won the damn thing." Like it or not, it is a simple fact of life that almost every coach on the planet uses profanity when talking to his players. Dean Smith is the exception to that rule. In 1977, when Kentucky's Rick Robey accused Smith of calling him a son-ofabitch, Smith vehemently denied the charge, saying, "I smoke and I drink. If I cursed too my parents would never speak to me again."

Smith doesn't curse. Other coaches do, some frequently, some only when they are truly angry, and some because they understand that profanity is part of the language for most college athletes. The word "motherfucker" is one coaches use often. It is considered a high form of praise. Every team needs a motherfucker, someone who is tough and mean and willing to do anything to win. That can mean getting in the other team's face or getting in the face of a teammate if necessary. Michael Jordan was a motherfucker, even if his college coach wouldn't use the term. Christian Laettner was a motherfucker and his college coach wouldn't hesitate to use the term. Years ago, Maryland center Buck Williams, who carried a Bible with him everywhere he went, was a motherfucker. His coach, Lefty Driesell, liked to say of Williams: "Off the court, he's the nicest person you'll ever meet. 'Yes sir, no sir, yes ma'am, no ma'am.' On the court, he'll kill you if he has to."

Barnes was convinced he had a burgeoning motherfucker in Buckner, someone who would do anything to win a basketball game and never back down from anybody. That was what he felt his team needed to compete in the ACC: an attitude, one that said, "We are motherfuckers and you can't scare us."

They weren't scared that night. They led from the beginning, withstood a couple of Duke rallies, and won the game fairly easily, 75–70. Every time Duke rallied, someone hit a three-point shot. For the game, Clemson hit 10 of 15 threes. They danced at midcourt to celebrate while the stunned Duke fans looked at them as if they were from another planet. They had been motherfuckers. It would become their motto and rallying cry.

As it turned out, there had been mitigating circumstances. Forty-eight hours after the game, Krzyzewski checked himself into the hospital, suffering from severe back pains and exhaustion. Later, he could hardly remember anything about the game because of the pain. He didn't coach again that season and Duke, which had been ranked ninth in the country with a 9–2 record going into the game against Clemson, would finish last in the ACC, winning only four of nineteen games after Krzyzewski's departure.

None of that mattered to Clemson that night. They had gone into a place where Clemson never won, and won. They were supposed to be a "dive" team on the road and they hadn't come close to taking one. They had beaten a team that had played in four of the last five national championship games. There was now no doubt that the system worked, that all the hard work in the summertime was paying off and that they could compete in the ACC.

They got to 10–0 with a victory over Texas A&M and woke up that Monday morning to find themselves nationally ranked. The bubble finally got popped — emphatically — at Virginia. Instead of shooting 10 of 15 from three-point range, they were five for 22 and the final was 62–44. Still, the foundation had been built by the slabbers and most nights they were able to stay in games. Barnes's goal in every ACC game was to stay close for thirty-five minutes and then watch the other team get tight. He never tried to convince his players that they were just as talented as the other league teams, only that if they shortened the game and wore the opponent out by making it work for thirty-five seconds on defense on every possession, they would give themselves a chance to win.

Three days after the Virginia loss, Clemson played its first ACC home game under Barnes against North Carolina. As always, the Tar Heels were loaded. They would finish the season in the Final Four and two of their players, Jerry Stackhouse and Rasheed Wallace, would leave school after two years to become the third and fourth picks in the NBA draft. Carolina led all night, but Clemson — smaller, slower, less experienced — wouldn't go away. The fouls piled up against the Tigers, and as they did Barnes got angrier and angrier.

"We did commit a lot of fouls," he said later. "But I had the feeling all night that the referees were calling the game the way they thought it was *supposed* to go. There was a feeling that Carolina has a certain place in the league and Clemson has a certain place in the league and Clemson's place is eighth or ninth. I wasn't going to accept that."

With five minutes left, Barnes turned to Shyatt on the bench and said, "It's time for me to make a point about all this."

Shyatt knew what he was planning. "Not yet," he pleaded. "We're only down thirteen. We could still have a chance if we foul and they miss some free throws."

Barnes agreed to wait. But with 28 seconds left and Carolina up 12, it was clear the Tigers weren't going to pull off any miracles. This time, Shyatt didn't have a chance to argue.

Lenny Wirtz, who some ACC people believe was the referee on the first day that James Naismith put up his peach basket, was standing in front of the Clemson bench. Barnes began railing at him, screaming about the disparity in fouls — 32 for Clemson; nine for Carolina.

"Rick, I know what you're doing," Wirtz said calmly. "And I'm telling you, it isn't going to happen."

"Oh yes it is," Barnes said, storming off the bench to confront Wirtz in the middle of the court.

Wirtz had no choice. He gave Barnes the technical he wanted. Barnes wasn't finished, though. He wanted more. He followed Wirtz to the scorer's table still screaming. The last thing Wirtz wanted to do was toss a coach in the final seconds of an already decided ball game.

"I'm not doing it, Rick," he kept saying.

"Yes you are," Barnes said. And he continued to scream and yell and wave his arms until Wirtz was left with no choice. He tossed him.

By now the crowd was going crazy. Clemson fans believe that the rest of the ACC looks down on them as some cow college in the middle of nowhere. They knew that no one from North Carolina, least of all Dean Smith, had any respect for them. And now, here was their new coach, who had already gone up to Duke and won, saying very loudly and very publicly that he wasn't going to accept all the old notions. They were on their feet screaming as Barnes was escorted off.

The final score was 83–66. Clemson's fans left feeling exhilarated anyway. Barnes had made his point. Clemson would not accept "being Clemson" anymore. "I was prepared," Barnes said, "to get thrown out of every game if I had to."

He did have one regret about the incident. In all the pandemonium during his exit, he had never congratulated Smith on his team's victory. The next morning he called Smith to apologize. "I had no problem at all with Dean that night," he said. "He didn't do anything wrong."

Smith appreciated the phone call, but wasn't thrilled with Barnes's on-court histrionics. He understood the point Barnes was trying to make and, naturally, didn't agree with it. If anything, he thought, his team could have shot *more* than 51 foul shots. What's more, he had read a quote in the paper from Clemson's Rayfield Ragland, who had said, "The coaches told us, if we were going to foul to make sure they were hard fouls."

Coaches say this sort of thing all the time. Nothing upsets a coach more than a ticky-tacky foul, a light push as a player is making a layup that leads to an easy three-point play. "If you're going to foul him," they will say, "then *foul* him." Often coaches will write on the blackboard before a game things like: "NO THREE-POINT PLAYS." That means, if someone has a layup, hammer him. Make him go to the line and earn two points.

"I have never told my players to hurt anyone," Barnes has said repeatedly. "And I never will."

Knowing that Clemson was outmanned, Smith couldn't help but wonder if Barnes hadn't told his players to be overly physical. He has always campaigned for officials to call games closer at least in part because his teams are usually more talented and are more likely to get fouled by slower players who have no alternative but to clutch and grab. For years, he was convinced that Virginia's MO against his team was to push, grab, and clutch whenever it could and he often made comments about Virginia's "style of play."

Now, he accepted Barnes's apology, but couldn't resist saying something about Iturbe, who he felt had been involved in a couple of questionable plays. Barnes quickly shot back, "What about Wallace?" He had just watched tape of the game and had seen Rasheed Wallace throw an elbow on the first play of the game that had cracked one of Andy Kelly's ribs. The conversation went no further.

But another foundation — different from the Slab Five's — had been laid.

A month later, Clemson went to play at Chapel Hill. The game wasn't nearly as close as the game at Clemson had been. Carolina won by 27 and it could have been more. Barnes had no problems with the officiating. It certainly wasn't their fault that his team could only score 14 points in the first half. He was answering questions in his postgame press conference when someone came into the interview room and said that a number of the North Carolina players had accused Clemson of dirty play. Barnes seethed. Wasn't it enough that the Tar Heels had humiliated them?

"Why don't you tell them to come in here right now and we'll sit down and look at the game tape," he said. "I'll show you some dirty play if you want to see it."

Now Barnes *was* angry at Smith. He knew the Tar Heels wouldn't make public comments like that unless their coach had said something to them. North Carolina players don't comment on what day of the week it is unless it has been cleared by Smith.

Naturally, as luck would have it, Clemson and Carolina drew one another in the first round of the ACC tournament. The Tigers had managed five conference wins — two over Duke; two over NC State, and one over Georgia Tech — to finish tied for sixth, their highest finish in four years. Carolina had finished in a four-way tie for first and drawn the second seed — and Clemson. Barnes knew his team had little chance to win the game. But he wasn't going to accept any more insults or put-downs — perceived or real — from Carolina.

The game was never really close, but it wasn't as one-sided as the game in Chapel Hill. The fouls were virtually even (17 for Clemson, 13 for Carolina) and the Tar Heels led comfortably most of the second half. But Carolina was a tense team. Rasheed Wallace's legendary temper flared midway through the second half and he screamed a profanity at referee Rick Hartzell, who promptly nailed him with a technical. Smith, having seen enough, yanked Wallace from the game.

Late in the game, Stackhouse, as good a citizen as Wallace was a shaky one, drove to the basket. Iker Iturbe, coming across the lane to help, fouled him. Stackhouse went down. It looked to most people like a routine play, a routine foul. Not to Smith. He was convinced Iturbe was trying to hurt Stackhouse. He jumped off the bench, face contorted in anger, screaming and pointing his finger at Iturbe. It was Shyatt who saw what was happening and pointed it out to Barnes. "Look at that," he said. "He's going off on Ikes."

Smith insists that all he was doing was yelling Iturbe's name. The Clemson version is that he was calling him a dirty player. Either way, there is no questioning the fact that Smith was screaming at Iturbe, pointing his finger at him, clearly enraged. That was it for Barnes. He walked to midcourt, called time-out, and waved referee Frank Scagliotta over.

"Get Dean over here," he said.

Scagliotta shook his head. "Let us handle it, Rick," he said.

"No," Barnes said. "No. If you don't get him down here, I'm going down there."

Barnes was in full shout almost before Smith arrived. "Don't you *ever* talk to my players again," he yelled. "If you have a problem with one of them, you come talk to *me!*"

Smith wasn't about to back down to anyone, much less a rookie ACC coach who had won about seven hundred fewer games than he had. "What do you want to do, Rick," he answered sarcastically, "hit me? Why don't you go ahead and hit me."

Barnes wasn't going to hit Smith, but he was prepared to go toe-to-toe with him. It took everything Scagliotta and Hartzell had to stay between the two men and keep the two benches separated as they yelled at each other. Smith tried to laugh it off as he went back to his bench, but he was shaken. Barnes got a technical foul for his efforts, but didn't seem to mind.

The last three minutes of the game were the most intense, physical three minutes of a one-sided basketball game ever played. Smith left his starters, except for Wallace, in the game and they kept trying to make spectacular plays. On the last play of the game, Carolina tried an alley-oop dunk play and Clemson's Bill Harder undercut Carolina's Donald Williams to make sure the play wasn't executed. Carolina freshman Shammond Williams raced in, wanting to fight Harder. The teams had to be pulled apart and security had to be called to prevent a riot.

Smith was asked after the game if he called Iturbe a dirty player. He denied it, then launched into a lengthy speech about "European players" (Iturbe is from Spain), the clear implication being that European players are dirty players. Later he would admit that he did think Iturbe was a dirty player and he had the tapes to prove it. Barnes was with the media for close to an hour telling his side of the story. When he finally walked out of the building, exhausted and drained, he walked onto the team bus and sank into his seat in the front row. He felt a hand on his shoulder. He looked up and saw Bruce Martin.

"Coach," Martin said, "I just want you to know how much the guys appreciate you standing up for us," he said. "You made us proud to be from Clemson."

Barnes smiled. Step one had been taken.

By winning fifteen games that first year, Barnes had set the bar higher for '96–97 than anyone at Clemson could have anticipated. But three seniors — Kelly, Martin, and Ragland — were leaving, meaning the Tigers would be even younger than they had been in year one.

But they would be far more talented. Barnes and his staff signed seven players. Their recruiting pitch was simple and direct. Come and be part of a basketball revival. They could offer immediate playing time to any player with talent. Two big men signed on — Tom Wideman and Harold Jamison. Both were wide-bodies, not the kind of players who would have to spend two years in the weight room before they could bang with ACC players. Their presence meant that Buckner, at six-four, wouldn't have to play inside as much as he had been forced to as a freshman. Barnes also reached back to his early days as an assistant coach at George Mason when he convinced Tony Christie and Andrus Jurkunas, both talented swingmen from St. John's Prospect Hall, in Maryland, to commit. The two played for Stu Vetter. Fifteen years earlier, the most important player Barnes had ever recruited was Carlos Yates of Flint Hill High School. Yates's coach had been Stu Vetter. He and Barnes had become friends and, as they both moved on to other jobs, they had stayed friends.

The most important signee that spring was the smallest. Terrell McIntyre was five foot nine if he stood up very straight. He was from Raeford, North Carolina, and had drawn some attention from both Duke and North Carolina in spite of his lack of size. Both coaching staffs were planning to see him play one night when they got a phone call from McIntyre's coach. McIntyre's father had died suddenly and he wouldn't be playing that night. McIntyre wasn't a prime recruit for either school and neither one could afford to take another recruiting day (they are limited in-season) to commit to another trip to see him. They backed off.

Barnes hadn't been too enthusiastic about McIntrye either. But he kept getting insistent letters from people saying he had to check him out, regardless of his size. Finally, he sent Shyatt to see if there was anything to what he was being told. Shyatt came back raving. "We've got to sign this kid," he said. Barnes trusted Shyatt implicitly. McIntyre became a prime recruit from that day forward.

"But we still didn't know just how good he was," Barnes said. "We brought him in figuring he would play fifteen or sixteen minutes a game as a freshman behind Merl Code and then we'd see what we had."

The Tigers were picked last in the league again. This time, they won their first eleven games, beating Duke and Virginia at home at the start of the conference season. Again, they were ranked. Then came a 33-point loss at North Carolina during which Barnes was booed throughout the game by the DeanDome faithful, still furious with him because of the ACC tournament incident. Then there was another loss, at Florida State, during which Code was hurt.

McIntyre turned out to be one of those players whose heart and guts overcome his physical limitations. In his first ACC game, McIntyre had hit two huge three pointers, including the game winner, in the win over Duke. Three games later, when Code went down for the season with a knee injury, McIntyre was the only player on the team with legitimate point-guard skills. In the first two games after Code's injury, he never came out. "We went from planning on him playing sixteen minutes a night to needing forty minutes from him," Barnes said. "He never flinched."

With McIntrye forced to play all the minutes at point guard, Barnes simplified the offense. But he didn't back down from the demands he made on his players. "You aren't freshmen anymore," he told them. "You can't use being young as an excuse. It's too easy."

They responded by beating sixth-ranked Wake Forest, 55–41, four days after Code's injury. They were competitive in every game for the next month except for a 30-point loss at Duke in a game the Blue Devils approached with a slightly different attitude than they had taken a year before. Three straight losses to a team will do that.

And then North Carolina came back to Clemson. The Barnes-Smith feud had simmered all season. Both coaches had been given token fines — $2,500 — for their behavior in the 1995 ACC tournament. Both had been told by Commissioner Gene Corrigan not to talk to the media any more about the incident. The first meeting of the season had been full of media buildup, especially with Clemson being undefeated going into the game. The Tar Heels had won so easily that there really wasn't much chance for any trouble.

Or so it seemed. Two days after the game, Clemson athletic director Bobby Robinson got a call from Fred Barakat. He wanted to know if Barnes had said anything to him about Smith talking to Bill Harder during the game. Robinson knew nothing about it. Neither did Barnes. In their game report, the officials had mentioned that Smith had been yelling something in Harder's direction late in the game. Barnes asked Harder about it.

"Yeah, he was saying something, but I didn't pay attention," Harder answered. "We were down thirty. Who cared?"

Barnes cared. But he decided not to do anything at the time. "I just decided when the season was over, I would confront Dean at the coaches meetings with everyone else there," he said. "There was no sense getting into the whole thing again during the season."

Then came the rematch in Littlejohn Coliseum. It was tense and low scoring throughout. When Littlejohn is packed, it is as tough and loud a place to play as there is in the country. Even at their angriest, the DeanDome crowd is about as mild as you will find, certainly in the ACC. Not so at Clemson, where the crowd is close to the court and the court is below ground level, meaning the noise stays right there at court level all night.

Midway through the second half, with the game seesawing, referee Stan Rote ran past the Clemson bench and said to Barnes, "Tell Bill not to worry. I saw it. I'll take care of it."

Barnes had no idea what he was talking about. During a break, he asked Harder what had happened. "Coach Smith was calling me a dirty player again," Harder answered, not appearing to be too shaken by the accusation.

Again, the Clemson version and the North Carolina version of the story diverge. Smith remembers saying to Harder, "Stop playing with your hands. You're a good player. Play with your feet." In other words: quit grabbing my players.

But again, there was no disputing the fact that Smith was lecturing Barnes's players. Barnes called a twenty-second time-out and started walking toward the scorer's table. Referee Tim Higgins, who knew all about what had happened in Greensboro and what had just taken place, put his hands up as Barnes approached. "No, no, no," he said. "Rick, we aren't doing this now. We're finishing this game." Barnes didn't argue. The game was too close to cause a scene. But when it was over and Carolina had pulled out a 53–48 victory, Barnes shook hands with Smith and then, as they were walking toward the tunnel, he said, "We need to talk."

"Not now," Smith said. "Call me."

"I'm not calling you," Barnes said. "I want to talk right now."

At that point, security people and assistant coaches got between the two men as they crossed from the court — where they were still visible to the TV cameras — into the tunnel leading to the locker rooms. Barnes was fuming — again. Smith was furious — again. In his postgame press conference, Smith said he didn't know what Barnes was upset about, insisting that he had merely been telling Harder to play with his feet. When Barnes heard that, he called Harder from the locker room into his office. Until that moment he had not allowed his players to talk publicly about any of the incidents or accusations. Now, he lifted the ban and told Harder to repeat what Smith had said.

"He called me a dirty player," Harder said.

When Gene Corrigan read his newspaper the next morning and saw the two coaches going at it once more, he was angrier than both of them put together. An unprecedented summit meeting was called — at Corrigan's house. Enough, Corrigan decided, was enough. The specter of two ACC coaches trading barbs and accusations and, in effect, calling each other liars, was unseemly. Smith and Barnes both showed up for the meeting armed with tapes. Smith's had a series of plays showing Clemson players doing dirty deeds. When he pulled it out, Barnes laughed.

"I've got *four* tapes with me," he said. He wasn't kidding. He had one tape showing every foul committed in the five games between the two teams during his Clemson tenure. He had another one showing what could be considered "bad" fouls committed by Clemson and another showing "bad" fouls committed by North Carolina. The fourth tape was of Carolina players accusing Clemson of dirty play.

"NO TAPES!" Corrigan roared. Normally, Corrigan is a conciliator and a mediator. But he thought the time for that had passed. He had tried it that way the previous summer with the token fines and a warning to both coaches. He knew now he probably should have suspended them for their behavior in Greensboro. He told them in no uncertain terms that the next time either one of them opened his mouth to say something about the other he would be suspended. There would be no more talking to the media about what had gone on. The league would be issuing a statement the next day signed by both men saying that all their troubles were behind them. They would stand behind that statement — or else.

Barnes didn't argue. He knew Corrigan was right. Smith didn't argue either, but he couldn't resist a couple of jibes. Smith is not used to anyone telling him what to do. After Corrigan had finished, he turned to Barnes and said, "You know, I really admire what you've done the last two years. I'd love to watch one of your practices someday to get an idea how you teach your players to hold the way they do."

Two weeks later, with an NCAA tournament berth at stake for Clemson, the Tigers came from behind in the first round of the ACC tournament to stun Carolina, 75–73. McIntyre made the play that won the game, beating a double-team to feed Buckner for a dunk with one second to play. There were no shouting matches. When the game was over, Smith came into the Clemson locker room looking for McIntyre to offer congratulations.

Peace was at hand. And Clemson was in the NCAA tournament for the first time in six years. There were no seniors on the team.

When practice began the following October for the '97 season, for the first time in history Clemson decided to stage a Midnight Madness celebration. It was scheduled at the last minute but close to 5,000 people showed up at Littlejohn. During Barnes's first year there had been *games* with fewer than 5,000 people in the building. The Tigers would open the season against Kentucky, the defending national champions. That was a far cry from Barnes's two previous openers against Charleston Southern and UNC-Asheville.

They had come a long way in a short time. "This is your time," Barnes told his players on the eve of their first practice. "You've worked too hard to get to this point to not keep on going. Every day we practice, you should be thinking about winning the national championship. There's no reason not to think that way."

3

The Triangle

ELECTION DAY 1996 was cloudy and mild in North Carolina, the kind of day that is supposed to produce high voter turnout. Politically, the state is radically — and racially — divided. If you drive straight down the 234 miles of I-85 that bisects the state and carries a driver from Virginia to South Carolina, you will find a moderate to liberal electorate, including a large number of black voters, in the state's five cities: Raleigh, Durham, Greensboro, Winston-Salem, and Charlotte. Veer east or west — especially east — and you will find an older, more conservative, almost all-white population. These are the voters who keep returning Jesse Helms to the United States Senate every six years.

In the area known as the Research Triangle, so named because three major universities are located within a thirty-mile radius of one another, there is always hand-wringing on election day when all the pollsters are again proven wrong and Helms is again sent back to Washington.

"It doesn't matter what the polls say," Dean Smith said a couple of days before the 1996 election. "When all is said and done, Helms gets his people out and he wins."

No one would have been happier to see Helms lose than Smith. He had worked behind the scenes in past campaigns and on rare occasions had made public appearances to try to help defeat Helms. Some friends had encouraged him to run against Helms. "Even if I wanted to run, I couldn't get elected," he said. "I'm much too liberal for a lot of people in this state."

Smith was probably right. One of the grand ironies of life in North Carolina is the fact that a majority of Smith's loyal fans, including many who filled the 21,444 seats in the palace named in his honor, would be far more comfortable politically with the man they considered evil incarnate: Duke coach Mike Krzyzewski.

Krzyzewski wouldn't vote for Helms either. Like Smith he considered Helms a racist and, like Smith, he thought anyone who coached black players and voted for Helms was a hypocrite. But where Smith was liberal and Democrat on most issues, Krzyzewski was conservative and Republican. In his office, Krzyzewski has pictures of his Duke team being greeted in the White House by George Bush after it won the national championship in 1991 and 1992. The last thing Krzyzewski said to Bush as they left the second time was, "I hope we're back here next year and you are too."

He got neither wish. Instead, it was Smith who made the trip the following year with *his* national championship team. Much to Smith's delight, he was welcomed by Bill Clinton, who had beaten Bush in his final a lot more easily than Smith's Tar Heels had beaten Michigan in theirs.

Krzyzewski got his chance to meet Clinton a year later after his team had lost the national championship game to Clinton's beloved Arkansas Razorbacks. Clinton came into the Duke locker room to congratulate the Blue Devils on the game and their season. The White House later sent Krzyzewski a picture of Clinton shaking hands with him that night. He put it in a drawer.

Both coaches voted early on this election day, Smith for Clinton, Krzyzewski for Bob Dole. That meant in the mini-election among college coaches in the Research Triangle, Herb Sendek had the tie-breaking vote. "I didn't vote," Sendek said. "No time."

And who, Sendek was asked, would he have voted for? He smiled. "I'm not sure. I didn't really have time to study the issues closely enough."

Sendek never goes into *anything* unprepared.

At thirty-four, Sendek was the new kid on the ACC block in 1996, stepping into what had once been one of the most glamorous jobs in all of college basketball. North Carolina State has two national championship banners hanging from the rafters of ancient Reynolds Coliseum, one for 1974 and another for 1983. The two titles had been won in entirely different ways by two entirely different coaches. But both represented a time when State could go into battle with anyone and have a chance to win. It had been the '74 Wolfpack, led by the incomparable David Thompson, who had upset UCLA in double overtime in the national semifinals, ending UCLA's unfathomable seven-year string of national titles. The '83 Wolfpack, which barely made it into the NCAA tournament, pulled off one improbable upset after another before finally beating supposedly unbeatable Houston in the national championship game on a buzzer-beating dunk by Lorenzo Charles. That game still ranks as one of the great upsets of all time.

The star of that game wasn't Charles or the three State seniors — Sidney Lowe, Derrick Whittenburg, and Thurl Bailey — who made one play after another during State's miracle run to the title. The star was Jim Valvano. In truth, back then, there was no bigger star in college basketball than James Thomas Valvano. He was a wisecracking New Yorker with thick black hair, a prominent nose and foghorn voice, who was so quick and so funny that he was impossible not to like. He could do shtick off the top of his head for an hour and leave any audience rolling in the aisles. He was also quicker on the draw with a one-liner than anyone alive.

"Hey, Hank," Valvano yelled at Hall of Fame referee Hank Nichols one night as Nichols ran past his bench, "can I ask you a question?"

"Sure, Jimmy. What?"

"Can you tee me up for what I'm thinking?"

"No," answered Nichols, baffled, "I can't tee you up for what you're thinking."

"Good," Valvano said. "In that case, I think you suck."

"I couldn't give him the tee," Nichols said later. "It was too good a line."

Valvano could also coach. Really coach. A lot of basketball people would tell you then and tell you now that if they had one game to play with their entire life on the line, their first choice to coach that game would be Valvano.

Not Bob Knight. Not Dean Smith. Valvano. He was that good.

He was also smart. Scary smart. Often, people got so caught up in the shtick and the one-liners that they didn't get to the smart part of Valvano. He was an insatiable reader with a prodigious memory. He could quote poetry or recall stock market trends as easily as he could list the country's top ten high school players. More easily in fact. He wasn't all that interested in the top ten list.

When he won the national championship in 1983, he was thirty-seven years old. He had been at NC State for three years. At that moment, he was a bigger star than Dean Smith, who had been at North Carolina for twenty-two years and had won his first national title the year before, and he dwarfed Mike Krzyzewski, who had arrived at Duke at almost the same moment Valvano had arrived at State and had been coaching in his shadow since.

The numbers told a lot of the story: Valvano was 62–34 and had won a national championship. Krzyzewski was 38–47 and had yet to win a *game* in the ACC tournament, much less sniff a berth in the NCAA tournament. Krzyzewski was competing against an icon eleven miles to the south and a media megastar twenty-five miles to the east. He also had a lot of alumni who were urging his boss, Tom Butters, to get him the hell out of Duke and go find a real coach to rebuild the program before Valvano and Smith buried the school forever.

Thirteen years later, when Herb Sendek was introduced as NC State's new coach, the landscape had changed considerably. Smith was still an icon, closing in on the all-time record for victories, churning out excellent teams every year. But now Krzyzewski was also a coaching superstar, having turned Duke completely around. He had been to seven Final Fours during a nine-year span and had won two national titles. During the first half of the nineties, Duke had been the best program and Krzyzewski the best coach in college basketball. Dean Smith was fifty-one when he won his first championship. At forty-nine, Krzyzewski already had two.

What had changed more than anything, though, was NC State. Valvano had continued to win consistently throughout the 1980s, but he never had another miracle trip like the one his team took in 1983. The

Wolfpack reached the final eight in 1985 and 1986 and the Sweet Sixteen in 1989. By then, though, the program was coming apart. After fulfilling his dream of winning a national championship, Valvano felt as if he had done coaching. He began looking for new challenges. He did TV commentary — during the season — and did sports on the CBS Morning News, also during the season. He became an entrepreneur, selling everything from blue jeans to trophies to statues. He taped a pilot for a variety show in Hollywood. He had a daily radio show and hosted not only his own TV show but a ridiculous sports bloopers show. He even became State's athletic director, thinking perhaps that would motivate him. He made tons of money, became more and more famous and less and less happy. He spent little time at home with his wife and three daughters and he left a lot of the day-to-day running of his basketball program in the hands of assistant coaches.

He still loved the games. "That's the only forty minutes when everything in my life is real," he said one night. But he didn't particularly care about anything that came in between. He had always been a master recruiter, but he was bored by it. He had also come to believe some of his own press. He thought he could take almost anyone and win games. He also thought he could keep anyone afloat academically because he always had been able to do so in the past.

He could never sleep more than three or four hours a night and he almost never slept at all after a game. He would sit in his office, eating pizza and drinking white wine and tell side-splittingly funny stories. When it got very late, he would sit in a chair and say things like, "I keep wondering what I'm going to be when I grow up. Is this what I want to be? No. But what do I really want to do with my life?"

Valvano was far less envious of Smith, his overwhelmingly successful rival, than of Krzyzewski, who was struggling to stay afloat. "One thing I know I don't want to be is Dean," he would say. "I don't want to be in my sixties and still pleading with high school kids to come play for me. I don't like basketball enough to care that much about it for that long."

Valvano loved to joke about Smith's godlike status in North Carolina. "First week I'm here I go to get my hair cut on campus," he would say, starting a favorite story, one he swore was true. "I get in the chair and the barber says to me, 'So, you're the fella who replaced old Norman [Sloan], aren't you?'"

"Yes, I am."

" 'Well,' says the barber, 'I sure hope you have more luck around here than old Norman did.' "

"I'm shocked. So I say to the guy, 'Hey, wait a minute, didn't Norman win a national championship? Didn't he go 27–0 one year?'

"And the guy looks right at me with a straight face and says, 'Yes sir. But just imagine what Dean Smith would have done with that team!' "

When Valvano looked at Krzyzewski, even before Duke started winning, he saw a life more like the one he had imagined for himself. Valvano believed he would have fit in perfectly at Duke. He loved the boisterous, wise-guy nature of the crowd at Cameron Indoor Stadium almost as much as Smith despised it. One of the reasons State always played well at Cameron under Valvano (five wins, five losses in a place where the visitors win about 20 percent of the time) was because Valvano was always so comfortable there.

Valvano was the hare, Krzyzewski was the tortoise. While Valvano whizzed around becoming more rich and more famous by the minute, Krzyzewski doggedly kept working to get players, to become a better coach, to win more games. Theirs was a unique relationship, one that went back to their playing days in college. Valvano had walked on the team at Rutgers and become part of a high-powered backcourt with All-American Bob Lloyd. Krzyzewski had been captain of very good teams at Army. Their teams met every year and the big-mouthed Italian kid from Queens was often matched up against the intense Polish kid from Chicago.

Valvano was a year older than Krzyzewski. He graduated and became an assistant coach at Rutgers. Krzyzewski went into the army for five years. Valvano married his high school sweetheart and they had three daughters. Krzyzewski married a stewardess he met through a friend in college and they had three daughters. Valvano coached for one year at Johns Hopkins, then for three at Bucknell before being named, in 1975, as the coach at Iona College, a Jesuit school in Westchester.

Later, Valvano would swear that he had gone to a party shortly after getting the job and introduced himself to someone there by saying, "Hi, I'm Jim Valvano, Iona College," and the person looked at him and said, "You look awfully young to own your own college."

That same year Krzyzewski, after one year as an assistant at Indiana under his old coach, Bob Knight, was named coach at his alma mater. Iona and Army played every year in those days. Valvano's teams won three times, Krzyzewski's twice. The two young coaches could not have been more different: Valvano was the showman, the media darling, living in — and loving — the New York spotlight. Krzyzewski was quieter, his wit more subtle. He earned the respect of the media with his penchant for absolute honesty. Tony Kornheiser, a *New York Times* reporter at the time, remembers the young Krzyzewski as "the first coach I had ever met who *never* went off the record. You asked him a question, he answered it. He was incapable of BS-ing you."

Krzyzewski built a solid program at West Point. Valvano produced a miracle, turning Iona into a national power. In his fifth season, Iona played Louisville in Madison Square Garden in front of a sellout crowd of 19,500 people. They beat the Cardinals by 17 — the last loss that season for a team that would go on to win the national championship. For years, Valvano had ended his coaching clinics at summer camps by telling the campers that his dream was to someday win a big game in Madison Square Garden and cut down the nets. That night, he and his players cut down the nets.

Iona reached the NCAA tournament that year, losing in the final minute to Georgetown in a second round game. Krzyzewski, after three straight winning seasons at Army, went 9–17 that year. When he was selected to replace Bill Foster at Duke, most basketball people around the country shook their heads and said, "Who?" Two weeks later, when Valvano was chosen to replace Old Norman at NC State, those same people nodded knowingly and said, "State got itself a star."

Krzyzewski and Valvano had always respected one another as coaches, but they had never been friends. Friendly rivals, but never friends. That didn't change during the ten years they coached against one another in the ACC.

Once Valvano had cut down that net in Madison Square Garden, his dream changed. Now, he wanted to cut down a net at the Final Four. That was one of the reasons he left a very comfortable situation at Iona for NC State. He believed his best chance to cut down the last remaining net was at an established program in the ACC. He never imagined it would happen so quickly. Or change his life so dramatically.

After winning the championship, Valvano and his assistants got careless in recruiting and brought in far too many players who had no chance to succeed academically. A book published in 1989 made numerous allegations about cheating and grade manipulating and, in general, a program running amok. NCAA investigators began looking into the program, and Valvano, even as his team continued to win, was under attack in the media and among State alumni.

In March of 1990, he resigned under pressure. That same spring, Krzyzewski went to his fourth Final Four in five years although he still didn't have a national championship. Valvano went to work as a commentator for ABC and ESPN and found stardom there, which surprised no one who knew him. He felt betrayed, though, because he didn't think the problems at State were so serious that he should have been forced out. State was placed on probation for one year and Valvano's successor, Les Robinson, was given a new set of academic standards to work with that were more stringent than those of any school in the ACC — including Duke.

A little more than two years after his resignation, Valvano began having severe back pains. When he finally went to see a doctor that summer, he received stunning news: he had cancer. It was terminal.

Valvano was being treated at Duke hospital. He was there a lot, often in great pain. His most frequent visitor, other than his family, was Mike Krzyzewski. The two men would sit and talk for hours about life and coaching and families and basketball. They said things to one another that men don't usually say to one another, especially men who have lived their lives in the macho world of sports. Even near the end, when Valvano was in terrible pain, he could still make Krzyzewski laugh. More important, Krzyzewski could make him laugh.

On the morning of April 28, 1993, Valvano died. He had said all his goodbyes the night before, knowing there was very little time left. His family was in the room with him. So was Mike Krzyzewski. Krzyzewski left the hospital and walked back across the Duke campus. It was a beautiful morning, the kind that makes you happy to be alive. He cried, not just for Valvano, but for his friend's family and for himself. He and Valvano had become friends only near the end and yet they had become achingly close. Why, he wondered, had this happened to Jim? It could just as easily have happened to him. It was like a giant lottery, nothing more than luck of the draw. Valvano had drawn the short life straw — forty-seven years. Barely more than ten years after he had been on top of the basketball world, his whole life stretching out before him, his life was over. He would never see his daughters marry; never be a grandfather.

Krzyzewski remembered a practice earlier that season that Valvano had attended. When it was over, he had asked Valvano if he would like to speak to the team. Valvano had said he would love to. And so, speaking to the team he never did get to coach, Valvano talked about how lucky they were to have Krzyzewski coaching them. He talked about being aware of life beyond basketball and how long it had taken him to understand it. "Life changes when you least expect it to," he said that day. "Right now, my goal in life is to be able to come back here and talk to you guys again next season."

Those words stuck in Krzyzewski's brain. Here was a man not yet fifty hoping to squeeze twelve more months out of his life. And not being able to do even that. Less than six months after speaking to the Duke team, Valvano was dead.

Krzyzewski was forty-six. He was on top of the basketball world. But for how long? For the first time in his entire life, he wondered if he was doing the right thing with his life. Maybe he should be using his fame to fight cancer. Maybe he should be working in the inner city. The games that had meant so much didn't seem quite so meaningful anymore. He thought about tears that had been shed after wins and after losses and wondered if they had been misplaced. No one had died at the end of those games. Now, someone had died. These tears were worth crying.

Valvano's illness and death cast a pall over an already sobered NC State campus. The glory years seemed lifetimes away as Robinson and his undermanned teams struggled to win in the ACC. In his first year, with a team built around Valvano-recruited players, Robinson went 20–11, but then dropped to 12–18 and 8–19 the next two years. Recruiting was at a standstill. The few players State did recruit had trouble dealing with the new academic standards. By the end of the 1996 season, the Wolfpack had endured five straight losing seasons. In 1992, when Florida State joined the league, the ACC had added a play-in game to the conference tournament, matching the bottom two teams in the league. The winner had the dubious honor of playing the top seed the next day in the quarterfinals. State avoided the play-in game in 1992 — by one game — then finished ninth, ninth, eighth, and ninth the next four years. Thus, the play-in game was jokingly renamed the "Les Robinson Game."

No one in Raleigh laughed very hard at the joke, although Robinson tried to make light of it when State finally won a play-in game in 1996. "If a game is named after you," he said, "you ought to be able to win it at least once."

That victory turned out to be Robinson's last at State. The Wolfpack lost to Georgia Tech the next day to finish 15–16 in what had started out as a promising season. A week later Robinson resigned to take a job in the athletic department and Todd Turner began searching for a new coach. A month went by before a new coach was named. At one point, it looked as if Oklahoma's Kelvin Sampson would become only the second minority coach in ACC history (Bob Wade at Maryland had been the first), but he eventually decided to stay put. Turner also talked to Dave Odom, but he ended up staying at Wake Forest — with a lucrative new contract. Turner went back to the drawing board.

His wandering eye eventually turned north to Miami of Ohio. Since Kentucky's Rick Pitino was the coach of the moment, Pitino assistants were a hot commodity. Herb Sendek had worked for Pitino at both Providence and Kentucky. He had struck out on his own at Miami three years earlier and had put together a gaudy 63–26 record that included an NCAA trip in 1995 and a first round upset of Arizona. Sendek had the right bloodlines and a proven record of his own. Turner called him.

Sendek's immediate response was to call Pitino. "If it's there, you have to take it," Pitino told him. "It's the ACC. It's a program that's been great and can be great again."

Sendek is cautious by nature. He told Turner that he didn't want to make the trip to Raleigh unless Turner had decided he was the first choice for the job. He knew that rumors that he was leaving could hurt his recruiting. When Turner finally called and said, "You're my first choice," Sendek made the trip south.

He was introduced as State's new coach on April 17, 1996. From the first minute on the job it was apparent to everyone that State had hired the anti-Valvano. Sendek was about as likely to do shtick as to fly to the moon with a jetpack on his back. He was intense, introspective, and shunned the spotlight at least as much as Valvano had craved it. He wasn't comfortable with the media, approaching press conferences the same way most people treat trips to the dentist. He handled each question as if it were a bomb that could go off at any second and answered most of them with slightly more caution than a Pentagon spokesman discussing troop movements in a war zone. Practices, he announced, would be closed to everyone, including the media. This was a slightly different approach than Valvano, who not only welcomed the media at practice but often asked reporters if they would like to *run* practice.

State people didn't really care if the media liked Sendek. The media had loved the folksy, friendly Les Robinson and that hadn't won them any games. All they wanted was a winner, and Sendek pledged to work twenty-four hours a day — more, if possible — to produce a winner. There would be no joke-telling on Sendek's watch.

While Sendek was throwing himself into his new job preparing for the '96–97 season, Mike Krzyzewski was still adjusting to his old one. Valvano's death had triggered a confusing, frustrating, and, at times, frightening period in his life. Krzyzewski's greatest strength, as a coach and as a person, is his self-confidence. He is never boastful and doesn't come across as conceited, but he has complete faith in his abilities and almost never second-guesses himself.

The only time in his life that he had questioned himself was during his first days as a plebe at West Point. Even then, it was his parents he questioned. "I wouldn't have gone if not for them," he said. "I didn't want to be in the army. No way. But every night they would stand around the kitchen and say to one another, 'Can you believe we have a son who is so foolish that he turns down a chance like this.' I finally got so sick of it, I said, 'All right, I'm going. Just leave me alone.' "

To Bill and Emily Krzyzewski, the notion that one of their sons could attend college for free and be guaranteed a job when he graduated was nothing short of a godsend. They were first-generation Polish-Americans who lived on the North Side of Chicago. Bill Krzyzewski used the Americanized name Kross when he worked as an elevator operator, while Emily worked many different jobs to make certain her two sons, Bill and Mike, had everything they wanted. Bill would go on to be a fire captain in Chicago. Mike would go to West Point because he could play basketball.

Like any plebe, Krzyzewski hated his early days at West Point — especially swimming class. "We didn't do a lot of swimming on the North Side," he said. "The closest we ever came to water was an open fire hydrant on hot days in the summer."

He survived, though, and, eventually, he thrived. He came to understand his parents had been right, even on those days when the academy's tyrannical twenty-five-year-old enfant terrible of a basketball coach made life miserable for everyone. By the time he graduated, he was Bob Knight's captain and Bob Knight was his friend and mentor. It was Knight who flew with him to Chicago on that awful day during his senior year when his father died suddenly of a heart attack. And, after five years in the army, it was Knight who gave him his first job in coaching as a graduate assistant at Indiana. A year after that it was Knight who suggested to the powers-that-be at West Point that they hire a twenty-eight-year-old alumnus with one year of coaching experience to run their program.

Of course Krzyzewski was an ideal choice for the Army job because he understood what it was like to play at the academy and try to survive academically. He knew how to sell West Point to recruits because he had bought into the package himself as a high school senior. Most important, perhaps, his experience at West Point had taught him to deal with failure. Military academies force you to deal with failure early on because they believe that it is the only way to teach you how to succeed when failure seems inevitable. Coaching a team that was almost always outmanned, Krzyzewski knew there would be nights when nothing he could do as a coach was going to produce a victory. But he also knew that there were nights when being tougher mentally could win a game against a team that was more talented physically.

Krzyzewski was 73–59 in five years at West Point, a remarkable record if you understand that in the seventeen years since his departure, Army has had one winning season (1985) and the record that year was 16–13. His team's hard-nosed style, reminiscent of the way Army teams had played under Knight in the sixties, drew some attention nationally.

Krzyzewski was still evolving as a coach during his days at Army. Technically, his teams were clones of the Knight teams of the sixties. They played man-to-man defense and ran motion offense (meaning the players reacted to the defense rather than simply calling out a set play regardless of what the defense was doing) and prided themselves on wearing the opponent down, physically and emotionally.

At Duke, Krzyzewski began to come into his own as an innovator. He never changed the basics, but he put wrinkles into them — especially on offense. Each summer, he sits down and evaluates his team, then builds an offense based on their skills. If he has a big man who is more comfortable playing away from the basket — like Danny Ferry or Christian Laettner — he will move him there and create plays designed to take advantage of those skills. If he has a big man who doesn't have the outside game — like a Greg Newton — he will keep him in the low post with his back to the basket. He does that with each player, figuring out how to maximize his skills. Even on defense, Krzyzewski will occasionally stray from his beloved man-to-man, depending on his team's strengths and an opponent's.

That came later, though, when Krzyzewski began to recruit players with multiple talents. At Army, everyone had one talent above all others: toughness. So, that was what the young coach emphasized.

Midway through the 1979–80 season, which would turn out to be Krzyzewski's worst at Army (9–17), he got a call from Knight telling him that he had recommended him for the job at Iowa State. It was time to move up, he said, after five years. Krzyzewski was intrigued. He was more intrigued, though, when he received a call from Tom Butters, the Duke athletic director, wanting to know if he could fly to Lexington, Kentucky, to meet with him about the Duke job.

Krzyzewski knew that Bill Foster had resigned after six years to take the job at South Carolina. Duke was playing in the NCAA tournament in Lexington, and Butters wanted to meet there because it was less likely to get out that he was interviewing a coach there than if someone came to Durham. Butters had called Krzyzewski after talking to Knight, who had recommended both Krzyzewski and another of his former assistants, Bob Weltlich, for the job. Butters thought Krzyzewski was much too inexperienced and too young, at thirty-three, for a job as high profile as the one at Duke. But he respected Knight's judgment enough that he felt he should at least meet Krzyzewski.

"After I met him, I kept talking to other coaches and to people about other coaches," Butters said. "But I couldn't get Mike out of my mind."

Butters was impressed most by Krzyzewski's self-confidence. He wasn't cocky or boastful, just self-assured. He came across as someone who knew he was good — but who also knew he was still learning and maturing as a coach.

While Butters was pondering his next move, Krzyzewski was offered the Iowa State job. He called Knight to ask him what he thought. "I think you have to take it," Knight said. Krzyzewski wasn't certain. He sought another opinion, that of Col. Thomas Rogers, who had been Knight's director of operations when he played at West Point and was now doing the same thing for Krzyzewski. "I think you need to follow this Duke thing and see where it goes," Rogers counseled.

Krzyzewski's gut told him that Rogers was right. He called Iowa State and told the people there that he couldn't say yes until he found out what was going to happen at Duke. He didn't want them waiting around for him when the answer might be no. Then he sat back and hoped he would hear from Butters again.

He did. Butters wanted him to come to Durham for a second interview. This time he felt certain Krzyzewski was his man. But he was concerned about what it would look like if he hired a young coach coming off a losing season. After Krzyzewski left the office, Butters went to talk to his top assistant, Steve Vacendak, telling him how impressed he was with Krzyzewski, yet how concerned he was about public reaction to his hiring.

"What's your gut tell you?" Vacendak asked.

"That this guy is the best young coach in America."

Hearing himself say that, Butters made a decision. "Go get him," he told Vacendak. "Go out to the airport and bring him back."

Krzyzewski was at the airport talking to his assistant coaches on the phone when he heard a page mispronouncing his name (it is pronounced "jejevski," although TV announcers usually say "sheshefski"). It was Butters.

"If I offer you this job, will you take it?" he asked.

"Are you offering it to me?"

"Yes."

"I accept."

"Stay right where you are. Vacendak should be there in ten minutes."

That ended the negotiations.

Butters's concerns about the way the media and the public would react to the hiring were correct. Many people had wanted him to hire Foster's top assistant, Bob Wenzel, for the sake of continuity in what had been a successful program. At the very least they had expected a more experienced coach with a more impressive record. Why not, some people wondered, this guy at Iona who had just won twenty-nine games?

The wondering turned to whining quickly. Duke was 17–13, 10–17, and 11–17 in Krzyzewski's first three years. The third season ended with a humiliating 109–66 loss to Virginia in the ACC tournament. After the game, Virginia superstar Ralph Sampson and his coach, Terry Holland, accused Duke freshman center Jay Bilas of dirty play for trying to knee Sampson early in the game. When Krzyzewski was informed of Holland's comments, he was furious.

"It's not their fault that they beat us by that score," he said later. "We were bad in the second half, really bad. But when you humiliate somebody that way, you don't rub it in by whining about a freshman trying to push you around. It was Ralph who threw an elbow, not Jay."

Krzyzewski was angry enough that he confronted Holland in the hallway on the way back to his locker room. Holland brushed the scene off as reflecting the frustrations of a young coach and soon forgot about the incident. Krzyzewski did not. Later that night, sitting in a Denny's at two o'clock in the morning, Duke sports information assistant Johnny Moore held up a glass of water and said to the small, quiet group assembled around the table, "Here's to forgetting tonight."

Krzyzewski picked up his glass. "Here's to *never* forgetting tonight," he answered.

He didn't. It would be seven years and sixteen games before Virginia beat Duke again.

Krzyzewski's fourth season was the turnaround year. The freshman class that he had recruited the previous year — Bilas, Johnny Dawkins, Mark Alarie, and David Henderson — had all been forced to play too early and too often to succeed in the ACC. Now, as sophomores, joined by a precocious freshman point guard named Tommy Amaker, they began to mature. Not that it was easy. After a 14–1 start that included an encouraging win at Virginia, the Blue Devils lost four straight conference games — three of them at home. The whiners had now become wolves. Butters heard them. Krzyzewski had only one more year left on his five-year contract at the end of the season. On the spot, Butters announced he was extending the contract. That was when he started getting death threats.

By the end of the 1984 season, the threats had ceased and the wolves had quieted. Duke had won twenty-four games, had beaten a Michael Jordan–led North Carolina team in the ACC tournament, and had reached the NCAA tournament for the first time since 1980. A year later, the Blue Devils won twenty-three. But they were upset in the second round of the NCAAs by Boston College. OK, Krzyzewski had proven he could build a solid program, but what about a national contender? The answer came swiftly. Duke was 37–3 in 1986, losing the national championship game 72–69 to Louisville only because their semifinal with Kansas was so grueling that Alarie and Henderson had nothing left in their legs.

The next year, picked to slide back toward the bottom of the ACC, they finished third and won twenty-four and reached the Sweet Sixteen. And then the dynasty was born. The five years from 1988 to 1992 produced: Final Four, Final Four, runner-up, national champion, and national champion. People began calling the Final Four the "Duke Invitational." During those five seasons Duke *averaged* 30.2 victories a season. Its *worst* record was 29–9.

The Blue Devils became America's Team. Not only were they good, but they had players who spoke in complete sentences and seemed to have fun playing the game. They graduated. Their coach took graduation so seriously that when his three seniors didn't graduate on time in 1990, he refused to hang their Final Four banner in Cameron Indoor Stadium. Two have since graduated. The banner still isn't up and won't go up until — and unless — the third graduates.

They also had a flair for the dramatic. In 1988, playing top-seeded Temple in the East Regional final, they upset the Owls when defensive specialist Billy King held Temple's shooting star Mark Macon to an incredible six of 29 shooting, including eight air balls. A year later they upset another number one seed — Georgetown — in another East Regional final. And a year after that they stunned yet another number one — Connecticut — when Christian Laettner hit an off-balance buzzer-beating jumper to win by one in overtime.

That was the year that UNLV humiliated them in the championship game. In Chapel Hill, the *Daily Tar Heel* wrote a pre–Final Four editorial saying that the basketball world wouldn't be safe until Duke was put in its proper place by losing — as it always did — in the Final Four. The loss to Vegas made Duke zero for eight in Final Fours, Krzyzewski zero for four. One joke making the rounds that summer in the ACC was: "Why does Mike Krzyzewski quit after fourteen holes when he plays golf?"

"Because he doesn't like the Final Four."

At the time, Krzyzewski didn't play golf. But, like any competitor, he was disappointed by the losses in the Final Four, He was not, however, discouraged. He had come a long way from that Denny's in Atlanta and was convinced that his — and Duke's — time would come. No one in the world expected it to be the next year, though, not with three senior starters leaving Duke; not with Vegas bringing all five starters back; and not with North Carolina bringing in the most highly touted freshman class in the history of college basketball.

When Duke made it back to the Final Four in 1991, even his harshest critics had to concede Krzyzewski had done a superb job with only one senior — Greg Koubek — playing any kind of significant role. No one gave Duke any chance to beat the 34–0 juggernaut that was Vegas in the semifinals, but it had still been one hell of a year.

One person thought Duke could win the game: Krzyzewski. He knew his team was better than it had been a year earlier, especially his sophomore point guard Bobby Hurley, who had gone from pouter to leader during the latter stages of the season. When Keith Drum, an old friend who was scouting for the Portland Trail Blazers at the time, came by practice that Monday, Krzyzewski told him, "I really believe we're going to win the game. We're good enough to stay close with them, and if it's close they won't know how to handle it because they haven't been in a close game all year."

Drum remembered those words the following Saturday when Hurley drilled a critical three with 2:14 left and Vegas up five. He heard them again when freshman Grant Hill threw a gorgeous pass to Brian Davis with a little more than a minute left to put Duke up by one. And, after Larry Johnson had tied it for UNLV, he heard it one last time when Christian Laettner scored the last of his 28 points with two free throws to put Duke ahead for good, 79–77. When Vegas's last shot bounded off the rim, the Blue Devils celebrated as if they had won the national championship.

Which they hadn't. Two days later, though, they bounced back emotionally and physically to hold off a Kansas team that had upset North Carolina in the semifinals. That was the weekend that took the Duke–North Carolina rivalry to a new level. It began with Smith's infamous ejection from the Kansas game. As he left the court, many of the Duke fans either cheered or mockingly waved goodbye to him. Many Carolina fans, already upset by the loss and the ejection, were angered by the Duke fans taking such pleasure in the humiliation of their coach. If nothing else, they felt, he deserved their respect. What made it worse was Duke's stunning victory in the second game over UNLV. When Duke then won the national championship, Carolina fans could no longer take solace in the fact that Duke and Krzyzewski were 0 for the Final Four. Duke's second title a year later only made it worse. When Smith walked into Cameron Indoor Stadium in 1993, he was serenaded with a chant of "Mike's got two, Dean's got one." By the end of that season Smith had evened the score at two apiece, but nonetheless, the bitterness that sometimes afflicted the rivalry had reached new heights.

The Carolina fans were used to being on top. Even though Duke had been good, very good at times, it had always been like the pesky little brother who would battle you and battle you, but sooner or later would lose the battle. North Carolina is a state school with almost 25,000 students. Duke is a private school with 6,000 undergraduates and 10,000 students total. There are more North Carolina graduates living in the state than there are Duke graduates in the world. Duke could win ten straight national championships and still not begin to compete with Carolina as an obsession in the state.

Carolina won most of the time in nonrevenue sports and, except for a three-year period when Steve Spurrier was Duke's football coach and went 3–0 against the Tar Heels, almost all the time in football. But basketball has been and always will be the signature sport for both schools, no matter how many national championships Carolina wins in women's soccer. Duke's back-to-back titles hurt many Carolina fans almost as much as it thrilled Duke fans. And even though Krzyzewski lectured the Duke faithful at the 1991 basketball banquet not to become arrogant, many did. What had been a great rivalry began to take on an undercurrent of ugliness.

In 1994, North Carolina was favored to go back-to-back the same way Duke had done in 1991 and 1992. It had lost only one starter — George Lynch — off the '93 championship team and Smith had brought in a ballyhooed freshman class that included Wallace, Stackhouse, and a talented point guard named Jeff McInnis. As it turned out, their presence probably cost Carolina a second title. The Tar Heels were racked by dissension all year, most of it caused by the freshmen believing they were better than the upperclassmen and deserving of more playing time. Smith wasn't about to start benching seniors, especially seniors who had keyed a national championship team, but as the season wore on, it became harder and harder to keep the younger players happy.

The scene that defined that Carolina team took place in Cameron Indoor Stadium on the final night of the regular season. Every time Carolina's senior point guard Derrick Phelps had the ball outside, Duke's Grant Hill played off him. Hill kept daring Phelps to shoot, knowing he wouldn't. "Come on, Derrick, put it up, put it up," he kept saying. When McInnis came in to relieve Phelps, Hill moved out a little more, knowing McInnis would shoot. A few minutes later, when Phelps returned, McInnis passed Hill on the way to the bench and said softly, "Keep after Derrick."

He was imploring his opponent to continue taunting his teammate.

Carolina won the game that night, completing a sweep of the season series. But Duke won the regular season title in large part because the Tar Heels didn't perform nearly as well against other teams as they did against Duke. "The one thing that unites them is playing against us," Duke assistant coach Mike Brey said. "We're the only thing they hate more than each other."

Carolina's '94 season ended shockingly two weeks after that game in the second round of the NCAA tournament. Seeded number one in the East Regional, the Tar Heels were upset by number nine seed Boston College. It was the first time since 1980 that Carolina had failed to reach the Sweet Sixteen. Duke made it back to the national championship game, losing a taut final to Arkansas. It was Krzyzewski's seventh Final Four in nine years, the greatest postseason run any coach not named Wooden had ever had. Amazingly, there were actually fans that spring calling for Smith to retire. He was sixty-three and, the thinking went, the game had passed him by. It had been twelve months since he'd won a National Championship but some of his fans were doubting him. Smith wasn't going anyplace, though. He was as competitive as ever and determined to come back and prove his doubters wrong.

The coach who was thinking of leaving was the one sitting atop the pedestal at that moment: Krzyzewski. Even though his team had pieced together a remarkable 28–6 season, keyed by the brilliance of Grant Hill, Krzyzewski had been restless. His wife, Mickie, who had always been his principal adviser on any key decision, wasn't happy either, feeling that a lot of people at Duke, notably new school president Nannerl Keohane, didn't appreciate how much her husband meant to the school. Throughout the season she talked constantly about leaving Duke. Sometimes she thought the NBA would be nice; other days she talked about a TV job. And, on occasion, she would sigh and say, "I'd like to see Mike coach a Division III team so we could get some privacy back in our life."

That was really the crux of the problem. It wasn't being unappreciated — Krzyzewski was the most revered figure in the history of the school — and it wasn't about needing new challenges. In truth, Krzyzewski had too many challenges. The two titles had made him the most visible, popular, and sought-after coach in the country. Every coach who was out of work called him for help. When the National Association of Basketball Coaches needed a spokesman on any issue, they sent for Krzyzewski. No national team could be put together by USA Basketball without Krzyzewski's input. Everyone on the planet wanted him at their banquet or to do a clinic. Every charity needed a signed basketball or picture or just a few minutes of his time.

The two groups that needed him the most — his family and his team — weren't getting nearly as much of him as they had in the past. This was the Valvano syndrome in a different form. Krzyzewski still wanted to coach. He didn't need fame or fortune. But he hadn't figured out how to deal with having both thrust upon him.

"All my adult life I trained to do one thing," he said a few years later, "and that was coach. I never once for one minute trained to be a celebrity. I never planned on being a celebrity. And when I became one, I had no idea how to handle it."

Krzyzewski's biggest problem was his inability to say no. He didn't want to appear to be big-timing old friends or other coaches. He didn't want to say no to charities or to anything involving kids. No one wanted that much time: a few minutes on the phone for an interview; a quick flight in and out in a day to give a speech; fifteen or twenty minutes of advice on how to handle a job interview.

The more Krzyzewski said yes to the outside world, the more he was saying no to his inside world. His recruiting slipped — not noticeably at first, but significantly. Duke was still bringing in talented players, but because Krzyzewski couldn't take the time to get to know them as well as he had gotten to know players in the past, some of them didn't fit in at Duke or under Krzyzewski. Even when he did spend time with his players, he was often distracted. "I didn't stop having individual player meetings," he said. "But a lot of times when they were talking, I wasn't listening. I needed to listen more."

The '94 season hid a lot of the problems. Hill was such a good player and Krzyzewski such a good coach that they were able to take a team with some serious deficiencies to the championship game. Moments after that game had ended, Mickie Krzyzewski stood in a hallway outside the locker room with her three daughters and said, "I wanted Mike to win a third championship and then leave."

A month later, he almost did. Both the Portland Trail Blazers and the Miami Heat were willing to pay him millions to become their coach. Krzyzewski had become fascinated by the notion of coaching NBA players in 1992 when he had been an assistant coach with the so-called "Dream Team" during the Olympics. But when it came time to pull the trigger, neither he or Mickie really wanted to leave Duke.

That summer, playing tennis and racquetball, Krzyzewski began to have serious back pains. Doctors told him he had a degenerative disc and needed surgery. He put them off for a while, but when the pain persisted, he decided to get it over with before the season started. He had the surgery just before practice started and returned to work ten days later. The doctors had suggested he wait six weeks. He said that was impossible. He had a team that had lost three starters, including the national player of the year, and he needed every minute he could find to prepare them for the season.

By December, his back was killing him. The doctors told him he had to take it easy on the bench during games, not jump up all the time. He tried that for two games, then decided he was worthless to his team that way. He would fight through the pain. "I honestly believed it was mind over matter," he said. "It was like going without sleep. I had always been able to do that when I had to. I thought this was the same. If I believed I could handle the pain, I could handle the pain."

Duke's trip to Hawaii just before New Year's made it clear that was not the case. The team won twice in three games but played poorly. Krzyzewski was convinced they were not ready for ACC play and he and his coaches stayed up all night on several occasions trying to come up with answers. By the time Duke's plane landed back in North Carolina, Krzyzewski was gray with pain and fatigue. After the loss to Clemson to open the conference season, he met with his coaches after the game. For the first time, he conceded defeat. "I just don't think I can do this," he said. "I don't think I can make it."

Two days later, after Mickie threatened to leave him if he didn't go to see a doctor, he checked into the hospital. He was in awful shape: exhausted, in terrible pain, strung out with frustration because he couldn't handle what was happening to him. The Blue Devils flew to Atlanta without him that day and lost to Georgia Tech the next night. No timetable was set for Krzyzewski's return, but he knew he had to get back soon or the 1995 season was going to be lost.

He went home a week later, but things really weren't much better. The rest had helped his back a little, but not his psyche. He couldn't sleep. He lay awake in bed, racked with guilt about his players. They had come to Duke to play for him and he wasn't there. They were struggling and he couldn't help them. He had screwed up — big time — and they were paying for it. Why, he wondered, wasn't he getting better? The doctors had run every single test there was and had found nothing wrong. Valvano's cancer had started with back pain that wouldn't go away, maybe he had cancer too. Maybe he was going to die young just like his friend. Maybe he would never be a grandfather either.

While Krzyzewski was in seclusion trying to get himself back to his team, rumors were rampant. Later, he and Mickie would put together a list of the Top Ten Best Rumors About Coach K. Among them were: AIDS, cancer, Mickie having an affair with a player, Mike having an affair with a cheerleader, and Mike having a nervous breakdown. By then, they were funny. In January, they were like a forest fire out of control.

Eleven days after he had checked into the hospital, the Krzyzewskis went to dinner at Tom and Lynn Butters's house. Krzyzewski was still exhausted and frightened and frustrated. He was spending more time each night sitting on the edge of his bed, beating himself up for not getting better, than he was sleeping. His team still hadn't won a conference game. He had sat the previous Saturday and watched a 23-point lead go down the drain against Virginia in a double-overtime loss. He wanted to throw something at the TV but was too weak even to do that. It was all his fault. He was convinced of that. He was a military man and he knew that in war when the battle has been lost, the honorable thing is for the general to fall on his sword.

"Maybe I should resign," he told Butters. "If you think that's what is best for Duke, that's what I'll do."

Butters looked him in the eye. "Mike, this is your job whenever you're ready to come back. I don't care if it's tomorrow or six weeks from now or six months from now or six years from now. It's *your* job. I don't want anyone else as my basketball coach."

Butters then told Krzyzewski that he needed to stop trying to rush back. "The difference between you and me is that my sport was baseball," said Butters, a former major league pitcher. "There's no clock in baseball. In basketball, you're always aware of the clock. You need to forget the clock. There is no clock."

That night was critical for Krzyzewski. Five days later, Duke announced that Krzyzewski wasn't coming back to coach for the rest of the season. From that moment on, Krzyzewski stopped trying to get back; he started trying to get better. It was a turning point. Slowly but surely he began to feel stronger. As hard as it was to watch his team struggle without him, he was now thinking about the future, about next season. He knew now that he wanted to coach and he wanted to coach at Duke. Absence had made the heart grow fonder. So had rest.

The '95 season was a complete disaster for Duke. Associate coach Pete Gaudet, Krzyzewski's first lieutenant throughout the glory years, took over the team. Duke was in one close game after another and lost one close game after another. There was a double-overtime loss to Carolina, two last-second losses to Maryland, an aggravating defeat at Clemson. And on and on. By the time the wreckage was cleared away, the Blue Devils had gone 2–14 in league play and finished ninth. They did manage to win the Les Robinson game (against Les Robinson of course), but the next day they were embarrassed by Wake Forest, losing by 17 after having led by 18.

The season also did irreparable harm to Krzyzewski's friendship with Gaudet. Watching his team fail night after night, Krzyzewski decided he needed to make changes. His coaching staff — including the head coach — had become too comfortable. All the success had softened them. He knew Mike Brey would be leaving for a head coaching job at Delaware at the end of the season. Because of NCAA rules, Gaudet could not remain in what was technically the part-time slot forever. He would eventually have to move up to a full-time slot (which meant recruiting) or out. Krzyzewski wanted a younger coach in that recruiting slot.

"I always believed the theory that every staff needs an older coach," he said. "One morning I looked in the mirror and realized I was the older coach, whether I wanted to admit it or not." It was not an easy or amicable parting. Krzyzewski felt he had to choose between a friendship and what he thought was best for the program. He chose the program.

During the last week of the season, Krzyzewski had formally announced that he would be back at the most heavily attended press conference ever called for someone to say, "I'm staying in my job." Actually, it was the second such press conference Krzyzewski had held. The first had been a year earlier when he had announced that he wasn't leaving for the NBA.

Krzyzewski came back to coach a team that, because of the recruiting mistakes, was not nearly as talented as the teams he had coached in the late eighties and early nineties. The Blue Devils were probably fortunate to go 18–13 in '95–96 and sneak back into the NCAA tournament. They were beaten easily in the first round by Eastern Michigan; it was Krzyzewski's first loss ever in the opening round.

Krzyzewski suspected that his team would be better in '96–97 but he didn't know how much better. Trajan Langdon, a shooting guard with loads of potential, was coming off major knee surgery that had cost him the entire season in '96. There were three talented freshmen, but how ready they would be for the ACC was tough to say. The only thing he knew two weeks into practice was that he had been wrong about Steve Wojciechowski, his five-foot-ten-inch junior point guard. During the summer, Krzyzewski had projected Wojo as his third guard behind Langdon and senior Jeff Capel. From the first day of practice, though, it was apparent that Wojo had to be on the floor as much as possible. He had lost fifteen pounds and was noticeably quicker. His suspect outside shot had improved. And, most important, he always played hard and made the others play harder.

Wojo would start and so would Langdon, if his knee held up. Greg Newton would start because he was a senior and the team's only legitimate big man. Capel would start even though he had gone through a disappointing junior year. The fifth spot and playing time off the bench were wide open.

Krzyzewski had signed a new seven-year contract to be Duke's coach that summer after a lengthy negotiation. He had made his peace with school president Nan Keohane. He had gone back to the recruiting style that had built the program: picking a small group of players who were both quality players and quality students and spending as much time as the NCAA rules allowed getting to know them as thoroughly as possible.

Krzyzewski was convinced that recruiting was the area in which the program had slipped the most since the back-to-back titles. It wasn't that Duke had stopped recruiting highly touted players. Quite the contrary. Each Duke recruiting class had players ranked and lauded by all the recruiting gurus. The difference was that Krzyzewski hadn't had the time to get to know them as well as he had in the past. Then, he sometimes flew with a recruit back to his hometown after a campus visit so he would have extra time to talk to him alone, to get a feeling in his gut about him. But after '91 and '92, he had stopped doing that. There just wasn't time. If he had had the extra time he might have figured out that Greg Newton and Joey Beard were ill-suited for Duke academically and socially. He might have thought twice about Tony Moore's and Ricky Price's ability to handle the school's academic rigors.

Instead, he read the reports on them, saw them play a couple of times, and recognized that each had talent. The rest, he figured, would come. The players were eager to come to Duke, so they were signed. Then, the problems started.

In the fall of '96, Krzyzewski was using his pre-championship formula again. Three of the players he was recruiting — Elton Brand, Shane Battier, and Chris Burgess — were excellent students. This was no coincidence. Duke was often at a disadvantage with shaky students. Some couldn't get into school. Some, who could get in, would never be comfortable. Others could get in but were scared off by other coaches telling them about how tough Duke would be academically. But with a good student, it was "advantage Krzyzewski." He could go into the home and say to the player and his parents, "At Duke, your son will have every chance to make it to the NBA if he's good enough. But, if by some chance he's not, he'll leave with a Duke degree." He could then cite his graduation rate — over 90 percent — as proof that the player would almost certainly get that degree.

Krzyzewski was comfortable recruiting kids like Brand, Battier, and Burgess, and even though William Avery wasn't nearly as good a student as the other three, Krzyzewski's gut told him he was the kind of kid he wanted to coach. He liked the fact that he had a gut feeling about Avery. That meant he knew Avery, really knew him. It had been a while since he had felt that way about a recruit — or a recruiting class.

Eleven miles away, Dean Smith quietly prepared for his thirty-sixth season at North Carolina. He had never been sick and hadn't been through a losing season since 1962 — his first. People wondered occasionally when Smith would retire, but it wasn't really a burning question. The answer was that he would retire when he stopped having fun coaching basketball.

Smith had given a good deal more thought to that question in recent years than most people suspected. This would be a critical year for Mike Krzyzewski because he had to find out if coaching could be fun for him again. It would be just as critical for Dean Smith. Surprisingly enough, for the same reason.

4

Comeback Kids

"COACH, WHAT'S your goal for this season?"

It was the first time all night anyone had asked the question. Jumping from house to house along fraternity row at the University of Maryland, Gary Williams had given his set speech a dozen times already, talking about how his team looked going into the 1996–97 season and how important it was that the student body get out to Cole Field House for every home game. He had never forgotten his playing days at Maryland, when Cole was less than half filled for most home games and there was no home court advantage. He loved walking into the old building nowadays and seeing it packed. He was comfortable in that setting, girding for battle, the way he was comfortable in this one, surrounded by kids who saw him as a hero, one of their own made good. He was a Maryland grad who had come home. He was more at home talking to the student body than in any other setting, other than the practice floor.

"My goal for this season?" Williams asked, repeating the question as if stalling for time. Then he told them the same thing he had told his team. "My goal is the national championship."

They stared at him for a split second as if he had lost his mind. Then they erupted. Cheers and whistles. They loved it. Why not? After all, that group of underachieving whiners we had last year was still good enough to beat North Carolina in Chapel Hill and Georgia Tech in Cole and should have beaten Massachusetts when the Minutemen were ranked number one back in December. Why not? After all, Gary loved challenges. He loved coaching a team that would do anything to win a game because he would do anything to win a game. That's why they had nicknamed Cole Garyland when he came back to Maryland in 1989.

Williams smiled at the response. "You don't have to be the best team to win the national championship," he said. "You just have to be good enough to beat anybody you play once. I think we'll be good enough to do that."

It was difficult for Williams to believe that he was about to start his thirtieth year as a basketball coach. He didn't look fifty-one, and, most of the time, he didn't feel fifty-one. He still brought as much passion and intensity to the game as he had back in the sixties, when he had played at Maryland. That was why the students loved him. Kids are into causes and Williams has always seen basketball and the team he coaches as a cause. No compromises, no pretending that the opponent is your pal.

"I see one of my players talking to another player during a game, I yank him," Williams always says. "We aren't out there to make friends."

And yet, many of Williams' best friends are other coaches, many of them men he has competed with for years, like Syracuse's Jim Boeheim and former Seton Hall coach P. J. Carlesimo. Williams likes being around people who understand competition because his entire life has been built around competing. "I always liked playing ball," he said, "because no one cared who you were or where you were from or what color you were. The only question was, could you play. The scoreboard doesn't lie very often. There's no way you can BS the scoreboard."

Unlike a lot of kids who grow up around games, Williams didn't come from a family that was involved in sports. His parents were never involved in sports and neither were his two brothers. The only family member he can remember ever having any interest in sports was his mother's dad, Herbert Lilly. "He was a very good baseball player," Williams said. "He was the one who took me out in the yard when I was little and played catch with me."

Williams grew up in south Jersey, in the Camden suburb of Collingswood. His parents, Bill and Shirley Williams, were strict Presbyterians. Sundays were spent in church, where his father was a deacon, his mother a Sunday school teacher. Bill Williams worked as a check processor at the Federal Reserve Bank in Philadelphia. His shift was from midnight to 8 A.M. Every night, the family had dinner together. Every Sunday, they went to church together. Beyond that, it was not a close home. "My brothers were into cars," Williams said. "I was into sports."

One morning, when Gary was fourteen, he awoke to find that his father was home. That was a surprise. It was a bigger surprise when he announced that he would be driving Gary and Donald to school. "Something had to be up," Gary said.

It was. Bill Williams told his two oldest sons that he was moving out of the house, that things were not good between him and their mother. The boys asked no questions. Their father offered no details. He dropped them off at school and moved out that day. He lived nearby and he still came and picked the boys up for church every Sunday. But things were never the same. His mother stopped going to church. The family dinners also stopped. The Williams brothers went their separate ways.

Sports became Williams's escape hatch. He had a freshman basketball coach named Neil Thompson who seemed to understand the fourteen-year-old's need for a friend. He and Thompson spent hours together, working on Gary's game, or sometimes just playing one-on-one. When he wasn't playing games, Gary went to games. On weekends, he went to the college doubleheaders in the Philadelphia Palestra and dreamed of playing there one day. Maybe for Penn. Or St. Joseph's. The Big Five was still about as big as it got in college basketball in the late fifties and early sixties and Williams wanted to be there.

No one in his family had ever gone to college. But Neil Thompson and the varsity basketball coach at Collingswood, John Smith, had told him he was good enough to go to college on a basketball scholarship if he worked at his game. Williams was barely six feet tall and he wasn't a great shooter, but he could get into the lane with his quickness and strength and he would just as soon die as let someone beat him on defense. His grades weren't great, but they were good. "Not good enough for Penn," he remembered. That was where he really wanted to go, especially after his high school pal Stan Pavlek went there. "You needed A's and B's. I had B's and C's."

That was good enough for a lot of places. For a while, he wanted to go to Duke, which was just emerging as a national power under a young coach named Vic Bubas. But on the night that Duke assistant Bucky Waters came to see him play, the opposition, Audubon High School, threw a zone at Collingswood and took away Williams's penetration. "I kept missing jump shots," he said. "I was devastated. I knew I would never hear from Duke again."

He did hear from Clemson and Maryland. They came to see him play against Trenton and he scored 27. He visited both campuses and came home from a spring visit to Clemson ready to go there. But John Smith thought Maryland would be a better fit. It was closer to home and the coaching staff had said they were going to play up-tempo. Williams liked the idea of being closer to home since he had his first serious girlfriend, Diane McMillan, and wanted to be able to get home to see her.

"So I was only two and a half hours away by car," he said. "The problem was, I didn't have a car and neither did she. I might as well have been at Clemson."

He played for Bud Millikan at Maryland with mixed results. As a sophomore he started on a very good (18–8) team that tied for second in the ACC; he came off the bench as a junior; and he started most of the time as a senior. He never averaged more than six points a game, although he did establish a Maryland record for consecutive field goals made (eight), a record that stood for more than thirty years. "My one moment of glory," he said. "Of course we lost the game."

There wasn't a lot of glory or all that much joy during his three varsity seasons. Millikan believed in a walk-it-up offense and drop-back defense. It had worked well for him for years, but as basketball changed, it became a less effective way to play. The Terrapins were 14–11 in Williams's junior year and 11–14 when he was a senior. By then, he had figured out that he wasn't going on to a pro career and had decided he wanted to coach and teach high school. He did play briefly in the Eastern League after finishing his senior year, but when Frank Fellows, who had replaced the fired Millikan as coach, asked him to come back to Maryland to be an assistant coach on the freshman team, Williams said yes.

"I hadn't finished my degree and I wanted to get that done," he said. "Plus, I figured it was a way to get into coaching."

It turned out to be more than that. The freshman coach that season was Tom Davis, who liked an up-tempo style as much as Millikan had hated it. Williams enjoyed coaching that way and knew that the players preferred it. He and Davis became friends. "If I ever get a college job," Davis told him. "I'll hire you."

Williams was flattered, but didn't think much of it. Davis was a freshman coach on a staff whose job status was shaky. Williams was about to go be a high school JV coach. "I figured, 'Yeah, sure, we'll be college coaches together someday.' "

Williams graduated from Maryland that year, married Diane, who he had continued to date through college in spite of his lack of transportation, and took the job as the junior varsity coach at Camden High School. He went off to coach high school ball and teach history, figuring that's what he would do for a long, long time.

He lasted three years. In his second year, he was promoted to varsity coach and with a senior-dominated team went 27–0 and won the state championship. Nothing to this coaching stuff, he thought. A year later, with the seniors gone, the record was 14–13. Williams had learned a valuable lesson. "You can coach your butt off, be a genius, scout the hell out of every opponent," he said. "Players win games. Not coaches."

That summer, his phone rang. It was Tom Davis, keeping his word. He had been hired as the coach at Lafayette College in Easton, Pennsylvania. For the first time, Lafayette was going to hire a full-time assistant coach. Davis offered Williams the job. "I'll take it," Williams said. There was one hitch. The assistant basketball coach also had to coach the soccer team.

"Soccer?" Williams said. "I don't know anything about soccer."

"Doesn't matter," Davis said. "You have to do it or I can't hire you."

"No deal," Williams said.

He and Diane were new parents. He knew that coaching on the college level would take hours and hours of time. Throw in coaching a sport he knew nothing about and he would never be home. He was happy where he was. South Jersey was home.

A week later, Davis called back. "Look, I know it's your life," he said, "but you're an idiot if you turn this down. We're going to be good. You'll get noticed. You'll work the soccer thing out." Then he added the clincher: "If you turn this down, you may never get another shot at college coaching."

Williams went out the next day and bought a book on how to coach soccer. "I figured I better at least know the rules before my first practice," he said.

To this day, he believes that what Davis said to him that day was true. "I didn't know anyone in the college game except Tom," he said. "If I hadn't gone with him to Lafayette, I might very well have spent my whole life as a high school coach."

Davis had — and still has — a unique style of coaching. He believes in constant pressure, almost continuous substituting, and bounce passes. Williams doesn't care how his players pass the ball, "as long as it gets where it's supposed to be," but beyond that, much of his style is adapted from Davis's. Williams likes his teams to pressure the opponent's offense for as close to ninety-four feet and forty minutes as is possible. He understands that to play that style, you must have depth. He also understands that some coaches believe that a gambling defense catches up to you eventually, especially against good teams.

"When I was in college, we walked the ball up the floor and played drop-back defense on every possession," he said. "That way of playing worked for Bud Millikan. But it never worked for me — as a player. I was better in a full-court game than a half-court game. So, I was probably inclined to coach that way anyway. Then, when I got with Tom, I saw his style work. I could also see that most players enjoyed playing that way. I've changed what I do over the years" — occasionally nowadays he will back off the press if he feels it isn't working — "but that's still the way I like to play the most."

He spent six years at Lafayette and actually came to enjoy coaching the soccer team. A couple of years they were very good. The basketball team was always good and Williams put in hours and hours in his car, driving around looking for kids who could play *and* read and write, since Lafayette was an academically oriented school that didn't offer athletic scholarships. On the road, he often encountered another young coach who worked at Lafayette's archrival, Lehigh. His name was Pat Kennedy.

Kennedy vividly remembers the young Williams. "One night, we're playing them and I go to the scorer's table to check something, time-outs maybe. I look up and there's Gary, about six inches away from me, making sure he can hear everything I'm saying. I said something like, 'No big deal, Gary, take it easy,' and the next thing I know, he's in my face and

I'm right back in his. Over nothing. He was just that intense. And I guess I was too."

After six years at Lafayette, Davis was hired at Boston College. Williams probably could have succeeded him at Lafayette, but he accepted the chance to move to BC with Davis because he felt he needed to recruit big-time players at a big-time school if he was ever going to have a chance at a major head coaching job. A year after he arrived at BC, the chance came — at American University.

Williams was familiar with American because it was located in northwest Washington, D.C. During his playing days at Maryland, AU had solid teams and, during the early seventies — when Davis was an assistant coach there — it had a kid named Kermit Washington, who one year led the country in both scoring and rebounding. It also had no on-campus gym, something Williams wasn't aware of when he went to Washington to interview for the job.

"Somewhere in the back of my mind, I must have known that they played at Fort Myer," he said. "But I had forgotten. When I asked where the gym was, they just pointed towards the Potomac."

Fort Myer was across the Potomac in northern Virginia. It was cold and creaky and didn't even have locker rooms. American changed in a weight room. Williams saw what "the Fort," as everyone at AU called it, looked like and then took the job anyway. "I was ready to be a head coach," he said. "I really didn't care what was involved."

As it turned out, the Fort was one of the great home court advantages in all of college basketball. "Teams would take one look at it and say, 'We can't possibly play here,' " Williams said. "We were used to it. We were comfortable there. It was so cold, we were usually ahead 10–2 by the time the other team got used to it. Then we'd win by four. We always thought we would win when we played there."

Williams and his teams had some memorable games in the Fort. There was the night the Eagles beat West Chester on a shot at the buzzer and West Chester coach Earl Voss was convinced the shot shouldn't have counted. He chased the officials off the floor, and when it became apparent nothing was going to change, he kicked an old iron gate in frustration. The gate broke. Voss went back to his locker room, spoke to the media, and got ready to leave. Only he couldn't. The military police were waiting for him. He had damaged U.S. government property. He had a choice: he could pay for the gate or go to jail. It was 3 o'clock in the morning before Voss could track down school officials to send him a check to pay for the gate. It could only happen at the Fort.

Williams knew when he arrived at AU that he couldn't compete in the recruiting wars nationally or even locally with Maryland and Georgetown. "If they wanted a player, they were going to get him," he said. What he could do was provide a fallback position for local players who left home and were unhappy. He could also piece together a team that was perenially undersized — because any true big man who could put one foot in front of the other was going to end up in a power conference — but played a style that gave other teams fits. The Eagles pressed up and down the floor, got in your face for forty minutes, and generally made your life miserable. In 1982, John Thompson brought a Georgetown team that would play in the national championship game later that season into the Fort and got out with a two-point win. Williams got a technical foul in that game when, in response to a call, he did a full pirouette that sent dollar bills flying all over the court.

"It was the postgame meal money," he said later. "We were allowed to give each kid three dollars. I had thirty-six singles in my jacket pocket and they went all over the place."

By then, AU was making waves in DC. People were coming to the Fort to watch the Eagles play. They won twenty-four games in 1981 and twenty-two the next. In 1981, they came up a missed jump shot shy of making the NCAA tournament. Both years they ended up in the National Invitational tournament.

Basketball people noticed the little school with no gym that was competing against Georgetown and Temple and La Salle and St. Joseph's and winning some of the time. They noticed the intense young coach who seemed to get his players to play better than they should be able to play. Duquesne offered a lot of money, but Williams didn't think it was the right move. He knew he had a good team coming back for his fifth season at AU and he wasn't jumping unless something special came along.

Something did. Again, Tom Davis was involved. He had been lured from Boston College to Stanford. BC called Williams. It was a chance to coach in the Big East and the Big Time. The money was more than double what he was making at AU. "I had to do it," he said. "I had lived in Boston for two years and liked it. Diane liked it too. It made sense."

It made perfect sense, especially the first year, when BC won the Big East regular season title, reached the final of the Big East tournament and the Sweet Sixteen of the NCAAs before losing a three-point game to Virginia and Ralph Sampson. Williams can still see in his mind's eye his team down two points with the ball in the final minute. "Dominic Pressley went baseline and dunked the ball," he said. "But the official called him for stepping out of bounds. He was right. But that's how close we were."

Even with the loss, life was a joyride. Williams was a star in Boston. The media loved him because he was accessible and funny and he was winning games. For the first time in his life, he was a star. He wasn't Larry Bird or Kevin McHale, but he wasn't that far behind. He enjoyed the attention. He had worked hard for a long time to get it. But while he was basking in his newfound glory, he was also beginning to lose touch with his wife.

"It's the classic 'If I had it all to do over again' story," he said, years later. "Life's not that way, though. You don't get do-overs."

Diane Williams had dealt with the vagaries of being a coach's wife since those early days in Camden. She had dealt with the travel, the nights spent buried in film, the times when Dad couldn't be there for Kristen so she had to be both Mom and Dad. Gary Williams felt pangs of guilt all the time. But he was busy climbing the coaching ladder. There would be time for family when he got to the top.

But the time never came. He could feel his marriage drifting in Boston but didn't really know how to piece it back together. What's more, things got tougher after the first year. The team struggled the second year and, for the first time in his life, he had a serious problem with a player. A senior named Martin Clark, unhappy with diminished playing time, went after Williams en route to the locker room after a game and then, after Williams had allowed him back onto the team following a suspension, went on a local TV station to blast his coach. Things got better the next year — another Sweet Sixteen trip — but the team struggled again a year later, not making postseason play for the first time since Williams had arrived.

It was a battle keeping things together in what was then the toughest league in the country at a school where basketball ranked not only behind football in importance but also behind hockey. At least at AU, Fort or no Fort, basketball was the sport. When Ohio State called at the end of the 1986 season, Williams jumped at the chance to move. That was tough on Kristen, who was in high school, but he knew he had to go. He also hoped that a move might revive the marriage.

Coaching is tough on marriages, especially when the coach is as driven as Williams. Even those who make their marriages work will tell you that it is hard going. In the ACC, three of the nine coaches have been divorced (Williams, Dean Smith, and Jeff Jones) and the others talk openly about strains caused by their profession and their own hunger to succeed.

"Diane did nothing wrong," Williams said. "I wanted to be a good husband, I wanted to be a good father. But I also wanted to be a good coach. I couldn't make them all happen at once."

Once again, at Ohio State, he revived a sagging program. Once again, he was an instant star. Even more so this time because in Columbus, Ohio, the only person more important than the Ohio State basketball coach is the Ohio State football coach. Since football coach Earle Bruce was struggling to keep his job, Williams was treated as a conquering hero. He replaced Eldon Miller, a solid coach who showed about as much emotion during a game as the chair he was sitting on. Williams, up and down through the entire game, always bursting with energy, became a local phenomenon almost overnight.

That was the good news. The bad news was that his marriage was now falling apart completely. Midway through their third season in Columbus, Gary and Diane separated. There are few secrets in a town the size of Columbus, especially when they involve the second-best-known man in town. The split made the local papers. Kristen, now a freshman at Miami of Ohio, had to deal with having all her friends read about her parents' filing for divorce. They also got to read reports that there was another woman in her father's life.

In the midst of all that turmoil, Williams began getting phone calls from people at Maryland. Bob Wade, who had replaced Lefty Driesell three years earlier in the wake of Len Bias's cocaine-induced death, was about to be fired. Wade had broken NCAA rules and then lied to NCAA investigators about what he had done. Maryland was in big trouble and Wade was going down with the ship.

Williams was truly torn. It had always been his dream to go back to Maryland as the coach. If the school had called him when Driesell had been fired, he might have walked to College Park. Now, the situation was different. He had spent three years putting the players in place who he thought could win the Big Ten and challenge for the national title. He had just won a huge recruiting battle for shooting guard Jimmy Jackson, regarded by some as the best high school senior in the country in 1989. The Buckeyes were going to be very good the next year and beyond.

Maryland was in trouble. It was facing probation and that would mean starting from square one, or close to it. Williams had already been through that at AU and at Ohio State and had faced a different kind of struggle at Boston College. He wasn't sure what to do.

But Lou Perkins, the Maryland athletic director, told him he didn't think the NCAA sanctions would be that serious. Wade had been the problem and he had been fired. Maryland had cooperated with the investigation. Perkins figured there would be no more than one year of sanctions — if that.

There was also the messy matter of his divorce. In College Park, it wouldn't be the story it was in Columbus. He could start fresh. He wouldn't be as big a man in the Washington, D.C., area as he had been in Columbus, but that was fine with him. He would also make less money in endorsements. He was making plenty already. He could handle it.

Last, but not least, was the Dream. Even as a Maryland player, Williams had dreamed of coaching the Terrapins. He had looked around Cole Field House on the few nights that it was full back then and thought it was a magic place to be. Flawed though it might be, Maryland was home.

He said yes.

And, once again, the first year was about as good as he could have hoped for. Even though the NCAA investigation was still going on, the team played well. It beat North Carolina twice and won eighteen games during the 1990 regular season. That put the Terrapins on the NCAA bubble going into the ACC tournament. If they could win their first round game against Duke, they would be a lock to get in. Even a loss and Williams thought there was still a chance.

And then the NCAA hammer came down. Perkins had guessed wrong. The sanctions were for two years and included no TV at all for a year, no postseason play for two years, and cutbacks in scholarships and campus visits. It was about as close as you could come to a death sentence without turning on the gas.

Williams got the news on the eve of the ACC tournament. He was stunned. All year long he had been telling recruits that — worst-case scenario — they might not be able to play in the NCAA tournament as freshmen. One year out of four is a lot different than two years out of four. He was angry and said so publicly. He thought the sanctions were unfair. The NCAA does not like those who have been punished to complain about their punishment. When the NCAA bids came out that Sunday, Maryland was left out. "It was as if they added another year to our probation because we complained about it," Williams said. "It hurt because we had worked all year to get in, knowing there was a good chance we were going to be unable to go the following year."

Things didn't get any better when the season ended. The woman he had gotten involved with during his last year in Columbus had moved to College Park. They had decided to get married in the spring. Two weeks before the wedding, she broke things off and left. A few weeks after that, Williams was driving home after an afternoon of golf, which had been followed by dinner. He'd had a few drinks with dinner; nothing crazy, but enough. A cop pulled him over, saying he had been weaving. He was charged with DUI. More embarrassing publicity.

"The worst part of the whole thing was having to call Kristen," he said. "We were just starting to get better after the divorce and then I had to tell her about that."

Williams felt as if his entire life had crashed all at once. He had gone from the coach of a rising program to the coach of one facing two years of NCAA sanctions. He had gone through a divorce and the end of another relationship. Both had been messy; the divorce had been expensive. He was virtually estranged from his daughter. Sometime that summer he picked up a magazine and read an article about the things that cause the most stress in one's life: divorce, moving, changing jobs. He had done all three at once. His lifelong dream, to come back and coach Maryland, had turned into a nightmare almost overnight.

"I really thought my career might be over," he said. "People said all the right things at Maryland, but I'm a realist. Sanctions or no sanctions there was going to come a time in a year, two years, maybe three, where if we didn't show improvement they were going to say, 'Time for a change.' That's the way the game is played. I looked at where we were and how hard we were going to get hit in recruiting and I didn't see how we were going to get out of last place. This was the ACC we were talking about. It wasn't as if there were some soft touches we'd go by easily."

Amazingly, they didn't finish last the next year. They finished seventh — one game out of fifth — and 16–12 overall. Williams finally caught a break when his best player, Walt Williams, decided not to transfer even though the sanctions meant he would never play in the NCAA tournament. With Williams and a bunch of players who went out each night to prove they were better than people thought, the Terrapins surprised people throughout the season. They weren't allowed to play in the ACC tournament (since all those games are on TV and Maryland was banned from TV), but they ended the season with an upset victory at Virginia that left Williams feeling as if perhaps there was still hope for the program.

The next season produced a 14–15 record, but with the sanctions being lifted for '93, Williams recruited a class that had everyone talking NCAA tournament the next fall. Victories over Louisville and Oklahoma in December convinced everyone that the freshmen were ready to step in and compete with the best in the ACC.

They won three games. All against NC State. Welcome to reality. "We were a little bit shell-shocked," Williams remembered. "I looked back though at the Duke team that played all those freshmen [1983] and got hammered. Three years later, they were in the Final Four."

Williams scored another recruiting coup that spring when he signed six-foot-five-inch Keith Booth out of Dunbar High School in Baltimore. The Booth signing was critical for reasons that went beyond Booth's potential as a player. Baltimore has always produced quality high school players and, as Maryland's only real city, should be a productive recruiting base for the state's university. But Maryland hadn't recruited a player out of Baltimore since the early 1980s, in large part because Ernest Graham, another Dunbar graduate, had been unhappy playing at Maryland for Lefty Driesell. One of the reasons for Bob Wade's hiring in 1986 was his connection to Baltimore as the longtime coach at Dunbar. Wade's firing had created another rift between the school and the city, since many in the

black community there saw Wade's firing as the work of a white administration making a black man the fall guy.

Booth's decision to come to Maryland was a critical step toward
opening Baltimore up again. Williams had insisted that Maryland play at
least one game a year in Baltimore and had worked Booth and all of his
various advisers very hard. Even with Wade, still an influential figure in
the city, working hard against Maryland, the Terrapins had won the
battle.

One day into practice the next season, Williams knew that although
Booth would be a fine player, he wasn't even close to being the best
freshman on the team. The previous fall, with little notice or ballyhoo, the
Terrapins had signed a skinny six-ten center from Norfolk named Joe
Smith. He had first been spotted by assistant coach Art Perry. When
Williams went to see him play, he loved his enthusiasm and his quickness
around the basket. If North Carolina had recruited Smith, he undoubt-
edly would have gone there. But no ACC school other than Maryland
showed interest in him until very late in the recruiting process. By then,
Smith was all but locked up for Maryland.

Watching Smith in practice, Williams realized he had something
special. Each day, he was the best player on the court, even though the
previous year's freshmen now had a year of ACC experience under their
belts. In the season opener, Maryland's first game against Georgetown in
fourteen years, Smith scored 26 points against Georgetown's star center
Othella Harrington, outplaying him on both ends of the floor. Maryland,
a double-digit underdog, won the game in overtime on a scoop shot at the
buzzer by sophomore point guard Duane Simpkins. While Simpkins
jumped on the press table to celebrate, Williams leaped for joy, re-
creating his pirouette of fourteen years earlier at the Fort. This time,
though, there was no money and no technical. And this time, he was the
winning coach.

Maryland was back. It wasn't going to dominate the ACC, but it was
competitive every night, which was all Williams could hope for, especially
with two freshmen and three sophomores in the starting lineup. They
were a long way from the dark days of 1991 when he had wondered if they
could beat anyone in the ACC with any consistency. With Smith winning
every freshman award there was, the Terrapins made it back to the NCAA

tournament — for the first time since 1988 — and then upset second-seeded Massachusetts in the second round of the Midwest Regional. They lost in the Sweet Sixteen to Michigan, but the game was tight until the end and the campus was alive with excitement the entire week leading up to the game. Everyone was high on being there.

This was what Williams had come back to Maryland for. He was finally living the dream to fill Cole every night and make it so loud that the teams from North Carolina would know how it felt to go down there. A year later, Maryland was picked in everyone's preseason top ten. When they opened the doors of Cole for Midnight Madness '94, the fans filled all 14,500 seats and then some to watch a scrimmage. Not since Lefty Driesell's glory days in the seventies and early eighties had it been like this at Maryland. Every time Williams walked on the floor, the entire student body gave him a standing ovation. Williams would shake his fist, the students would go nuts, and then the place would rock with noise and emotion for two hours.

Maryland finished tied for first in the ACC that season. Smith won several national player of the year awards. Before all was said and done, the '95 Terrapins won twenty-six games.

But it was not quite the season Williams had envisioned. For one thing, he missed part of it. Late in February, after a long trip to San Antonio to play a national TV game against Cincinnati, Williams began to feel sick. As he always did when he felt sick during the season, he ignored it. Like Krzyzewski — who was at that moment watching his team play from home because of *his* illness — he believed in mind over matter. Like Krzyzewski, he paid the price for that attitude.

He got home from practice on the last Monday in February feeling so chilled and sick that he went right to bed, still wearing his clothes and his overcoat. Even so, even huddled under every blanket he could find, he was shivering. The next morning, he called his trainer, J. J. Bush, and said he thought he needed to see a doctor. Bush took him to the Maryland infirmary. There, they told him in no uncertain terms to get to a hospital. He had pneumonia. "If I had tried to travel that day" — the team was going to Duke — "they said I might have died," he said.

Instead, he lay in bed, essentially unaware of anything for several days. The Terrapins, coached by assistant Billy Hahn, went to Durham and beat the Blue Devils, coached by Pete Gaudet, in the first ACC game in history in which neither head coach was well enough to show up. That Sunday, with a chance to win the ACC title outright, the Terrapins went to Virginia and got hammered. When Hahn walked in the next morning, Williams was on the phone screaming about the team wimping out and not showing any guts under pressure. That was when Hahn knew Williams was feeling better.

He wanted to coach in the ACC tournament that week, but the doctors said no. They let him go home, but made him wait another week to travel. Maryland lost in the ACC semifinals to North Carolina, then got sent west as a number three seed. Williams returned, still on medication, but wound up and ready to go. The Terrapins won their first two games, then played Connecticut in the round of sixteen. The Huskies, playing a pressing defense similar to Maryland's, jumped on top early, and never looked back. The final was 99–89.

It was a crushing loss for Williams. He hadn't expected an easy game, but he felt as if his team had been timid in the early going and he couldn't figure out why. He questioned himself, his preparation, his ability to make them understand that this year the Sweet Sixteen wasn't good enough, that they were good enough to go farther, that they should want to go farther — need to go farther.

He knew Smith was going to turn pro. He had hoped against hope that he could keep him for at least another year because everyone else would be back. But the agents and their bird dogs had been all over Smith throughout the season. On the season-opening trip to Hawaii, Williams had noticed one of the bird dogs lurking around the locker room after each game. When he saw him walking down the beach one afternoon with Smith, he called Smith to his room.

"Joe, why are you hanging around with that guy?" he asked.

"Coach, he's my friend."

Williams knew at that moment he was going to lose the battle. If Smith believed any of these guys were his friends, nothing he could say would change things.

Williams was so aggravated about the whole situation in Hawaii that he screamed at Chuck Walsh, his sports information director, when he saw Walsh handing the bird dog a Maryland media guide. Walsh thought he was just being courteous to someone the players had been hanging out with. Williams didn't see it that way. "Don't you understand who that is?" he yelled. "That's the enemy! The enemy! You don't associate with the enemy!"

He knew this was one war he couldn't win. In Washington, the agents are more omnipresent than in almost anyplace else in college basketball. Three of the major management companies — ProServ, Advantage International, and FAME — are headquartered in Washington. The head of IMG's basketball division works in Washington. Every night, Williams looked up and saw agents in the stands. After the games, they were in the tunnel outside the locker room, buddying up, not just to Smith, but to everyone on the team.

"In a small town, you don't have to deal with that," he said. "Here, you can't get away from it."

Smith's announcement that he would turn pro was inevitable. In his case, the agents weren't lying when they told him he could be the number one pick. He was. He left behind a team that would return four starters — three seniors and Booth, who had steadily improved during his first two seasons. Even with Smith gone, Maryland was picked by many to win the ACC.

The '95–96 season was a nightmare. To begin with, the other four starters were accustomed to playing with Smith. Because he was always double-teamed, they had open shots. Not anymore. Because he was there to block shots if a defender beat them, they could let their man get by them and know help was there. Not anymore.

But it was more than that. All the agents and scouts had spent so much time sucking up to the other players that each of them was now convinced he was on his way to the League right behind Smith. Williams felt from day one that Exree Hipp, a three-year starter, was out of shape and never worked hard in practice. He had a miserable season. Simpkins, the starting point guard for two years, somehow managed to accumulate more than $9,000 in parking tickets. Then when he borrowed money to pay the fines, he ended up getting himself a three-game NCAA suspension even after Williams had told him he couldn't accept the loan.

It was that way all year. Williams didn't like his players, they didn't like him. After one galling loss at Wake Forest, Williams looked at the seniors the next day in practice and said, "By the way, have you guys seen any of those agents who were your best friends last year around here lately? I wonder where they went?"

He hurt them with that line and he felt a little bit guilty about it later. But he meant it and he meant to make a point with it. It wasn't until he started playing his three freshmen in February that Williams saw any improvement from his team. Maryland scrambled to tie for fourth in the ACC and squeezed into the NCAAs for a third straight year. But Williams thought the seniors — with the exception of Johnny Rhodes — quit against Santa Clara in the opening round and the Terrapins were upset, 91–79, by a team a lot of people didn't even think deserved a bid.

"They got me back," Williams said later. "Their way of getting me was to not play hard. Which is sad. Because I'll be coaching for a long time. It was their last chance as college basketball players."

The embarrassing ending left Williams angry and hurt. He knew that some of what had happened had been out of his control, but ultimately he knew he was responsible for what happened to the team — good or bad. None of the four seniors graduated that spring, and a *Baltimore Sun* story about that only made things worse. Two of them — Rhodes and Simpkins — had been close to graduating, which wasn't bad after four years — if they came back to finish.

For the first time since he had returned to Maryland, Williams was publicly criticized. The team had underachieved and that was his fault. There had been no big-name recruits for a couple of years. That was also Williams's fault. The fact that the three freshmen — point guard Terrell Stokes, forward Laron Profit, and center Obinna Ekezie — had all shown outstanding potential late in the season didn't seem to matter. Maybe it was time for Williams to move on, went the thinking. Williams was discouraged enough that if the right offer had come that summer, he would have considered it.

But he liked the team he had coming back for '97. Booth would be the only senior starter, and it would be, without question, his team. For two years it had been Joe Smith's team. Then it had been nobody's team. Now it would be Booth's team. That was good. A team needs a clearly defined leader. The freshmen would be sophomores and there would be no doubt they would be starting. He wouldn't have to soothe egos anymore, worrying about playing freshmen ahead of seniors.

When he walked downstairs on the first day of practice, the women's team was on the floor. It was thirty minutes before his team was scheduled to begin working out. When he reached the tunnel outside the locker room, he was shocked by what he saw: most of his players were already there, in their practice uniforms, loosening up, ready to get going.

"Last year, we had guys getting to the locker room most days five minutes before practice," he said. "These guys were ready to go. Eager to go. It made me feel good."

They were there early, ready and eager every day throughout preseason. Like most coaches, Williams always has a gut feeling about his team before the opener. A year earlier, on the day the team had left to play its opener against Kentucky, he had learned about the Simpkins parking ticket fiasco. He had gone into the Kentucky game with a sick feeling in his stomach. This year the opener was a little less daunting: a home game against Howard. Walking onto the floor that night to the usual ovation — the students hadn't quit on him even if some of the alumni had — Williams felt great.

His team had been picked eighth in the ACC by the media. That was fine with him. He loved being the underdog. Especially with a team that seemed to want to win as much as he did.

5

Openers

ONCE UPON A TIME the college basketball season began on December 1. And, more often than not, it began with the so-called power schools playing at home against weak opposition. Pad the record early, most coaches figured, and build toward your conference schedule.

All of that began to change in the late 1970s when television began to take over the sport. Preseason tournaments began to spring up in far-flung places like Alaska and Hawaii and, for a while, Japan. The NCAA had long ago mandated that any games played outside the continental United States did not count toward the twenty-seven games a team was allowed to play. Once, that rule existed to allow the Rainbow Classic, an annual post-Christmas tournament played in Honolulu, to be able to recruit seven teams to join the University of Hawaii in the event. As time went on, more and more events were sanctioned in Hawaii. As the glut grew, they began to expand into November and to places other than Hawaii. Everyone wanted to play in these so-called "exempt" events because exempt games were bonuses, a chance to add experience and victories early in the season. By 1996, there were no fewer than eight major exempt events with slots for sixty-two teams. And no conference had more willing — or more invited — participants than the Atlantic Coast Conference.

The ACC was entering its forty-fourth basketball season. As is so often the case in college athletics, it was football that brought about the radical change in the spring of 1953 that led to the formation of the conference. Back then, the seventeen-school Southern Conference was divided over the issue of cutbacks enacted in the wake of the betting and cheating scandals that had beset many schools in the early 1950s. When Maryland and Clemson accepted bowl bids at the end of the 1951 season even though the conference had denied them permission to play, both schools were placed on probation by the conference. Maryland's Jim Tatum and Clemson's Frank Howard, both of whom doubled as football coaches and athletic directors, began looking to break away from the conference. Throughout the next school year, they recruited five other conference members — Clemson's archrival, South Carolina, and the four schools located in North Carolina — North Carolina, NC State, Duke, and Wake Forest — to join them. On May 8, 1953, at the Sedgfield Inn in Greensboro, the seven schools voted unanimously to leave the Southern Conference and form a new league called the Atlantic Coast Conference. Seven months later, Virginia, which had left the Southern Conference in 1936 to become an independent, joined the fledgling ACC.

Thus, from the seeds of a football revolt, the strongest basketball conference in history was born. Since then, the league has undergone three changes. In 1971, South Carolina withdrew from the conference. Again, the reason was football. The ACC had a rule that prohibited schools from offering scholarships to anyone who did not make at least 800 on the SATs. South Carolina football coach Paul Dietzel, who was also — surprise — the school's athletic director, decided to get the Gamecocks out of the ACC to get around the rule. Basketball coach Frank McGuire pleaded with Dietzel and the school's trustees not to leave, but was overruled. Three years later, Dietzel resigned under pressure. But the damage had been done.

The ACC operated with seven teams until 1979, when Georgia Tech joined the league. For once, the decision was not football-only. Although the Yellow Jackets were down in basketball at the time, the school believed that joining the ACC would give it a chance to rebuild. The school's football tradition was, of course, a lure for the ACC, which by then was well known as a conference that kicked butt and took names during the winter, but was usually little more than a wannabe outside the borders of Clemson during football season.

Finally, in 1991, the league expanded again. This time the decision was as much about football as the breakaway that created the league in the first place. With most major conferences expanding, ACC commissioner Gene Corrigan saw his chance to put the ACC on the football map by recruiting a power. He flirted with both Miami and Florida State, independent powerhouses, before finally settling on Florida State. If Corrigan was at all bothered by the unwieldy nature of a nine-team basketball conference or by the fact that Florida State was not exactly a bastion of academia, he never mentioned it. All he knew — or cared about — was the fact that Florida State would bring significant TV and bowl revenue into the league and force bowls and TV networks to make deals with his league in order to get to Florida State.

The ploy worked. Florida State has brought huge football revenues into the conference. It has also lost exactly one conference game — to Virginia in 1995 — in five seasons, essentially turning the ACC into a two-tier conference: Florida State and everybody else. The rest of the league is so upset about this that it laughs all the way to the bank each January.

One thing that neither Corrigan nor any of the schools had counted on or given much thought to in admitting Florida State was the quality of the school's basketball program. In 1991, their final year in the very solid Metro Conference, the Seminoles had won the league title and reached the Sweet Sixteen. Their coach, Pat Kennedy, had put FSU's program on very solid footing after arriving there in 1986. Even so, no one in the ACC dreamed that Florida State would step in that first season and finish second in the conference. In their conference debut, the Seminoles waltzed into the DeanDome, shot the lights out, and easily beat North Carolina, 96–84.

After the game, when someone asked shooting guard Sam Cassell about coming into the DeanDome and winning so handily, he shrugged.

"It's not really a tough place to play," he said. "It's kind of a wine and cheese crowd."

One game into life in the ACC and Florida State had made an indelible mark.

Three things made the ACC special: geography, the tournament, and the coaches.

Until Florida State's arrival, one could drive from the northernmost school — Maryland — to the southernmost — Georgia Tech — in a comfortable ten hours. The four North Carolina schools were located within ninety minutes of one another, and three of them — NC State, North Carolina, and Duke — shared the same community and were less than thirty minutes apart. It was a tightly packed conference, if not always a closeknit one. From the beginning, the Big Four schools, as they came to be known, were intense rivals. The two public schools — Carolina and State — were always resentful of the two private schools — Duke and Wake Forest — viewing them, especially Duke, as rich-kid schools filled with northerners. The private schools were always jealous of the facilities and the finances available to the state-funded schools. And State and Carolina were always at one another's throats, State people believing that Carolina people looked down their noses at them (which many did) and Carolina people seeing the State people as a bunch of jealous hayseeds.

To the non–North Carolina schools, though, the Big Four schools seemed like one overwhelming entity. The league's headquarters have always been in North Carolina and, until 1976, the ACC tournament was always played in Greensboro or Raleigh. It has now been played outside of North Carolina six times in forty-four years, with no plans to do so again before the year 2003. The Big Four schools have won thirty-seven of the forty-four tournaments and all seven of the league's national titles.

The non–Carolina schools believed at the beginning and believe now that the Big Four schools control the league. "We're like a satellite orbiting the earth," Gary Williams often says.

And so, the Carolina schools battle each other and the non–Carolina schools battle them.

Of course, they are all also business partners. They share in one another's bowl revenues, NCAA tournament revenues, and television revenues. They all understand that the stronger the league is, the more likely they all are to make money. They also know that one of the main lures in recruiting is not only their own strength, but the strength of their competition. Basketball coaches sell the ACC to recruits as much as they sell their individual school — unless they are recruiting against another ACC school, which is often the case.

The geography has always made for intense, often bitter rivalries. Those rivalries were sharpened each of the first twenty-one years by the fact that no matter what a team did in the regular season, it had to win the ACC tournament to get into the NCAAs. Back then, the ACC was almost unique, one of only two conferences in the country that decided its champion on a three-day, winner-take-all basis. Some of the conference's most memorable games took place in the tournament, most notably the last final that was played on a winner-take-all basis, in 1974. That year, NC State, led by David Thompson, Tom Burleson, and Monte Towe, beat Maryland, led by Tom McMillen, Len Elmore, and John Lucas, 103–100 in an overtime classic that many basketball people viewed for a long time as the best college game ever played. The two teams played to an 86–86 tie at the end of regulation *without a turnover.* State went on to win the national championship two weeks later on the same Greensboro Coliseum court. Maryland went home. The next year the NCAA rules changed to allow more than one team from a conference to qualify and the tournament was never quite the same.

Even so, the ACC tournament is still a huge social event every spring. There has not been a public sale of tickets since 1966, and to the schools involved, even when their coaches try to view it as just a warm-up for the NCAAs, it remains a big deal. Now, almost every conference has a postseason tournament for the simple reason that they are moneymakers. But none of them has the tradition and feel of the ACC tournament. And none of them makes money like the ACC tournament. Most ACC schools use tournament tickets as a carrot for their big-bucks contributors. In fact, during the 1970s, when Carolina dominated the conference, some Carolina fans joined the booster clubs of schools like Clemson and Wake Forest as a cheaper way of getting tournament tickets. Duke would also have been cheaper, but most Tar Heels fans drew the line there. They would rather pay the extra money than risk being called a Dukie.

And then there are the coaches. From Everett Case (NC State), Bones McKinney (Wake Forest), and Frank McGuire (North Carolina) in the 1950s to Dean Smith, Mike Krzyzewski, and Bobby Cremins today, the league has always been full of driven, highly successful coaches. The list of famous ACC coaches is long: Vic Bubas, Norman Sloan, Lefty Driesell, Terry Holland, Bill Foster, Jim Valvano. Of the nine men coaching in the league in 1996–97, two had won national championships (Smith, Krzyzewski), a third had been to the Final Four (Cremins), three others had been to the Elite Eight (Kennedy, Odom, Jones), and two had been to the Sweet Sixteen (Williams, Barnes). Only Herb Sendek, who has been at NC State for just one year, has not yet gotten at least to the Sweet Sixteen.

What's more, ACC coaches have always been characters. Smith, who has been involved in the league for thirty-nine years, has done battle at one time or another with almost everyone who has passed through. One of the most famous encounters between Smith and Maryland coach Lefty Driesell occurred in Chapel Hill in 1983. The previous year, North Carolina had finally broken through and won the national championship in Smith's seventh Final Four. That season, Maryland had its weakest team in years, having lost four starters, including Buck Williams and Albert King, who were both among the first ten picks in the 1981 NBA draft.

Weakened to begin with, Maryland went to play in Chapel Hill in '82 without its best player, Charles Pittman. On the day before the game, Driesell all but predicted a win. "If I was smart like Dean, I'd talk about how I ain't got no players and he's got [Michael] Jordan and [Sam] Perkins and [James] Worthy," he said. "But I ain't that smart. I think we're gonna go in there and whup 'em."

Amazingly, they almost did. Leading most of the second half, Maryland finally went down, 59–56, after Worthy stole the ball in the last minute with the Terrapins leading by one and dunked to put the Tar Heels ahead. After the game, someone asked Smith how it was that Maryland, without its best player, could come so close to pulling what would have been an astonishing upset. "You know I always say you can play one great game without a key player," Smith answered.

Smith does always say that. But when that line was repeated to Driesell, he went ballistic. "I come in here with no players and he's got three All-Americans, the best team in the country and we almost beat 'em and that's all he can say! What a bunch of crap that is!"

Driesell didn't think anything more about the incident until the ACC meetings that spring. Smith always assigns someone in his office to clip newspapers from around the country and keep a file for him to read any stories that mention North Carolina or the ACC or anyone or anything that might be relevant to him or the school. When he walked into the coaches meeting, he was carrying a clipping from the day after the game in Chapel Hill. Highlighted in yellow were Driesell's comments.

"Lefty, I'm very disappointed you would say something like this . . ." Smith began.

Driesell blew up again, telling Smith he had one hell of a nerve showing up with some clipping about a game in February when he had just won the national championship and Driesell had struggled to his worst season in ten years. After he got back from the meetings, still angry, Driesell wrote Smith a letter telling him not to bother shaking hands with him after they played the next season. Smith wrote back saying he would shake hands — win or lose — after any game with any coach.

The first game between Maryland and North Carolina the next year was in Chapel Hill. As luck would have it, Carolina pulled out another in a continuing series of miracle victories against the Terrapins. This time, Jordan flew in from the top of the key on the last play of the game to somehow block an open layup that Driesell's son Chuck was about to make to win the game. The only player in the sport who could have possibly made the play was Jordan. Driesell screamed goaltending but no call was forthcoming — or called for. The game ended. Final score: North Carolina 72, Maryland 71.

True to his word, Driesell headed for the exit without looking for Smith. True to *his* word, Smith followed him, coming up behind him to offer his hand. Driesell pushed his hand away and turned angrily to face Smith. "Get away from me, Dean. I told you I wasn't shaking your hand anymore."

Before Smith could answer, his assistant, Bill Guthridge, enraged by what he had seen and heard, began to charge at Driesell. Driesell's assistant, Mel Cartwright, grabbed a chair and a melee seemed inevitable.

But before Guthridge could get to Driesell, North Carolina sports information director Rick Brewer got in between the two men. There was a lot more shouting and shoving from both sides, but it ended there.

Of course three years later, when Driesell was made the fall guy at Maryland for Len Bias's death, Smith was one of his most vocal defenders.

That's the way it is in the ACC. The coaches battle one another, get angry with one another, often don't speak to one another for periods of time. But when one of their own is in trouble, they tend to close ranks.

Nowadays, the league is more fraternal than in the days when Norm Sloan and Driesell were doing battle with Smith. Smith is still the focal point for much of the contentiousness that does exist, in large part because he has been on top for so many years. When you are on top or near the top every single year — North Carolina has not finished lower than tied for third in the ACC since 1964 — you are going to make enemies, especially when you are as competitive as Smith. Clearly he and Barnes, although they have stopped their public sniping, are not exactly close.

But because Smith is sixty-six and one of the game's icons, the other coaches, who range from twelve years younger (Odom) to thirty-two years younger (Sendek) view him with a kind of respect and awe that the Sloans and Driesells — who were his contemporaries — never felt. The only relationship among the coaches that remains respectful but contentious is the one between Smith and Krzyzewski. Much of it is only natural. They coach at schools that are eleven miles apart and have been archrivals forever. They recruit against one another all the time; each constantly hears from the other's fans about how superior the other coach and the other school is.

Krzyzewski is not the first coach to challenge Smith's dominance in the ACC. At different times, Driesell, Sloan, Duke's Bill Foster, Terry Holland, Valvano, and Wake Forest's Carl Tacy and Dave Odom have had runs of several years where they were extremely competitive with Carolina. But Krzyzewski has stayed and, other than during the period when he was ill, has been a consistent winner since his fourth season. Sloan and Valvano both won national titles at State, but never returned to the Final Four. Holland went to two Final Fours at Virginia but never won a championship. Krzyzewski won two titles and went to seven Final Fours in nine years. Even Smith couldn't match that. His best Final Four string was five in eleven years (1967 through 1977) and seven in sixteen.

The bottom line, though, is that the two men are entirely different. Krzyzewski wears his emotions on his sleeve; Smith works to never show emotion. Krzyzewski is blunt; Smith obtuse. Smith likes scotch, used to be a chain smoker, and never uses profanity. Krzyzewski is profane, will occasionally drink a glass of wine, and wouldn't be caught dead with a cigarette in his mouth. Krzyzewski plays tennis and racquetball and, only recently, took up golf in order to spend more time with his wife. Smith loves golf, studies it, putts on hotel-room carpets, and according to friends will never be heard saying, "That's good."

The beginning of the end of their relationship came in 1984 when North Carolina had a dominant team, led by Jordan, Perkins, Brad Daugherty, and Kenny Smith. It was ranked number one nationally for most of the season. Duke was just starting to find itself under Krzyzewski. When the two teams met for the first time that season in Cameron Indoor Stadium, the Blue Devils surprised Carolina by playing them to the wire. Always uptight in Cameron, Smith actually banged on the substitution horn because he was convinced the officials at the scorer's table were trying to prevent him from getting a sub into the game. He and Krzyzewski exchanged angry words throughout, and the game ended with Krzyzewski getting a technical (Smith was not teed up for his horn banging) after telling the officials that they had taken the game away from his team.

Afterward, Krzyzewski made his infamous comment that there were two standards of officiating in the ACC: one for North Carolina and one for everyone else. Smith was furious. Krzyzewski didn't back down. When Clemson coach Bill Foster was quoted as saying in the mildest terms that there might be something to what Krzyzewski was saying, Smith sent him an angry note. Years later, the comment still rankles Smith.

"You know [former St. John's coach] Looey Carnesecca told me that he [Krzyzewski] made the same claim about St. John's when he was coaching at Army," he says. "Maybe it worked for him then too."

Krzyzewski makes no apologies for the comment and sees Smith's reaction as an example of the difference in their philosophies. "I said it because I thought it was true," he says. "I was protecting my players. Dean always talks about standing up for his players. That's what I was doing. I didn't do it for any hidden reason. I don't have a bunch of hidden agendas like some people do."

Those "some people" are one person. Krzyzewski often jokes that if he ever becomes President his first appointment will be Smith — "as head of the CIA, because he's the sneakiest guy I know."

The Smith-Krzyzewski relationship is perhaps best summed up by an incident in the DeanDome in 1993. Duke was the two-time defending national champion. Carolina was about to win the ACC regular season title and go on to the national title. The two programs were, by any standards, at the top of the college basketball heap and so were the two coaches. Duke had won the earlier game in Cameron, meaning it had won five of the last seven meetings. Even though Grant Hill was hurt and not playing, even though Carolina had already clinched first place, it was a huge game for the Tar Heels; a big one, because it was Carolina, for the Blue Devils.

During the first three minutes of the game, Smith and Krzyzewski, both wired, were on the officials every time they blew a whistle. Finally, Lenny Wirtz, the lead official, called them both to the scorer's table. "Look, guys, I know it's a big game and you're both a little hyper," he said. "But you have to let us work the game. You can't be up on every call."

Krzyzewski smiled at Wirtz and said, "Lenny, there are twenty-one thousand people in here who are all against me. You three guys are the only ones I feel comfortable talking to."

Seeing Wirtz smile at the wisecrack, Smith jumped in. "Lenny, don't let him do that, don't you see what he's trying to do?"

Before Wirtz could say anything, Krzyzewski waved a hand at Smith. "Dean, you know, you're just full of shit," he said and walked back to his bench. When he arrived, he looked at his assistant coaches and said, "If I ever for one minute start to act like him, don't ask a single question. Just get a gun and shoot me."

The 1996–97 college basketball season began on November 15 in the same place where it was scheduled to end 136 days later, The RCA Dome in Indianapolis. The season opener was a doubleheader sponsored by the

Black Coaches Association, an exempt event. The first game was Indiana-Connecticut; the nightcap Clemson-Kentucky.

This was not the kind of opener Clemson was accustomed to. The Tigers had become notorious through the years for playing the softest December schedule imagineable. But Rick Barnes thought this team was ready to play top teams early. In fact, he wanted to play top teams because he thought that was the best way to make it clear to outsiders that his program had arrived.

In his third year, Barnes was easily the most popular man on what was normally a football-crazed campus in a football-crazed state. Unlike a lot of basketball coaches at football schools, Barnes never fought football. He did demand a separate weight room in Littlejohn Coliseum for his team and new locker room facilities. He got both. Then he became one of the hosts of the *football* pregame show, driving around the parking lots in a golf cart and interviewing tailgaters.

"I enjoyed it," he said. "What's more, it meant that every week at every football game people were reminded about basketball. It was almost like an ongoing promotion all fall for the basketball team."

Barnes was a big man on campus at Clemson, but he knew he wasn't that big. He enjoyed telling the story about the football game that Senator Strom Thurmond had come to earlier in the fall. Barnes was in the president's box at halftime when someone told him that Thurmond was eager to meet him. Barnes hustled over to meet the ninety-four-year-old senator. Thurmond gripped his hand warmly and said, "So happy to see you. So proud of what you've done. So proud." Then he turned to an aide standing behind him and said, "Who is this?"

Whenever Barnes started to think he was a big shot, he reminded himself of that scene.

Clemson was scheduled to play its last home football game the afternoon after the Clemson-Kentucky game. With his team's charter due to arrive home at about 3 o'clock in the morning, Barnes was planning to be on the air at 9 A.M.

Barnes knew this was a great time to play Kentucky. The Wildcats were still loaded with talent, but they had lost four starters from their national championship team. They would still be adjusting to new roles in November, while his team, with all five starters back, should be comfortable.

Barnes's theme for this game was much the same as his theme would be for the whole season: "It's your time, guys," he told his players. "This is what you've worked for. This is what all that running in the summer was all about. This game. This season. You deserve it."

For one night at least, they not only deserved it, they took it. Down nine early in the second half, they stayed calm, continued to get good shots, and actually led by four with five minutes to play. Kentucky tied the game in the final minute, but the Tigers controlled the overtime and walked away with a 79–71 victory.

Barnes was ecstatic, not just with the victory, but with the way his team had won. The Tigers had handled the Kentucky press, only turning the ball over fifteen times in forty-five minutes. Four players had scored in double figures and eight in all had scored. They had shown maturity, a byproduct of the experience they had gained with their late run the year before. They had shown everyone — most importantly themselves — that they were ready to play with, and beat, the game's big boys.

As Barnes tooled through the football parking lot the next morning, he was like a conquering hero. He hadn't gotten to bed until 4:30 but there was no way he was going to miss this pregame show. When the new national rankings came out the following week, Clemson was number six, not in football, but in basketball. That was higher than North Carolina, higher than Duke.

During the break between the end of regulation and the start of overtime, Barnes had leaned into the huddle, smiled, and said to his players above the din, "You got to love this, guys. This is what we're in it for. Let's just play all night if we have to. This is fun."

Six of the nine ACC schools played in an exempt event. Maryland would travel to Hawaii at the end of December to play in the Rainbow Classic. Everyone else was playing early. North Carolina traveled to Springfield, Massachusetts, basketball's birthplace, to play in the Hall of Fame Tipoff Classic against Arizona. The Tar Heels were surprised in that game by the Wildcats, who had lost four starters from the previous season and were without their only returning starter, Miles Simon, who was academically ineligible for the first semester. Playing his old attacking defense, Dean

Smith was surprised and disappointed by how easily Arizona beat his team down the floor to get good shots. Arizona won, 85–73.

Wake Forest went to Chicago to play in the Great Eight, a three-year-old event that was supposed to match the eight teams who had reached the Elite Eight the previous March. Since Syracuse was playing in Alaska, the Orangemen opted out of the Great Eight and were replaced by Purdue. This didn't affect the Deacons, who were assigned a game against Mississippi State even though Dave Odom's first choice would have been a game against Kentucky. "If we're going to play in the thing, we might as well play the best team available and find out where we are," he reasoned. He also thought it would be a good idea for his team to get a December look at Kentucky's press in case they had to deal with it again in March. There was one other reason — unspoken — that Odom wanted to play Kentucky. When he and his coaches had watched the tape of the Midwest Regional final, which Kentucky had pulled away to win, 83–63, they had counted 38 fouls committed by the Wildcats against Tim Duncan. Not ticky-tack stuff, but hard, solid fouls. The officials had called seven of them. Odom may look like a mild-mannered college professor, but he doesn't think like one. Friend or no friend, he wanted another shot at Rick Pitino's team.

He didn't get it because Pitino didn't want it. Like a lot of coaches, Pitino doesn't like competing against friends except when he has to. He asked to play someone else, and his wish was granted. The Deacons were left to play a Mississippi State team that, like Arizona, had lost five starters, but unlike Arizona hadn't been able to come up with strong replacements. The game was a debacle, Wake winning, 83–54.

"That certainly didn't tell us very much," Odom said when it was over.

Duke and Virginia were both in November tournaments and both had mixed success. The Cavaliers went to Maui and played very well for two and a half games, beating South Carolina and Massachusetts and playing top-ranked Kansas to a 30-all tie at halftime in the final. Then the roof of the tiny Lahaina Civic Center fell in on them and the Jayhawks blew to a 75–55 win. Still, coming off a disastrous 12–15 season that had been marked by one off-court controversy after another, Jeff Jones felt good about what he had seen in Hawaii. For most of the weekend the Cavaliers had played the kind of defense that had been the trademark of their best teams. They had played three teams that would be in the NCAA tournament and beaten two of them. The third might be the best team in the country and they had just run out of gas against their depth in the second half. It wasn't a complete turnaround by any means, but it was a start.

Mike Krzyzewski had no idea how he felt at the end of his team's four-game run in the preseason NIT. The Blue Devils played very well in their two home games against St. Joseph's and Vanderbilt, winning both games easily. They struggled, but survived, in their semifinal in Madison Square Garden against a very good Tulsa team.

That victory put them into the final against Indiana. Like it or not, that was going to mean a difficult, emotional evening for Krzyzewski. His relationship with Bob Knight was a complicated one, dating back to the first time Knight had come to his parents' home to recruit him in 1965. Much of what Krzyzewski had become was because of Knight. He had taught him toughness as a player and a system he believed in as both a player and a coach: hard-nosed, man-to-man defense; a motion offense tailored to allow smart players to make smart decisions; and a nononsense approach not only to games but even to practices and meetings. He had gotten him started in the business as a graduate assistant at Indiana and had played a role in getting him both of his head coaching jobs, at Army and at Duke.

They had remained close friends for years, doing clinics together in the off-season, talking often on the phone. Krzyzewski had never forgotten what Knight had done for him, and more importantly for his mother, when his dad had died during his senior year at West Point. In 1986, when Krzyzewski took Duke to the Final Four for the first time, he had Knight speak to his team prior to the semifinals. Knight walked around Dallas that weekend like a proud father, wearing a Duke button everyplace he went.

When Duke lost the final to Louisville, Knight was on the phone with Krzyzewski every night for a week. "Are you OK?" he kept asking. Krzyzewski was fine. He takes losing hard, but he has never taken it as personally as Knight. Still, he appreciated his old coach's concern. A year later, the student and the mentor met in the Sweet Sixteen. Duke, a decided underdog, played Indiana tough before losing to a team that would go on to the national championship. After the game, Knight's first comment was, "It's hard for me to enjoy this very much thinking about Mike."

But the relationship now wasn't what it had once been. The 1992 Final Four in Minneapolis had been the turning point. By then, Krzyzewski had won a national championship and become, arguably, a bigger star in coaching than Knight. He won just as consistently — in fact, he had been to one more Final Four at that point — and he did it without any of the baggage that Knight brought to the table. Knight was uptight about the matchup and told friends before the game that he believed that Krzyzewski had changed with his success, had somehow become less loyal to him.

Krzyzewski heard all this but ignored it. He was convinced Knight was playing a mind game with him, trying to soften his approach to their semifinal. The game was a war, Indiana jumping way ahead, Duke coming back. Knight hurt his team's cause with an ill-timed technical foul in the second half and Duke pulled away and appeared headed for an easy win. Then the Hoosiers rallied, actually getting to within three points, with the ball, in the final minute. But Duke hung on for an 81–78 victory.

The postgame handshake was not what you might expect between student and teacher. In fact, it was more along the lines of what coaches call a "blow-by," a handshake so quick that no words are exchanged as one coach blows by the other. Krzyzewski was surprised, but not shocked. He knew how much the game meant to him and he assumed it meant just as much to Knight. He hadn't expected a blow-by, but he was prepared for something less than warm and fuzzy.

What he wasn't prepared for was what happened twenty minutes later. At each Final Four, the NCAA curtains off a walkway between the locker rooms and the interview room so coaches and players can walk unimpeded from one to the other. As the losing team, Indiana went to the interview room first. Krzyzewski was walking into the interview room with Christian Laettner and Bobby Hurley just as Knight was leaving. Knight stopped and shook hands with both Laettner and Hurley and wished them luck in the championship game. OK, Krzyzewski thought, he's got his emotions under control, now we'll shake hands like men and talk for a moment about the game.

Wrong. This time, Knight didn't even look at Krzyzewski. Instead, he looked past him as if he wasn't even there and walked right by him without so much as a nod. Krzyzewski was devastated. Intellectually, he understood what was going on. Knight was a bad loser; always had been. The list of coaches who have turned from good guys into bad ones for having the audacity to beat Knight — especially in a game he really cared about — is a long one. But even knowing all that, Krzyzewski was blown away by the blow off.

He stumbled through his press conference, barely able to keep his mind on the questions. When he walked back to the locker room, he found Mickie and his daughters waiting for him. When Mickie put her arms around him to give him a postgame victory hug, she was shocked to find him racked with tears.

"What is it?" she asked, completely baffled.

"Knight" was the only answer she got.

While his players dressed and answered questions in the Minnesota Twins locker room, Krzyzewski sat in the back with his coaches, his eyes still glistening. "There are days," he said, "when life's not fair."

His team had just qualified for a third straight national championship game and a shot at back-to-back titles and Krzyzewski was completely undone emotionally by his old coach's behavior.

By the next day, he was fine. A number of former Knight players and coaches, having witnessed the initial blow-by in the arena, came by the Duke hotel that night to make sure Krzyzewski was all right. When he told them about the incident in the hallway, they were unsurprised, but nonethless disappointed — in Knight. To a man, they told Krzyzewski to ignore it. "Coach will get over it," one friend said.

"I don't really care if he gets over it or not," Krzyzewski said. "That was it for me."

Ten months passed before the two men spoke again. When word began to leak to the media about a Knight-Krzyzewski schism, it was Knight who took most of the heat. Knight will never admit a battle is lost, but he is always smart enough to understand when it is time to cut his losses.

Shortly after New Year's 1993, he called Krzyzewski. Krzyzewski wouldn't take the call. He kept calling. Finally, on the afternoon that Duke was to play North Carolina in Cameron, Krzyzewski took his call. They talked for about an hour. Knight never said, "I'm sorry," because he never does. What he did do was "explain" to Krzyzewski why he had behaved the way he had. The story was lengthy and convoluted, full of imagined slights, most of which led back to Krzyzewski having had the audacity to win the game in Minneapolis.

Krzyzewski listened and didn't argue. What was the point? He knew this was as close to an apology as Knight would ever come, and he appreciated the effort. "I'll always love Coach Knight," he said later. "I will always appreciate everything that he did for me. But I think the time has come for us to go our separate ways in life."

Which is exactly what they did. Krzyzewski made a point of never criticizing Knight publicly. In fact, whenever Knight got into trouble one of the people his media sympathizers ran to looking for pro-Knight quotes was Krzyzewski.

Duke and Indiana had played in November of 1995 in the semifinals of the Great Alaska Shootout. That had been Krzyzewski's first weekend back on the bench since his illness the previous season. Duke had won the game 70–64 and had gone on to win the tournament. Facing Knight again — and beating him again — had been cathartic for Krzyzewski. There had been no blowups or blow-bys. Of course a preseason tournament played in near privacy in Anchorage is a lot different than a Final Four. There was almost no media, and Knight had been cordial.

This was also a November game, but it was a little different. New York was a long way from Anchorage and both teams were nationally ranked. It still wasn't the Final Four by any stretch, but it was important to both coaches as an early-season test of where their teams were and how good they might become. And it was important because they knew the whole country would be watching.

"This is the kind of game you came to Duke to play," Krzyzewski told his team during their afternoon shoot around in Madison Square Garden on the day after Thanksgiving. "Did you see *USA Today* this morning? Banner headline: Duke-Indiana. Anyone who cares about college basketball will be watching this game tonight. That's good. That's the way we like it. That's where Duke basketball is supposed to be."

Indiana was 4–0 and Duke was 3–0. Neither school had won an NCAA tournament game since 1994, which, for these two coaches, represented a major drought. Each suspected that his team was better this year than it had been and each was eager to find out how much better that evening.

This was the matchup that NIT officials had hoped for when they put together their sixteen-team draw in the summer. The preseason NIT was twelve years old and, on a number of occasions, attendance in The Garden on Thanksgiving weekend had been embarrassing, with announced crowds of under 10,000 that looked a lot more like 5,000. That was not a problem for this final. The attendance was 17,930, just shy of a sellout.

Krzyzewski had decided that he was going to take the high road with Knight before the game. He would play the role of dutiful student and greet his old mentor when he arrived at his bench. Knight likes to come out of the locker room at the last possible moment. Krzyzewski knew that. With about two minutes left on the pregame clock, he walked to the Indiana bench to wait for Knight to arrive. He talked to the assistants, even sat on the bench briefly to make things look as informal and comfortable as possible.

The clock ticked down to zero. Still no Knight. The PA announcer began introducing the lineups. Krzyzewski was squirming. Part of his pregame routine is to kneel in front of his bench and give each starter a pat on the back as he is introduced. Still, he waited. Knight finally emerged, walking with famed horse trainer D. Wayne Lukas, a pal of his who was in New York hanging with Knight and the Hoosiers for the weekend.

Krzyzewski was now standing next to the Indiana bench, almost at attention, waiting for his old coach to show up. Knight saw Krzyzewski, stopped, threw an arm around Lukas, and launched into a story. Then he made a point of shaking hands with a few other people. By the time he got to Krzyzewski, the teams had been introduced.

Krzyzewski put out his hand. "Good luck," he said.

"You too," Knight answered, turning away quickly.

If it wasn't a blow-by, it was pretty damn close to it. Krzyzewski walked back to his bench angry, but forced himself to forget about it and focus on the game at hand.

Both teams were tight throughout the first half, shooting the ball poorly. Both coaches were on the officials early and Knight, showing what the game meant to him, drew a technical with 5:11 left in the half. That led to a four-point play for Duke and a 28–22 lead. They were still clinging to a six-point margin at halftime, even though Indiana's Andrae Patterson had been virtually unstoppable, scoring 17 of Indiana's 31 points.

"If we get him under control, we'll win the game," Krzyzewski told his assistants at halftime. "None of their other guys are hurting us."

But they never figured out how to stop Patterson. What's more, in the second half, he did get help, most notably from freshman point guard A. J. Guyton, who consistently beat Duke's defense into the lane and ended up with 16 points, six rebounds, and five assists. Patterson had 39 on one of those nights college players dream about.

No one from Duke came close to matching Patterson or Guyton. All five starters shot less than 50 percent and as a team the Blue Devils shot a miserable 35.6 percent. The second half got uglier and uglier. Indiana opened with a 10–2 run to take the lead. Krzyzewski picked up a technical of his own during that stretch, arguing over starting center Greg Newton's fourth foul. "You got the second foul," he kept yelling at referee Joe Mingle, implying that Newton had been fouled first. Mingle ignored the comment and ran down the court. "Joe, you guys missed the first foul," Krzyzewski insisted. "You got the second one. Come on!"

For some reason, Mingle decided that comment was worth a technical. When he made the signal and walked to the scorer's table, Krzyzewski really lost it. "Oh fuck you!" he screamed in complete exasperation, loud enough to be heard at least ten rows up. That line didn't earn Krzyzewski a second technical, no doubt in part because Mingle knew he had been trigger-happy on the first one, but also because officials are loath to toss a coach (two techs and you're gone), especially a famous one, in front of 17,930 people and a national television audience.

As it turned out, Mingle would have been doing Krzyzewski a favor if he had sent him to the locker room. The Blue Devils were awful down the stretch. Trailing 50–49 with ten minutes left, they managed to get outscored 35–20 the rest of the way. Krzyzewski was on the officials right to the end, but his tone was more plaintive than angry. He knew his team was being outplayed. He just didn't want to concede until he had to.

"What makes me angry is you were outfought," he said to the players when it was over. "I can live with losing if the other team is just better than we are. But you let yourselves get outfought. That's not acceptable."

He didn't get angry or even raise his voice very much. He was frustrated. The entire evening had been frustrating. Sitting with his assistants after he had said all the right things about Indiana in his press conference, he shook his head. "It could be a long season. That just wasn't very good. But we can't afford to jump this team too much. They can't handle it. We've got to almost baby them right now."

The subject of Knight's pregame behavior came up. Krzyzewski sighed. "I'm almost glad it happened that way," he said. "It lets me put a period on the end of the sentence. The end. You know, it's really kind of sad. He keeps turning his friends away. I'm not the first or the last. I tried to do the right thing. I'm over it now. Five years ago, that would have hurt me. It doesn't hurt anymore."

In fact, the most painful part of the evening had much more to do with what Knight's team had been able to do to Krzyzewski's team than anything Knight had done himself to Krzyzewski.

"We play like this," he said finally, "and it's going to be a very long winter."

6

Back from
the Near-Dead

THE ONLY THREE ACC teams that did not begin the season with exempt games were Georgia Tech, North Carolina State, and Florida State. This wasn't all that surprising, since each was in need of a softer early schedule to build confidence.

No place was that more true than at Florida State. The Seminoles were beginning their sixth year in the ACC and Pat Kennedy was starting his eleventh as their coach. The first eight had been good enough that Kennedy's name constantly popped up in connection with big-name, big-money jobs around the country. In the right-hand drawer of his desk, Kennedy kept three things to remind him about the vagaries of basketball: the scouting report done on him as a high school junior by recruiting guru Howard Garfinkel, a picture of the first team he ever coached at King's College, and a 1992 contract proposal from Nevada–Las Vegas for a compensation package totaling $582,105 a year.

"That's basketball right there," he said. "Three sentences that are supposed to tell a coach everything there is to know about who you are and what you might become; a team I coached for nothing and, eighteen years later, an offer for that kind of money that I *turned down*. The wheel is always turning in this business — one way or the other."

The wheel had not turned all that well for Kennedy in the past three seasons. The offer from Vegas had come after FSU's remarkable first season in the ACC, in which it finished second behind a Duke team that went on to win the national title. Kennedy turned Vegas down because his best players from that team were coming back in '93 and he thought the Seminoles might do even better. He was right. Again they finished second in the league behind a national championship team (this time North Carolina) and they advanced all the way to the final eight of the NCAA tournament. There, they met a Kentucky team that was on a roll and got blasted, 106–81.

Even so, with a 25–10 record and the school's best performance in the NCAA tournament since the 1972 team had reached the championship game, Kennedy was a hot coach. Kennedy wasn't really looking to go anyplace. His family liked living in Tallahassee and FSU was paying him a lot of money — $500,000 a year — thanks to offers like the one from Vegas.

But the next three years didn't go nearly as well. The Seminoles went 13–14, 12–15, 13–14. They were 6–10, 5–11, and 5–11 in the ACC and the '96 season had ended with a humiliating 80–65 loss to NC State in the Les Robinson game. In that debacle, the Seminoles fell behind 19–0 and the rest of the night was thirty-five minutes of garbage time. "It was embarrassing," Kennedy admitted. "We went in there actually thinking we were playing well enough to do some damage and the next thing we know it's 19–0 and the game is over."

Things were not good off the court either. Cory Louis, who had been a highly recruited prospect two years earlier but had never become the player everyone expected, had been suspended for a game after testing positive for marijuana. Naturally, that incident led to rumors that drug use on the team was widespread. Kennedy was suspended for a game too after being ejected from a game against Georgia Tech. Kennedy was embarrassed by the ejection and by Athletic Director Dave Hart's decision to suspend him. More rumors swirled: Hart, who had come to FSU three years earlier, was reportedly unhappy with Kennedy and the relatively loose ship he ran. Kennedy, so the stories went, felt underappreciated by Hart and was angered that Hart had shown him up by suspending him.

As is often the case with rumors, there was some truth to those surrounding Hart and Kennedy. Hart had expressed concern to Kennedy about the academic performance of some of his players and had told other athletic directors in the ACC that if Kennedy couldn't improve the quality of the program off the court, he would look for another coach, regardless of the team's performance on the court. Kennedy wasn't happy with the suspension and he and Hart were not likely to socialize with one another very often. But Kennedy and Hart did respect each other professionally. They might not always agree, but they tried to understand each other's reasoning.

Kennedy had signed a five-year contract after the Vegas offer that included a rollover clause. That meant, at the end of each season, the contract was automatically extended for a year, unless the school informed him otherwise. At the end of the '96 season, Hart called Kennedy in and did just that. No rollover. He now had four years left on his deal.

Again, Kennedy wasn't happy, but he understood. "Dave wants to see some positive things," he said. "I don't have a problem with that. So do I."

The non-rollover did make him do some thinking about his future at Florida State. Although he was only forty-four, Kennedy had been a head coach for sixteen years. He had been only twenty-eight when he succeeded Jim Valvano at Iona and he already had 306 career victories. Until the previous three seasons, he had only had one losing record (14–15 at Iona in 1986) in his first twelve years. He had won twenty games on ten different occasions and been to seven NCAA tournaments.

Now, though, for the first time, he saw himself approaching a possible crossroads. Florida State was a good job, a very well-paying job, but it was never going to be an easy job. It was always going to be a school where the most important sport was football and the second most important sport was either football recruiting or spring football. To some degree, baseball was more important than basketball because the Seminoles were almost always a national title contender. "People around here tend not to know we even have basketball until after New Year's," Kennedy said. "Then, in February, a lot of people are focused on baseball — not to mention football recruiting. We get squeezed a lot."

Florida State played its home games off campus, in the Leon County Civic Center, a distinctly undistinctive building that they filled on rare occasions to its capacity of 12,800. Most of the time, FSU had less home court advantage than any other ACC school — even less than the wine and cheese crowd provided in the DeanDome. Although the building was due for renovations, it would still be off-campus and the crowd would still be one that would take its cue from the team, rather than vice versa.

Being in the ACC certainly helped recruiting, but it also meant that you had to recruit higher-quality players because the competition night in and night out was so much tougher than in FSU's old league, the Metro. That meant that any recruiting setbacks put the program in a precarious position. Two years earlier, Kennedy had been convinced he was going to get Vince Carter, who went to high school in Daytona. Carter chose North Carolina. That was the kind of loss that a North Carolina or a Duke could bounce back from fairly quickly. Not Florida State. The last three seasons had been evidence of that.

With all that in mind, Kennedy had been willing to listen when he got a phone call from St. John's the week before the 1996 Final Four. Would he be willing to meet? Yes. St. John's is one of the great traditional programs in all of college basketball. What's more, Kennedy was a New York/New Jersey guy. He had grown up on the Jersey shore and had cut his teeth as a head coach in the New York area at Iona. He knew that coaching at St. John's would involve a lot more pressure from the New York media than the Iona job, but he was confident he was equipped to handle it.

Kennedy met with the St. John's people shortly before the Final Four semifinal games, which were being held across the Hudson River in the New Jersey Meadowlands. He thought the meeting went well. In fact, they asked him if he could meet with the school president before he left town. The second meeting never took place. Kennedy still isn't certain what happened, but he is convinced that the apparent change of heart was due in part to a *New York Daily News* story the next morning that alleged that Cory Louis was buying and selling drugs on campus. The story was completely inaccurate and the *Daily News* ran a lengthy retraction, but by then — at least in Kennedy's mind — the damage was done.

"Someone didn't want me to have the St. John's job and planted that story," he said. "The reporter didn't even call me to confirm or deny what he had been told."

Would Kennedy have taken the St. John's job if it had been offered? Probably. It would have meant a fresh start in his home area. He and his wife, Jeannie, own a home on eastern Long Island where they spend as much time as possible. The commute from Queens (less than two hours by car) is a lot less than from Tallahassee. All of that and the non-rollover almost certainly would have added up to Kennedy packing and heading north. But he never got the chance.

Instead, he was back in Tallahassee, a bit wary about the situation; chastened by the fact that the St. John's interview had become so public. A lot of people at Florida State thought he had pursued the job and they found that insulting. Kennedy — and his team — would have to reprove themselves to the locals.

The good news was that all five starters were back for '96–97. Of course, as the old joke goes, that could also have been the bad news. Kennedy had known at the end of the '96 season that he needed a point guard. He had tried everyone but Chief Osceola (the school mascot) at the spot with absolutely no luck. College basketball is a game dominated by guards. Kennedy's best teams had been blessed with three great guards — Charlie Ward, Sam Cassell, and Bob Sura. All three were now in the NBA. In senior James Collins, he had a solid shooting guard. But he had to have someone who could run the team.

Although he knew that going the junior college route was always risky, Kennedy felt he had no choice. He had recruited a freshman named Devonaire Deas who he thought had potential, but the thought of handing the ball to him right out of the box terrified Kennedy. He had to have an experienced point guard, not a shooting guard bringing the ball upcourt because no one else could do it.

He settled finally on Kerry Thompson, a New York kid whom he and his coaches had watched play at nearby Tallahassee Community College. Thompson was six one, 180. He was powerfully built and appeared to have the kind of quickness FSU hadn't had since the NBA three had been in the backcourt.

After one day of practice, Kennedy was on the verge of panic. Thompson had looked awful: slow, scared, unwilling to shoot an open shot. "We can't go through another year like this," Kennedy told his coaches. Twenty-four hours later, his thinking was 180 degrees different.

Thompson had obviously had a case of opening-day jitters. He was a different player the second day, clearly in charge on the floor, getting into the lane, beating people off the dribble. "He went from prop plane to jet in one day," Kennedy said.

Although Kennedy spends time each day preparing a practice plan with his assistant coaches, almost everything he does is based on emotion, gut feelings. In that sense, he is exactly like his mentor, Jim Valvano. Florida State has the ACC's smallest practice facility, a tiny gym underneath the mammoth football stadium, with walls practically on top of the court, and Kennedy's booming voice echoes around it throughout practice. He can run the emotional gamut in a span of less than a minute: a good pass will merit applause and cheers; a physical mistake may bring about a whistle, followed by a quiet teaching point; a silly mental error will bring on full-throated screaming.

On that second day of practice, watching Thompson find a comfort level and make play after play, Kennedy's voice and intensity seemed to go up a notch with each passing minute.

The other players understood. They knew how important Thompson's development would be to their season. Each time Thompson whizzed by him, Kennedy played cheerleader: "That's it, Kerry Thompson, that's it. Keep going, keep pushing. Perfect! That's it! You've got it!"

At one point, he even turned to his assistants and, without apology to Professor Henry Higgins said, "By God, I think he's got it!"

If Thompson could be a solid ACC point guard, everyone else would improve. Collins and LaMar Greer, who had been asked to do far too much ballhandling, could concentrate on what they did best. And the team's three inside players — senior Kirk Luchman; Louis, now a junior; and sophomore Randell Jackson — would know that if they got themselves open the ball would be there. Louis, sobered by his failures of the previous two years, was working harder than he ever had in practice. If he and the six-eleven Jackson ever played to their potential on a consistent basis, there was no telling how good the Seminoles could be.

All through preseason, Kennedy was pointing his team toward December 5, the fourth game of the season, at Duke. Cameron Indoor Stadium was the only place in the ACC where FSU had not won at least once since entering the league. A year earlier, the Seminoles had gone into

Durham with a 10–4 record, including 2–2 in the league. They had led by nine early in the game and then done a complete dive in the second half, losing 85–65. That was the start of a five-game losing streak from which they never recovered. Kennedy had joked with Mike Krzyzewski that summer that everyone could save a lot of time and money if the Seminoles just mailed the final result in to the ACC office each year, rather than go through the ritual of actually flying north to play the game.

That wasn't what he was telling his players as they raced through laughers against Southwest Louisiana, Rice, and Florida Atlantic. Those games were supposed to be warm-ups, confidence builders, and that's exactly what they were. In truth, Florida State's December schedule looked a lot like an old Clemson preconference schedule. Kennedy felt his team needed wins and he had scheduled a bunch of them. The only quality nonconference game on the schedule was against Florida, and the Gators were in a rebuilding mode and would not be nearly as tough as normal. That made the Duke game even more important because whatever came out of it — good or bad — the feelings were likely to linger until January.

Normally, ACC teams don't play league games in December. But the addition of Florida State six seasons earlier had created a league schedule of sixteen games instead of fourteen, and with the calendar falling in such a way in both 1997 and 1998 that the season was a few days shorter than normal, the only way to get the entire conference schedule played was to have eight of the nine teams play one conference game in December. North Carolina had drawn the December bye. Everyone else would play.

Florida State at Duke would be on Thursday, December 5. Then, on Saturday, Clemson would play at Virginia and Wake Forest would be at NC State. The following Thursday Georgia Tech would be at Maryland.

There was a part of Kennedy that wanted to open with a home game, preferably against someone in the lower half of the league. Another part of him figured that confronting the school's jinx building right away was a good thing. If they lost, well, it was nothing new. But if they won . . . "Huge," he said. "The kind of win people notice. It would stir up some excitement around here for our team. And it would tell everyone that this wasn't the same old Florida State team."

It took Mike Krzyzewski about sixty seconds to figure out this was not the same old Florida State team. The Seminoles were in his players' faces on defense from the moment the game tipped off. They were aggressive and eager. He had hoped that his team would have an advantage because it had played four good teams in the NIT and this was FSU's first game against a quality opponent. No such luck. The Seminoles came out flying even though Cory Louis, who had been forced to undergo minor knee surgery just before the start of the season, still wasn't ready to play.

Kennedy had been blunt with his team before the game. Having learned much of his coaching technique from Valvano, his pregame talks often sound a little bit like revival meetings. His voice booming around the room — even though, like Valvano, he is perpetually hoarse — Kennedy will go over plays and matchups while a manager stands next to him at the board to erase for him as he moves on to the next diagram.

Often, Kennedy will ask rhetorical questions: "Are we going to let them dominate us in this building the way they have in the past?" he will shout.

"NO!" They will shout back in unison.

"We must — MUST — take care of the basketball, fellas. If we do that, if we play smart basketball for forty minutes, I promise you we will walk out of here with a win!"

Claps, cheers, and whistles.

"We have something to prove tonight, fellas, not to anyone outside this room, but to ourselves! Do you understand?"

"YES!"

They did understand. And they played exactly that way the entire first half. Duke never had the lead. Jackson was superb inside from the beginning and the entire team shot well (14 of 27). By contrast, Duke couldn't throw the ball in the ocean from a surfboard. The Blue Devils were seven of 30 from the field, and the only reason FSU's lead was just 36–29 at halftime was center Greg Newton, who had 12 points and eight rebounds. Everyone else was horrendous, especially senior guard Jeff Capel, who was zero for six. Krzyzewski had kept him in the starting lineup despite a poor NIT because he felt that benching him might mean losing him forever. Capel's self-confidence was identical to his shooting percentage: zero.

The second half started out much like the first. Two Jackson free throws with 17:40 left stretched the lead to 42–32. But then Thompson, a bit nervous in his ACC debut, missed two free throws that could have made the lead 12. Given a tiny opening, with the crowd imploring them to make a move, the Blue Devils did. A three-point play by Newton capped a 16–5 run and put Duke ahead for the first time at 48–47 with 11:13 to go. The rest of regulation turned out to be a harbinger of what most nights in the ACC were going to be like the rest of the winter. No one could take control. FSU went up four, but Duke came back. Steve Wojciechowski, having a miserable shooting night, made a huge three with 2:45 left to put Duke back up, 62–59. FSU came back to lead 63–62 with 54 seconds left on two Luchman free throws. Langdon, a 90 percent free-throw shooter, made one of two with thirty-eight ticks left, and the game was tied at 63.

Kennedy could not have asked for much more than this. On the road, in their jinx gym, his team would have the last shot to win the game. He called time to set up a shot. Thompson would drive and either shoot or dish, depending on what the defense did. Thompson dribbled the clock down, pushed into the lane, and went up with his shot. It rolled off. But Jackson beat everyone to the rebound and had a layup. The shot hit the rim, rolled around, hung there for what felt like forever — and fell off.

Kennedy couldn't believe it. The Cameron crowd screamed, not for joy, but in relief. The ball had been no more than an inch from falling in.

Watching the game on television, Gary Williams felt for Kennedy. Every coach knows what it feels like to have your team ready to play, to have it perform, and then, somehow, not to win. "I hadn't seen them play as hard or as well on defense for four years," Williams said. "I was impressed. And I felt for Pat. They deserved to win that game."

He would get no argument from Krzyzewski, who knew he was lucky to be sending his team out to play an overtime. FSU led once in the overtime, on a Geoff Brower free throw. The rest of the extra period belonged to Duke: specifically to Carmen Wallace and Trajan Langdon. Wallace, only six five and sore-kneed, was all over the boards, with four of the 11 he had for the game. His two free throws put Duke ahead at 65–64 and with the issue still in doubt in the final minute, Langdon buried a three to make it 70–66. On a night when the other team deserved the game more than they did, the Blue Devils had survived.

Both coaches knew the outcome was deceiving. Kennedy's team had lost, but it walked out of the building feeling good about itself and about the season ahead. "If you are good enough to go into Duke and come within an inch of winning," Kennedy told his players, "then you are good enough to play with anyone in this league, maybe anyone in the country."

Krzyzewski might not have agreed with that statement. Newton and Wallace had been superb. Wojciechowski had played an excellent floor game. But his key shooters, Capel, Langdon, Ricky Price and Roshown McLeod — players who had to score for his team to be any good — had shot a combined six for 32.

"Florida State's a lot better," he told his coaches. "We got lucky. Extremely lucky."

Duke was ranked tenth in the country. Florida State was unranked. If you had watched the two teams play on this night, you might have thought it should have been the other way around.

Maryland was also unranked at that moment. That was fine with Gary Williams. He loved reminding his team how little the rest of the world thought of them. More than that, he liked knowing that his early suspicions that this team would be far better than last year's team were correct.

The Terrapins had opened their season with four breathers. Like Kennedy, knowing he had an inexperienced team, Williams liked the idea of getting his feet wet with some teams that weren't likely to cause problems. What's more, after two years as a glamour team that had led to made-for-TV games against teams like Kentucky, Massachusetts, UCLA, Utah, and Kansas, Maryland was now considered a second-echelon ACC team once again. That too was just fine with Williams.

The Terrapins' first true challenges came on the second weekend in December in the Franklin National Bank Classic, a four-team charity tournament that included George Washington, Mississippi State, and California. The Terrapins would open against California. Although Cal had been devastated during the off-season by player defections and the firing of coach Todd Bozeman in the midst of an NCAA investigation, the Golden Bears still had excellent size, a great shooter in Ed Gray, and an outstanding new coach in Ben Braun, who had left Eastern Michigan in the fall to take over for Bozeman.

"Today, we begin," Williams told his players in the locker room. "Those other games were fine, but you know and I know that this is different. This is the kind of game we'll be playing for the rest of the season."

A Williams-coached team arrives at the arena two hours before tip-off. Most coaches don't want their players in the locker room any more than ninety minutes before game time. Some prefer even less than that. Dean Smith has his players arrive — as he does everything else — according to class rank: freshman ninety minutes early; sophomores eighty; juniors seventy; seniors sixty. Williams has always gone the other way. Early in his career, he interviewed with Chuck Daly for an assistant's job at Pennsylvania. He remembered Daly telling him that a lot of what he did as a coach came from the book *The Art of War,* by Sun Tzu. One thing the book had said was that most of the famous ground battles in history had been won by the army that arrived at the scene of the battle first.

Maryland always arrived at the scene of the battle first.

Every team has a pregame ritual. Maryland's begins with a brief chalk talk while the players are still in street clothes, Williams making a couple of points about the scouting report and throwing out a theme for the day. Then he leaves the players to themselves. While they dress, music blasting around the locker room, he will find a spot to sit by himself and think up the four game themes he plans to write on the board. Every game has four themes. Most are basic. For California, they were: team rebounding (Cal's size being a concern); offense (being careful not to quick-shoot against Cal's zone); transition (easy baskets would be key against a bigger, slower team); and effort. The last of the four themes is almost always an intangible. It is also, most of the time, the most important message Williams wants to deliver. In this case, effort meant that they were now stepping up in class. Everyone they played from here on in would be talented. Often, effort would be the decisive factor. Who wanted to win the game more.

Like most coaches, Williams speaks to his team twice before each game — once about thirty minutes prior to tip-off, before they go out to warm up, and then again after they come in a few minutes before the game starts. In most locker rooms, a manager is assigned to know precisely how much time is on the scoreboard clock. He (or she) will stand in the back of the room and hold up fingers so the coach can see how much time is left. At Maryland, assistant coach Billy Hahn fills that role, since managers are not allowed in the locker room while Williams is talking to the players. Hahn doesn't hold up fingers. He just calls out the time as it winds down.

Williams is the only coach in the ACC who does not participate in some kind of pregame prayer with his players. Although he was brought up as a devout churchgoer, Williams hasn't attended church on a regular basis for years. When he got to college, he found himself questioning a lot of the church's teachings. "Maybe my parents' divorce had something to do with it," he said. "They spent all that time in church but it didn't seem to protect them or us from what happened to our family."

When Williams finishes his first pregame talk, his players huddle in the hallway outside the locker room and say the Lord's Prayer. They go out to warm up while Williams sits in the locker room with trainer J. J. Bush and waits.

"If there's anything that will drive me out of coaching," he said one night, "it's waiting for the games to start."

Most coaches will echo that sentiment. The waiting on game days is brutal, especially nowadays, when so many games are played late at night. Coaches sit in the locker room thinking of what they have forgotten to do or say, worrying about what the other coach is doing, wondering if their team is ready to play.

The good news about the Cal game was that it was in the afternoon, so the wait came early in the day. Laron Profit would not be in the starting lineup because he had been a few minutes late for a team meeting the previous day. That made Williams nervous. So did the half-empty arena his team walked into. USAir Arena, on its very best days, is drafty and dank. On a cold Sunday in December with fewer than 10,000 people inside, it has all the warmth of an airplane hanger.

Even so, Williams was pleased with the first half. Cal jumped to an early lead, but the Terrapins began to wear them down with their quickness near the end of the half. Profit, unbothered by not starting, came off the bench to hit four of seven shots. Maryland led 40–36 at the break. Williams was pleased. He was convinced Cal could not keep up with his team's quickness. They had been outrebounded 22–18, but that was OK. They could handle that kind of margin.

The second half was all Maryland. Profit hit three three-pointers in the first four minutes to open the lead to 52–40. From there, it was the Profit–Keith Booth show. Cal had no answers for either. The lead grew to 22 before Williams went to his bench and the Terrapins cruised home with an 80–64 victory. Even Williams couldn't know at the time how impressive the win was. Cal would go on to be one of the surprise teams in the country, reaching the NCAA Sweet Sixteen. On this day, though, the Bears were completely outplayed.

Williams spent a good five minutes, maybe even ten, reveling in the victory. Then his mind was on the next night, when his team would have to play crosstown rival George Washington. Although Maryland and Georgetown were Washington's traditional powers and the schools who received the most attention, it was GW that had started the season with a national ranking (twenty-fifth). Mike Jarvis had built his program to the point where it was a perennial NCAA team or contender. It had been the Colonials who had ended UMass's long unbeaten string the previous February, going to Amherst to beat the Minutemen.

With most of their key players back from that team, the Colonials were ranked by everyone in preseason and were dying for the chance to play Maryland. A year earlier, in the tournament's consolation game, Maryland had hammered GW in the first meeting between the two schools in seventeen years. Jarvis was now convinced his team was ready to play with Maryland.

He was right. But playing with someone is different than beating them. Maryland started the game tight, even though Williams had made a point of telling his players that GW was the ranked team and therefore the one with more to lose. The players knew better. Maryland was Maryland. It was the ACC team. It was supposed to beat GW. The Colonials jumped out front 16–4. Williams called a twenty-second time-out and called his players several unflattering names. They regrouped and led by halftime, 34–29. GW rallied to take two brief one-point leads midway through the second half, but couldn't figure out a way to stop Booth when the game was on the line. He ended up with 29 points and 12 rebounds and was chosen as the MVP of the tournament. Maryland won, 74–68.

Williams was thrilled. His team had dealt with two good teams and had responded well to its first close game of the season. What's more, he could see the kind of personality he wanted developing: Booth was clearly the leader and go-to guy, sophomore center Obinna Ekezie was far stronger than he had been as a freshman, and Profit, although still flighty, had explosive potential.

"This was good," Williams said when the night was over, savoring this win for perhaps fifteen minutes. "But Thursday we'll really have an idea of where we are."

Thursday, Georgia Tech would come to Cole Field House for the last of the ACC December games. On Saturday, Clemson had won at Virginia, an indication that the Tigers' victory over Kentucky was no fluke, and Wake Forest had won a surprisingly tough game at NC State. The warm-up games were over.

7

Chemistry Problems

COLE FIELD HOUSE is one of college basketball's grand old places. Once, it was one of the sport's jewels, a 14,500-seat colossus built, in 1960, long before most people thought about putting that many seats into a basketball arena.

Twice, Cole hosted Final Fours. In fact, what is generally considered the most important college basketball game ever played took place in Cole on the night of March 25, 1966, when Texas Western beat Kentucky, 72–65. All five Texas Western starters that night were black. All five Kentucky starters were white. It was a watershed event for the college game.

Gary Williams was in the building that night. He was a Maryland junior at the time, and he remembers wandering among the Kentucky fans before the game and hearing the word "nigger" over and over. Two of his Maryland teammates — Billy Jones and Mike Johnson — were black and the word upset Williams. "We sat there all night and rooted like hell for Texas Western," he said. "Then, after the game, I remember hearing the Kentucky people saying, 'We gotta get us some of them.' "

Four years later, Adolph Rupp finally broke down and recruited a black player, Tom Payne. By the early 1970s, everyone in the once-segregated South was recruiting blacks. If it hadn't all started that night in Cole, it had certainly picked up considerable momentum.

Throughout most of the 1960s, virtually all of Cole's highlights were NCAA tournament games, if not Final Fours, then Eastern Regionals. Maryland rarely played in front of a full house. "Once or twice a year," Williams remembered. "Even then, it wasn't that big a deal because there were no seats on the floor. Everyone was like a million miles away."

All of that changed when Charles G. "Lefty" Driesell came to College Park in 1969. Driesell was a bald, six-foot-five-inch dynamo who had been a little-used substitute at Duke in the 1950s before going on to turn tiny Davidson College into a national power. Ironically, his last game as Davidson's coach took place in Cole: the Wildcats losing the East Regional final to North Carolina on a Charlie Scott jump shot. Scott was the first black to play for North Carolina. Initially, he had committed to Davidson before changing his mind and going to play for Dean Smith. It was the first time — but not anywhere close to the last — that Smith would torture Driesell.

Driesell came to Maryland vowing to create "the UCLA of the East." The Bruins were in the midst of their run of ten championships in twelve years at the time and Driesell was promising comparable success. That wasn't going to happen. But he did turn Maryland basketball around, bringing in high-profile recruits — most notably six-eleven Tom McMillen, whom he spirited away from North Carolina at the last possible moment — and he began filling Cole. Whenever Driesell walked out of the tunnel, the Maryland band would play "Hail to the Chief," and he would flash the "V" sign to the student body. It was superb theater.

Driesell came agonizingly close to greatness throughout his seventeen years at Maryland. There were two trips to the final eight, but no Final Fours. There were two ACC regular season titles and one ACC tournament championship. The championship came after the Terrapins had lost in the finals five times — the last four by a grand total of seven points. "When I was younger," Driesell said after finally winning in 1984, "I'da taken this trophy, slapped it on the hood of my car and driven up and down North Carolina honking at people to make sure they saw me. Now, I'm too old for that."

Not really. But two years later, when Len Bias died of a cocaine overdose on the night after the Boston Celtics made him the number two pick in the NBA draft, all hell broke loose on the Maryland campus. When the dust finally cleared, Driesell had been exiled to a tiny office on the other side of Cole from the basketball office and Bob Wade, a former high school coach, was sitting where Driesell had once sat. Three years later, Wade was gone and Williams, twenty-two years after his graduation, was back.

It had taken Williams five years and a survived probation to get the program back on track. Now, he was in his eighth season. And with Maryland off to a 6–0 start, Cole was rocking again the way Williams wanted it to be. "This is as good a place as there is to play in the country," he would tell his players. "We do not let people come in here and beat us."

Defending your home court is important in all of college basketball, but especially important in the ACC. Winning on the road is extremely tough in the league, in part because the teams are so good, in part because older buildings like Cole, Cameron Indoor Stadium, Reynolds Coliseum, and Littlejohn Coliseum are so tough to play in because of the close proximity of the fans to the playing floor. Any loss at home was a body blow, any win on the road a major coup.

Sitting in Cole's tiny visitors' locker room, Bobby Cremins knew that the task facing his Georgia Tech team on a snowy December night was a daunting one. A year earlier, Cremins had enjoyed one of his most gratifying seasons in the twenty-one years that he had been a head coach. After starting 6–7, including an embarrassing three-game losing streak against Mount St. Mary's, Bradley, and Santa Clara, the Yellow Jackets had righted themselves and gone 13–3 in the ACC to win the regular season championship. After two years out of the NCAA tournament, they had gone to the Sweet Sixteen before losing to Cincinnati and finished 24–12. Cremins was overwhelmingly voted ACC Coach of the Year.

It was an important year for Cremins. The two years following his 1993 "midlife crisis," which had led to him taking the South Carolina job for two days before changing his mind and returning to Tech, had been mediocre. After making the NCAA tournament for nine straight years, the Yellow Jackets missed twice in a row. Cremins had made it his mission in life prior to the '95–96 season to win the recruiting war for Stephon

Marbury, an extraordinary guard from Brooklyn. Guards, especially New York guards, had been the foundation of Cremins's program. His most important player, Kenny Anderson, had come from Brooklyn. Like Marbury he was a point guard who could lift other players to a different level.

Cremins won the Marbury battle. That was the good news. The bad news was that Marbury and his father had all but announced in a book three years earlier that whichever college program wanted Stephon would have to pay heavily to get him. Reporters came in to investigate, as did the NCAA. And Marbury made it clear to everyone that he was unlikely to stay at Tech for more than a year.

Was he worth all the trouble?

"Oh yes," Cremins said a year later. "We needed the year we had to get ourselves back on track. I needed that year. But we didn't do a good job preparing for Stephon to leave. I fooled myself a little."

In 1991, when Kenny Anderson was a sophomore, Cremins had known he wasn't going to be back as a junior. As a result, he signed a point guard, Travis Best, to replace Anderson. But he had held out hope early in 1996 that Marbury would come back for a second season. By the time he realized in the spring that Marbury had stopped going to class and had no intention of returning, most of the best point guards were signed or committed to other schools.

"It was my fault," Cremins said. "I got caught up believing what I wanted to believe instead of believing reality."

If that sentence sounds a bit confusing, it is also pure Cremins. There is no one in coaching like Bobby Cremins. He is still very much the kid from the Bronx who relies on his Catholic faith and his inherent belief in people to get him through life. "I been lucky all my life," he often says. "People have been good to me."

Cremins has lived in the South since he was eighteen, but his accent is still pure Bronx. When he talks about the winningest coach in history, he talks about, "Dean Smit at Naut Cowlina." His team always needs to work on "tree trows." And when he talks about religion, he will earnestly tell you he was brought up in the "catlic fait." Many of his friends insist that he is an effective recruiter in large part because none of the players can understand a word he is saying.

What is most remarkable about Cremins is that he has thrived in a cutthroat profession, one filled with jealousies and rivalries, without making enemies. "Maybe a couple," he says. Norman Sloan, the old NC State coach who didn't like a lot of people, never liked him. In 1987, Sloan took Florida to the Sweet Sixteen. This was two years after Sloan had lost a hot recruiting battle to Cremins for Tommy Hammonds, a top player from Florida. Cremins ran into Sloan that spring the week after Tech had been eliminated from the NCAAs. Florida was en route to New Jersey for the Eastern Regionals.

"Congratulations, Norm," Cremins said when their paths crossed in an airport.

"Yeah, thanks, Bobby," Sloan answered. "It's great to still be playing when sonsofbitches like you are sitting home watching."

There had also been some harsh words between Cremins and Syracuse's Jim Boeheim after their battle over Anderson. Boeheim had publicly accused Cremins of cheating to get Anderson, and Cremins confronted him about it at a summer camp.

But that's about it. In the ACC, where almost everyone seems to snipe at everyone else at some point, no one has anything really bad to say about Cremins. Ask almost any ACC coach who he considers a friend among the league's coaches and almost all of them will think for a moment and then say, "Well, Bobby, of course." They may or may not add other names.

Two days after the 1996 Final Four, ACC commissioner Gene Corrigan asked the league's coaches to come to Greensboro for an impromptu meeting. Cremins burst into the meeting late, out of breath, but excited. "Boy, did I see a terrific player yesterday," he told the other coaches. "I think we finally found the guard we need."

The other coaches looked at each other. Finally, Dave Odom spoke up. "Bobby," he said, "yesterday was a dead period."

That meant it was against the rules for Cremins (or any coach) to be looking at a potential recruit that day.

Cremins slapped his forehead with his hand. "You're kidding?" he said. "A dead period? Jeez, how could I not know that?"

Everyone in the room cracked up. "If it's anybody else," Gary Williams said later, we'd have all been saying, 'Yeah, sure you didn't know it was a dead period.' But it was Bobby. We knew he wasn't lying. If he wanted to lie, he never would have brought seeing the player up in the first place. We ended up getting on Dave for bringing it up."

The next day, Cremins turned himself in to the NCAA. He was ordered not to have any more contact with the player until after the player had chosen a college. The player, Kevin Morris, chose Georgia Tech.

Everyone who knows Cremins has a Bobby story. During one ACC meeting, Cremins was talking about all the pressures basketball coaches face. His theory was that football coaches had it better than basketball coaches because there are so many spots open in bowl games and a coach can go 7–5 but still end his season with a win in a minor bowl game.

"Oh, come on, Bobby, it's not that bad," Gene Corrigan said. "After all, sixty-four teams make the NCAA tournament every year."

"Yeah," Cremins responded, "but how many Division I teams are there?"

"About three hundred."

Cremins looked at Dean Smith, the resident math major among the coaches.

"Dean, what percentage is that?"

"A little less than twenty-two percent," Smith answered.

"OK, Gene," Cremins said, "how many teams go to bowl games?"

"Thirty-six," Corrigan answered.

"And there are how many Division I-A football teams?"

"About one hundred."

Cremins looked at Smith again. "Thirty-six out of a hundred, Dean," he asked. "What percentage is that?"

Like Mike Krzyzewski, Cremins would turn fifty in 1997 (on the Fourth of July). His hair had turned prematurely gray so many years ago that during his early years at Tech, the Duke students always serenaded him with chants of "Grecian Formula" when he walked into Cameron. He was third in seniority among ACC coaches, having come to the league in 1981, one year after Krzyzewski and twenty years after Smith. Tech's second win of the season over Morgan State had been his three hundredth at the school and his four hundredth overall. And yet, Cremins still came across to people as boyish. He had an easy smile and a friendly manner. He was terrible at remembering names, but brilliant at recovering. The road that Cremins had taken to being a successful coach was different from most of his colleagues'. He had grown up in the South Bronx, the third of Robert and Margaret Cremins's four children. His dad was a longshoreman until an injury forced him to take a job as an elevator operator in a Manhattan apartment building. His parents were Irish immigrants, strict Catholics who said a rosary every night. Bobby went to Catholic schools through the eighth grade but, because his grades weren't very good, seemed bound for a public high school.

In those days, though, Catholic high schools openly recruited athletes and Cremins was already a very good basketball player. He tried out at three schools — Power Memorial in Manhattan and Rice and All Hallows in the Bronx. "If I'd gone to Power, I'd have played with Lew Alcindor," he remembered. Power didn't offer him a scholarship. But All Hallows did.

Bobby continued to star on the basketball court at All Hallows, but his schoolwork got even worse. By the end of his junior year, he was in big trouble. "I flunked everything," he said. "The Irish Christian Brothers who ran the school told me there was nothing they could do but throw me out."

When he informed his father that he had been thrown out of All Hallows, he got a beating. "Hands only," he said thirty-three years later, the memory still vivid. Then Bobby Sr. and Bobby Jr. went back to school. While Bobby waited in the hall, his father negotiated with the Irish Christian Brothers. A deal was cut: Bobby would be allowed to return to school, but he would have to repeat junior year. It was an embarrassing experience, sitting in class with kids who had been a year behind him, but he got through it. He even worked at it a little bit, and his grades improved.

But that was his last year of eligibility in New York. His coach, Dick King, thought he was good enough to get a college scholarship. But he couldn't play for All Hallows as a senior and he needed another year of classes to graduate. King called an old friend, Bill Kenney, who was a local basketball guru. Kenney offered Cremins a spot at Frederick Military Academy in Portsmouth, Virginia. No way, Cremins said. But it was the only way he could play. He went. He watched a number of other players drop out the first week, but he stuck with it.

Midway through the season, Frederick traveled to suburban Maryland to play Bullis Prep. Bullis's two best players were Corky Carnevale and

Tommy Terry. Their fathers were close friends with Frank McGuire, who had recently returned to the ACC as the coach at South Carolina. The game was in the afternoon. South Carolina happened to be playing at Maryland that night. McGuire came to the game to see his friends' sons play. What he saw was Cremins scoring 27 points. After the game, he introduced himself to Cremins and asked him if he had any idea where he wanted to go to college.

Cremins was thinking he might have a chance to go to Old Dominion, although Sonny Allen, the coach, kept telling him he was too skinny at six two, 135 to play college ball. A few days later, Cremins got a call from McGuire's assistant, Donnie Walsh. They were interested in him. Did he have an 800 on the SATs yet?

No. Cremins had been dreading the SAT. Walsh told him he had to have a score of 800 to get into an ACC school. Cremins did what a lot of athletes in those days did: he paid someone fifty dollars to take the test for him. But the night before the test, he was having dinner with a man named Hook Hillman. Hillman worked in the Portsmouth Navy Yard and loved basketball. He often informally adopted the local prep school players, knowing they were away from home for the first time. Cremins told Hillman his plan. Hillman pleaded with him not to do it, to take the test on his own at least once.

"Probably the best advice I ever got," Cremins said. "Because if I'da shown up with a score of like 1000, they'da known something was up."

He took the test on his own and got an 810. When his score came in it was the happiest day of his life. Just before Bobby left for Columbia, his mother bought him his first suit. The suit was made of wool. Cremins got off the plane in Columbia in one-hundred-degree heat wearing the wool suit and carrying his pool cue. Walsh picked him up and drove him to McGuire's house to see the coach. "Nice pad, Frank," Cremins said. When they were back in the car a few minutes later, Walsh told him, "Never call Coach McGuire 'Frank.' And lose that suit. You're sweating like a pig." Cremins never wore the suit again.

Freshman year, he almost flunked out first semester. At midterm, he had three F's and a D. "I hung out with the wrong guys," he said. "I never went to class." When he was about to see McGuire to explain himself, Corky Carnevale, now a fellow freshman, gave him some advice: "Just tell him you spent all your time on one subject — the D." McGuire and Walsh explained to him that he'd better diversify or he was going to be headed back to the Bronx. He put his pool cue away, studied up a storm the rest of the semester, and emerged with three D's and a C.

He also didn't have much of a social life that year. "Girls would hear my accent and be scared of me," he said. "I didn't eat grits, I didn't know how to shag, and I talked funny. I had no chance."

Things got better his sophomore year. His grades improved. He was playing well. And Dean Smith gave his social life a huge boost. The Gamecocks closed their regular season road schedule at North Carolina. Trailing down the stretch, Smith kept fouling South Carolina's worst foul shooter — Cremins. He made 16 of 17 free throws and ended up with 23 points and 15 assists. South Carolina won, 87–86. "When I got back to campus, girls were all over me," he said. Cremins credits Smith with an assist on his first collegiate sexual encounter.

South Carolina won the regular season title his junior year, but was upset in the ACC tournament. That sent the Gamecocks to the NIT. There, in the quarterfinals, they were beaten by an unheralded Army team. When South Carolina fell behind in the second half and was forced to switch from a zone defense to man-to-man, McGuire asked Cremins whom he thought he should guard. "I'll take the guy with the big nose whose name I can't pronounce," Cremins answered.

The nose and the name belonged to Mike Krzyzewski.

Cremins's college career ended in disaster. South Carolina was 14–0 in ACC play his senior season. It was a star-filled team with John Roche, Kevin Joyce, Tom Riker, John Ribock, and Cremins's old pal from the Bronx, Tom Owens. But in the ACC tournament semifinals, Roche fractured an ankle on a fast break. He played in the final the next night, shot up with drugs, but shot four for 17. NC State played slowdown and won the game in double overtime.

Totally distraught, Cremins dropped out of school and joined the Carolina Cougars training camp the next fall, but he was the last player cut. He went home and his dad got him a job as a bellhop at the Waldorf-Astoria. Then one night at dinner, his father looked at him and said, "Four years you go to college, you come home with no degree and I have to find you a job."

Bobby quit the next day, went back to Columbia, re-enrolled in school, and began working for a real estate company. He graduated that summer. By then, his pal Carnevale was working for McGuire as a graduate assistant. When a South American talent scout called to ask about Tom Owens's availability, Carnevale told him he couldn't have Owens, but he knew somebody better.

"How tall?" the scout asked.

"Six eight," Carnevale answered.

Two days later, Cremins, stretching his six-two frame as much as possible, was at the Plaza Hotel in New York, knocking on the door of Omar Quintana. "You're too short!" Quintana screamed. "Go away."

Cremins really wanted to play ball. "Come with me," he said to Quintana. He led him to a schoolyard basketball court where he gave a kid five dollars to borrow his basketball. Then he took a few dribbles and dunked.

"OK?" he said to Quintana.

"OK," Quintana said.

A day later, Cremins was in Guayaquil, Ecuador, suiting up for the Emelec club. He was their leading scorer, once scoring 47 points in a game. There were no other Americans on the team so Cremins spent a lot of time hanging out with Peace Corps volunteers. One day he came back from a workout starving and found them cooking brownies. "I loved brownies," he said. Before anyone knew it, Cremins had eaten about a dozen brownies.

"Bobby," someone asked. "How many of those did you eat?"

"About twelve."

"Uh-oh."

They were, of course, loaded with marijuana. Cremins was so sick he thought he was going to have to go to the hospital to have his stomach pumped. "It was fifteen years before I could even look at a brownie again," he said.

He came back from Ecuador in the spring of 1972 and played on an AAU team in Columbia. He was thinking about going back to Ecuador when he got a letter from a man named Jerry Conboy, who was the coach at Point Park College in Pittsburgh. Conboy had a lot of friends in the ACC area and he was looking for someone to coach his freshman team. Cremins's name had come up. Was he interested?

"I never thought about coaching," he said. "I was a player, not a coach. But my options as a player were used up. I figured, what the hell, I'd try it for a year."

He liked it. He liked Pittsburgh too. Point Park was affiliated with the Pittsburgh ballet and Cremins dated ballerinas all year. At the end of the year, McGuire called. If he was going to coach, he should be at South Carolina. He went back as a graduate assistant. "By then, I was falling in love with coaching," he said. "I loved being around the players, still being in basketball even if I couldn't play anymore."

He was a full-time coach at South Carolina a year later, and a year after that he was the head coach at Appalachian State. Press Maravich — father of the legendary Pete — had resigned midway through the 1975 season, and South Carolina's tennis coach knew the Appalachian athletic director because he had once been the tennis coach there. He recommended Cremins and Cremins got the job. He was twenty-seven years old and a little more than three years removed from Ecuador.

In the next ten years Cremins's career rocketed. Before moving to Appalachian State he got married. Naturally, as with all things Cremins, it wasn't easy. He had met Carolyn James on the tennis courts at his apartment complex. She had just divorced a South Carolina professor and moved in with her two little girls. They began dating, fell in love, and decided to get married. Since Carolyn was divorced, she couldn't be married in the Catholic Church. When Cremins informed his parents that he was marrying a divorced woman who was five years older than he, his mother was not happy. They were married in a private ceremony in Columbia, then headed off to Boone, North Carolina, so Cremins could begin his career at Appalachian.

But he knew his mother was unhappy. He spoke to a priest he had befriended named George Kloster. What could be done? Kloster agreed to remarry the couple in the church but in a private ceremony. That satisfied Margaret Cremins.

Six years, one son, and one hundred victories later, Cremins was the coach at Georgia Tech. "I got the job," he said, "because no one else wanted it."

Tech was a dead end for coaches in 1981. The Yellow Jackets had been in the ACC for two years and had a conference record of 1–29. They were overmatched. Tom Davis, then at Boston College, turned the job down. So did Penn's Bob Weinhauer. Homer Rice had been the athletic director at North Carolina when Cremins made all the free throws in Chapel Hill in 1968 and he had always remembered him for that. Now, looking at his record at Appalachian, he called. Cremins didn't care if the job was a dead end or not. It was in the ACC and it would pay $60,000 a year, twice what he was making at App. He accepted the job, moved into a hotel room with his top assistant George Felton — "we had to share a bed the first few nights because they had no doubles; it wasn't too good" — and began looking for players while Carolyn took the children (now including four-year-old Bobby III) to look for a house.

A year later, while Tech was improving to 3–11 in the ACC and 10–16 overall, Cremins convinced a baby-faced guard from Oklahoma named Mark Price and a skinny, six-ten kid from the Bronx named John Salley to come to Georgia Tech. By the time they left four years later, their numbers were hanging from the rafters in Alexander Memorial Coliseum and Bobby Cremins was one of the hot names in coaching.

Tech won the ACC tournament in 1985 and went to the Elite Eight before defending national champion Georgetown managed to shut Price down and get by the Yellow Jackets, 60–54. With all their key players back the next season, Tech was picked number one in every preseason poll. Cremins and Price and Salley were on magazine covers everywhere. At forty, Cremins was the Next Great Coach. Sure enough, the prognosticators were right. When the Final Four assembled in Dallas that season, the ACC was represented by a hot young coach. But it was the kid with the big nose and the unpronounceable name. Picked third in the ACC in preseason, Duke faced none of the pressures Tech had to deal with. The Blue Devils won the regular season title, beat Tech 68–67 in a classic ACC tournament final, and went to the championship game before losing to Louisville.

Tech went out in the Sweet Sixteen, to LSU. It was the most devastating loss for Cremins since the NC State game his senior year. "I didn't coach very well that year," he said. "The pressure got to me. It was all too much. It happened so fast. I wanted Price and Salley to win it all before they left because they had meant so much to me."

One of Cremins's most endearing traits is his willingness to accept the blame for his teams' failures. Unlike many coaches who give "I coached good, they played bad" speeches after losses, Cremins always takes responsibility. If the players weren't good enough, he reasoned, well, he was the one who recruited them.

Tech made the NCAA tournament the next three seasons after the '86 disappointment, but won only one game. Then came the epic recruitment of Kenny Anderson. "I must have written Kenny two hundred letters," Cremins said. "I never worked a kid harder. I thought he was the player who could take us to a national championship."

He almost did. In 1990 with Anderson as a freshman, Dennis Scott a junior, and Brian Oliver a senior, Tech evolved into a wonderful team. The trio was dubbed Lethal Weapon III and they lived up to it. They won the ACC tournament, then avenged the '86 LSU game with a victory over a Shaquille O'Neal–led team in the second round. They needed a kind whistle to beat Michigan State (a buzzer-beating shot by Anderson to tie the game at the end of regulation actually came a split second after the buzzer) and then beat Minnesota. They were in the Final Four — at last. They met Nevada–Las Vegas in the semifinals and put a scare into the Rebels, leading by five at halftime before Anderson picked up his fourth foul on a charge and had to go to the bench. "That was the one time when Kenny's yoot [youth] showed up," Cremins said.

They lost the game, 90–81, but Cremins walked out of the building almost as thrilled as if his team had won. He suspected Vegas was the best team — it would go on to kill Duke by 30 in the final — and he knew his team had given him everything it had. He was a Final Four coach. Scott and Anderson would be back and would only get better.

But Scott didn't come back, he jumped to the NBA. Anderson stayed one more year and then he too was gone. Finally, in 1993, after a difficult season, Cremins left too, lured back to his alma mater, South Carolina, by friends who begged him to rebuild a fallen program. Only he couldn't go through with it.

"I felt like Judas," he said. "Georgia Tech didn't do anything wrong. It was wrong for me to leave."

He called Homer Rice in the middle of the night and asked for his job back. Rice took him back. And then, with all hell breaking loose in Columbia and Atlanta, Cremins fled to Florida. He was in counseling for weeks and on antidepressants for three months. Finally, he woke up one morning in July and threw them all out. It was time to move on. Even so, for months, whenever he saw someone he knew, he would — unsolicited — retell the story. He still felt guilty about what he had done to South Carolina, although he was relieved when Eddie Fogler, a coach he greatly respected, took the job after he had left.

The next two years were, by Tech's standards, mediocre. That was why Marbury was so important. It was also why his departure, along with senior shooting guard Drew Barry, had left Cremins concerned about this team. He and Kevin Cantwell, his alter ego and top lieutenant, had liked Kevin Morris in the spring. He would have to step in for Marbury at point guard.

Things had not gone well in the fall. There had been a problem with Morris's high school transcript and he had not been declared eligible to play until a week after practice had started. Sophomore Gary Saunders, slated to take Barry's spot at shooting guard, was ineligible first semester. Cremins first considered redshirting him for the entire year to see if he would improve academically, but had decided by mid-November that he needed Saunders playing as soon as possible.

The front line looked solid: Eddie Elisma, a six-ten senior, had pro potential; Mike Maddox, a six-eight junior, had showed marked improvement late last season; and Matt Harpring, the six-seven junior, was as good as any player in the ACC not named Tim Duncan. Harpring was a workhorse, willing to do anything to win. The only reason Harpring was at Tech was because Cantwell had pushed Cremins to go back and see him again after Cremins had initially thought him too slow for the ACC. "He should go to Davidson or Furman," Cremins told Cantwell.

He went to see him again only because Harpring played on the same high school team as his son. Finally, he agreed to give him a scholarship. "My goodness," he said as his team got ready to play Maryland, "where would we be if Kevin hadn't made me take Hopping?"

It was a reasonable question. Tech was 4–1 going into the game, but Cremins wasn't happy with what he had seen so far. Morris was having serious trouble running the team and Maddox and Elisma weren't playing nearly as well as they had a year before. The other three freshmen, all of whom were getting playing time, were not ready for the ACC. Cremins knew that. They would be learning on the job. That was potentially disastrous for a freshman unless his name happened to be Price or Anderson or Marbury. Tech had managed to pull out a win over Georgia, but had been beaten badly the previous weekend by Temple.

"That game scared me," he said, sipping a coke in the locker room. "We played bad. We had no chemistry at all."

Cliché though it might be, chemistry has always been a key word in the Cremins coaching vernacular. He thinks it is critical that his players like one another off the court if they are to work well together on the court. Cremins doesn't try to beat anybody with X's and O's or with multiple defenses. He beats them by recruiting good players who fit well together as a unit. The Price-Salley teams had that. So did Lethal Weapon III. For that matter, Marbury and Barry had also had it and they had been so hard to guard that Harpring constantly got good shots.

This team had none of that. Harpring was being forced to work like crazy for his shots because teams were double-teaming him every chance they got. They were more than willing to give up a shot to Morris or the other freshmen or even Elisma or Maddox, rather than to Harpring. Already, Harpring was becoming frustrated.

Cremins always seems to have friends with him in the locker room before a game. On this night, two priests he had known for years were there and so was Ed Janka, the traveling Nike rep whose job was to schmooze the coaches Nike paid to promote their shoes and clothes. This was a twofer for Janka, since Gary Williams was also a Nike coach.

"How's Gary?" Cremins asked Janka.

"Tight," Janka replied, which was like saying that Williams was breathing. Cremins laughed. "Guess he hasn't seen us play."

Cremins delegates a lot of the pregame duties to his assistants. Gary Leiner writes matchups on the blackboard — at least in part because Cremins's handwriting is virtually illegible — and Cantwell does the scouting report. Georgia Tech is the only ACC school that doesn't give its players a written scouting report to study. Cremins, like Dean Smith, has always focused most of his preparation on his own team. Specifically, he works on offense. Cantwell is in charge of the defense. Rarely does Cremins speak for very long in pregame.

"Fellas, we have got to meet the challenge tonight," he said after

Cantwell had finished going over Maryland's personnel. "We have to play with guts and courage. We didn't do that against Temple. I don't want to see your heads go down if things go wrong the way they did on Saturday. It's a young season. Your attitude is important."

He paused. "You need to like each other, fellas. Don't play with your heads up your ass tonight. We have to rebound against this team and we *must* be aware of Keith Booth." (Actually, he said "Keit Boot.") "Eddie, you're the senior. You have to be the leader."

He walked to the center of the tiny room — it took about three steps to get there — and the players surrounded him. They said the Lord's Prayer. "Good luck, fellas," Cremins said and they headed into the raucous Cole atmosphere. Cremins's final words on the bench before tipoff were direct: "We haven't earned anyone's respect yet this year. Let's start right now."

Cremins works with a magnetic board, constantly pushing the little pieces around to show his players where he wants them. He moved the pieces around one more time to show them how he wanted them aligned on offense. Then he sat down next to Cantwell, who had told him that afternoon that Maryland was about the last team Tech should be playing right now.

"They do so many different things," he said. "We still haven't figured ourselves out, much less a team like this. I'd rather play Duke at Duke right now. At least with them, you know how to prepare."

As it turned out, Tech would have been better off anyplace but in Cole Field House.

It was 7–0 before Tech even got a shot to the rim — four turnovers and an air ball. Harpring finally hit a jumper to get his team on the board, but Maryland scored the next 11 to make it 18–2. It got to 29–9 a few minutes later and was 33–16 when the last TV time-out of the half was called.

Cremins was as close to angry as he ever gets on the bench. "Guts, fellas, you have to show some guts," he said. "Do that and we'll crawl back into this thing."

His frustration showed a minute later when he yelled at referee Steve Gordon for missing what he thought was a pushing foul. Cremins never gets on officials. ACC referees tell one another, "If Bobby Cremins gets on you, then you're really having a bad night."

On this occasion, it was Cremins who was having the bad night.

The Maryland lead was 15 at halftime and never less than double digits in the second half. When it got to 64–40 with ten minutes left, Cremins sat on the bench, leaned back, put his hands behind his head, and let out a deep sigh. It had been a long night.

The only person in the building who was at all uptight was Gary Williams, who was furious with his subs for letting the margin dwindle to 11 with two minutes left. It got that close because the Terrapins got sloppy and because Harpring wouldn't give up. The final was 77–63. Williams, his shirt soaked through, was almost pleased. His team had played three tough games in five days and had won all three impressively.

Cremins had no such comfort level. "Fellas, I hope you're as pissed off by what happened tonight as I am," he said. "That was embarrassing. We play like that all winter and we're going to be in trouble. Big trouble. Think about it."

They would think about it. But not as much as Cremins would. As he walked out of the locker room, he looked at Cantwell. "Might be a long season, Kevin," he said. Cantwell wasn't arguing.

8

The Road Back

SITTING IN an empty locker room across the hall from where his players were getting dressed in Philadelphia's brand-new Core States Center, Mike Krzyzewski looked tired. The season was only eight games old, but already he felt a little worn out.

The trip to Philadelphia had something to do with that feeling. The Blue Devils had left Cameron Indoor Stadium after lunch on Friday afternoon, expecting to arrive in Philadelphia at 4:30. That would have left plenty of time to practice in the new arena, eat dinner, and be in bed at a reasonable hour. But their charter had been canceled. Attempts to bring in another plane had failed. The team had finally gotten onto a jam-packed commercial flight that had gone through Baltimore before finally arriving at 11:30 on a rainy, windswept night.

"We can do two things," Krzyzewski said to his players the next morning. "We can use the travel as an excuse or we can say, 'What the hell, we still got a good night's sleep, we got to watch *Martin* in the airport even though Coach K had no idea what was going on, and we're ready to play.'"

Krzyzewski was convinced his team was going to take the latter approach. "I think we're fine," he told Tommy Amaker and Quin Snyder, his two full-time assistant coaches. "If they've really listened this week, I really think we'll win the game. I think we can make life very hard for this team."

The team in question was fourth-ranked Villanova and there were not many reasons to be as confident as Krzyzewski was. The Wildcats were big and talented. They had experienced guards and they would be playing in front of a partisan crowd of close to 20,000 people in the first college basketball game in the new building in South Philadelphia. This was a made-for-TV game, scheduled because CBS promised to televise it nationally. Villanova wanted to bring a big-name team to town for a game in the new arena and Krzyzewski always liked to schedule at least one tough road game in December to prepare for playing on the road in the ACC.

As tired as he was, Krzyzewski was excited about the game. To Amaker and Snyder that was an important sign. Both had played for him at Duke, Amaker graduating in 1987, Snyder in 1989. Neither had started out to be a coach. Both had gone to graduate school before their love for the game had turned them to coaching.

Both had watched Krzyzewski go through the nightmare that was 1995 — Amaker as an assistant, Snyder as an administrative assistant. When Krzyzewski had remade his staff after that season, Amaker had been promoted to associate coach and Snyder had taken the spot vacated when Mike Brey became the head coach at Delaware. Each had wondered at times during the next season — as had their boss — if Krzyzewski really wanted to be back coaching, if he could love what he was doing as much as he loved what he had done.

The fall had not been easy for anyone in the Duke basketball office. It had started just before Labor Day when Krzyzewski got a call from his older brother, Bill, in Chicago. Emily Krzyzewski had been fighting cancer for a year. She was failing quickly now. Bill told his brother he needed to get there as soon as possible. Fortunately, Mike did get there soon enough that he was able to spend several days with his mother while she was still lucid. She slipped into a coma on the fifth of September and died the next day.

She was eighty-four and she had been ill, and yet, her death came as a complete shock to her second son. "I wasn't there the way Bill was," he said. "I didn't see her getting worse as the year went on. In a lot of ways, I was in denial. Intellectually I understood that she had cancer and she was very frail. Emotionally, I never prepared myself."

There is no way to prepare yourself emotionally for the death of a parent, especially a parent who was as close to her sons as Emily Krzyzewski was. Mike Krzyzewski was never that close to his father, who worked long, difficult hours and came home exhausted most nights. His mom had always been his rock. He knew how hard she had worked to take care of her two sons. He never lost sight of it.

One summer night, when Emily Krzyzewski was visiting Mike and Mickie and the three girls at their beach house, mother and son found themselves alone at the kitchen table. "Look at you, Mike," Emily said. "Look at the success you've become. Who would have thought you would ever become so important and famous."

Mike Krzyzewski shook his head at his mother. "Mom, don't you understand, if I'm a success, it's because you were a success. Your goal in life was to make Bill and me happy. No one has been more successful at what they do than you are. No one."

That was the bond that existed between Emily Krzyzewski and her sons. Her death devastated them and the entire Krzyzewski family, including her grandchildren, who adored her. Mickie Krzyzewski barely knew Mike when his father died. She was fully aware of the closeness he felt to his mother. But she wasn't prepared for the complete devastation he felt when she died.

"I haven't lost a parent, so maybe I had trouble *really* understanding it," she said. "He was a mess, a complete mess. I had never seen him that way."

When Krzyzewski came back from Chicago, his assistants could see that he was still hurting. There was also the additional insult of finding that their home had been broken into while the family was in Chicago. Bill later told his brother that it was common practice for burglars to check the obituaries, note the death of a person's out-of-town relative, and then break into the person's house. Often, in meetings Krzyzewski would bring up his mom, openly wondering sometimes if he should have found more ways to spend time with her.

His mother's death also changed Krzyzewski's attitude toward one key recruit: Baron Davis, a superb point guard from California. Over the summer, Krzyzewski had raved about Davis. He had taken a week off from recruiting after his mother's death, telling Amaker and Snyder to explain to all the players they were recruiting that he would be back in touch just as soon as he could put himself back together emotionally. Only one recruit complained about not hearing from Krzyzewski during that period: Baron Davis.

"After that, he just couldn't feel the same about the kid," Amaker said.

Even without Davis, Duke had put together a remarkable recruiting class in the fall. Four players had committed: six-eight Shane Battier, six-eleven Chris Burgess, six-nine Elton Brand, and six-two point guard William Avery, who had become a lot more important after Davis became less important. Battier and Burgess had signed letters of intent during the November signing period. Brand would sign in the spring. So would Avery, assuming his grades improved. Krzyzewski was excited about the potential of the incoming freshmen, but didn't want them coming into the program viewed as saviors. "We need to establish something with these kids this season," he said. "The freshmen should be important additions to the team next year, not the keys to the team."

The early returns were not that encouraging. After the loss in New York to Indiana, the Blue Devils had won a breather against Lehigh and then been lucky to escape Florida State. That had brought Michigan to town for the traditional December game that the two schools had played since 1989. For several years, Duke seemed to have Michigan's number. The fabled Fab Five had faced Duke three times — in December '91 and '92 and in the '92 national championship game. They had gone 0–3. Duke had then won in '93 and even in '94, one of the few highlights of that ill-fated season.

Michigan had finally broken Duke's six-game winning streak the prior December in Ann Arbor. But that had been a struggling Duke team. As it turned out, this was also a struggling Duke team. For almost thirty minutes, that didn't appear to be the case. When Steve Wojciechowski fed freshman Mike Chappell for an easy layup, Duke led 58–46 with 10:32 left and Cameron was rocking in anticipation of a win over a top ten team.

Only it never happened. Duke didn't score again from the field. Its offense for the rest of the game consisted of three Trajan Langdon free throws with 6:30 left. That was it. One open shot after another clanged off iron. "We had six three-point shots that were wide-open," Krzyzewski said later. "We make any one of them and we win the game."

But they made none of them. Michigan chipped and chipped and finally took the lead at 62–61 when two Duke defenders collided in the lane, leaving center Robert Traylor wide open for a dunk with six seconds left. To make things worse, the Blue Devils panicked and called time-out — which Krzyzewski didn't want because it gave Michigan a chance to set its defense. After the time-out, they failed to get a shot off. As fate would have it, the ball was in Jeff Capel's hands when the game ended. After his zero-for-nine performance against Florida State, Capel had only played fifteen minutes against Michigan. He had improved to two for seven.

Capel was no more responsible for this loss than anybody. He just had the misfortune to have become the symbol for all the troubles of the past two — and now three — seasons. Krzyzewski was angry with his team for panicking. He could accept a loss, but he couldn't accept panic. He told the players that they would meet the next day just to talk and try to figure out what they needed to do to get back on the right track.

When Krzyzewski got home that night, he found a message from Jeff Capel Sr. He knew the call probably wasn't social. Jeff Capel Sr. is an outstanding coach in his own right, the head coach at Old Dominion University. He understood better than most fathers the ups and downs players went through. But he was still a father and his son was hurting. He hurt for him too. Krzyzewski could hear the hurt in his voice when he called back.

"He's become an outcast," Capel Sr. said. "You're giving the freshmen predetermined playing time and it's cutting into Jeff's chances."

Krzyzewski knew he couldn't talk to Capel coach-to-coach. This had to be father-to-father. "Jeff, do you know how many starts the freshmen have had so far?" he asked. "Two out of a possible thirty-five. Mike Chappell played eleven minutes today. That's not the problem. Let me ask you a question. Has Jeff ever told you that he's afraid?"

"No he hasn't," Capel Sr. said.

"Yes he has," Krzyzewski said. "And he's probably telling me the same thing. He's not an outcast, but I'm sure he feels guilty because he's not playing better, so he sees himself that way. He's afraid like most college seniors are afraid because the future's uncertain. That's a perfectly reasonable way to feel. But we have to work with him to get rid of that feeling."

After that, the tension between the two coaches lifted. They talked about the Michigan game and the problems other players — like Ricky Price — were having. "I'll never give up on Jeff," Krzyzewski said finally. "Because I think he's a great kid."

The next two days were intense and emotional. The players and coaches met for two hours on Monday. For an hour, one player after another stood up and talked. It was Wojciechowski who talked the longest, telling his teammates — Capel and Price in particular — that they had to stop playing scared and just play. The next day, Krzyzewski and Amaker had a long meeting with Capel. It was emotional and draining. But Krzyzewski was convinced they had made progress.

On Wednesday, they beat Davidson, then practiced well on Thursday and Friday before the trip to Philadelphia to play Villanova. Krzyzewski felt as if he had been through an entire season in the last week. But he was convinced the work was going to be worthwhile.

"You know, every outstanding team I've coached at Duke loved games like this," he told his players before they went out to warm up. "This team we're facing is as big as any we'll see. But you know what? We're as quick as anyone they'll see. We need to use that quickness and beat them up and down the court all day."

Krzyzewski almost never uses a blackboard in his pregame talks. The players have seen the other team on tape and they have been walked through the opponent's plays by whichever assistant coach has done the scouting report earlier in the day. Now, though, he turned to the board and wrote one word on it: FUN.

"Basketball, guys, should be this," he said, pointing at the word. "The way you make it fun is to work together. Help each other out on the floor, call out screens, pick each other up, outwork the other team. If you're playing well, there comes a point in the game where you see a look in the other team's eyes that tells you you've got them. It's a great feeling, guys, you know that. We need to get that feeling back starting today. This is a championship-caliber game. Let's enjoy it."

Krzyzewski looked around the room. He is an intent reader of body language and he liked most of what he saw. No one looked more ready than Jeff Capel, who wasn't going to start. That, he thought, was a terrific sign. But he still felt some tension. The assistants had commented on how cold the court felt. It was another rainy, nasty day and, in the not-yet-full building, it was nippy on the court.

"Cold out there?" he asked.

Everyone nodded. "Did the ball still go in the bucket when you shot it?"

They all nodded.

"So it works here then, just like back home."

That got a laugh. That was what he wanted. They moved together for their prayer. Krzyzewski says the same prayer before each game, asking for health and optimum performance. His last words are always the same: "Let's go, Duke!" saying the word "Duke" not the way a cheerleader might, but as if "Duke" is everyone in the room's name. Once the players have started for the floor, he circles the room, shaking hands with everyone present: assistants, managers, trainers, doctors. He says the same thing to everyone: "Let's get 'em." Then he puts on his jacket and follows everyone else onto the floor.

The Core States Arena was packed. Even after two mediocre seasons, Duke was still a big name in college basketball. And Villanova was a hot item in Philadelphia. Steve Lappas had been an assistant under Rollie Massimino when Villanova pulled off its miracle national title run in 1985. He had come back to Villanova when Massimino had fled to Nevada–Las Vegas in 1992. He had steadily rebuilt the program, and when he signed six-ten Tim Thomas the previous spring a lot of people had penciled the Wildcats in for a Final Four slot in 1997. They were 6–0, including a pair of Big East victories over Providence and St. John's. Most in the crowd had come to see them beat up on a once-proud team fallen on hard times.

A thunderous dunk by center Jason Lawson three minutes into the game put Villanova up 11–7 and had Krzyzewski squirming. His team had been outrebounded by Michigan and, against any opponent, lacked size. He had visions of Villanova pounding away all afternoon. But there are no rebounds if you make all your shots, and for the next few minutes, Duke did just that. Trajan Langdon hit a three and Greg Newton posted for a bucket. That put Duke up 12–11.

Krzyzewski went to the bench for Capel. The first time he touched the ball, he went right to the basket and got fouled. Swish, swish. The next time he touched it he was open for a three. "Take it, Cape!" Krzyzewski screamed, even though Capel couldn't hear him at the far end of the court over the crowd noise. He took it anyway. Swish! Krzyzewski looked at Amaker. Neither one could remember the last time they had seen Capel so assertive.

The lead actually grew to 27–13 before Villanova, responding to the pleading crowd, ran off an 8–0 run of its own to get back to 27–21. "Hey, guys, we've given them four points on loose balls," Krzyzewski said during a TV time-out. "We have to be the ones doing that. Not them. Want the ball!"

Another Capel three stretched the lead back to 32–25, but Wojciechowski picked up his third foul with 3:56 left. Krzyzewski was concerned because Wojciechowski had become absolutely invaluable to his team. Frustrated, he started to get on the officials. He was thrilled to get into the locker room at halftime still ahead, 40–33. In spite of Wojo's three fouls, he was pleased with what he had seen. They hadn't been intimidated by the crowd or Villanova's size. The only offensive adjustment he wanted to make was to convince his perimeter players to drive the middle rather than baseline. "The baseline's not there, guys," he said. "There's clear air in the middle. Let's go there. We dealt with enough air traffic last night."

Every coach tells his team that the first five minutes of the second half is critical. Actually, these days, coaches talk about the first four minutes, since college basketball is now played in four minute blocks — from one TV time-out to the next. Rick Barnes goes so far as to tell his team it's going to play ten four-minute games. The first four/five-minute theory is especially important when an underdog has the lead on the road. The home team is bound to receive a fire-and-brimstone talk in the locker room and come out wound up, determined to take control of the game. Villanova tried to do just that, but Duke was shooting the ball too well to allow it. Wojo hit a three. Price hit another. Wojo made a steal and two free throws and the margin was back up to 50–37 when the whistle blew for the first TV time-out with exactly sixteen minutes to play.

They wobbled briefly and Villanova cut the gap to 10. But Price and Capel, the invisible men of the first seven games, came up with two big plays: a Price drive, followed by Price stealing the ball and feeding Capel, who went to the basket and made a tough off-balance layup while being fouled. Villanova called time with 9:54 left. The lead was 64–49.

It was almost eerie how similar the circumstances were to the Michigan game. Just under ten minutes left and the lead was 15. Against Michigan it had been 12. A lot of coaches would have steered clear of any memories of the debacle. Krzyzewski has always believed that failure makes people stronger.

"Fate is funny," he said during the time-out. He turned and pointed at the scoreboard. "This is Michigan all over again, isn't it? Ten minutes to go and we're in control. Only now, we're going to kill them. We're better now than we were then."

He was right. Every time Villanova tried to make a move, Duke had an answer. A Malik Allen layup got the margin to 10, but Langdon hit three free throws. Villanova fouled down the stretch and Duke never blinked. The final was 87–79, only because Thomas, the heralded freshman who had been held in check almost all day, made a meaningless three in the final seconds. It really wasn't that close.

The locker room was jubilant. There were hugs, the kind usually reserved for late in the season, but after the week they had been through, they were appropriate. Krzyzewski, a huge smile on his face, walked in and wrote one word on the board again: FUN.

"Now," he said, "do you see what I was talking about?"

They did. "It couldn't have worked out better, guys. Not only did we win, but we dealt with that Michigan ghost right away. That's why I brought it up. We're better now because of Michigan. You see, sometimes in life, you have to embrace adversity." He paused, then smiled. "You just don't want to become too intimate with the sonofabitch."

Krzyzewski was thrilled. Price had scored 17 points and Capel 13, easily their best performances of the season. Wojciechowski had dealt with his foul problems and finished with 13 points and eight assists. More important than any numbers, they had beaten a quality team on the road and done it emphatically. "That may be the best game we've played in three years," he said. "At the very least, it was as important a game as we've played in three years. Now we know we can beat quality teams. Before today, I don't think these kids were convinced they could do that."

It was important for the kids. But as Krzyzewski stood talking to friends afterward, an ear-to-ear grin on his face, it was apparent that it was equally important to the coach.

9

School Days

JEFF JONES stared at the plate of food in front of him as if that act would somehow transfer it to his body and give him the nourishment he was going to need for the next few hours. When that didn't work, he picked at it for a few minutes, pushing a couple of bites of chicken into his mouth. Finally, he gave up.

"OK, fellas, give your attention to Coach Herrmann."

Pete Herrmann, Virginia's part-time assistant coach, pushed back from his chair and began handing out scouting reports. The cover sheet said:

LIBERTY

DECEMBER 18, 1996

It was followed by fourteen pages that Herrmann had compiled in preparation for the game. Each Liberty player had been broken down individually. There were diagrams of their offensive sets and their defensive sets; diagrams of out-of-bounds plays; and, finally, team statistics and a box score from Liberty's most recent game, an 84–70 victory over Howard.

Each time Virginia played a game, Herrmann prepared a scouting report just like this one. That was the way it had been at Virginia since the Terry Holland era, the part-time assistant coach preparing and giving the scouting report. For years, the job had fallen to Tom Perrin. Now, though, Perrin was a full-time assistant and the scouting duties fell to Herrmann, an intense, fiery man who had been the head coach at the Naval Academy during David Robinson's senior year.

As Herrmann got up to talk, Jones sat back in his chair. He had been listening to scouting reports like this since 1978. In many ways, little had changed since that fall when he arrived at Virginia, a wide-eyed kid from Owensboro, Kentucky, who had been so shy in high school that his father had once offered him ten dollars if he would ask a girl out on a date.

Back then, pregame meals had been served in the back room of the Aberdeen Barn, the exact same spot where this pregame meal was being served. Back then, the part-time assistant coach gave the scouting report, just as Herrmann was doing now. And back then, Jones had to force himself to eat, knowing that he needed nourishment with the game four hours away but also knowing that his nervous stomach would make it very difficult to keep more than a few bites down.

There were pictures on the wall of the young Jones, wearing his orange-and-white Virginia uniform, the number 24 on the back, brown hair flying as he raced down the floor. Jones had been a good player on good teams, perhaps the best teams in Virginia history. The Cavaliers, led by Ralph Sampson, had gone to the Final Four in 1981 — Jones's junior year — and had lost in the Sweet Sixteen his senior year when his backcourt mate Othell Wilson was injured in the ACC tournament.

That loss had torn Jones up. He was angry and depressed. For days, he had trouble talking to people. He just wanted to get off by himself and try to forget what had happened. Shortly after that game, someone had asked Virginia coach Terry Holland how he thought Jones, the only starting senior on that team, would handle having his career end on such a down note.

"J.J. will handle it," Holland said. "J.J.'s a rock."

But J.J. wasn't a rock. Even Holland, who knew him as well as anyone on the Virginia campus, didn't understand that. Just as Holland's stoic demeanor hid a constantly churning stomach that would eventually land him in the hospital near the end of his coaching career, Jones had a poker face too. Years later, a Virginia newspaper would do a cartoon depicting all the varying emotions of Jeff Jones, ranging from joy to anger to grief to glee. The look on his face never changed.

"A lot of times," he said, "people don't really get what's going on with me. When I read that quote from Coach Holland years ago, I laughed. I was about as far from being a rock as you possibly could be."

Fifteen years later, a lot had changed. And, as with the pregame meals, a lot had not. Jones was still working for Holland, only now he sat in Holland's old seat as Virginia's coach and Holland was the school's athletic director. By now, Holland had figured out that J.J. wasn't quite the rock he had once thought he was. But that didn't mean Jones was sitting in his old coach's office pouring his heart out.

"You know there's a lot there," Holland said. "But sometimes you have to pull it out of him."

Looking at Jones as he sat listening to Herrmann, one might have thought the most pressing concern in his life at the moment was his team's ability to stop Peter Aluma, Liberty's leading scorer, that evening. Jones could only wish his life was that simple.

At thirty-six, he had the same boyish features as he had when he was still in uniform. He was heavier, constantly starting exercise regimens, then abandoning them, but his hair was still brown and only a close-up look revealed any lines on his face.

Inside, though, Jeff Jones was churning away. The last year of his life had been complicated and difficult. He and his wife, Lisa, were going through a divorce that had become the subject of all sorts of gossip in Charlottesville, the kind that is unavoidable when you are the basketball coach at the college that is the centerpiece of life in a college town. Ironically, George Welsh, Virginia's football coach, was also going through a gossip-filled divorce. One rumor in town had it that Welsh and Jones, who were separated by twenty years and entirely different approaches to life, were sharing a bachelor pad.

That one Jones could laugh at. Some of the others weren't so funny, especially when he realized that his three children, who were now eight, six, and three, were bound to hear some of them.

Jones had learned to deal with all that. He and Lisa had been separated for two and a half years. He had figured out that while it might be all right for most separated men to be out socially, it wasn't all right for a separated man who coached the Virginia basketball team to be out socially. So he had stopped going out.

His refuge had been his team. In 1995, when the rumors about his marriage had been swirling like the snow in the Virginia mountains, the Cavaliers had gone 25–9, tied for the ACC regular season title, and reached the Elite Eight of the NCAA tournament. That performance made Jones, at thirty-four, a hot young coach. In five years at UVA he had won 105 games — an average of 21 a year — and had kept Virginia competitive in the country's most competitive league.

But the next season had been a complete disaster. Not only had Virginia stumbled to a 12–15 record — only the school's second losing record in twenty years — but there had been a series of embarrassing incidents off the court, including two players being picked up for shoplifting; an incoming recruit's jailing after a pickup basketball game had somehow led him to severely slash an opponent with a knife; and finally, star guard Harold Deane's arrest after a scuffle with police at a party.

Someone had asked Jones late in the season — even before the Deane arrest — if he would try to forget the season quickly.

"I doubt very much that I'll forget this season anytime soon," Jones answered.

Melvin Whitaker, the recruit who had been involved in the slashing incident, had been convicted of malicious wounding. Instead of being Virginia's starting center, or at least a major contributor as had been projected, he was in jail. Deane, who had been suspended from the team after the party incident, was now back as the starting point guard. Jeff and Lisa Jones were waiting for the final details on Jeff's Reebok contract to be worked out before they signed their divorce papers.

And Jeff Jones, the hot young coach of 1995, had two years left on his contract and an uncertain future at a school he had been a part of for eighteen of his thirty-six years. Nine months earlier, at the end of the season, he had finally gone to see a doctor after the stomach pains that had plagued him all winter forced him to walk out of an NCAA tournament game in Richmond doubled over in pain.

"Maybe it was seeing the tournament going on without us that did it," he said. The doctors couldn't find anything wrong. Other than the usual pregame butterflies, Jones hadn't had any problems so far in the new season. But the Cavaliers had only played eight games.

They had played well on the trip to Hawaii but hadn't been as sharp since then. Jones had been distressed by the way they had lost their conference opener to Clemson, a come-from-ahead, 62–52 loss at home. The Cavaliers had led the game 27–19 at halftime and still had a nine-point lead after a Deane three pointer with 12:53 left. Clemson dominated from that point on, outscoring UVA 37–18 the rest of the way.

"What bothered me more than anything was that they were just tougher than we were," Jones said. "When we're good, we win games like that. We like close, hard-nosed games, at least we used to. In that game, when things got tight, Greg Buckner was tougher than our guys every single time. That's not a good sign."

Jones was very aware of good signs and bad ones at this stage of the season. Although Virginia had played reasonably well the previous December, Jones had been very concerned about what he was seeing. When he tried to tell the beat writers covering the team that he was uncomfortable with the way the team was playing, they had shrugged his skepticism off as coachspeak. Unfortunately, Jones's gut — which was paining him in both a literal and figurative sense — had turned out to be correct.

He wasn't sure just yet how he felt about this team. The best news was that Deane seemed back to being the player he had been his first two seasons, a hard-nosed floor leader willing to take important shots down the stretch, and the defense had been very good at times. "Even though we didn't maintain it, we played thirty minutes of very good defense against Clemson," Jones said. "If we can do that consistently, we'll be OK."

There were, however, other concerns.

Virginia's most talented player was sophomore guard Courtney Alexander, a gifted shooter who put the ball so far behind his head when he took his leaning backwards jump shot that it was unblockable. That meant when he was on he was virtually unstoppable. But Alexander didn't always appear that interested, especially on defense. There were already rumors that he was planning on leaving early for the NBA, rumors that Jones dismissed because he thought Alexander's game was a long, long way from the NBA level. Of course, that hadn't kept other college players from leaving early.

What's more, no one had really established themselves inside. Norman Nolan, the six-foot-eight junior from Baltimore, had the most experience and the most game, but he was having serious problems finding the basket. Freshman Colin Ducharme had potential and seven-four Chase Metheney had height. Jones had hoped that six-ten Australian Craig McAndrew would be able to help right away, but he had lost seven games because of an eligibility tussle with the NCAA over a brief stint he had done with an Australian pro team. Sophomore transfer Monte Marcaccini played as hard as anyone on the team, but he was just six five, and Kris Hunter, another freshman, had plenty of athletic ability and raw potential but was still learning how to play.

Jones felt a little bit like a mad scientist, mixing different things in the pot, hoping something good would eventually bubble up. There were five games left before ACC play began. Four were at home: Liberty, Maryland Baltimore County, Delaware, and Loyola-Baltimore, all games the Cavaliers should win comfortably unless they completely forgot to show up. In between UMBC and Delaware was a trip to Connecticut that everyone was dreading, not so much because UConn had beaten the Cavaliers by 41 and by 30 in their last two meetings, but because it was two days before Christmas and because the trip there a year ago had been one of the bumpiest plane rides on record and had taken forever because of the bad weather and headwinds.

That trip was in the back of Jones's mind as he sat in his team's meeting room, reading a game program to kill time prior to tipoff. Because the locker room itself is so narrow in University Hall, the team meets in a separate room before, during, and after games. Jones will often sit there by himself while the team warms up, reading anything he can find or, occasionally, closing his eyes to try and relax.

He didn't feel the least bit relaxed about this game. His concern wasn't really losing, although every coach facing a major underdog worries at least a little bit about lightning striking. If another ACC team had been playing Liberty that night, the thought would never cross Jones's mind that an upset could happen. When it is your team playing, the mind-set is different. That is especially true at Virginia, since the Cavaliers were the victims, in December of 1982, of what may be the biggest upset in the history of college basketball. On that night, in Hawaii, the top-ranked Cavaliers, led by Ralph Sampson, were beaten by Chaminade University. It was a game scheduled largely as an excuse to stop over in Hawaii en route home from two games in Japan. Jones had been a graduate assistant on that team. To this day, when coaches want to bring up a game that is proof of the "on any given night" theory, they bring up Virginia-Chaminade.

Even so, Jones didn't give an upset more than a few seconds of serious thought. The point of this game was to get better, to come out of it with confidence going into the Connecticut game. The two games after UConn were, like this one, warm-ups for the ACC, a time to solidify a rotation and get into the best possible frame of mind for ACC play.

For most of his life, Jones had enjoyed the challenges provided to him by basketball. His dad had been an athlete, both a basketball and baseball player at Georgetown College of Kentucky. While he was at Georgetown, Bob Jones had married his high school sweetheart, Carol Trotter. Their first child, Jeff, was born in June of 1960. In spite of his genes, he didn't start off life as a likely candidate for athletic stardom. Before he was two, he had to wear thick horn-rimmed glasses because of a lazy left eye and special shoes because he was severely pigeon-toed. It wasn't until high school that he could wear regular sneakers to school.

Even so, athletics were a big part of Jeff's life almost from the start. Bob Jones went into coaching after graduation, first as an assistant at Georgetown, then as a high school coach, and then back to college coaching at Kentucky Wesleyan in Owensboro. Jeff was always around ballplayers and teams and was drawn to the games they played.

By high school, he had eliminated football and baseball from his repertoire because he was good enough to make the varsity in basketball as a freshman. By the time he was a sophomore, he could dunk the ball at six two and was the best player on the Apollo High School team. Recruiting started later in those days, but the letters started coming in during his junior year. Jones was interested in schools like Louisville and Evansville, but not Kentucky. He had too many memories of his father's players, many of whom were black, telling him that they would have liked to have played for Kentucky but couldn't because Adolph Rupp wouldn't recruit black players.

He wasn't exactly enamored with the ACC either. "I always thought it was a wimp league," he said. "All that four corners [Dean Smith's delay offense] stuff. It wasn't basketball as far as I was concerned. The Big Ten and the SEC, now that was basketball."

Jones may not have liked the ACC, but the ACC liked him. Maryland, Virginia, and North Carolina were all interested. By then, he was six four and the point guard on an undefeated team. He also had a 3.7 GPA and just under 1200 on the college boards, making him the kind of player almost anyone would want to recruit.

Maryland dropped out of the race early because it had a commitment from another point guard, Reggie Jackson. Jones had put off all recruiting visits until after his season was over because his father had been in the hospital all season, fighting a mystery infection that left him so ill that he lost close to one hundred pounds. For a while, it had looked as if he might die. Carol Jones was spending a lot of nights at the hospital because the winter weather made driving home late treacherous. That left Jeff in charge of his brother and sister at home.

"I got to a point where I just said, 'Forget this' about the recruiting process," he said. "I couldn't deal with basketball and school and Dad and taking care of Doug and Kelly, even though they were teenagers" — fifteen and thirteen — "and I didn't have to do all that much. It was still more than I could handle."

By the time March rolled around, Bob Jones had been to the Mayo Clinic and, even though the doctors still didn't know exactly what had happened to him — one theory was Legionnaires' disease — he was well enough to come home. By now, Jeff had narrowed his choice to Virginia and North Carolina, although Western Kentucky probably could have had him if it had made any effort, since his first serious girlfriend was a freshman there.

Jones was interested in Virginia because there was a Kentucky connection there: Terry Holland had recruited both Jeff Lamp and Lee Raker out of Louisville's Ballard High School the year before, and in one of those coincidences that seems to occur when star players are involved, their coach, Richard Schmidt, had been hired at UVA as an assistant. Their presence at a school Jones knew almost nothing about intrigued him.

He knew plenty about North Carolina, especially about Dean Smith, who was a legend even then, in the late seventies. It was exciting when first

Eddie Fogler, then Bill Guthridge, turned up to see him play. Then word got around that Smith was coming to visit. By then, the season was over and Jones was playing pickup games with friends after school each afternoon. On the day that Smith came to watch, one of his friends, a college senior, kept knocking Jones down every time he tried to make a move to the basket.

"I finally got up and yelled at him, 'You're out of eligibility! Cool it!' "

Perhaps Smith liked seeing Jones keep getting back up after getting knocked down. In any event, he left convinced he wanted him. Jones made plans to visit North Carolina and Virginia. The visit to Chapel Hill overwhelmed him. Carolina sent Fogler down in a Lear jet to pick him up, and when Smith met them at the airport, he was driving a Cadillac that had a car phone. This was 1978. Jones had never seen a car phone, much less been in a car that had one. He enjoyed the weekend and the Carolina players. He ate bagels and lox for the first time in his life when he went to Smith's house for Sunday breakfast. For all he knew they had been flown in from New York just for him.

When he left, he was convinced he was going to Carolina. But he still had a visit to make to Virginia. He wasn't as overwhelmed there as he had been at Carolina. But he did hit it off with Lamp, Raker, and Schmidt — especially Lamp. "I just felt comfortable around those guys," he said. "Maybe it was the Kentucky background, I'm not sure. But my gut feeling when I left was that I had probably had more fun at Carolina, but I was more comfortable at Virginia."

A few nights later, he chose Virginia. Telling Smith was the hardest part.

Jones ended up starting throughout most of his freshman year and played solidly on a rapidly improving team. But it was a traumatic year for him. Shortly after Christmas, he was sitting in the suite he shared with several people when the phone rang. It was his parents — both of them. They had news: they were splitting.

"It was pretty devastating," Jones remembered. "My first thought was that it was something I had done wrong, that I should have stayed closer to home to go to school or maybe even gone to Kentucky Wesleyan to play for Dad after he had missed all that time. I never saw it coming. It hit me hard."

Of course he didn't tell anyone how hard it had hit him. That night, he hung up the phone and went out into the cold night to shoot some baskets by himself on an outdoor basket. It wasn't until several hours later, when one of his suite mates came out and asked him what the hell he was doing, that he thought to come back inside. The next day Holland, who had also gotten a call from Bob and Carol Jones, called him into his office to ask him if there was anything he could do.

"I'm OK," Jones told his coach. "Really, I'm just fine."

J.J. was a rock. At least on the outside.

His last three years at Virginia, Jones played on great teams, due in no small part to Ralph Sampson's decision to stay in his home state to attend college. Jones was home on spring break when he heard Sampson had decided to go to Virginia. "It was on live television in Owensboro," he said, "because everyone down there thought he was going to Kentucky. I remember running out of the house and screaming, 'Yes!' It was a very personal thing. I thought with Ralph we could be great. I also didn't want to lose him to Kentucky."

Virginia struggled for much of the next season, failing to make the NCAA tournament, with everyone expecting Sampson to be Samson. They did win the NIT, then started the next season with twenty-three straight wins. That team made it to the Final Four, before losing to a North Carolina team that it had beaten twice in the regular season. A year later, the Cavaliers won thirty games, but, forced to play Alabama-Birmingham on its home floor without Othell Wilson in the round of sixteen, they lost, 68–66.

Once Jones got over that disappointment, he had to decide what he wanted to do with his life. He had gotten married the previous summer to Lisa O'Donnell. They had met when Jeff was a freshman and had started dating when he was a sophomore. About three dates into the relationship, Jeff was convinced he wanted to get married. They were engaged the following summer and married a year later.

Jones had never given any serious thought to coaching. Following his dad's career had been sobering. Bob Jones had been a part of two Division II national championship teams at Kentucky Wesleyan as an assistant coach and had won the national championship in his first year as head coach in 1973. But recruiting had been hurt during the year he was ill and the team had never fully recovered. In 1980, two years after the illness, Bob Jones was fired.

"It certainly made me realistic about coaching," his son said, years later. "I've always understood that no one remembers or cares what you've done in the past. All they want to know is, not even what you've done lately, but what you're doing *now*. And, what you're going to do in the future. But when I graduated from college, I wasn't thinking in those terms. I was thinking about being a ballplayer."

He was smart enough to know that he was no lock to play in the NBA. And he didn't want to spend a lot of time knocking around in minor leagues. So, when Holland told him he could have a job as a graduate assistant that fall if he didn't make an NBA roster, he accepted. He was in camp with both the Golden State Warriors and the Indiana Pacers and made it to the last cut with the Pacers. When he was finally cut, his coaching career was launched.

Although he moved quickly up the ladder from grad assistant to part-timer to full-time assistant in just four years, no one — Holland included — dreamed that he would be Holland's successor. Initially, Holland had hoped that Athletic Director Jim Copeland would commit the job to Dave Odom in the spring of 1989. When Copeland balked at that and Odom went to Wake Forest, the job was thrown wide open. By the middle of the next season, Holland had become convinced that Jones, even though he was only twenty-nine, was the right man for the job.

"I was so sold that I seriously considered resigning before the ACC season started so that J.J. would have to be allowed to take over the team," he said. "I was convinced he was ready. But then when I looked at our ACC schedule starting out, I thought there was a decent chance we could be 0–4 no matter who was coaching the team. And an 0–4 start probably would have sealed J.J.'s fate before he even had a chance to prove himself."

Holland proved prophetic. The Cavaliers did start 0–4 in the ACC although they bounced back to finish with 21 victories and made the second round of the NCAAs before losing at the buzzer to second-seeded Syracuse in the Southeast Regional. Holland left in triumph and Copeland began a national search for a coach.

He brought Mike Montgomery in from Stanford and asked Jones to be his tour guide. At first Jones was insulted. Then he realized that Copeland was hoping that Montgomery would like him enough to keep him on as his top assistant. After Montgomery left, Rick Barnes came in from Providence. Copeland offered him the job. That was when Holland asked Barnes to consider keeping his staff intact. Barnes had no intention of doing that but felt uncomfortable with the notion of jettisoning the staff of a very popular ex-coach. That, and Dave Gavitt's powers of persuasion, caused him to change his mind.

Jones had gotten a call from Holland the day after Barnes left town with Copeland's offer in hand. He wanted him to know what was going on before Barnes returned to Charlottesville for a press conference. Upset and angry, Jones did the only thing he could think to do: he got in his car and drove over to Richmond to look at some high school players in an AAU tournament. He wasn't sure why he was looking at them but he couldn't think of anything else to do.

As he sat and watched one of the games, he was joined on the bleachers by Richmond coach Dick Tarrant.

"So, I guess you heard about Barnes," Tarrant said.

"Yeah, I did," Jones said mournfully. "We're all pretty bummed out about it."

Tarrant gave Jones a funny look. "Are you sure you heard what I heard?"

"Barnes is taking the job," Jones said. "Coach Holland told me this morning."

"No," Tarrant said. "Barnes turned the job down. I just heard it driving over here."

Jones jumped to his feet. Was it possible? He excused himself from Tarrant and ran for a pay phone to call the basketball office. It was true. Barnes had said no. Suddenly a coach again, Jones forgot completely about watching any more games. He raced to his car — he still hadn't gotten to where Dean Smith was in 1978, so he had no car phone — and drove home as fast as possible. By the time he got to his house, there were twenty messages on his answering machine. The first nineteen were from reporters, all wanting to know if he thought this put him back into the running for the job. Jones had no idea. The twentieth message changed that. It was from Copeland. Could he meet with him the next morning?

Copeland needed to move fast. The Barnes about-face had been embarrassing for him, especially because he had been forced to admit that he had offered Barnes the job after he had pleaded with Barnes to say it hadn't been offered to him. The job had been open since the previous June. It was now April. Dave Odom was at Wake Forest, Mike Montgomery at Stanford, Rick Barnes at Providence. And Terry Holland's office was empty while everyone else in the country was on the recruiting trail.

Two days later, just prior to the basketball banquet, Copeland offered Jones the job. There was one stipulation: he couldn't tell anyone, even Holland, until Monday. There couldn't be any more leaks. Jones agreed, then spent the whole night jumping out of his skin wanting to tell people. When Holland asked him at a post-banquet farewell party if he had heard from Copeland, Jones just said, "I think we're going to talk again Monday."

Holland understood. "Good," he said, smiling.

Jones was ten weeks shy of thirty when he was introduced as the new Virginia coach. That made him the youngest head coach in the history of the ACC. Another ACC coach had been only thirty when signed — Dean Smith at North Carolina. But that had been two weeks after Jeffrey Thomas Jones turned one.

Jones's first five seasons at Virginia were about as good as anyone — even Jones — could have hoped for. The Cavaliers reached the NCAA tournament in four of those years and the only year they missed (1992) they went on to win the NIT. Virginia won 21, 20, 21, 18, and 25 games. In 1993, they reached the Sweet Sixteen and in 1995 they upset top-seeded Kansas in the Sweet Sixteen before losing to Arkansas, the defending national champions, one game short of the Final Four.

By then, every player in the program had been recruited by Jones, so no one could say he was winning with Holland's players. Copeland had given Jones a contract extension after the third season, so he was making considerably more than the $90,000 he had been paid initially. "I didn't mind being paid less than other ACC coaches at first because I had done less than they had done," he said. "But once I established that the program was still going to be pretty good, I thought I should be paid more. Fortunately, Jim agreed."

The new deal, which ran through the end of the 1998 season put Jones closer to $300,000, including his shoe deal and his camp. That was still a lot less than Dean Smith and Mike Krzyzewski made but more in the ballpark with the other coaches in the league. At least back then it was in the ballpark.

By the time the 1996–97 season started, Jones was back at the low end of the ACC pay scale. In addition to Smith and Krzyzewski, Gary Williams, Dave Odom, Bobby Cremins, and Pat Kennedy were all making more than $500,000 annually. Rick Barnes was making more than $400,000. Jones was in the same league as Herb Sendek, who was in his first year at NC State. He had already spoken to Holland, who had come back to UVA as athletic director in the spring of 1995, about a new deal. Holland had told him they would sit down at the end of the season.

Jones wasn't concerned with his contract situation. After all, he had only had one bad year in six. But in the back of his mind was the memory of what had happened to his father. He was also aware of the fact that politics could get ugly at UVA in a hurry. The breakup of his marriage had been viewed rather dimly by some of the old-line grads. Jeff and Lisa had actually split on June 29, 1994 — Jeff remembered the date because it was his thirty-fourth birthday.

The rumors had been whispers during the '94–95 season, quieted in part by the fact that Lisa still showed up at most games and by the fact that the Cavaliers were winning. But with the team losing the next winter and everyone in Charlottesville aware of the fact that Jeff was seeing other people — and all of them talking about that fact — the whispers had turned to roars. Jones knew that another losing season would not go over well with the faithful. He knew that even a good season wouldn't clear his name with some people. He and Lisa had an amicable separation and Jeff saw his kids often. He lived in a townhouse ten minutes away from Lisa and the kids and they often stayed overnight with him. That was one of many reasons why he had no desire to coach anyplace but Virginia.

The game against Liberty would be Jones's 196th as Virginia's coach. To most outsiders, he appeared to be the same stoic J.J. who had played point guard and then sat on Holland's bench for eight seasons. The only crack in that veneer had come in 1995, when Jones had gotten so upset with his team at halftime one night at Maryland that he put his fist through a blackboard, breaking his hand. "Given the way that season turned out, maybe I should do that more often," he said.

But the Jones the public saw, the one Holland thought he knew, was neither a rock nor a stoic. The stomach problems of the previous winter were evidence of that. What's more, Jones was convinced this was a team that needed to be pushed and prodded, that it could not be allowed to accept mediocrity, because if it did it could slide quickly in that direction. Jones did not want to go through another losing winter.

"I expect you guys to play for forty minutes tonight," he told his players after Herrmann had gone through the matchups one more time on the blackboard. "We have to establish some things. First, we have to make it clear to Liberty that this is our building and our game. But beyond that, we have to establish a tempo and play at that tempo, tonight and as we prepare for January."

He paused. "Now I know we're not going to have a wild sellout crowd out there" — the building was about half full and would sound like a morgue most of the evening — "but that doesn't matter. We generate our own enthusiasm right from the start."

He looked around the room to make sure he had everyone's attention. "OK then, everyone in his own way."

With that, he stood, head bowed, hands in his pockets in silent prayer for one minute. The silent prayer is a tradition left over from Holland, who first began a silent pregame prayer when he was at Davidson and was concerned that non-Christians on his team might find a Christian prayer offensive. Both of his former assistants who are now ACC coaches — Odom and Jones — ask their players to pray in their own way before each game. Some players remain still, eyes shut, for the entire minute. Others get up and begin to walk around. When Jones (or Odom) says, "Amen," it is time to head for the floor.

The basketball atmosphere in University Hall ranges from good to lousy, depending on the opposition. Big ACC games sell out and a UVA run will get the crowd going, but this is not a wild crowd. It is almost a dignified crowd, which fits with the image of the school — except in the old days when the only reason to go to a Virginia football game was the antics of the band at halftime. With Liberty in town and the students on break, U-Hall had all the atmosphere of a Florida shopping mall on a July afternoon.

Still, the Cavaliers played reasonably well the first twenty minutes. Jones wasn't terribly happy when a jump shot by Liberty point guard

Marcus White cut his team's margin to 27–21 with 4:22 left. He called a twenty-second time-out and got into his players faces in no uncertain terms. They responded, outscoring the Flames 12–2 the rest of the half for a comfortable 39–23 lead.

Jones was anything but comfortable. He was angry. They had played as hard as they needed to — nothing more. "That was a sorry effort!" he screamed. "Sorry! If you played the first sixteen minutes like the last four, the game's over. I am sick and tired of having to yell at you guys to get you to play! You're on cruise control. No one is in a stance. Jamal, Courtney, just step up to the line and make your free throws. You're good shooters, quit worrying about things and shoot the ball. You guys off the bench come in and *you* don't play hard. How is that possible?

"It's all in your heads, fellas. You've got plenty of talent. You just aren't using it."

Jones was trying to send a message. He knew his team was going to need to perform at a higher level not only against Connecticut but in ACC play. He didn't want to wait until after a couple of losses in January for them to realize it.

But the second half was no better than the first. In many ways, it was worse. Liberty actually closed to within 43–39, forcing Jones to call time-out and plead with his players not to panic. A Curtis Staples three and a Deane steal got things back under control, but the Cavaliers were lurching and stalling the rest of the night. Only in the last five minutes did they finally pull away, but even then, there was trouble. With 2:37 left in the game, Courtney Alexander went up for a three-point try with the 35-second clock running down. The shot was late and wouldn't have counted if it had gone in. No one really cared about that. What they did care about was the sight of Alexander crumpled on the ground, clutching at his left ankle. He had come down on somebody's foot and had sprained the ankle. He was helped off the floor. Trainer Ethan Saliba's initial diagnosis was a sprain, but there was no way to tell how serious it was until the next day. Knowing that Alexander did not have the highest threshold of pain in the world, the coaches were pretty convinced he wouldn't be back soon enough to play against Connecticut in five days.

The final was 67–54. Jones wasn't angry, just frustrated. "We don't expect you to be perfect," he told the players. "But you have to come a lot damn closer than this. We're playing a game Saturday" — Maryland Baltimore County — "we're supposed to win. Forget one game at a time. We have a very tough game coming up Monday at UConn. That's a chance to beat a good team on the road. We'll have to be a lot sharper than this, though. A lot sharper."

His comments to the media were much calmer than those to the players. They had been sloppy, yes, but there had been progress. Alexander had played well before he had gotten hurt; Staples had shot the ball well; Nolan had made some progress. They would just have to wait and see about Alexander's injury in the morning.

His voice in the press conference was a monotone. It had been a routine night, another brick in the preseason wall. No big deal, one way or the other. They would come back in forty-eight hours for another game just like it against UMBC.

As always, win or lose, early season or late season, J.J. was a rock.

Or so it seemed.

10

Deck the Halls

CHRISTMAS WEEK is always a difficult one for basketball teams and basketball coaches. Basketball players don't get holiday breaks the way most college students do. Everyone plays on Thanksgiving weekend, often on the road. In 1996, for example, Duke had spent Thanksgiving in New York, Virginia had spent it in Hawaii, and Clemson had been in Puerto Rico. The ACC teams that didn't travel all played on either Friday or Saturday. No one spent Thanksgiving at home.

At Christmas, almost all coaches make a concerted effort to get their players home for a few days. Exams are over and the campuses are depressingly empty. It is one thing to be on an empty campus for four days at Thanksgiving, it is quite another to do so for four weeks during Christmas and New Year's.

"You have to get them out of here for at least a little while," Dave Odom said. "Otherwise, they'd go crazy, you'd go crazy, and you'd walk into January feeling exhausted and wrung out. That's not what you want."

That doesn't mean coaches see Christmas break as a vacation period. Just the opposite. Since there are no classes to worry about and the NCAA rules that restrict teams to twenty hours of practice time a week are not in force, most coaches practice twice a day during the break. Since teams have played several games by then, coaches know what their teams' strengths and weaknesses are and what they need to focus on.

No coach took the Christmas break more seriously than Odom. To him, it was almost like a second round of preseason practice. He had turned down a chance to take his Wake Forest team to Spain over the break even though he would have loved to have given Ricky Peral a chance to play in front of his countrymen. Making the trip would have meant having no chance to go home for the players at all and it might have meant going to Utah for a New Year's Eve TV game with a case of jet lag. A lot more would get done by staying in Winston-Salem and getting everyone home for five days before the trip west.

Odom had pieced his schedule together carefully, scheduling only one game between December 14 (UMass at home) and December 31. That would give him plenty of time for extra work and a break. If he had any regret about his first semester schedule it was that the two nonconference games he had thought would challenge his team had not. Mississippi State and UMass had both been Final Four teams in 1996 and if they had returned all the players they were supposed to return, they would have been formidable again. But Mississippi State had lost its two best players to the NBA draft and its point guard to a jail sentence. UMass lost the national player of the year, Marcus Camby, also to the draft. A year earlier in a game at UMass, Camby had outplayed Tim Duncan and the Minutemen had won easily. Now, with Camby gone, Wake jumped to a big early lead and cruised to an easy victory. Odom had been hoping for more.

He had no such thoughts about the last game before Christmas break — a Saturday afternoon game against Campbell. If the Camels played a perfect game and Wake played a perfectly awful game, the Deacons might win by only ten. It was a classic early-season mismatch. But that didn't mean there were not important things going on at Wake Forest during that weekend.

First — and foremost — was the annual Christmas party at the Odoms': "It doesn't get any bigger than this," said Odom, repeating one of his favorite phrases. The party had become an annual highlight in the schedule in large part because of the gag gifts the assistant coaches bought for the players. Odom was a little concerned about this year's gift-buying. The man who had perfected the art of the gag gift, Jerry Wainwright, had departed two years earlier to become the head coach at North Carolina–Wilmington. A year earlier, veteran assistants Ernie Nestor and Ricky Stokes had filled in admirably for Wainwright. This year Nestor and Stokes both had to be at high school games on the night of the party and the weight of buying and, just as important, presenting the gifts had fallen to Odom's two young coaches, part-timer Russell Turner and administrative assistant Bill Old.

"Lot of pressure," Odom said. "I hope they can handle it."

They could. Turner and Old had put considerable time and thought into the challenge presented them. They had gone so far as to buy multiple gifts for several key players.

Duncan, the team's superstar, made out better than any of his teammates — which, everyone agreed, was as it should be. For being a good boy all year, Duncan received:

- A pair of sleeves — since none of his shirts had them.
- A fake ID — guaranteed to get him into bars before his twenty-first birthday in late April.
- A pair of pom-poms, since his favorite thing in life was to sit on the bench and lead cheers for his housemate, Mark Scott.
- And most touching of all, a nose ring, an autographed picture, and a letter from his counterpart at Duke, Greg Newton. A year earlier, after Duncan had made every key basket down the stretch to beat Duke in Cameron Indoor Stadium, Newton had said afterward that Duncan wasn't really all that good, that he "floated" (didn't play hard) a lot of the game. When Duncan had been asked for a response, he smiled and said, "Peace to him. He's the best player I've ever seen." Newton wore earrings in, among other places, his navel, his eyebrow, and his tongue. Given Duncan's tremendous respect for Newton, the gifts clearly meant a lot to him.

Duncan was not the only one to receive more than one gift. Peral, who had trouble remembering to shave, received a shaving calendar. He also got an "American" kit that included a bandana, a football, a Travis Tritt tape, and a "Born in the USA" T-shirt. The other senior starter, Sean Allen, got a can of wood finish, to help him "finish" his moves in the lane. Mark Scott, who had broken every Wake Forest record for parking tickets, received a handicapped license plate. Steve Goolsby, whose car had been towed several times, received a miniature police car and tow truck. Joseph Amonett, who had announced that he planned to ask his girlfriend to marry him over break, received a book on a thousand and one ways to propose. Freshman Loren Woods received a pacifier in honor of his constant whining and a tape on how to tell time to help him make it to practice and meetings on time. And walk-on senior Kenny Herbst was presented with a yarmulke, which was then retired to honor the fact that he was the second-leading Jewish scorer in school history. The all-time leader, Ronny Watts, had scored 1,069 points and graduated in 1965. Herbst entered the season only 1,065 points behind Watts.

No one was spared — including the head coach. Once all the players had received their presents, Duncan and the other seniors handed Odom a box. On it was a note. "Coach, we wanted to give you something that no one in college basketball has," it said. "Major league baseball has this now and so do the NBA and the NFL. But it doesn't exist anyplace in college basketball."

Inside the box was a baseball cap. The front of the cap said simply: "$512,000." That was Odom's published salary since the signing of his new contract. Odom's gift was a salary cap. He would wear it proudly: around the house, at practice — anyplace where no one outside family, friends, and team members was around.

There was also business to conduct that night. The party broke up at around nine, which meant the players had an hour free before they had to report back for their night-before walk-through and meeting. Every coach approaches game preparation differently. Most coaches nowadays believe in at least one meeting and one walk-through of an opponent's offense and defense. The most notable exception to this rule among successful coaches is Dean Smith, who never walked through the opposition until four years ago and now only does it on occasion.

Odom likes to walk through everything twice: once the night before a game, then on the day of the game to reinforce anything that might have been forgotten. The night-before meeting is almost always at 10 o'clock.

That gives the players most of the evening free, but also makes it unlikely that they will do anything afterward, meaning they will get to bed at a reasonable hour.

The game with Campbell wasn't exactly circled in red on Wake's schedule, but Odom had put a good deal of time into preparing for it that week. He had surprised his players by putting in a new defense: full-court pressure. Wake almost never pressed. That wasn't Odom's style. He was a walk-it-up coach who liked to play half-court basketball at both ends of the court and beat you down with relentless execution, possession after possession. He knew that it was a potentially dangerous way for a power team to play because a low-possession game made it easier for an underdog to stay close and then have a chance to get hot late and pull an upset. But that was the way Odom was most comfortable. Nine of Wake's twenty-six victories a year earlier had been by four points or less. Only one of their six losses had been that close; in fact four of them had been by double digits. In short, the Deacons were a confident team in the endgame.

Odom was never going to be a pressing coach and he knew his players weren't suited mentally or physically to that style. But he also believed that to win the national championship there was going to come a night when his team was going to have to beat a full-court-pressure team. In both 1993 and 1996 Kentucky had thrown full-court pressure at the Deacons in the NCAA tournament, and both times they had crumbled: quickly the first time, gradually the second. Odom knew it was very possible his team would have to go through Kentucky at some point to win a title. He knew that practicing against pressure could only accomplish so much. Wake's second team, like all other second teams, just wasn't going to be as quick or as big or as talented as Kentucky's first team. The next best thing he thought he could do was have his own team press. "That way maybe they learn the mindset of a pressure team a little bit," he said. "I want them to have an understanding of how the other team is thinking when it's pressing us."

The other benefit of spending some time on a press was in case Wake had to use it in an important game later in the season because it had fallen behind. Odom was very curious to find out how his team would react to doing something new and different. He still wasn't certain if he had a handle on the group's emotional makeup. It was a veteran team — three seniors and two juniors started — that had accomplished a lot in the last two seasons. The players had won a lot of games and accomplished everything there was to accomplish except reach the Final Four. Odom wanted to be certain that they stayed interested and motivated throughout the regular season. He knew that sleepwalking through January and February and then trying to turn it on in March wouldn't work.

He was most aware of and concerned about the boredom factor with Duncan. Theirs was an almost unique relationship. Most coaches will lean on their seniors during a season and give them some say in the running of the team. Dean Smith consults with his seniors on everything from dress codes to halftime adjustments to how to travel. Rick Barnes will sometimes ask his seniors to critique the play of his underclassmen. Mike Krzyzewski will send seniors to talk to players who have been disciplined so they can explain why he got angry.

Odom and Duncan go beyond that. Their relationship is almost coach to assistant coach or friend to friend as much as it is coach to player. Almost from the first day of their relationship, Odom understood that Duncan was different from other basketball players. A lot of it has to do with Duncan's background: he grew up on St. Croix in the Virgin Islands and didn't really play any serious basketball until he was in high school. Prior to that he played some soccer and was a standout swimmer. But when he kept growing, reaching six nine by the time he was a high school sophomore, basketball became his main game. He attended Ohio State's basketball camp one summer, but was overlooked by the Ohio State coaches because he was so skinny and gangly and unpolished that they saw nothing special in him.

Odom first heard about him from Chris King, a standout forward on his first three teams, who had gone to the Virgin Islands to play for a U.S. junior team. When King came back from the trip, he went to see Odom to tell him how the trip had gone.

"So, did you see anyone we ought to recruit?" Odom asked jokingly.

"Yeah, one guy, maybe," King answered. "Real skinny kid we played against on St. Croix. Tell you what, though, he had some raw talent."

Odom was intrigued enough to make a few phone calls to see if anyone had heard of the kid. A couple of people had. Odom figured it was worth a trip. After all, the Virgin Islands wasn't that far away. Odom flew down and went to an outdoor court where he'd been told the best local players gathered to play each day. Odom sat down on a grassy knoll overlooking the court, looked down, and didn't see Duncan. He was about to get up to go and find out what had happened when Duncan appeared — sitting next to him.

"Stay calm, Coach," Duncan said. Then he explained the politics of street ball on St. Croix. When the word had gotten around that a big-shot American college coach was in town, everyone who had ever picked up a basketball on the island had shown up to play. Duncan was sixteen, which made him just about the youngest player on the court. "If I make them let me play the first game, they'll get upset and put me on a bad team," he said. "I'll lose and I won't get on the court for an hour. If I sit out the first game, though, I can pick my own team and once we get out there, we'll be there for a while."

That was Odom's introduction to Duncan's savvy. Duncan stood up to get ready to play. "One more thing, Coach."

"What's that?" Odom asked.

"I can play this game."

By day's end, Odom was sold. One other school was recruiting Duncan hard: Providence. Rick Barnes had been tipped about Duncan by the Ohio State coaches, and he and his assistants Dennis Felton and Larry Shyatt had been recruiting him even before Odom got to St. Croix. Duncan liked Barnes, Felton, and Shyatt a lot. He enjoyed Barnes's offbeat sense of humor and he got a kick out of Shyatt's intensity. When the fall rolled around, Duncan was ready to sign with Providence. He liked Odom and he liked Wake Forest, but Providence had been there first and, at that moment, he felt most comfortable going there.

But there was a problem. Providence didn't have a scholarship to offer. Barnes knew he was going to lose at least one player at the end of the season and he wanted to sign Duncan, then worry about finding a scholarship for him later. Providence said no. Duncan would have to wait until spring. Duncan didn't want to wait. Going to college in the states on a scholarship was a big deal for his family. His mother had died of cancer three years earlier and he knew how much it would have meant to her to see him go to college. He wanted a definite commitment, not someone saying, "We'll work it out." Wake offered a commitment. Duncan took it.

"Probably lucky for me in a lot of ways," he said later. "For one thing, I'd have frozen to death in Providence."

For another, he would only have played for Barnes there for one year. As impressed as Odom had been with Duncan, he still considered him a project. He even thought about redshirting him as a freshman. For one thing, he was only seventeen when he showed up on campus. For another, he was still rail thin and an extra year of development could only help. What's more, the ACC in 1993–94 was loaded with big, strong, tough, mean centers. The league had five centers who would go on to be first round draft picks: Joe Smith (number one in the '95 draft); Rasheed Wallace (number four that year); Sharone Wright (number six in '94); Cherokee Parks (number twelve in '95); and Todd Fuller (number eleven in 1996). Odom was afraid Duncan might get eaten alive before his eighteenth birthday.

Once practice began, though, it was obvious that Duncan was much too good to be redshirted. "The coaches told me I had better be ready to go or my tropical butt was going to get cooked," he remembered. "They weren't kidding."

Actually, he did just fine. He averaged 9.8 points and 9.6 rebounds a game. He also blocked just under four shots a game and was an intimidating presence inside throughout the second half of the season. It was almost scary how quickly he picked things up, improving on an almost daily basis. That was just the beginning. A year later, he averaged 16.8 points and 12.5 rebounds. By then, even though he was still just eighteen when the season ended, the pro scouts were salivating. If he had chosen to turn pro that year, he probably would have been the first pick in the draft — ahead of Brown and Wallace and well ahead of Parks — because his potential appeared to be unlimited. He was even better as a junior, when he would have been a lock number one pick.

He had come back for his senior year because he liked college. Duncan wasn't like kids who had grown up in the States dreaming of having their own shoe line or making millions of dollars. He was eager to test himself against the best players, but, especially at twenty, didn't see any need to rush into it.

Odom knew that Duncan enjoyed being around his teammates and the college atmosphere. But he also sensed that he was wearying of all that came with stardom. By coming back as a senior, Duncan had unwittingly turned himself into a symbol. He was the shining light in the darkness that surrounded a game being eaten up by defections to the pros. He was the role model, the good kid who put education ahead of money. In truth, Duncan just wanted to have a good time. He didn't see himself as a role model or a shining beacon for education. All the questions about his decision to come back bored him. On occasion, Odom sensed, practice bored him too.

So, he tried to do things to make it more fun. He told Duncan to range outside more on offense, to play facing the basket more often. He had spent three years camped in the low post, but now with seven-foot-one freshman Loren Woods on the team, he didn't have to do that all the time. Like most big men, Duncan believed he was a guard stuck in a center's body and he liked nothing more than running the break, making a pass on the wing, or pulling up to shoot a three pointer. It might not be the most effective way for him to play, and he was bound to make mistakes trying to do an imitation of point guard Tony Rutland, but Odom wasn't going to stop him. If he enjoyed it, if it made practice something for him to look forward to, then it was just fine with him.

"I owe him that," Odom said, wearing his salary cap into the Friday night Campbell walk-through. "He's given us too much and me too much for me not to let him work on developing other parts of his game. And if it makes the season go faster for him, then maybe he feels fresher in March and we all benefit."

Clearly, even though Odom wanted to build this team the way he built all his teams, piece by piece and game by game, part of him was thinking down the road to March. The present was precious, he would tell the players that almost every day, but preparing for the future was also very important.

That was why Odom was so happy after the Campbell game. If there had ever been a game set up for a sloppy performance, this was it. For a pre-Christmas Saturday, the 11,279 in the Lawrence Joel Coliseum (about 3,000 shy of capacity) was an excellent crowd, but it was hardly an electric one. Odom knew most of the players had airplane flights on their minds and were probably more excited about getting home than playing the game.

He had made certain that Russell Turner, who had scouted Campbell, had made the scouting report every bit as detailed as a scouting report for North Carolina or Duke would be: there were detailed descriptions of every Campbell player's strengths and weaknesses; a summation of the offense and the defense; and, at the bottom of the report, the four keys to victory. That was followed by all the usual diagrams and statistics. The message was clear: the coaching staff was taking this game very seriously.

And then Odom blew up the entire plan. After Turner had carefully written the scouting report on the board in the team's meeting room so that he could go through the matchups one last time, Odom complimented him on his work. "Just don't get mad at me when the players come in here," Odom said.

Then, as soon as they had walked in and taken their seats, Odom walked to the board and dramatically erased all of Turner's hard work.

"Why did I do that?" Odom asked rhetorically. (Odom is the king of rhetorical questions: Am I pleased? Yes. Can we play better? Yes. Do I think our offense is playing up to its potential? No.) "I did it because none of it really matters. That's not because Coach Turner didn't do a good job scouting these guys. But the fact is, this game is about us. How we play. How we respond to all the distractions. I know most of you have one foot on the airplane. I understand that. But this is the kind of game we may look back on late in the season as an important one. Why? Not because of the outcome. Is it possible for this team to beat us? Yes. Is it very likely? No. Not at all. But what we have the chance to do today is take a step towards becoming a great team. Are we a great team right now? No. Do we have the ingredients in this room to become a great team? I think so. Today, we'll find out a lot about ourselves. A lot."

What they found out was that this was a very mature group. The game was over almost before it started. The Deacons led 21–4 early and 48–27 at halftime. The margin could have been whatever Odom wanted it to be, but he made sure to get everyone in the game. Duncan scored 22 points and had 15 rebounds in 25 minutes, then spent the last nine minutes working his pom-poms for Mark Scott and the walk-ons. The final was 93–50.

Odom sent the players home with one last rhetorical question: "Am I pleased with where we are right now? Yes. Very much so."

Wake Forest was 8–0. It was ranked number two in the country behind Kansas. Christmas at the Odoms' would be very pleasant.

11

Struggling

FOR THE 1,109TH TIME in his life, Dean Smith sat on a bench designated for the University of North Carolina watching a team he was responsible for go through warm-ups. It was the first Saturday in January, and around him, the Lawrence Joel Coliseum was shaking with noise and glee as Wake Forest's fans worked themselves into their annual Carolina frenzy.

"Whether you want to admit it or not," Dave Odom had said driving to the arena that night, "the air feels different when they come to town."

Coaches love to claim that all games are the same. All victories only count once; the same for all losses. But they all know there are games and there are *games*. For more than thirty years now any game involving Dean Smith has been a *game*. That's because he has built one of the great dynasties in the history of sports in the thirty-six years that he has been in charge of Carolina basketball. The Tar Heels don't always win, but they do always contend.

John Wooden won more national championships — a lot more, ten to Smith's two — and Bob Knight has won three. Mike Krzyzewski and

Denny Crum, among current coaches, have, like Smith, won two apiece. But no one, not Wooden, not Knight, not Adolph Rupp or Phog Allen or Henry Iba, has won for as long or as consistently as Smith. And because he has won so often and so long, Carolina fans consider winning a birthright. Any chink in the armor brings howls of panic and incredulity from around the state.

Watching his team go through its layup line — with managers charting misses, of course — Smith was mentally preparing himself for some howling. Not that it really bothered him. He would be sixty-six years old in less than eight weeks and he was more than thirty years removed from worrying about screechy fans. He was seventeen victories away from surpassing Rupp as the all-time winningest coach in college history, but he wasn't concerned about that either. What was bothering him was his team. Carolina was 9–1, the only loss being in the Tipoff Classic back in November against Arizona. They had won nine straight games since then and had also won three exhibition games the previous week in Europe, but Smith wasn't terribly happy.

To begin with, he was beating himself up for scheduling the European trip. He had accepted the invitation to play two games in the Netherlands because it was a chance for his senior center, Serge Zwikker, to play at home. A third game, in Italy, had also been scheduled. Smith knew now that the time would have been better spent in Chapel Hill, preparing his team for the ACC schedule that was to begin with this game against Wake Forest.

"I made a mistake," he said, popping a pregame Nicorette into his mouth. Smith has been a Nicorette chewer since he stopped smoking on October 15, 1988. "We'd be a lot more ready for this if we had stayed home." He shrugged. "At least it was good for Serge. I have a feeling this will be tough for us tonight."

It is a required part of every coach's personality to be skeptical. Smith, however, has refined skepticism to an art. In 1981, when Georgia Tech was in the process of going 0–15 in ACC play, the Yellow Jackets came to Chapel Hill. That morning's paper carried a story by columnist Ron Morris with the headline: "Twenty-five Reasons Why Tech Will Beat Carolina." The piece was a hilarious litany of Smith's various reasons for being scared to death of a winless opponent. The Tar Heels eked out a 100–60 victory that day.

Smith's old rival Lefty Driesell once commented, "Dean Smith's the only man in history who's won seven hundred games and been the underdog in everyone of them." That number was now at 860 (all as the underdog) and counting.

Smith, who is married to a psychologist, talks often about "psychological advantages." He is constantly searching for them. His players are under strict orders to never say anything negative about an opponent, while at the same time always to talk up their own teammates — especially any and all seniors. If someone on an opposing team is foolish enough to say something disparaging about Carolina, those comments will be seen by all the Tar Heels. If someone in the media is foolish enough to count the Tar Heels out of a game, that too will make its way into the Carolina locker room. In 1995, prior to Carolina's Southeast Regional final against Kentucky, a *Washington Post* columnist handed the national title to the Wildcats. The Carolina players all had a good pregame read and a great postgame laugh after they won the game easily.

And if someone doesn't hand him a psychological advantage, Smith is apt to create one. After Carolina had beaten Duke in 1985 in the regular season finale to finish in a three-way tie for first place in the ACC, center Brad Daugherty said, "This is a great feeling, especially after everyone picked us to finish last in preseason."

It was pointed out to Daugherty that the Tar Heels had been picked no lower than third in the ACC in preseason. Daugherty shook his head. "That's not what Coach Smith told us."

Five years prior to that, before a game at Maryland, Smith thought his team needed some psychological help. He asked Art Chansky, then the sports editor of the *Durham Morning Herald* and a loyal Carolina/Smith disciple (he had roomed with Smith's assistant coach Eddie Fogler as an undergraduate and co-owned a restaurant with him) to write a column saying Carolina had no chance to win the game. Chansky did as he was told, the column made the bulletin board in the Carolina locker room just as Smith had planned, and the Tar Heels won the game.

Smith never used that particular tactic again, because, he said years afterward, he felt embarrassed about it later. Fortunately for him, he didn't need to.

A coach's son, Smith learned to look for edges early in life. His older sister, Joan, tells a story about a high school football game when young

Dean was quarterbacking. A howling wind blew the ball off the line of scrimmage and one of Smith's running backs instinctively ran over to pick it up and return it to the officials. "Let *them* do that," Smith screamed. "You save your energy."

Dean Edwards Smith is as reluctant to talk about himself as he is to let an opponent go into a game with an edge. Perhaps even more reluctant. "Born in Emporia, Kansas, went to Topeka High School, graduated from Kansas with a degree in math. Not much of a player. Dad was a coach. Though I might like coaching. Became a coach. Lucky enough to have good players and have some success. What more do you need?"

He is dead serious when he gives that synopsis of his life and hopes that will be enough. He has turned down multiple big-money offers to cooperate on an autobiography. In an era where it seems as if any coach who has back-to-back winning seasons has a book out someplace, the winningest coach of all time has no interest in doing one. "I don't think not wanting to talk about yourself is a bad thing," he says.

He loves to talk politics and issues, but will often stop in mid-opinion and say, "You aren't writing this, are you?" He will often cut off probing questions with a vehement shake of his head and a four-word answer: "None of your business."

"I'm beyond the point where I feel the need to do things I don't want to do," he said one night standing outside his team's locker room before a game. (The best time to talk to Smith is often just before a game when he is killing time.) "What's that saying? 'Been there, done that.' There aren't many things left I can't say that about."

Dean Smith was always an athlete, playing quarterback in football, point guard in basketball, and catcher in baseball. All the positions of authority. He was a good enough student in high school to get an academic scholarship to Kansas and a good enough basketball player to be offered a partial scholarship to Kansas State. His father, Alfred Smith, a minister's son, coached football, basketball, baseball, and track at various time during his career in Emporia, a small town on the Kansas prairie. He is believed to be the first high school coach in Kansas to coach an integrated basketball team, and when the school board asked him to remove the black players from his team, Alfred Smith said he would quit first. The controversy ended when Emporia won a state championship. Young Dean loved being around his father's teams and getting to know the players, but one thing always stood out to him as he got older: the ex-players. "I always remembered how good it made Dad feel when his former players would come back from college or the army or even from jobs someplace and make a point of coming by to see him," he said. "It just seemed to me like a nice way to live your life."

Alfred and Vesta Smith were strict Baptists and spent most of their Sundays in church. Smith remains religious to this day (he is a church deacon) but is as much a student of theology as he is a disciple of the church. Alfred Smith was a man of principle — witness his response to the school board — and discipline. Vesta Smith was the organizer. She was the one who always knew where everything was or where it should be. Today, one can see both parents' influence in Dean Smith: the important things in his life are organized to a tee. Off the top of his head in mid-November he can tell you that his team has practiced twenty-two times and he has walked off the floor satisfied four times out of twenty-two. He is as good a time manager as has ever lived. But if something isn't a priority — say, the inside of his car — his less-organized dad appears.

It was Rick Pitino who wrote the modestly titled book *Born to Coach* (at the age of thirty-seven, without a championship to his name), but the title seems more suited to Smith. He remembers drawing his first football play at the age of twelve — "It was a double wing play and Dad said I messed it up," he said. "I forgot to block somebody" — and by the time he was a junior at Kansas, his coach, the legendary Phog Allen, had made him an unofficial assistant, ordering him to teach the offense and the defense to the football players who would join the team late each year. "At first it made me angry, because the message was I wasn't that important as a player," he said. "Later, I realized he was doing me a favor."

Smith was a reserve on Kansas's national championship team in 1952 and the sixth man on a team that lost the national championship game a year later. Although Allen always said he had six starters that year, Smith didn't get to start his last home game. Nine years later, in his first season as a head coach, he remembered how that had felt and decided he would always start his seniors the last time they played at home. Unofficially, "senior day," now a tradition at almost every school in the country, was born on February 24, 1962 in the old Woollen Gym at North Carolina.

That wasn't Smith's first innovation — or his last. He is credited — or blamed, depending on your point of view — with creating the four corners delay offense, which drove many an opponent crazy in the closing minutes of games and was probably responsible for the creation of the shot clock in college basketball. He also came up with the notion of having players raise a fist to indicate when they are tired (and of allowing a tired starter to put himself back in a game when he felt rested); huddles at the foul line to call defenses; hoarding time-outs for the endgame; the run-and-jump scramble defense; and spending hours and hours practicing specific endgame situations. His passing-game offense was one of the first to give players the opportunity to freelance, although it is fraught with rules about who can and cannot shoot from specific areas of the floor.

Like most good teachers, Smith is always learning. He listened intently to his dad and then to Phog Allen when he was growing up. Later, he sat quietly while the two men he worked for, Bob Spear at Air Force and Frank McGuire at North Carolina, talked about basketball. To this day, he spends a week every summer with several coaching friends, sitting around talking X and O basketball, always looking for new ways to teach the game or trying to dredge up old ways that may have been discarded but are worthy of reconsideration.

Smith owed the Air Force two years after graduating from Kansas because he had been in ROTC and he spent a chunk of that time stationed in Germany. There, he started out as a player on the base team and ended up coaching it. The team went 11–0 under Smith, who gave himself a lot of playing time at point guard. The other players must not have minded. At the end of the stint, they gave him an engraved watch. He still has it.

"I think I did a pretty good job," he said. "I even put in the shuffle and they ran it very well."

More important than his team's success running the shuffle offense was Smith's meeting of a man named Bob Spear, who was also coaching in Europe. When Spear was named as the first coach at the new Air Force Academy, he asked Smith to join him as his assistant. Smith accepted. He learned a lot about the game during three years under Spear, but he also suffered the indignity of his first losing record as a coach: he was 1–4–1 as coach of the academy's golf team. "I knew we were in trouble right away," he said, "because I was better than some of the players."

That was then, when he was just learning to play golf. Now, Smith works hard at his golf during the off-season and has been as low as a six handicap. He still plays to a solid nine or ten most of the time and is every bit as competitive on the golf course as he is on the basketball court.

Smith first met Frank McGuire through Spear at the 1957 Final Four. Ironically, McGuire was in the process that March of coaching North Carolina to a historic triple-overtime victory over Smith's beloved Kansas team in the national championship game. A year later, McGuire offered Smith the job as his assistant at North Carolina. Smith barely knew where the school was, but he said yes.

By then, Smith and his wife, Anne, had two children. They joined the Binkley Baptist Church, a liberal spin-off from Chapel Hill's established Baptist church. Smith became close to the Reverend Robert Seymour, a civil rights activist in an era when the subject was a potential powder keg in a small southern town. At the time, most Chapel Hill restaurants were still segregated. Hoping to change that in the summer of 1959, Seymour enlisted the help of the young Carolina assistant coach. In a town that small, Smith was well-known, although certainly not as revered as McGuire. One night, Seymour asked Smith if he would be willing to take a black theology student who was spending the summer in Chapel Hill to his favorite restaurant, The Pines.

Smith agreed. The three men walked into the restaurant and sat down at Smith's regular table. "No one said a word," Smith remembered. "They came over and took our order and that was it."

It was a gutsy step for an assistant coach to take. Smith has never liked talking about it very much because to him, it's personal. "I did what I thought was right," he said. "Should I stand around and take bows for doing what was right?"

Three years after Smith arrived in Chapel Hill, McGuire quit. The NCAA was about to level Carolina with sanctions because of McGuire's extravagant spending on recruiting trips. McGuire had an offer to coach the Philadelphia Warriors and Wilt Chamberlain in the NBA. In the summer of 1961, he resigned, but only after telling Chancellor William Aycock that he thought Smith should succeed him. Aycock had worked with Smith preparing Carolina's response to the NCAA, since McGuire categorically refused to get involved, and he had been impressed with

Smith's diligence and his organization. He agreed with McGuire. On August 5, 1961, Smith was named the head coach at North Carolina.

If Aycock had searched the entire country he could not have found a coach more unlike the flamboyant McGuire. Smith was thirty years old and not even that sure he was ready to be or wanted to be a head coach.

"I thought, I'd try it," he said, "and if it didn't work out, I could always go back and be a high school coach."

As comical as that statement sounds thirty-six years later, Smith wasn't all that crazy about his new job and his future disciples weren't all that crazy about him. "I remember the first game we lost" — to Indiana — "I walked out of the gym that night thinking, 'The heck with this coaching.' " He smiled. "Of course now when we lose it's completely different. I think, 'The heck with this coaching.' "

Now, though, on the day when he does finally say, "The heck with this coaching," for real, it will be a historic day in the sport's history. Back then, he was a driven young coach trying to follow a legend. His first season produced his only losing record, 8–9, but no one was unhappy with that. Saddled by the probation, Carolina was still very competitive. Smith even got some votes for ACC Coach of the Year. "Back then," he said, "that actually meant something to me."

He had an excellent team his second year, one he still believes was good enough to win the national championship. But that was in the days when only the ACC tournament champion went to the NCAAs, and a 56–55 tournament loss to Wake Forest ended a 15–6 season. Then came bad times: a 12–12 record in 1964, including a 6–8 ACC record — Smith's first and last sub-.500 conference record and his first and last time in the second division of the league. A four-game losing streak early the next season left the Tar Heels 6–6. It was the night of the fourth straight loss, a 107–85 humiliation at Wake Forest, that Smith was hanged in effigy outside Woollen Gym by a group of Carolina students.

The story has been told and retold dozens of times because it is considered a turning point in Smith's career. Billy Cunningham, the team captain that year, charged off the bus and yanked the effigy down. Smith remembers that, but claims to remember little else about the incident. This is a man who can remember the names of all his managers, not to mention players, but that cold January night is a blur. No doubt because he wants it to be that way. "But I did give the best pregame pep talk of my life three days later at Duke," he said. Carolina won that day — Smith's first victory in Cameron Indoor Stadium. That team finished 15–9.

It was also during that season that Smith's sister, Joan, sent him Catherine Marshall's book *Beyond Our Selves,* which included a chapter called "The Power of Helplessness." Smith has said repeatedly that the book, specifically that chapter, helped him better understand how to deal with the ups and downs of coaching. From that point on, he worried far less about outside forces and critics and tried to focus more on the things he could control: recruiting, practices, game preparation, finding an edge.

By then, Smith's dogged recruiting was starting to pay dividends. He had beaten Duke's legendary Vic Bubas for a shooter out of Pennsylvania named Larry Miller and he had also brought in a wizard-like guard named Bobby Lewis. In 1963, hoping to integrate the team, Smith had convinced a young man from Charlotte named Willie Cooper to walk onto the freshman team, telling him he would give him a scholarship as a sophomore if he made the varsity. Cooper decided at the end of his freshman season to quit basketball to focus on his schoolwork. Three years later, Smith successfully recruited Charlie Scott, who became not only Carolina's first black player but a superstar.

By the time Scott enrolled in 1966, Smith was building a juggernaut. Carolina went 26–6 that year and began a string of three straight ACC titles and three straight trips to the Final Four. The Tar Heels reached the final in 1968, but in spite of Smith's efforts to slow the game down against Lew Alcindor and UCLA, they were eventually blown out, 78–55.

Those three years were the foundation for the Smith dynasty. After going 18–9 in 1970, Carolina began a string of twenty-seven straight seasons (and counting) in which it won at least twenty games. In 1975, when the NCAA opened the tournament to more than one participant from each league, the Tar Heels began a string of twenty-three straight seasons (and counting) in which they made the tournament. In 1981, they started a thirteen-season streak in which they reached at least the Sweet Sixteen. The numbers just kept mounting and mounting: there were two more Final Fours in the seventies, two more in the eighties, four in the nineties, making eleven in all. In the fall of 1981, when some people were wondering if Smith would ever win a national championship, a kid from Wilmington showed up on campus with a funny mannerism in which he stuck his tongue out when making a play.

The following spring, the kid hit a seventeen-foot jump shot in the national championship game to beat Georgetown, 63–62. Smith finally had his national title and the legend of Michael Jordan was born. Eleven years later, on the same Superdome floor in New Orleans, Smith won a second title.

Jordan was not, by any stretch of the imagination, the only great player Smith recruited. In fact, the case can be made that Smith is the most underrated recruiter in the history of basketball. From Lewis and Miller and Scott to Bob McAdoo and Bobby Jones and Walter Davis and Phil Ford to James Worthy and Sam Perkins and Jordan and Brad Daugherty to Kenny Smith and J. R. Reid and Eric Montross to Rasheed Wallace and Jerry Stackhouse and Vince Carter, Smith has successfully recruited more highly touted, hotly pursued players over a longer period of years than any coach in history. Some didn't become the stars they were supposed to become. Others who weren't as highly recruited became superb players. Smith has always said that the key to the program's success is the players. In truth, the key to the program's success has been his ability to keep top players coming to Carolina and then the job he has done coaching them after they have arrived.

Of course all that winning did not come without a price. Smith's first marriage was crumbling as his program was ascending, and he and his first wife were divorced in 1973. During the four years before he remarried, like any well-known man in a small town (ask Jeff Jones) he was the subject of all sorts of rumors. His friend, the Reverend Seymour, remembered that as the most difficult time in Smith's life, one in which he felt as if he had failed as a husband, a father, and a Christian. It was during that period that Smith began to fight his weight. He smoked more heavily and put on weight because he liked to eat, liked to drink scotch, and didn't like to exercise.

In 1982, when Carolina won its first national title, Smith kept a promise made prior to the national championship game to run (along with the other coaches) windsprints at the end of the first day of practice, instead of having the players run them. His second wife, Linnea, was terrified that her husband wouldn't survive. "She wasn't far wrong," he said.

Today, Smith still fights his weight. At five ten, he has been as high as "199½," and tries not to go over 195. He quit smoking in '88 after a series of nosebleeds and considerable pleading from his wife, family, friends, and doctors. Even his players got on him about it, watching him sprint out of the gym during practice breaks to grab a few drags under the stands. For years, Smith would wait until the last possible minute before walking on the court before a game so he could squeeze the time he would be forced to go without a cigarette to a bare minimum. Today, he always has a Nicorette in his pocket, although he tries to limit himself to a few a day.

Smith has always been a controversial figure in the ACC, in large part because he has been on top for so long, but also because of his peculiar style and his stubbornness. He will never — ever — let go of an issue, whether it is something vitally important like civil rights or something somewhat less important like the number of ex–Carolina players working as color commentators on ACC telecasts. How stubborn is Smith? "I will never sit down when the students are yelling, 'Sit down, Dean,'" he once said before a game at Duke. "I won't give them the pleasure of thinking they can tell me what to do."

Smith has done battle with several generations of ACC coaches — not just on the basketball court. He has been in verbal battles through the years with Norm Sloan and Lefty Driesell; with Terry Holland and Bill Foster — who uttered the famous line "I always thought it was NAISmith who invented the game, not DEANSmith" — with Mike Krzyzewski and Rick Barnes. The most personal of the battles has probably been with Krzyzewski, in part because it has gone on the longest (seventeen years), in part because the two have fought not just for ACC supremacy but national supremacy, and perhaps most significantly because they are both so intensely competitive and so different.

Even Smith admits that Krzyzewski's success made him work harder. "Maybe you look at one more tape, maybe you make the extra recruiting phone call," he said. "It probably made me a little bit better."

And while each respects what the other has built, there is always an unseen layer of hostility that lurks just below the surface. That was never more evident than in 1996 after Carolina had beaten Duke in the regular season finale in Durham. It was the Tar Heels' seventh straight win over the Blue Devils, and the Duke students, frustrated by losing again to their hated rivals, taunted Carolina point guard Jeff McInnis about personal animosity between him and assistant coach Phil Ford.

Smith was furious. He is about as close to Ford as he is to any of his ex-players. When Ford was going through treatment for alcoholism, Smith went to AA meetings, studied books on the disease, and memorized the twelve steps to recovery. The rumors about tension between McInnis and Ford had led to similar taunts at both Wake Forest and NC State, but hearing them at Duke drove Smith over the edge. McInnis was a cocky, in-your-face player who often jawed with opposing fans in a very un–Carolina-like fashion. Smith has always counseled his players that the best — and most pleasing — way to shut up an opposing crowd is to beat their team. That was never enough for McInnis. When he started giving it to the Duke crowd, the crowd gave it back to him.

Smith became even angrier when Duke walk-on Jay Heaps, in at the end of the game just to give a foul, overdid it, knocking McInnis into the press table. Heaps wasn't trying to hurt McInnis, but Smith didn't want to hear that. When McInnis screamed at Heaps for the shove, he was hit with a technical foul. Since he had already been teed up in the first half for taunting, that meant he was ejected. As he left, the hostile crowd (Carolina was in control of the game) serenaded him with chants of "Asshole."

"I'll tell you one thing," Smith said a year later, still upset. "If it had been me, I would have reacted a lot worse than McInnis did."

Smith exploded after the game, saying he was certain that the "esteemed" Duke faculty would be ashamed of the behavior of the students. Smith has never found the Duke students as amusing as most others do. His rivalry with them is probably as intense as with any coach or team. He was furious in 1977 when they posted a sign naming Carolina freshman Mike O'Koren to the "All acne team." He wasn't thrilled in 1988 when, after he had been in a fender bender with a Duke campus bus outside the Duke chapel (he was taking his parents to church there) they loudly chanted, "Dean Can't Drive" when he appeared in Cameron that season.

Smith knew McInnis was no angel. In fact, when Smith tried to talk to McInnis on the bench after the ejection to calm him down, McInnis turned away from him and TV cameras clearly showed him mouthing profanities. Smith wasn't thrilled by any of that but if he had to choose between one of his players (not to mention Ford) and the Duke students, there was no choice to make.

Three days later, on the eve of the ACC tournament, Krzyzewski fired back. He accused Smith of trying to divert attention from McInnis's behavior by criticizing the Duke students. "All they did," he said, "was make an accurate comment about McInnis."

This was just two weeks after the feud between Dean Smith and Rick Barnes had culminated in a meeting at Gene Corrigan's house. Shortly after Krzyzewski finished his tirade to a horde of reporters and TV cameras, Mickie Krzyzewski walked over to Corrigan and said, "So, what time do you want us over tonight?"

Corrigan laughed uneasily. The last thing he needed was another public feud between two of his coaches.

Smith and Krzyzewski have been sparring for years now. Even so, Krzyzewski was hurt when Smith was the only ACC coach who didn't contact him when he was sick. Every other coach called or wrote — most did both. Bobby Cremins called so often that Mickie Krzyzewski had to tell him to stop calling. When Smith broke the all-time record for coaching victories, every coach in the ACC wrote or called or personally congratulated him. Except one.

The team that Smith brought to play Wake Forest in Winston-Salem on an unseasonably warm January evening in 1997 — the temperature had hit seventy in the afternoon — was not what one would call a traditional Carolina team. The only two players in uniform who had graduated from high school four years earlier were walk-ons: Charlie McNairy and Webb Tyndall. The third senior, the only one who played, was Serge Zwikker, a fifth-year player Smith had redshirted during the 1993 national championship season. The three players Smith had recruited in the wake of that title were Rasheed Wallace, Jerry Stackhouse, and Jeff McInnis. The first two had gone on to NBA riches after their sophomore seasons. McInnis had left the previous spring even though he would not be drafted until late in the second round and would fail to make an NBA roster. He was the first player ever to leave Carolina to turn pro before his senior year without being a top ten pick in the draft.

Smith knew there was no sense playing the "what if" game that many fans and the media liked to play. Because he knew that sort of game cut both ways. Given Wallace's and McInnis's personalities, it was not unreasonable to think Carolina was better off without them. It did, however, make his team younger than Smith was comfortable with. In addition to Zwikker, the starters were a junior, Shammond Williams, and three talented sophomores, Antawn Jamison, Vince Carter, and Ademola Okulaja. The sixth man was a freshman, Ed Cota, who was the only pure point guard on the team. Cota was improving steadily, but still learning the system.

Jamison had been a stunning surprise as a freshman, making first-team all-conference while emerging as a dominant inside force. Conversely, Carter, who had arrived at Carolina publicized with all sorts of hype, had struggled, mixing fits of brilliance with stretches when he looked lost. Carter had been a good student in high school and was compared by some to Duke's Grant Hill, the sort of model student/great player every program tried to recruit. And yet Carter had proven to be something of a trash-talker, an arrogant chest-thumper, not at all in either the Grant Hill or the North Carolina Tar Heel mode. It was probably not a coincidence that in the Carolina media guide under the category of favorite book, he had listed Dennis Rodman's *Bad As I Wanna Be.* Jamison had slightly different taste. His choice was the Holy Bible.

Wake looked like a juggernaut. The Deacons had come back from their Christmas break and had won a tough, competitive game at Utah, 70–59. The game was a lot closer than that final margin. In fact, the Deacons had trailed 30–27 at halftime before guards Braswell and Rutland hit a couple of critical threes down the stretch. That was enough because Duncan was fabulous throughout — 23 points and 16 rebounds — and because Wake's defense was brilliant, holding the Utes to 33 percent shooting.

Carolina almost never goes to an opposing gym to shoot around on game day the way most teams do. Once upon a time, Smith didn't even walk through opposing offenses and defenses because he felt if his team could play the style of ball he wanted to play, the opposition wouldn't be able to run its normal offensive sets or get into its defense. That changed in 1993 when he decided that his run-and-jump defense, which emphasized attacking almost all the time, wasn't as effective as it had once been. "Once we backed off our defense, we did start to work more on what the other team was doing," he said.

He had started this season with more emphasis on attacking defensively. After talking to all of his former assistants about it during the summer he had decided to go back to that style because he was most comfortable with it. But four games into the season — the loss to Arizona and tougher-than-they-should-have-been wins over Richmond, Pittsburgh, and Southern California — Smith had made a difficult decision: this team, he decided, wasn't quick enough or deep enough to play defense the way he wanted to. Reluctantly, he returned to the more standard defenses, mixing a fair amount of zone in with the traditional man-to-man.

No coach likes to change his game plan for the season in December, least of all someone as successful and as stubborn as Smith. As innovative as he has been through the years, he is also a creature of habit. He readily admits that his game-day routines have changed little, if at all, in thirty-six years. When he does change a policy or abandon a habit, it is usually after a great deal of thought and only after he is convinced it is absolutely necessary.

Watching a North Carolina practice, Smith's organization and efficiency are easily apparent. There is absolutely no wasted motion. Players don't wander out and begin to warm up. They practice jump shots or passing drills with the help of the ever-present managers until Smith walks to the center-jump circle and blows his whistle. At that moment everything stops and everyone runs to the circle and stands surrounding the coach with their feet on the line of the circle. If someone fails to arrive promptly, everybody runs.

There are two kinds of visitors at a Carolina practice: family and non-family. Those who are part of the Carolina family — ex-players, coaches, or managers — are welcome to sit on the floor and observe. Everyone else sits in the upper deck. No exceptions. When Smith and North Carolina first signed a multimillion-dollar contract with Nike, Ed Janka, the company's chief coach schmoozer showed up for a DeanDome practice on his annual preseason swing through all the schools whose coaches are under contract to Nike. Almost everywhere he goes, Janka is given the royal treatment. He can sit just about anyplace he wants, chat up the coaches before practice — sometimes during practice — and will usually be taken to dinner at the best restaurant in town when practice is over. At North Carolina, Janka was politely asked to join the other non–family members in the upper deck. There, a manager collected the little card issued to him by the basketball office saying he was allowed to watch practice that day.

There is also no such thing as extended family. When Larry Brown, ex-player, ex–assistant coach, and one of Smith's closest friends through the years, came to practice he was — of course — escorted to the floor. His assistant coaches were given directions to the upper deck.

Each day, the players receive a copy of the day's practice plan. At the top is the practice number (for the season) and a thought for the day, which can be a famous quote, a not-so-famous quote, or a concept. Rarely is it something that is directly connected to basketball. Often, it has nothing to do with basketball.

Everything that happens at a Carolina practice is recorded: shots made and missed. Turnovers. Missed layups. Players are given plus marks for things like charges taken and minuses for bad passes, missed defensive assignments, or not hearing what the coach is saying. Minuses result in sprints at the end of practice; pluses can be used to get out of sprints. Players can actually "will" their pluses to younger players when they graduate. Everything is regimented. Water breaks are taken by class: seniors first, juniors second, and down the line to the freshmen, Smith blowing his whistle to indicate it is the next class's turn. If Smith gets angry during practice, the whole team may have to run on the spot. Occasionally, if he is really angry, an individual or the whole team may be sent to the locker room.

That had happened more often than Smith cared to think about during the '95–96 season. This team was struggling. It hadn't been able to play the way Smith really wanted it to play, but Smith liked the attitude.

"They've been a fun group to work with," he said. "Most of the time they listen. That's a start."

And apparently a change from a year before.

Odom expected to see a lot of zone in this game, which meant the way his guards shot the ball would — as usual — be crucial. Unlike Smith, Odom is a walk-through fanatic. When his team arrived for its 3 o'clock walk-through on game day, the Joel Coliseum had a Grand Central Station–like feel to it. ESPN technicians were everywhere, noisily setting up wiring and cables for the telecast, and Dick Vitale was holding court with the assistant coaches. Mick Mixon, the color commentator on Carolina's radio network, sat at the press table, waiting for Odom to finish with the players so he could do a pregame interview. Ushers and maintenance people busily readied the building for tip-off, which was five hours away.

Some coaches would lose their mind arriving for a walk-through — or any practice — and finding so many people around. Later in the season, during a morning walk-through at Clemson, NC State's Herb Sendek would attempt to banish the TV techs. Only after a lengthy argument with the producer did Sendek give up. He thought a closed practice meant closed to the world. He learned that day that in the ACC closed means closed to everyone except the TV people who pay the league millions of dollars.

Odom really didn't care who watched his team's walk-through as long as he had his players' attention. Most coaches would gag at the notion of having a member of the opponent's radio crew watch his team work. Odom didn't care. "I guarantee you one thing," he said. "Mick Mixon won't decide this game tonight. In fact, if Dean Smith wanted to come and watch this, that would be fine too because *he's* not deciding the game tonight." He pointed toward the floor. "Those guys" — the players — "will decide it. Not Mick, not Dean, not me."

"I need your minds right now, not your bodies" was Odom's standard walk-through opening line. Duncan's mind and body were often excused from the exercise. "He knows everything cold," Odom said, opting to give Loren Woods extra work with the first team while Duncan sat and observed.

Once he was finished, Odom gave Mixon his interview, then spent a few moments chatting with Vitale. Unlike some coaches, who are nice to Vitale because of the power he wields as college basketball's best-known TV voice but then snipe at him behind his back, Odom genuinely likes him. He remembers the pre-TV Vitale, a workaholic coach who built a very solid program at the University of Detroit. What's more he understands that Vitale's enthusiasm, even though it grates at times, is real. His one complaint with Vitale is his insistence on calling him "Little Davey Odom."

"People stopped calling me that in high school," he said. "And in the real world, five ten isn't little. In basketball, yes, but not anyplace else."

Vitale is always searching for anecdotes or vignettes he can use on the telecast. He and Odom chatted about the team and its progress for a few minutes. "Don't you worry about playing the way you do?" Vitale said, finally. "You get to March and it's one-and-out and you let a team stay with you, let it come down to a last shot, you can get beat. Isn't it risky?"

"Might be," Odom said. "But I can't change my style at this point in my life. I'm not comfortable coaching any other way."

"I think you need to go for the jugular more," Vitale said.

"You may be right," Odom said. "But that's not me."

While he talked to Vitale, the players headed to a nearby restaurant for the pregame meal. Odom goes to pregame meals on the road, but not at home. At home, the players tend to race through the meal so they can have some free time before the game. On the road, they are more likely just to be killing time around the hotel and will linger. Odom always tells the players to be back at the arena "no sooner than ninety minutes before tip-off." He doesn't want them hanging around the locker room any longer than that.

Odom was curious to see how his team would play against Carolina. The Tar Heels are always a measuring stick for ACC teams and Odom felt no differently about them this year than any other year, even though his team was in the unusual position of being the prohibitive favorite to win the league.

Carolina's presence also meant the return to Wake Forest of Makhtar Ndiaye (whose last name is pronounced "ji"). If the recruitment of Duncan had been the best thing that had ever happened to Odom in coaching, the recruitment of Ndiaye, that same year, had undoubtedly been the worst. Odom had first heard of Ndiaye through a friend who coached in France and had seen him play in a tournament there. Ndiaye was from Senegal, but his father was a diplomat living in Paris.

At that stage, Ndiaye was much more impressive to look at than Duncan. "He was six nine and had a pro body," Odom remembered.

Ndiaye moved to the United States the next year and enrolled at Oak Hill Academy, the basketball factory in Virginia where many high school stars go, especially when they are in need of a quick grade transplant. Ndiaye had no such problems, he just needed time to learn the language and American basketball. He graduated from Oak Hill and, along with Duncan and Peral, enrolled at Wake Forest in the fall of 1993.

But he never played a game there. Odom was accused of illegally recruiting him, of having "placed" him at Oak Hill (he had told coach Steve Smith about him, but that was perfectly legal), and of having made promises to Ndiaye through a maintenance worker at Wake whom he had used as an interpreter when he first made contact with him. Accusations flew back and forth for months. It looked as if Wake was going to get hit with sanctions. If so, President Hearn, as one of the leaders in the NCAA's alleged reform movement, would have no choice but to fire Odom.

"It was not a good time," Odom said. "Things were being said that I knew weren't true and they hurt. They hurt me, they especially hurt Lynn. I've never seen her like that. It was the only time in her life that I can remember where she just didn't enjoy being around a lot of people."

The NCAA eventually ruled that Ndiaye could not play for Wake Forest but could play anyplace else in the country. There were no sanctions against Wake. It was a typically curious NCAA decision. If Ndiaye was culpable, why should he be allowed to transfer without any loss of eligibility? If the school was culpable, why no sanctions? If no one was culpable, why couldn't Ndiaye stay at Wake?

Ironically, Ndiaye turned out not to be worth the trouble. He transferred to Michigan and played without distinction there for two years. Then, in a surprise, he transferred to Carolina. Smith, having lost both Wallace and Stackhouse late in the recruiting year, needed some inside depth. Ndiaye was big and strong and would be twenty-three years old early in the '96–97 season and would have two years of eligibility left after sitting out the '95–96 year. Smith figured he was a better risk than a freshman would be. Even so, the move surprised everyone in the ACC. Smith had sworn off of junior college players and transfers after Bob McAdoo had transferred from a junior college in 1971 and stayed just one year before turning pro.

Ndiaye was Carolina's seventh man and would not play much. But Odom was concerned about how he would be treated by the Wake Forest fans given the jeopardy that he had placed the program in three years earlier. He made a point during pregame warm-ups of walking over to Ndiaye and giving him a warm handshake.

Odom and Smith are the only coaches in the ACC who walk out to their benches during pregame warm-ups. Both like to try and pick up little things watching their team — and the opponent — warm up. Both also admit that sitting around the locker room alone drives them a little bit nuts.

"How do you like my suit?" Smith asked Odom as the two shook hands. "It's dark enough to be Wake Forest black."

Both men were wearing expensive suits. Coaches make a lot more money than they used to. They also wear much more expensive clothes, although rarely do they have to pay for them. Most have their suits made for them by someone who is thrilled to supply clothes for a famous coach.

Smith had been the coach at North Carolina since Odom was in high school. Although he had never been a Carolina fan and had competed against Smith at both Virginia and Wake Forest, there had never been any animosity between them. Odom has very few enemies in coaching.

"When I think about Dean I think about how many nights he's done this," he had said on the short drive over from his house that evening. "It boggles my mind. So many wins, a few losses too, but all that pressure on all those nights. Always the guy everyone wants to beat.

"I look at him, I look at Terry [Holland], and I see how tough it is to be that public a figure. I've always said that I never want to get to the point where I stop going out because I don't want to deal with people. I can remember at Virginia, we would go back to Terry's basement after every game. He never wanted to go out. I say I won't let that happen to me, then I find myself avoiding football games here because I don't want to hear the fans criticizing the coaches. I'm uncomfortable with that. It makes me realize that a lot of them don't really like me, they like what we've done. If we weren't winning, they would say the same things about me."

On this night, everyone in Winston-Salem was in love with Odom — and his team. Odom had been concerned that his players might be tight. "Try to remember, it's just a game," he said. "We want to win, we want to play as well as we possibly can and we've worked hard to be ready. But no one's going to die out there tonight. It's still just a basketball game."

Odom probably should have given that speech to his fans. Or Carolina's. Or Duke's. Or any others in the ACC.

Joel Coliseum was jumping from the start. The building can be an intimidating place when it is full and the Deacons are on a roll. Often, though, it is a crowd started by the team as opposed to a crowd that starts the team. Against Carolina, though, team and crowd were in synch. The Deacons never trailed, jumping to a 6–0 lead as the Tar Heels missed their first six shots. The game stayed close for fifteen minutes, before Wake went on a 10–4 run before halftime to lead 37–28.

Odom thought his team needed more emotion. "We play the first half to get to the second half, you know that," he said. "That's where games are won and lost." He sensed that they were only half listening, up nine, the game comfortably in their control. "Look at me!" he yelled. Odom doesn't raise his voice often. When he does, he gets his team's attention. "This thing is not nearly where it needs to be. You've got to go out there the first four minutes and send a message. If you want this one, you have to go get it."

Apparently, they wanted it. Even though Tony Rutland threw a scare into everyone, falling heavily on his surgically repaired left knee ninety seconds into the half, the Deacons dominated. They built the lead to 60–36 during the first nine minutes and coasted from there. The closest Carolina got was 67–52, and the Deacons responded by scoring the next 10 points. The final was 81–57, as thorough a loss as Carolina had suffered in years. Normally, even in a blowout, the Tar Heels make some kind of run. Not on this night.

"They're very, very good," Smith said when it was over. "Our goal is to be a top twenty team. No matter what the rankings say right now" — Carolina was ranked fifteenth — "we're not a top twenty team." As if Smith didn't have enough to worry about, Carter had gone down with a hip-pointer late in the game and had been helped off.

Odom could not have been happier with the way his team had played. Rutland's injury was just a twist — a relief to everyone. Duncan, even with a stomach virus, had scored 23 points and dominated the boards with 18 rebounds. They had shot 53 percent as a team and outrebounded a good rebounding team, 43–33.

It was almost a perfect night.

Odom did a postgame interview with Vitale (who had no comments about going for the jugular) and walked into his locker room feeling giddy. He rounded the corner to the players' dressing area and was stunned by what he heard: nothing.

"It was like a morgue," he remembered later. "We beat Carolina by twenty-four and there's no celebration, no joy. Not a thing."

Odom turned to Ernie Nestor, who knew exactly what he was thinking before Odom opened his mouth.

"I was just going to ask them," Nestor said, "if they were aware of the fact that we won the game."

Odom decided this wasn't the time or the place to lecture his players about the Precious Present.

"That was a great job tonight, guys," he said. "Believe me, that's a hell of a basketball team. And we have to play them again at their place. Keep that in mind when you're talking to the media. Beyond that, enjoy it." He paused, then repeated himself. "Enjoy it. You earned it."

He left them so he could go tell the media how thrilled he was with the 10–0 start and this performance. He knew his team was playing as well as anyone in the country. And yet, the locker room had left him feeling uneasy. He wasn't certain if he had a problem. Evidence thus far indicated he didn't. But if he did, he didn't know what the solution was. "You can't change a team's personality," he said.

He hoped he wouldn't need to.

12

Respect Yourself

ABOUT SIXTEEN HOURS after Odom had left his team to its non-celebration, Mike Krzyzewski was furious with his. He had spent three days priming his players for this day and this game and this road trip and they had walked into Alexander Memorial Coliseum and played scared. They had been outhustled, outworked, and completely dominated on the boards by Georgia Tech, and the halftime score reflected that: 37–26, Tech.

"I'm telling you," he said to his assistant coaches, "it is no fun to coach like this. We talk and talk and they don't listen. What did they expect Tech to do, just let us walk in here and win the damn game? I mean, goddamn, how many times did we tell them this week that they had to expect Tech to play its best game of the season?"

The assistants — Tommy Amaker, Quin Snyder, Tim O'Toole, and Jeff La Mere — didn't respond because they knew Krzyzewski wasn't expecting answers. He was blowing off steam before settling down to decide what to change for the second half.

Down the hall, in the Georgia Tech locker room, Bobby Cremins was congratulating his team on — as Krzyzewski had predicted — playing its best twenty minutes of the season. But he knew that an 11-point lead with twenty minutes to go was fragile — especially with this team.

Cremins was still searching, groping for answers that hadn't been there in December. After the embarrassing loss to Maryland, the Yellow Jackets had been blown out by Kentucky, 88–59, in a game in which they actually played better in the first half than they had played all night at Maryland. Then, they had gone to New York for the ECAC Holiday Festival. Often, trips to his hometown had provided Cremins's teams with a lift. Not this time. After barely escaping from winless Hofstra in the opening round, Tech had played a weak St. John's team in the final.

They weren't weak enough. Tied at halftime, Tech was horrendous in the second half, shooting seven for 29 from the field en route to an embarrassing 67–55 loss. Cremins had tried everything in that game. He had pleaded and cajoled from the bench. He even yelled at Matt Harpring at halftime for complaining to the officials too often. "Quit whining and play!" he told Harpring. "I told you guys not to worry about the officials and I meant it. I tell people what a great kid you are all the time, Matt, and then you go out and make me look like a hypocrite. Just play basketball!"

No one got on the officials in the second half. But they didn't play much basketball. Cremins was almost pleading for a new attitude after the game. Again, the chemistry issue continued to bother him. "Fellas, your teammates should be your best friends in the world, the people you trust most. You have to like each other more. I'm telling you, if we don't start to come together in these next few days before we play Duke we're going to be in trouble. I know basketball, fellas, and I know what a winning team feels like when it's together in the locker room. Right now, we don't have that feel."

Eight days later, they had that feel. The sniping between the older players and the younger ones seemed forgotten. Gary Saunders, who had played well in New York after becoming eligible at the end of the first semester, was giving them an outside threat. Eddie Elisma was destroying Greg Newton inside. They were playing at home and even though the nonsellout crowd was disappointing, they had control of the game.

"Twenty more minutes, fellas," Cremins said. "Twenty more like the first twenty and we'll be very happy."

"Twenty-seven to thirteen on the boards. Look at that. How can that happen?"

Krzyzewski was staring at a stat sheet just handed to him by trainer Dave Englehart. He looked at the coaches again. "I don't even know what to say to them at this point. We've beaten one quality team in the last three years" — Villanova — "and they come in here acting as if they're so good all they have to do is show up and that's it. What a bunch of crap that is."

He stared at the stat sheet again, adjusting the reading glasses he had started using in the last year as he looked at the depressing numbers. It was Tommy Amaker who finally spoke. Normally, Amaker was the quietest of the coaches in the locker room. Snyder and O'Toole were both wired, full of ideas, suggestions, and comments. Amaker, who had been with Krzyzewski the longest, knew that it took a few minutes for Krzyzewski to put the first half — good or bad — behind him. When it was time to focus on the second half, he would wait to hear where Krzyzewski was going before deciding what — if anything — to say. Now, hearing the anger and frustration in his boss's voice, he spoke up.

"I just have a feeling, Coach, that one way or the other this half will decide a lot about this team," he said. "I mean a lot. We'll find out now if we're tough, if we're any good. But they have to do it themselves. We can't do it for them."

Krzyzewski was silent for a moment. "You're right," he said finally. "We'll start all three seniors because this is their team. If they go in and lie down, then the other kids have permission to go in and lie down because that's the standard they've set." His voice was hoarse from all the yelling he had done in the first half. He stood up. "Let's go find out about this team."

He walked from the empty track locker room they had been using for their meeting back to the adjacent visitors' locker room. The players sat waiting, expecting an explosion. They didn't get one. Instead, they got a stern lecture. "You guys played the first twenty minutes like you were afraid," Krzyzewski said. "Every time I got on the referees, I felt like what I should be saying is, 'Please don't let them pick on my little boys because they aren't tough enough to deal with it.'

"You three seniors" — Newton, Jeff Capel, Carmen Wallace — "will start because this is a very big half and this is your team. Everybody else will take their cue from you guys — good or bad."

He paused. "Now you guys know that's a bullshit way to play. I told you yesterday that every team in the conference is going to test your toughness because the last couple of years, we haven't been a very tough team. That's what this game is about now. I have nothing for you X and O that will change this game. There's no play I can call to make you tougher. So here's my huge halftime speech to you: Go out and play like men!"

He hoped he had challenged them, gotten them to understand that, as important as this game was to them, it was probably more important to Georgia Tech. This was the Yellow Jackets' first ACC home game. They needed a win to negate their awful December, to build some confidence. Their next two games were against Wake Forest and at Louisville. They would be a clear underdog in both. They needed a win over Duke to stop sliding before the slide got out of control.

For five minutes, Tech looked as if it was still in command. But with the lead 45–36, power forward Michael Maddox, who had helped Elisma and Harpring control the inside, picked up his fourth foul and Cremins had to go to his wafer-thin bench. Sensing an opening, Duke crept back into the game. It scored six straight points to cut the margin to 45–42 before Elisma again beat Newton to a rebound for a follow-up basket. But that was Tech's only basket during an eight-minute stretch. If Duke's offense had been as good as its defense, the Blue Devils would have had the lead. Tech was clinging to a 47–44 margin when Elisma, who had never hit a three-point shot in a game, hit one with the shot clock about to run out. That bounced the lead back to 50–44 and brought the crowd back into the game.

Both coaches had the same thought at that moment: Maybe it's Tech's day.

It wasn't. Duke wouldn't go away. Trajan Langdon, who had been the team's best player all afternoon, made a circus shot falling down on a drive to cut it to 52–50 and then Capel bombed a three to put Duke up for the first time, 53–52. Tech kept trying to go to Harpring, but now Duke was doubling him whenever he made a move, daring the other players to shoot. The open men were the guards Kevin Morris and Gary Saunders, but they couldn't hit a shot when it mattered, combining to shoot five for 20. "You can't beat Duke if your guards shoot like that," Cremins said later.

The game came down to a Tech possession with under two minutes to play. Down 55–54, Cremins called a play for Harpring. But Capel read the play, dropped off Saunders, and stole the ball. He fed Langdon, who knocked down an open three to make it 58–54 with 1:32 left. That was Tech's last gasp. The final was a deceiving 66–56.

The Duke locker room was filled with joy and relief. Krzyzewski walked in, a broad grin on his face and wrote the number "19" on the board. "That's how many points you gave them in the second half," he said. "Less than a point a minute. That's playing tough basketball. That's the way Duke should be playing. You wore them down at the end, fellas. You won a brawl out there. You were tough and you were poised. You guys won the game. It wasn't us on the bench. I wanted to call a time-out a couple times, but I didn't because I had confidence in you guys.

"That's a hell of a win because that's the best Tech has played all year. By far. You won't face a better player all year than Harpring. You took their best punch and you came back and won the game." Krzyzewski was genuinely thrilled with the win, especially after the disastrous first half. What made him happiest was that his team had responded to adversity. That had been a trait often missing the previous two seasons.

Cremins wouldn't have argued with anything Krzyzewski said. He knew his team had played its best game of the year. Elisma had been superb and Harpring and Maddox had played well. But their guard play and lack of depth had done them in. He couldn't yell at his team, though, not after that performance. "If you play that hard every night, you're going to win games," he told them. "That was progress. That was better. We just have to keep working at it."

Tech was now 0–2 in ACC play. Cremins had never started a season 0–3. Wake Forest was next. The possibility of 0–3 was quite real.

Rick Barnes watched the end of the Duke–Georgia Tech game before his team practiced that day with mixed emotions. He wasn't sure if he preferred having Duke come to Clemson forty-eight hours later confident after a win or angry after a loss.

"Either way," he said, "it'll be wild."

Barnes grinned his best little-boy grin. His team was 12–1 — the only loss to Minnesota, six weeks earlier in Puerto Rico — and ranked third in the country. Only Kansas and Wake Forest, both undefeated, were ranked ahead of Clemson.

"Can you believe it?" he said, still grinning, "Little ol' Clemson ranked number three. We can't possibly be that good, can we?"

Just how good the Tigers were, Barnes wasn't certain. There were times when he was convinced they were as good as any team in the country. There were other times when he thought they lacked scoring depth and were still a year from being as good as they were going to get.

Right now though, Barnes was having the time of his life. His team was beating everyone in sight and the entire nation was taking notice of little ol' Clemson. That was exactly what Barnes had been planning when he arrived. He had never dreamed, though, that it would all happen in his third season.

Barnes hadn't gotten Clemson where it was because of his boyish charm. He and his assistants had worked maniacally in recruiting and Barnes had spent hours and hours driving to every corner of the state to drum up support for his team. In fact, he still took his Monday night radio show on the road, broadcasting from a different restaurant — all in the same chain — each week. Barnes and host Jim Phillips sat on bar stools in the middle of the restaurant, held microphones in their hands, and chatted for a while. Then they took some questions from the live audience and a few from callers. Afterward, Barnes would glad-hand for a few minutes before heading down the road with some take-out chicken sitting on his lap while someone else drove.

No other coach in the ACC spent as much time pursuing fan support as Barnes did. Of course the case could be made that no other coach needed to pursue it as much as Barnes, given Clemson's lack of basketball history. But it was more than just that. If Barnes ever landed at a school that didn't need him to do one minute of promotion for the team, he would probably do it anyway. Barnes likes being around people. He's as comfortable walking through a restaurant saying "hey" to the folks as he is running a practice. Most coaches put up with their fans; Barnes embraces his.

Perhaps that's because Barnes has always been searching for a place where he could be totally comfortable and has finally found it at Clemson. Growing up wasn't very easy, not with his parents splitting when he was four and his older sister, Sandy, who spent a lot of time taking care of Rick and his younger brother, Gary, being killed in an automobile accident when Rick was getting ready to start eighth grade.

Sandy was eighteen at the time of the accident and both her younger brothers worshiped her (there were also two older brothers) and were totally devastated by her death. Mary Barnes was smart enough to send her two youngest sons to grief counseling. Even so, Rick struggled in school. He didn't work very hard in eighth grade and his grades suffered. In ninth grade, he ran into a teacher who wouldn't accept his willingness to accept failure. "Alice Watts," he said. "Ninth grade algebra. She turned my life around."

Alice Watts made a simple deal with young Rick: Do your work and pass your tests and you can go to basketball practice. Don't and you can't. Both the principal and the ninth-grade basketball coach backed her up. Rick began getting his work done.

He was the first — and only — member of his family to go to college. Mary Barnes wanted her children to have high school diplomas but assumed they would go to work after that. She worked long hours in the hosiery mills around Hickory, North Carolina, to keep everyone fed, and there was no chance she could pay for college. But Bob Hodges, the coach at nearby Lenoir-Rhyne, offered Rick a partial scholarship and arranged for him to work for a man named Preston Rhyne (a nephew of the school's founder) in his hosiery mill. That worked out well for Rick because it meant he had enough money to get through school and because Preston had a daughter named Candace — Candy — whom he fell in love with. They were married Rick's senior year.

Rick's greatest influences had been coaches and teachers. He wanted to coach and teach. But there were no jobs. He went to work as a substitute teacher and loaded trucks for UPS from 4 A.M. to 8 A.M. Finally, a friend told him there was an opening for an assistant coach at a local private school. Rick jumped at it. Later that same year, Paul Lavitt, the friend who had helped him land the coaching job, suggested they drive down to Greensboro and see the ACC tournament. Barnes had seen one game involving an ACC team in his life, years earlier in the Charlotte Coliseum, between Clemson and LSU. "Pete Maravich scored forty-nine," he remembered.

He saw three games in the Greensboro Coliseum that day with Lavitt. One, between Maryland and NC State, went triple overtime. Walking to the car after the last game, Barnes turned to Lavitt and pointed back in the direction of the building. "That," he said, "is what I want to do someday. Coach in that tournament."

It took him seventeen years, with a lot of stops along the road, but Barnes got there. The story of how Barnes broke into the college coaching business is one that is still told by friends, acquaintances, and people who have never met him.

After working at North State Academy for a year, Barnes had decided that if he wanted to coach in the ACC, he needed to get into college coaching. He got in his car and drove to North Carolina, Duke, NC State, and Wake Forest, prepared to offer his services at any of those schools in any capacity. He had no résumé, just a lot of eagerness. Politely he was told thanks, but no thanks. A friend of his from Lenoir-Rhyne, Andy Anderson, was working as a part-time coach at Appalachian State, and he encouraged Barnes to make the trip into the mountains to meet Bobby Cremins and his assistant Kevin Cantwell. While he was there, Cantwell gave him some advice: "Volunteer somewhere," he said. "Anywhere. We've got someone here or we'd take you. But someone's going to need a coach who will work for nothing. That's the only way to break in."

Barnes tucked the advice away. A few weeks later, Eddie Biedenbach was hired at Davidson. His old friend Lavitt knew Biedenbach and called to see if Biedenbach would at least talk to Barnes even though Biedenbach said his staff was set. "Maybe you'll like him and hire him next year," Lavitt said. As a courtesy to Lavitt, Biedenbach agreed to meet Barnes.

It was a hot June day when Barnes arrived at Davidson at 7:30 for his 9 A.M. appointment. He wanted to be certain to leave extra time in case he got lost. Dressed in his only suit, he sat in the sweltering Davidson gym, waiting for someone to arrive and open the basketball office. Biedenbach's assistants, Tom Abatemarco and John Kochan, arrived. Barnes introduced himself. "Oh yeah, sure," they said. "Eddie will be here soon."

Nine o'clock came. No Biedenbach. Then ten o'clock. Eleven. The coaches went to lunch. "He called us," they said. "He's running late. But he'll be here in about an hour."

By now, Barnes suit was soaked. He took a chance and left long enough to go to the campus cafeteria to buy a bagel — "first one I'd ever eaten," he said — then came back to continue his vigil. The afternoon passed. Candy called the basketball office a couple of times wondering what had become of her husband. At 5 o'clock everyone went home. Abatemarco and Kochan were apologetic. "The day just got away from him," they said.

"Is he still coming in?"

"Yeah, but we really don't know when. You should probably call tomorrow for another appointment."

"I'll wait."

Six, seven, eight. The sun was setting. Finally, more than twelve hours after he had arrived, Barnes gave up. Exhausted, in desperate need of a shower, he walked out the door of the gym. As he opened the door, someone was opening it from the other side: Eddie Biedenbach.

Biedenbach stared at the rumpled, sweat-soaked young man in front of him. "Oh my God," he said. "You have to be Rick Barnes."

He led Barnes back to his office, apologizing all the way, explaining what had happened. Barnes didn't care. "I owe you a favor," Biedenbach said.

"Put me to work."

"I don't have a job."

"Let me volunteer."

Biedenbach thought for a moment. "Tell you what," he said. "Come and work my camp. I'll give you ten bucks for every camper you bring here. If you work out at camp, I'll find something for you to do in the fall."

"Deal."

Barnes shook hands, drove home, and took the longest shower of his life. That fall, he began working as a volunteer for Biedenbach. To make a living, he drove a forklift at the Hoch lumberyard all morning, went home and showered to get the sawdust out of his hair, then went to the basketball office or out on the road scouting or recruiting. "I fell asleep at the dinner table a lot," he said.

But he impressed Biedenbach with his work ethic. He was promoted to part-time assistant coach and then, with help from his old friends Kochan and Abatemarco, he was hired by Joe Harrington as the first full-time assistant coach at George Mason. Harrington had been hired in 1980 to take GMU from Division II to Division I. Kochan and Abatemarco, who were then at Maryland together, convinced Harrington (an ex–Maryland assistant) to consider Barnes. Harrington was skeptical. He thought he needed someone with more experience. You need someone who will work round the clock for you, they told him. No one works harder than this guy. You call him at 6 in the morning, he'll be in the office.

As luck would have it, Harrington was an early riser. The next morning, he woke up at 5:30 and called the Davidson basketball office. Barnes answered the phone.

"Is this Rick Barnes?" Harrington asked.

"It is."

"Good. You're hired."

Six years later, having helped Harrington put George Mason on the map, Barnes was hired at Alabama. A year later, Gary Williams, who had become friendly with Barnes when they kept running into each other at high school games while Williams was at American, offered him a chance to come to Ohio State as the number one assistant. Barnes accepted. He enjoyed working for Williams because of his intensity and figured he would stay with him for several years. He lasted one. He was sitting at home one night shortly after the season had ended when the phone rang. It was Harrington. "Ricky boy, pack your bags again," Harrington said.

"Huh?"

"I just got hired at Long Beach State and you're going to be the next coach at George Mason."

Barnes wasn't so sure. He was dying to be a head coach and he loved the idea of going back to George Mason. He called Athletic Director Jack Kvancz. "Just sit tight," Kvancz told him. "I have to deal with some red tape and some politics, but you're the guy I want to hire." Kvancz was as good as his word. Two weeks later, Barnes had the job. He was thirty-three.

"If I had stayed at George Mason for the rest of my career, I'd have been happy," Barnes said. "I liked the school, I liked the Washington area. I liked working for Jack. I figured I'd be there at least ten years."

He was off by nine. The Patriots were 20–10 in Barnes's first season. Barnes was shopping one morning a few weeks after the season had ended when he got an urgent message to meet Kvancz for lunch. "Jack never ran me down that way," he said. "I figured something was wrong."

Not exactly. "Would you be interested in the Providence job?" Kvancz said.

"I'm not sure," Barnes answered.

"The job will probably pay about two hundred fifty thousand dollars a year," Kvancz said. "I think you're sure." Kvancz didn't want to lose Barnes, but he knew he couldn't stand in his way if a chance like this came along.

Barnes's whirlwind tour of America's colleges, George Mason to Alabama to Ohio State to George Mason to Providence in a period of four years, ended a week later when he was named to succeed Gordon Chiesa at Providence. Chiesa had inherited the unenviable task of succeeding Rick Pitino, who had made himself into a godlike figure in Providence in just two years by taking the Friars to a totally unexpected Final Four in 1987. When Barnes was named to replace Chiesa he was immediately dubbed Rick II.

Rick II was still a coaching work in progress. Everywhere he had been, he had taken a small piece of his boss's philosophy with him: Joe Harrington's belief that you can never recruit a player long enough or hard enough, Wimp Sanderson's belief in quickness and physical man-to-man defense, and Gary Williams's drive and full-court pressure defense. Wherever he went, Barnes asked questions. He always wanted to know how the best coaches did things, whether it was handling a zone trap or the media or a recruit's mother.

Above all, Barnes had learned to believe that the one thing you could not be inflexible about was being flexible. Certain rules were inviolate — like being prompt, getting to class, and treating everyone with respect. Others were more flexible. A mistake that might cause him to scream and yell at one player might be ignored if made by another. "I learned over the years that I needed to figure out their personalities as much as they needed to figure out mine," Barnes said.

He also learned to control his temper. These days, most Barnes outbursts are calculated. Not at Providence. More than once he chased officials off the court after losses. After one incident — a loss at Villanova — Big East commissioner Dave Gavitt lectured him long and hard about his behavior in public. As always, Barnes listened. And learned.

Even so, the fans in Providence never attached themselves to Rick II the way they had to Rick I. No doubt not reaching the Final Four had something to do with it. But just as surely the Southern accent had something to do with it, and so did the fact that he never came across as hungering to win the way Pitino did. "I think they always thought of me as a short-timer," Rick II said. "Seems like there were rumors about me leaving almost from the day I got there."

He almost left for Virginia after the second season, but ended up staying six before Clemson came along and offered the chance to return to the league he wanted to coach in, in a place where he could claim not to have an accent. When he finally coached his first game in the ACC tournament, all those years after dreaming about it, he found himself opposite Dean Smith. That was the night when he ended up toe-to-toe with him before the game was over. Now, Barnes had built a team that could stand in with the powers of the ACC on the court and on the scoreboard, and he was enjoying every minute of it.

"I'm still not sure if the rest of the league is ready to deal with the idea of Clemson being at the top or near the top," he said. "But it may have to."

Once the ACC begins conference play in January, there are eight league games played each week: four on weeknights, usually spread out from Tuesday to Thursday for TV; four on the weekend, also spread out across Saturday afternoon and evening and Sunday afternoon for TV purposes. During each sequence, one of the nine teams has a bye from league play. North Carolina had drawn the December bye. Clemson had the bye the first weekend in January. The Tigers had taken a week off and, since it was between semesters, Barnes had run two-a-day practices.

"I guarantee you one thing," he said. "We're in shape. Now, though, we start finding out just how good we are."

Duke coming to town was still a major occasion even though the Blue Devils had been a shadow of their former selves the previous two seasons. Krzyzewski was still Krzyzewski and the uniforms still said Duke even if the players in those uniforms weren't quite as imposing as the players who had worn them in the late eighties or early nineties. A win over Duke at home was, in one sense, an absolute necessity — after all, the number three team in the country isn't supposed to lose at home. In another sense, it was still a very big deal because beating Duke was always a big deal.

Duke was accustomed to being a team everyone wanted to beat. During the run of seven Final Fours in nine years, it had become as big a target as — at times even a bigger target than — North Carolina. In fact, in 1992 and 1993 when the Tar Heels beat the Blue Devils in Chapel Hill, their students had poured onto the floor of the DeanDome and cut the nets down. In '92, they had celebrated on Franklin Street in a manner usually reserved for national championships or, at the very least, Final Four trips.

Now, Carolina was again the league's biggest target, along with Wake Forest. Krzyzewski saw his team as the one that had something to prove, especially on the road, even though most opponents didn't see it that way. He had told his players that the Georgia Tech–Clemson trip, two difficult games in a little more than forty-eight hours, was an opportunity to prove to themselves that they could play, as Krzyzewski liked to put it, "Duke basketball."

And so, when the Blue Devils and Tigers walked into jammed-to-the-rafters Littlejohn Coliseum on a cold January Tuesday, each carried an almost identical message from their coach: be tougher than the other guy.

If you play basketball, coach basketball, or just watch basketball, there are certain places on certain nights that give you chills just walking into the building. Duke-Clemson had that atmosphere. Even with a 9:10 tipoff, the sort of late made-for-TV game that players and coaches hated, the electricity in the place made you forget quickly that it was much too late at night to be starting a basketball game.

The Clemson locker room just before tip-off was, as is the case in most locker rooms, a study in contrasts. The players sat quietly waiting for the coaches, who were gathered down the hallway in Barnes's office watching the movie *Braveheart,* starring Mel Gibson, for the umpteenth time of the week. The blood and guts helped get them psyched for battle. Love scenes were fast-forwarded; the goriest scenes replayed over and over in slow motion.

Barnes watched *Braveheart* for a while, then wandered into the coaches' bathroom to gather himself. Barnes can go from loose to tense and back again in a matter of seconds before a game. One minute, he will be stuffing wet toilet paper into someone's shoes, the next he will be sitting on the floor, staring straight ahead, saying, "I'm not sure how many more years I want to do this."

Of course every coach, especially at this level, would gladly hand in his resignation during the waiting period before a game — especially a 9 o'clock game. "You just wait forever and ever," Krzyzewski says.

Krzyzewski had taken his team home on Sunday night from Atlanta, then flown into Clemson very late Monday night so the players would sleep in on Tuesday. The initial plan had been to make the two-hour drive up I-85 from Atlanta after the Georgia Tech game, but Krzyzewski had changed his mind, figuring extra travel was preferable to spending forty-eight hours in Clemson.

Clemson is one of those places where it is better to live than visit. It is a pleasant little college town, scenic in many spots, and the campus itself is quite pretty. But the Clemson that a visitor sees usually consists of the Ramada Inn or the Holiday Inn or the newer Hampton Inn — which doesn't have a restaurant. Pat Kennedy remembers the first time he brought Florida State to Clemson to play. "The drive over from the hotel I kept thinking, 'This is the darkest place I've ever been.' "

Clemson *is* dark at night because there aren't a lot of streetlights away from the main drag. Dean Smith, who has been playing games at Clemson for thirty-six years, houses his team in Greenville, forty-five minutes away. The Tar Heels bus in from there, play the game, then bus out. "When I was younger we used to tell our wives that if they wanted to go to Hawaii with us they had to make the trip to Clemson with us first," Smith said, laughing.

Of course it is that sort of humor, combined with the jokes about the occasionally embarrassing off-field behavior of the Clemson football team, that puts the chip onto Clemson's collective shoulder. That's the chip Barnes had been playing with since his arrival, talking about people expecting Clemson to be eighth or ninth in the ACC in basketball. "I don't see any reason why Clemson people should have to accept that," he says.

And Clemson people loved him for saying it, thinking it, and, most of all, doing something about it. To be fair, it is not as if Clemson never fielded a team before Barnes arrived. In 1990, the Tigers won the ACC regular season and were a buzzer-beating jump shot by Connecticut's Tate George away from the final eight. But the last few years of the Cliff Ellis era had been difficult ones and Barnes's aggressive, in-your-face approach was one Clemson fans related to more than Ellis's usually calm demeanor. They had sold out Littlejohn for the season and the students had taken to lining up to pick up their tickets on the night before big home games. Barnes, taking a page from Krzyzewski's book, had bought them all pizza the night before the Duke game.

Now, with people literally sitting in the aisles and all the local fire marshals apparently looking the other way, the two teams went after each other as if the game would decide a Final Four spot. The two coaches were so wired that Duke Edsall, the lead official, had to tell both of them to back off early. "Let us work the game," he said. "Give us a chance."

The first half seesawed. Duke was up six, then Clemson was up four. The two point guards, Terrell McIntyre and Steve Wojciechowski, were trying to carry their teams emotionally. Each was making life miserable for the other defensively. They were like a couple of attack rats, each so low to the floor that you would swear the floor was part of their uniform. In the last minute of the half, with Clemson up 33–30 and holding for the last shot, Wojciechowski made a diving steal and fed Chris Carrawell for a dunk just before the buzzer.

Barnes was furious with Rick Hartzell for not calling a foul. As the teams exited the floor, the three officials stood at the center jump circle waiting for them to get into the tunnel before they followed. That's the way it works at halftime: the teams leave, then the officials. At the end of the game it's just the opposite: the officials get out as soon as the buzzer sounds while the teams and coaches shake hands.

As Barnes passed the officials, he barked at both Hartzell and Larry Rose. They kept walking, Barnes a few steps ahead, turning to get in one more shot. Finally, Rose put a hand up. "That's enough, Rick."

Those three words are code. They mean shut up. When an official says, "That's enough," he's warning a coach that the next thing out of his mouth is probably going to cause him to get teed up. Barnes didn't need a technical in a one-point game. He turned away and walked into the tunnel. Once in the tunnel at Clemson, the officials turn left into their locker room, the visiting team goes a few steps farther and turns right into its locker room, and Clemson goes all the way down the hall and up a flight of steps to its locker room. Barnes had gotten a few steps past the officials' locker room when he decided he had to get in one last volley. He turned back and, just as Hartzell was following Rose and Edsall through the door, he screamed, "There's no way, Rick, no fucking way."

Barnes turned on his heel to head for the steps. Hartzell stopped, turned around, and put his whistle in his mouth. A technical seemed inevitable. Hartzell stared after Barnes, as if waiting to see if he was going to turn around one more time. Barnes was through. Hartzell stared for a few more seconds, then decided to let it go. "If he'da called it," Barnes said later. "I would have gone back and gotten another one." Which would have meant ejection.

In other words, Hartzell had avoided complete chaos by keeping his temper in check. If Clemson had walked back on to the court for the second half without Barnes while a Duke player walked to the foul line to shoot four technical free throws, there might have been a full-scale riot.

Instead, Edsall called the two coaches together when they walked back on the floor to warn them once more that enough was enough. This was not an easy game to officiate. Both teams were playing very aggressively on defense, hand-checking whenever they could, putting their bodies on people all over the court. The officials had to decide which knock-downs were fouls and which ones were incidental contact. It wasn't easy, especially with both coaches up constantly.

Take a poll of ACC officials and they will tell you that Barnes and Krzyzewski can both be difficult to work with. Both are generally considered fair and they are well liked by the officials, in large part because they don't just criticize. They also praise. But in the heat of a game like this one, each man wanted every call because they were all so important. "Mike's like a football coach," one longtime referee said. "If you take a possession away from him, you better have a damn good reason for it." Barnes probably didn't get up as much as Krzyzewski, but when he did he could be very blunt. At one point later in the game he would call Edsall over and say simply: "Do you know just how bad that last call was?"

Krzyzewski and Barnes took Edsall's warning to heart. The second half swayed back and forth, neither team ever leading by more than six. Clemson led by three with nine minutes to go before Duke pieced together an eight-minute stretch of near perfect basketball, scoring on twelve straight possessions. The only reason the Tigers hung close was that their offense was almost as good. Even so, when Roshown McLeod hit a short bank shot with 1:03 to go, Duke led 76–70 and appeared to have a huge victory within sight.

But then, after playing so flawlessly for so long, the Blue Devils played about as flawed a final minute as was possible. McLeod committed a silly foul, his fifth, and was gone. McIntyre converted the two free throws to make it 76–72. Carmen Wallace, in for McLeod, committed a cardinal error on the inbounds — throwing the ball into traffic under his own basket. Greg Buckner intercepted, was fouled, and made two more free throws, giving Clemson four points in four seconds and, most important, turning the emotional momentum completely around. Later, looking at the tape, Barnes would see that Buckner had pushed Trajan Langdon in the back just before making the steal. "Some nights you get the calls," he said, "Other nights you don't."

Especially, as it would turn out, in 1997 in the ACC.

Clemson played great defense again to force one more turnover and then, with the clock under ten seconds and McIntyre trying to set the offense for a tying basket, Greg Newton foolishly came thirty-five feet away from the basket and bumped McIntyre coming around a screen. Krzyzewski would insist later that no advantage had been gained by the contact and no foul should have been called. But the bottom line was Newton had put himself in an untenable position.

McIntyre drained the two free throws. It was tied at 76. Unlike in the Michigan game, the Duke players kept their cool and didn't call time-out. Wojciechowski raced down the floor before Clemson could set its defense.

As he went to the basket, Harold Jamison was forced to cut him off, leaving Newton wide open. Wojciechowski alertly shoveled the ball to him and Newton had a wide-open dunk.

Only he forgot to catch the ball. It slipped through his hands and rolled out of bounds with 1.3 seconds left as the crowd screamed with relief. Clemson had escaped. "If you don't love this you shouldn't be playing basketball," Barnes told his team during the break. "This is what we've worked for, to play this game in this atmosphere."

Duke led early in the overtime and was still clinging to a 79–78 lead with a little more than a minute left when McIntrye and Code double-teamed Wojiechowski. He went down, the ball came loose, and Krzyzewski screamed for a foul. No call. Krzyzewski went ballistic. Code was fouled on the ensuing fast break and his two free throws put Clemson ahead to stay, 80–79. The final was 86–82.

The celebration was as wild as the game, fans spilling onto the court while the teams tried to escape in one piece. Barnes was thrilled — and drained. It had been a great game, one his team easily could have lost. "I hope that if we had lost, I would still feel like it was a great game," he told his coaches. "But it's a lot more fun this way." They popped the *Braveheart* tape back in.

Krzyzewski had lost a lot of tough games in his career. He had lost national championship games. But he took this one just about as hard as any. He honestly felt that a couple of calls — especially the noncall on Wojciechowski in overtime — had cost his team the game. He was uncharacteristically curt and short in his press conference. Only one sentence that he spoke was longer than two words: "I thought my team played its heart out."

Both teams had. Both were drained. It was January 7 in the ACC. It was going to be a long winter for everyone.

13

Early Crises

WHEN THE ACC admitted Florida State as a member in 1991, the reaction of most of the basketball coaches was, "Why the hell do we need Florida State?" The answer, as they all knew, was football. Their second reaction was a rationalization: "Well, at least it means we get a trip to Florida once a winter."

They soon learned that wasn't exactly the case. Technically, Tallahassee is in Florida. In fact, it is the capital of Florida. But when people think of Florida as a winter escape, they do not have Tallahassee in mind. The city is located in the western panhandle of the state, a lot closer to Alabama than to Miami. It may not snow in Tallahassee in January but it can get cold and it is almost always overcast, foggy, rainy, or all of the above.

The second Wednesday in January was all of the above.

That was perfect weather for the Virginia basketball team, given its collective mood. The Cavaliers were 0–2 in the ACC and were looking at a week that included the trip to Tallahassee and a home game against North Carolina. After that came the always easy swing through Wake Forest and Duke. In short, if they didn't get their act together in a hurry, they could be staring at 0–6 in the league before anyone could say déjà vu all over again.

The first thing Jeff Jones had to do was figure out a way to get some production inside. The second — and most important — thing he had to do was get everyone in his locker room back to speaking to one another.

The problem — again — was Courtney Alexander. As the coaches had predicted, Alexander had not been able to play in the game at Connecticut, an overtime loss. He was back in uniform for the team's last pre–ACC games against Delaware and Loyola of Baltimore. Since he had only practiced briefly before the Delaware game, Jones didn't start him. When Alexander got into the game, he was clearly sulking about not starting. He didn't work on defense, he was predictably rusty on offense. Virginia played well enough to win — by 10 over a team that would finish in the middle of the pack in the less-than-powerful America East Conference. What galled Jones most was the sight of his big men being pounded by Greg Smith, a six-seven kid from nearby Ashland, Virginia, whom he and his staff hadn't recruited. Why not? Because they thought the players they were recruiting were better than he was. Now, he was outplaying them.

Two nights later, against Loyola, things got no better. In fact, they were worse. The Cavaliers, facing a team that was 2–6 coming in, actually trailed 28–26 at halftime. Before Jones even had a chance to express his disgust, Harold Deane did, screaming about players being selfish, saying he was sick and tired of "guys" worrying more about themselves than about the team. He was looking directly at Alexander as he spoke. Alexander had not scored in seven first-half minutes and had done even less on defense. Alexander's response to that was to not take part in two time-out huddles in the second half. He sat on the end of the bench until teammates prodded him to his feet to stand outside the circle while Jones was talking.

Jones was so busy trying to straighten his team out (the Cavaliers finally won the game, 67–61) that he didn't even know about Alexander's behavior until he read about it in the newspaper the next morning. He was shocked and angry. When he met with the team that morning, he made it clear that any behavior like that was intolerable and that if it happened again, serious action would follow. He decided not to do anything else — meet with Alexander or suspend him — because he thought Alexander deserved the benefit of the doubt, at least for the moment. "It can be hard to deal with an injury when you haven't been through it before," Jones said later. "I wasn't happy with what he had done and neither were his teammates. The most important thing for me was to get them all back together, get the guys to feel as if Courtney was with them, not against them. Or, more accurately, to get them not to be against Courtney."

Alexander didn't start the following day at Maryland, but this time he was ready to play when his chance came. He came in off the bench to play 28 minutes and scored 18 points. That wasn't enough. Maryland was a hot team, playing in front of a hyped crowd. The Terrapins led by 14 at the half, let Virginia close to within six in the second half, then pulled away again, winning 78–62. Jones was disappointed that his team had been so flat at the start, but encouraged by the fact that they had rallied and by the return of Alexander's shooting touch. He and his teammates appeared to be on the same page again. Or at least reading the same chapter.

But they were flying into Tallahassee to face a team that was 9–1 and, like themselves, eager to make amends for the past.

"The only thing that worries me," Pat Kennedy said to his coaches, "is playing a desperate team. I want our kids to be confident, I like that. But I think we have to remind them that as of this minute, they haven't beaten a soul."

Kennedy was sitting in what he calls the War Room, a small office across from his own where he and his assistants meet every day to plan practice or recruiting visits or, on game day, that night's game. Tom Carlsen had been with him forever. He was a friend and a relative — his sister was married to Kennedy's brother — and had known Kennedy since their days growing up on the Jersey Shore. Donnie Marsh had been on the staff for two years; Jim Baxter was in his first year.

The Seminoles still had only one loss — the overtime heartbreaker at Duke in early December. They had reopened ACC play the previous Saturday with an easy 71–51 victory over NC State. The game had been at home and the Wolfpack was picked to finish ninth in the league. That was what Kennedy meant about not having beaten a soul. Virginia was struggling but Kennedy knew the Cavaliers were better than anybody his team had beaten so far.

Kennedy was confident, but apprehensive. "If our inside guys play, we should really kick their butts inside," he said. "They can't run the floor with us. The only thing they do that really scares me is make jump shots."

At times, Kennedy sounded as if he was trying to convince himself that this team and this season were going to be better than the last three teams and seasons had been. He was smart enough to understand that this was a potential crossroads year in his career. "The funny thing is, I'm only forty-four and I look around at where I've been and where I've come from and I have trouble dealing with the idea that maybe I am at a crossroads," he said. "I haven't enjoyed the last three seasons. But I think I understand why we haven't been good, and I think we've taken the right steps to get back to where we were. Now, we've just got to go out and win the games."

Like most of his brethren in the ACC, Kennedy began setting his sights on becoming a coach very young. The youngest of four children, he came from a family of athletes. His dad, one of the few Democrats ever elected to any office in the Jersey Shore town of Keyport, had been a semipro baseball player. His brothers, Wally and Bobby, were both excellent football players. Wally, ten years older than Pat, went into coaching after college. By then his youngest brother was giving up his baseball career to concentrate solely on basketball. His dream was someday to play at Seton Hall. His teams occasionally played games on campus there in Walsh Gym, and Pat would often close his eyes and imagine himself playing there wearing a Seton Hall uniform.

But when he graduated from high school he was only six feet tall and barely weighed 140 pounds. What's more, even though his grades were good, his board scores were awful — under 800. He enrolled at Staunton Military Academy, in Virginia, hoping to add pounds to his body and points to his board scores. He did better at the latter, going up to 1,100 after a year of intensive math and English courses. He put on some weight, but lacked the quickness Division I schools were looking for. He got a Division II scholarship to Kings College, in Wilkes-Barre, Pennsylvania.

His coach there was Ed Donahue, something of a legend in eastern coaching circles, since he was generally credited with convincing Calvin Murphy to enroll at Niagara while he was an assistant coach at the school. In Kennedy, Donahue found a coaching soul mate, if not a point guard, someone who spent a lot of his class time drawing up practice plans and offensive and defensive sets.

By the time Kennedy was a junior, it was apparent he was never going to play much. He was the third-string point guard. On opening night, Kings was supposed to travel to Philadelphia to play Pennsylvania in the Palestra. As the team was getting ready to board the bus, Donahue pulled Kennedy aside. "I've got an idea," he said. "Instead of going to the game tonight and sitting on the bench, why don't you drive up to Jersey City and scout St. Peter's" — Kings' next opponent — "and put together the scouting report for the game."

Kennedy was torn. As a kid, one of his dreams had been to play in the Palestra. This was going to be his chance. Then again, chances were he wasn't actually going to play in the game unless it became a rout. Donahue knew he wanted to coach. He was offering him a chance to get a head start. "I went back inside, got a clipboard, and drove to Jersey City," he said. "In the end, it wasn't that tough a decision."

Donahue put him in charge of the junior varsity that year and the team went 17–4. It is that team's picture, the team he coached for nothing, that Kennedy keeps in his desk next to the proposed UNLV contract for $582,105 a year. As a senior, Kennedy was Donahue's top assistant.

By the time Kennedy graduated from Kings, his brother had gotten out of coaching and opened a summer basketball camp in the Poconos. This was in the days before basketball camps became the rage everywhere. The entire Kennedy family worked the camp most of the summer. Famous coaches and players came to the camp to lecture, and Kennedy hung on their every word. One of the coaches he became friendly with was Jim Lynam, who was then the coach at American University. When Kennedy learned during his senior year that Lehigh had just hired Brian Hill to coach and that Hill was looking for an assistant, he asked Lynam to call Hill on his behalf. Kennedy spent two years at Lehigh, often competing in recruiting with another aggressive young assistant working at a small, academic school in Pennsylvania: Lafayette's Gary Williams.

While he was at Lehigh, Kennedy met another up-and-coming young coach through his family's camp. "We were looking for some new speakers," he remembered. "We didn't want to get stale bringing in the same guys all the time. Someone said there was a young guy coaching at Bucknell who they had heard was good. We called him up and offered him twenty-five bucks to come up and do a clinic."

The Bucknell coach accepted the offer. He came to camp on a Tuesday. Kennedy introduced him to the campers, then went back to the camp's offices to do some paperwork. "Forty-five minutes later, I hear what sounds like a riot outside my window," he said. "I go back down to the courts and the campers have this guy up on their shoulders and they're all chanting, 'V-V-V-V-V!' And they take him over to one of the nets and he cuts the net down! And he's waving the net over his head and screaming, 'Someday, I'm going to do this in the Garden! I promise you, one day, that's what I'm gonna do!'"

Thus was born the legend of Jim Valvano — clinician extraordinaire. By the end of the summer, Tuesdays at the camp were known as "V-Day," and no one went back to their offices when it was time for Valvano to speak. When he talked about "attack rats," the kids loved it so much that they found a stuffed rat, stuck it on a skateboard, and gave it to Valvano, who used it as a prop: attack rat taking a charge — on the skateboard. One week, Valvano met a helicopter pilot in a bar and made a deal to have the guy fly him into the camp for his speech the next day.

"The guy kept swooping in and Jim's got his face up against the window and he looks like the attack rat," Kennedy said. "The third time through, he went a little too far, tried to stick his face out of the helicopter, and he got sick all over the place. The guy landed the copter, the kids carried Jimmy into the showers, cleaned him up, and then he came back and did his talk."

By the end of the summer, Valvano was making $250 a speech, and he and Kennedy had become good friends. And so, a year later, when Valvano had moved on to Iona and was looking for an assistant, he hired Kennedy. They became inseparable. Kennedy was Valvano's designated driver — morning, noon, and night. He would pick Valvano and his two daughters up at 7 A.M., drop the girls at school, then head to the office. At night, they would go out recruiting, always ending up at Saporito's, an

Italian restaurant in New Rochelle that would stay open late. Sometime between 2 A.M. and 4 A.M. Kennedy would drop Valvano at his front door. Then they would start the whole cycle again a few hours later.

"Jim didn't need sleep," Kennedy said. "Couldn't sleep most of the time. He was too wound up, had too much to do. I needed sleep. But I hung in there because I had no choice."

Kennedy met his future wife at Iona — and that was also because of Valvano. "Jeannie was in charge of a Special Olympics program that used our gym in the afternoons," Kennedy said. "They tended to run a little longer than Jimmy wanted them to because he wanted the kids on the floor for early shooting, things like that. But there was no way he was going in there and tell a bunch of Special Olympians to get out of his gym. So, he sent me to do it. I think it's probably fair to say I didn't make a great first impression on Jeannie."

Eventually, though, he convinced her to go out with him. The first date was a disaster. But he was too attracted to her not to try at least one more time. "By the end of the second date, I knew I was going to marry her," he said.

Life was good. He had convinced Jeannie to marry him, Valvano was building a pint-sized juggernaut and getting more media than anyone at Iona would ever have thought possible. On most Sundays, Valvano and Kennedy would drive into New York and go listen to Norman Vincent Peale. "Jimmy loved that power-of-positive-thinking stuff," Kennedy said. "He really believed in it because for him, as a coach, it worked."

They beat Kentucky, North Carolina, and most of the college basketball powerhouses for six-ten Jeff Ruland and became a factor nationally. In February of 1980, little Iona went to Madison Square Garden to play top-ranked Louisville, the Doctors of Dunk, led by All-American Darrell Griffith. The place was packed, a rarity for college basketball in New York.

Walking into the building, Valvano turned to Kennedy and said. "You know what tonight is, don't you?"

Kennedy, who had looked at about a hundred tapes of Louisville that week, was bleary-eyed with exhaustion. He wondered if he had forgotten a birthday or an anniversary. "No, what is it?" he asked.

"Tonight's the night I cut down a net in the Garden," Valvano answered.

Then he went into the locker room and gave the players his whole cut-down-the-net speech. "It was one of those old-time Knute Rockne pep talks," Kennedy said. "You know the one, by the end, the assistants are all crying and the players are all asleep."

Not this night. Iona walked into the sold-out Garden, and with the crowd raising the roof all night, pounded Louisville, 77–60. As soon as the game was over, the players had Valvano up on their shoulders. They chanted, "V-V-V-V-V," and he cut the net down. Kennedy had tears in his eyes. That summer, when Valvano came back to camp, he still talked about dreaming of cutting a net down. Only now, it would be after winning the national championship. The net from the Louisville game was in his office.

Valvano left Iona shortly after that historic night in the Garden to become the coach at NC State. Kennedy, who was twenty-eight at the time, was hired to succeed him. With Ruland coming back for his senior year, it seemed like a dream situation. But the dream ended quickly. Ruland, it turned out, had signed a contract with an agent. That made him ineligible. There was also considerable controversy surrounding Valvano's departure. The school was bitter about it; Ruland was bitter about it. Valvano was ordered to stay away from the basketball banquet by the school president.

Without Ruland — "but playing a schedule made for Jeff Ruland to play," Kennedy pointed out — Iona was 15–14 the next year. But during the next four seasons, the Gaels averaged 24 victories a year. They made two trips to the NCAAs. Kennedy did a good job of keeping the program very close to where it had been under Valvano. But things had changed. Valvano's last year at Iona had been the Big East's first year. As the league got stronger, recruiting got tougher. In the fall of 1985, Iona was heavily involved with two New York City kids, Gerald Greene and John Morton. Even though Kennedy and his staff thought they had done a good job recruiting them, both opted for Seton Hall.

"Seton Hall!" Kennedy screamed, years later, still stunned. "They were at the absolute bottom of the Big East. We would have beaten them by twenty. But they beat us for those kids because kids wanted to play in that league. I said to my assistants after that, 'Fellas, this Iona thing is over.'"

Kennedy had been on the short list for other jobs before. Now, though, when other schools expressed interest, he was more willing to listen. Florida State had a proud basketball tradition, but it had been fourteen years since its only Final Four appearance and the program had fallen on hard times. When Joe Williams was fired at midseason, Kennedy — by coincidence — was in Florida on a recruiting trip. He called his friend Tom Carlsen, who was coaching at a local high school, and asked him what he thought about the school. "It can be a great job," Carlsen said.

En route home, Kennedy stopped in Raleigh to see another potential recruit. There he ran into Bobby Cremins in his hotel. "You should go after Florida State," Cremins told him. "It's a sleeping giant." The next day, Kennedy had lunch with Valvano. "I want you to go after Florida State," Valvano said.

The clincher came when he returned home. There was a message waiting for him from Fred White, who had broadcast some Iona games in the past and was now the radio voice of the Kansas City Royals. The manager of the Royals was Dick Howser — a Florida State graduate. "I can have Howser call for you," White said. Sure, Kennedy said, why not? After all, everyone on the planet was telling him to go after the job.

Howser got Kennedy an interview with the search committee. Shortly after that, the committee met to vote on who to hire. It chose Kennedy. The following morning, Kennedy was driving to work listening to the all-news station in New York, WINS. The last item during the sports update was about Florida State hiring a new basketball coach: "Iona's Pat Kennedy."

"I almost drove into a telephone pole," Kennedy said.

Since Florida has sunshine laws that prevent state-funded organizations from holding closed meetings, the search committee meeting had been attended by a couple of local reporters. They had reported that Kennedy was the committee's choice. The radio report had made it into a fait accompli. Kennedy quickly pulled over to find a phone booth. "This was Iona," he said. "I didn't have a car phone."

He called the school president, Brother Driscoll, hoping he could get to him before anyone told him about the radio report. "Brother," he said breathlessly, "we need to talk."

"I know," Driscoll said, "I was just listening to WINS."

The money was too good to say no to, especially given what Kennedy thought about Iona's future. He accepted the job and moved south, equipped with his Jersey shore accent and a lot of enthusiasm. The first seven years could hardly have gone better — five NCAA bids, the trip to the final eight, the smooth transition into the ACC. Kennedy was making more than $500,000 a year and his family — he and Jeannie now had three children — liked living in Tallahassee. But the non-rollover of his contract the previous spring had been a jolt. It was the first time in his coaching career that anyone had even hinted at the possibility of not wanting him around.

"Fellas, we've put last year behind us once and for all," he told his players after their shoot-around before the Virginia game. "We've closed that chapter on FSU basketball. Now, the whole country is waiting to see what we're going to do. It's all mental right now. Tonight is when our tough games really begin. NC State will probably finish ninth in the league. This team is a lot better than they are. But if you play your butts off on defense for forty minutes you will kick their ass."

This would be a meeting between the two teams who gave their players the most scouting information on opponents in the league. "I've always been a preparation freak," Kennedy said. FSU's handwritten scouting report included details on each player's strengths and weaknesses, his statistics and tendencies. Underneath was the defensive strategy to use against that player. For Courtney Alexander, the report said: "Attack him on the defensive end, he doesn't like physical play."

Jeff Jones would no doubt have agreed with that analysis.

The Leon County Civic Center is located about two miles from the FSU campus. It is a fairly typical older city-owned building. The lighting isn't great and it feels drafty when it is less than full. Renovations are planned, but in 1997, on a night when a women's game was played prior to a men's game, the FSU men and women had to share a bathroom at the rear of their adjoining locker rooms. Some might call that intimate.

The Civic Center seats 12,800 but only sells out a couple of times a season. Even with the Seminoles off to a good start, the crowd was an announced 9,452 with rows and rows of empty seats evident in the end zones. To the average fan, the big ACC game of the night was Maryland at North Carolina. That game would be on ESPN. So would Wake Forest at Georgia Tech. This was one of the few league games all year that wasn't on any kind of TV.

And yet, for both teams, it was a huge game. Kennedy had said on his pregame radio show that his goal was "that magically mysterious 8–8 league record." Valvano had always said that a .500 record in league play was all he wanted or needed because that would clinch an NCAA berth for any ACC team. Kennedy had picked up on that theme. To go 8–8, FSU certainly couldn't afford any home losses to teams picked to finish in the lower half of the league. Virginia wasn't thinking about 8–8 or any other record — other than 1–2. It needed a win, any win, in the ACC.

Kennedy was as wound up as ever in his pregame pep talk. "This will be our biggest win of the year, fellas, it will be another step towards reopening the door to greatness. Do you understand that?"

"Yes!"

"What will our record be after we win this game?"

"Ten and one!"

"And what should our record be, if we had made one more play at Duke?"

"Eleven and 0!"

Donnie Marsh says the pregame prayer for Florida State. The players gather in a circle after Kennedy is finished talking and Marsh gives thanks for the opportunity to play and asks for the health of everyone in the game. As the players break, the four coaches form their own brief huddle for a handshake. Every team says something as it breaks its huddle. At Maryland, it is "Don't get beat," something Gary Williams came up with prior to the '97 season as a reminder not to get beaten on defense. North Carolina's players simply say, "Heels." Duke's players say, "Win." Wake Forest's say, "Together." So do Virginia's, another manifestation of Odom and Jones being former Terry Holland assistants. All are variations on a theme. At Florida State, where a student dressed up as a Native American — specifically, Chief Osceola of the Seminole tribe — is the mascot, the players say, "War!"

The Virginia locker room was more subdued than Florida State's. Jones took the unusual step of calling Norman Nolan aside for a private pregame chat to remind him that this was a team he had played well against in the past and how important his play was to the team's chances of winning. After the Liberty game, Jones had benched Nolan and Chase Metheney and had given freshman Colin Ducharme and sophomore transfer Monte Marcaccini a couple of starts. When Marcaccini walked in and saw Jones writing his name on the blackboard, he had assumed it was because his locker was dirty. When a player's locker gets too dirty, Jones writes the player's name on the blackboard to remind him to clean it. Ducharme and Marcaccini were immediately dubbed "the dirty lockers." One of them, Ducharme, was still starting.

The game began exactly as Kennedy had hoped and envisioned. James Collins stole a Harold Deane pass on Virginia's first possession and dunked. Cory Louis, healthy again, drop-stepped and dunked, then took a pretty pass from Kerry Thompson for a layup. It was 6–0 and Virginia hadn't even caught its breath.

But then Kennedy's fears began to kick in: jump shots. Specifically, Courtney Alexander jump shots. Swish-swish-swish, he went. Then swish again. Nine points in four minutes and Virginia had the lead, 13–11. The rest of the half was Kennedy trying to figure out a way to slow Alexander while also working the officials to try and get them to stop Virginia's big men from pushing his big men away from the basket. Louis and Jackson were considerably quicker than Nolan and Ducharme, but not as strong. Strength was giving quickness trouble. Even so, a Kerry Thompson three put the Seminoles back ahead and they led 35–31 at the half. Alexander had 16 of his team's points on seven-of-nine shooting.

"We're turning Courtney Alexander into an All-American tonight," Kennedy told his coaches. "He's killing us."

Unlike the other coaches in the league, Kennedy always talks to his coaches before he talks to his players — both at halftime and after the game. They decide what changes, if any, to make and then go in to see the team. There wasn't much they could do about Alexander. Collins, who was guarding him, was their best defender. What needed to improve was the offense, which had been stagnant inside. "If we hadn't made a bunch of threes we'd be in serious trouble," Kennedy told the players.

Kennedy at halftime is more clinical than rah-rah. He reminded the inside players not to worry about finishing their cuts in the lane.

"No one's calling three seconds," he said — correctly — "so don't worry about it."

The second half was a lot like the first. FSU led early, Virginia came back. It was one of those games in which neither team could gain control. As the clock dwindled, Virginia's confidence began to grow. FSU might be better than it had been, but they were still very beatable. The crowd wasn't much of a factor. Kennedy's normally ruddy complexion reddened as the night wore on. At every time-out, he pleaded for more movement on offense. When backup guard Geoff Brower snapped at one of the assistants during a time-out, Kennedy smashed a clipboard while telling him he had better not *ever* talk back to an assistant coach again.

Both coaches were tense at that point. When Chase Metheney fouled out, Jones was up screaming at Duke Edsall, who, having done Duke-Clemson twenty-four hours earlier, was having a second straight long night working a whistle in the ACC.

Down three, Virginia went up three when freshman Kris Hunter came in with the Cavaliers in brutal foul trouble inside and produced five points in three minutes. It would be his most productive stint of the entire season and it came in his hometown. A Deane baseline jumper put Virginia up 62–58 with 2:31 left, but a Thompson three — his fourth — cut it to 62–61 with 59 seconds left. Kennedy called time to set his defense. The Seminoles, knowing that Deane was Jones's go-to guy even on a night when Alexander was white-hot, were ready when he made his move into the lane. They double-teamed him and he threw up an off-balance force that barely drew iron. But Norman Nolan, responding to the pre-game pep talk, beat the FSU big men to the rebound and dunked for a 64–61 lead with 45 seconds to go.

FSU had one last chance, but LaMar Greer missed a three. Nolan rebounded. It was over. Final: Virginia 64, FSU 61.

The Cavaliers raced from the floor elated. It was their biggest road win in two years. Alexander had been brilliant — 26 points — and Nolan had come up with 12 key points and eight rebounds. Everyone had contributed in some way, right down the bench to Kris Hunter.

"We're breathing again," assistant coach Tom Perrin said. "Now, if we can play this well against Carolina Saturday . . ."

Jones wasn't thinking about Saturday yet. It had been a difficult three weeks, with the Alexander saga and the lineup tinkering and the tension in the locker room. Now, he hoped, all of that was behind them.

Down the hall, the mood could not have been different. Before they even walked into the locker room, senior Kirk Luchman stopped his teammates. "Last year we lost early to NC State just like this," he said. "And then we died. We can't let that happen this time."

The coaches were thinking about the past too. "We haven't had any real adversity this year," Kennedy said. "Duke hurt, but we knew we played well. I wonder how we'll react to this." He paused and looked at Carlsen. "God, this could be just like last year. Now we're 1–2 in the league, we've got a loss at home and Clemson coming in here Saturday. We can't let this team fall apart like last year. We just can't."

Forty-five minutes later, after talking to the media, doing his postgame radio show, and making plans for the next day, Kennedy walked to his car in a soaking rain. He barely noticed.

About seven hundred miles to the northeast, another coach was walking to his car that night in something approaching a state of shock: Dean Smith.

There weren't many nights when Smith walked out of the building named for him a loser — Carolina was 122–16 in its first eleven years in the DeanDome — and the number of nights in his life when he had watched his team blow a 22-point lead could be counted on one hand. But that was what he had just witnessed. With 14:24 left in the game, Carolina freshman point guard Ed Cota had split the Maryland defense for a layup to make the score 66–44. Nine minutes and 52 seconds later, a shell-shocked Smith called a 20-second time-out. The score at that point was Maryland 72, Carolina 68. The Terrapins had outscored the Tar Heels 28–2.

In the DeanDome.

In front of the usual sellout of 21,444.

More important, in front of Dean.

If Smith was stunned, Gary Williams was amazed. He had been all over his team at halftime for letting Carolina bring the game to them, for not being aggressive, for being intimidated by their first game in a hostile arena. The score at that point was 50–38. The tirade didn't help. For the first six minutes, Carolina, which had shot 58 percent in the first half, continued to dominate the game. Then, when a rout seemed inevitable, the game suddenly turned 180 degrees with extraordinary swiftness. Maryland ripped off 14 straight points in a little more than three minutes. Still, the Terrapins trailed by eight. Serge Zwikker stopped the bleeding for Carolina with a rebound basket, but Terrell Stokes went right through the defense for a layup to cut the margin to eight again.

Smith, who hates to call time except in the endgame, called a 20-second time-out to calm things down. It didn't help. Maryland kept forcing turnovers and making shots. It took the lead at 69–68 with 5:07 left on a Laron Profit layup. When Profit drained a three pointer 32 seconds later, Smith called his second 20-second time-out. By then, it was so quiet in the building you could hear sweat drops hitting the floor.

Carolina teams are famous for their resiliency. For them to be 22 down and come back to lead was almost commonplace. Even after the 28–2 run, there was still plenty of time left to turn it around. It wouldn't happen on this night. The Tar Heels never got even again. Maryland pulled away in the final minute for an 85–75 win. The score of the last 14 minutes of the game was 41–9.

When the buzzer sounded, Williams found himself staring at the scoreboard, almost unable to believe the numbers could be accurate. He walked down the court to shake hands with Smith and felt a little bit shaken. Smith looked gray to him, his hair looked gray, his face looked gray. He looked old. "I've never thought of Dean as old," he said later. "At that moment, he looked old to me."

It was the second time that evening that Smith had caused Williams to think about the fragile nature of their profession. Prior to the game, as he walked past the Carolina bench, he had stopped to chat with Smith. Seeing Vince Carter in street clothes as a result of the hip-pointer he had suffered late in the Wake Forest game, Williams casually asked Smith how long he thought Carter would be out.

Smith arched an eyebrow. "If this were fifteen years ago," he said, "he'd probably be playing tonight."

The comment rocked Williams. He had never heard Smith put down one of his players in any way. To him the implication was clear: today's kids aren't as tough as yesterday's. That wasn't a new concept by any means, but for Smith to apply it to one of his own players was brand-new. At least to Williams. It made him wonder if Smith wasn't getting a little fed up with the way the game had changed. He had lost an entire class to the NBA and there were rumors that Antawn Jamison was leaving at the end of this season. He couldn't help but think, even in the gleeful aftermath of the victory, about how Smith had to feel that night.

"I had the sense before the game that he was frustrated," he said. "I can only imagine how he felt after the game."

Awful was the correct answer.

Smith never says anything to his team in the locker room after a game — except when it is the last game of the season. He will walk in, pick up a Diet Coke, offer a brief prayer — "to a general creator, not any specific religion" — and then go to meet with the media right away. It is a policy he has had since December 9, 1967. After an 89–76 loss at Vanderbilt, Smith angrily blasted Bill Bunting and Joe Brown in the locker room for poor play. He had to take a single-engine plane home that night so he could get back in time for his TV show the next day. The little plane rocked and rolled crossing the mountains. "I was so angry that I didn't really care if we made it or not," Brown said. "The next day, when I looked at the film, I found out that Bunting and Brown hadn't done anything to deserve singling out. I told myself afterwards that I was never going to critique my players right after a game was over when I was still emotional and wound up — win or lose."

He smiled. "Of course we did win twenty in a row after that game."

Smith is nothing if not resilient. He calmly answered all the media's questions about the Maryland collapse, took the game tape home with him, and, as he does after every game, sat and watched the entire tape. Then he had to make a decision: "Did I make the players go through what I had just gone through?"

The answer was yes. He thought they needed to see how good they had been and how bad they had been. The early part of the Maryland run had been more about Maryland than Carolina — "we still got good shots for a while," he said — but the last 12 minutes of the game had been about as bad as a Carolina team can be. Part of Smith wanted just to pretend it hadn't happened. But he thought the players needed to understand how tough it was going to be for them in the ACC all season, how hard they had to work for 40 minutes — not 20 or 26 or 36 — to win games.

Painfully, he took them through the tape the next afternoon. Then he pulled it out of the VCR, held it up, and said, "Now we burn this and go on."

14

Trendsetting

COACHES LOVE to blame the media for their problems, as if reporting that a team has been losing games is some kind of conspiracy cooked up to get them fired. The media is an easy target. Players today look at most members of the print media as if they have some kind of infectious disease. TV is different, in part because players watch TV and know that their family and friends watch TV and in part because most TV people tend to be less than critical. So, if a coach wants to create an us-versus-them atmosphere in his locker room he will often talk about what "they" are saying about "us" in the papers. Or on talk radio or the Internet.

On some occasions, the coaches are absolutely right — especially when it comes to talk radio, where hosts and callers who wouldn't dare set foot in a locker room to ask a tough question say outrageous things about people they have never met and games they know little about. As basketball and all sports have grown more popular in recent years and, as media coverage has exploded, more and more fans have come to consider themselves experts.

Terry Holland remembers being at a party late in his tenure as the coach at Virginia when a local doctor approached him and said, "Terry, you mind if I give you some advice about your team?"

"As a matter of fact," Holland answered, "I do."

At first, the man thought Holland was kidding. He wasn't. "Let me ask you a question," he continued, "how many years did you train to become a doctor? Eight, nine, ten? If someone walked in off the street and said they'd watched you work a few times and thought they could tell you how to be a better doctor, what would your response be? You would think he was nuts, wouldn't you? Well, guess what? I trained just as long and hard to learn my job as you did to learn yours."

The reaction to the Maryland–North Carolina game was a perfect example of why coaches often have trouble dealing with fans and the media. In the Washington, D.C., area, Gary Williams was suddenly a hero again. Fans and media who had been whispering the previous summer that it was time for Maryland to find a new coach were now fighting for places on the Maryland bandwagon. Rick Barnes often says that during the course of a basketball season every coach hears thumping noises. "It's the sound of people jumping on the bandwagon, then jumping off, then jumping back on," he says.

The Maryland bandwagon was now filled to near capacity. The Terrapins had cracked the national rankings in late December. Now with a 3–0 ACC record and a 13–1 overall mark, they were headed for the top ten. The local papers were full of stories about the comeback against Carolina; about Keith Booth's emergence as a potential first-round draft pick; about the improvement of the three sophomores (Terrell Stokes, Obinna Ekezie, and Laron Profit); and about how difficult it had been for Williams to deal with the previous year's senior class. Poor Johnny Rhodes, of whom Williams had often said, "I'd go to war with him," was being lumped with the other three members of that now-judged-guilty class.

The reaction to the game in North Carolina was quite different. To say that panic set in would not be a stretch. The talk shows were full of callers wondering if Dean Smith had finally lost his magic touch, if it wasn't time for him to retire and pass the baton to Roy Williams or Eddie Fogler or George Karl. Maybe, they said, the game had passed him by.

The papers weren't quite as hysterical, but there was talk about all of Carolina's remarkable streaks — 22 straight NCAAs, 26 straight 20-win seasons, 30 straight top three finishes in the ACC — being in jeopardy.

Mike Krzyzewski:
Seeking to recapture old glory —
and the joys of coaching.

Pat Kennedy:

Eleven is enough — twenty victories weren't enough to keep him at Florida State.

Rick Barnes:
The practical jokes and
outgoing personality mask an
insatiable desire to succeed.

Bobby Cremins:
A nightmare season, but not
another midlife crisis.

Gary Williams:
A winner in a league where
you can never win enough.

Dean Smith:
The winningest coach of all time
— but don't remind him.

Herb Sendek:
Rookie of the Year — now
comes the hard part.

Jeff Jones:
Five NCAA tournament appearances in seven years and still
under fire from his own people.

Dave Odom:
The present was precious
but the finale came much
too soon.

Clearly, Smith wasn't going to break Adolph Rupp's record this season. Maybe he wouldn't break it at all. Maybe he would just walk away at the end of the season, even if he was a few victories shy of Rupp's 876.

Smith was a lot more concerned with getting ready to play Virginia than any of the talk around the state. He knew that things weren't nearly as bad as they appeared. He blamed himself for the Wake Forest debacle. The team just hadn't had enough time to get ready for a game at that level after the long European trip. What's more, Wake was far more advanced at this stage of the season, with three seniors and two juniors starting, than his team was. The last 14 minutes of the Maryland game had been so bad they almost had to be an abberration. And with a team that wasn't deep to begin with, not having Vince Carter had certainly been a factor.

Still, he knew they needed to improve soon. He was concerned enough with keeping the team together and focused on the job at hand that he took the unusual step of riding the team bus to Charlottesville. Normally, he would drive his own car and let the assistants go with the team. "Of course the last time we lost up there [1995] I got a speeding ticket going through Lynchburg," he said. "They knew who I was too. I heard them laughing."

Smith wouldn't have to worry about a speeding ticket on this trip. He figured he had enough to worry about already.

Jeff Jones wasn't the least bit concerned about Dean Smith's troubles with state troopers in Virginia or with the convulsive reactions in and around Chapel Hill to the Tar Heels' 0–2 league start. But when he woke up on Saturday morning and heard ESPN's Chris Fowler talking about the game in Charlottesville being "an absolute must" for Carolina, he had heard enough. As his players finished their pregame meal that afternoon at the Aberdeen Barn, he told them what he thought.

"All we've heard the last couple of days is how crucial this game is to Carolina," he said. "They're 0–2 and they've never been 0–3. Fine. But have you heard one word about this being a crucial game for Virginia? About how we can't afford to be 1–3? No. What does that mean? It means people think they have a chance to contend for the league, win the league, and we don't. That is a damn insult.

"Now, we can just say, 'that's OK,' and go on from there, or we can take it personally and go out and kick somebody's butt. Because you see, this is a big game for *us*. Every bit as big as it is for them. Maybe bigger, because we're playing at home."

Playing at home didn't seem like that much of an advantage in U-Hall these days. Even with Carolina in town there were empty seats in the upper reaches of the building and the crowd was less than electrified when the teams came on the court. Jones had been hoping that his team, which had grown accustomed to playing in front of quiet crowds at home, might have a chance to feed off the emotion of a wired sellout. That would not be the case.

While Jones sat in his locker room prior to the game reading up on how much better his team had played defensively in the first half than in the second half (100 fewer points given up), Smith leaned against a wall in the hallway outside his locker room killing time. He had finished his pregame radio show and was waiting to go back inside to talk to his team. A U-Hall usher walked up and welcomed Smith back to Charlottesville.

"It's good to see you again," Smith said. "You've been here forever, haven't you?"

"Sure have," the man said. "Been working here sixteen years."

That only put him twenty years behind Smith — who was too polite to point that out.

Smith hadn't changed his pregame routine in thirty-six years — except that now he chewed Nicorettes instead of smoking — and when he was at home he skipped lunch. For many years, he had eaten lunch with the same group every day, but the death several years before of one of the group's members and Smith's concern about watching his weight had ended that tradition. He did sometimes eat the pregame meal with his team on the road because there were fewer chances to meet before a road game and the end of a meal was a good time to do that.

Jones always attended pregame meals, but rarely ate. He was too nervous. But his stomach problems had started up again after the Delaware game and his doctor had suggested he try to eat something before games so he wouldn't be dealing with the stress of a game on an empty stomach. He had forced himself to eat some chicken. The Aberdeen Barn served about as good a steak as you were going to find up and down the length of the ACC. Jones figured chicken was about all he could handle.

His big concern against Carolina was rebounding. His inside players — especially Nolan — had improved against Florida State but they couldn't afford to get into foul trouble. Knowing Carolina lacked depth, he urged his players to make them work, to play them physically. "Wear their asses out," he said.

It was not a pretty game. Neither team shot the ball well early and, as often happens in the ACC, the defenses knew the offenses so well, it was tough for anyone to run anything. Carolina was trying to pound the ball inside, figuring — correctly — that Zwikker was bigger than Virginia's inside players and Jamison quicker. When Colin Ducharme picked up two quick fouls, Jones brought in the one player he had who could match Zwikker's size, seven-four Chase Metheney.

Metheney had almost left Virginia the previous summer, intending to transfer to South Carolina. But at the last minute he had decided he didn't want to leave and he had returned. Jones desperately wanted to get minutes, rebounds, and fouls out of him. But to date he had only provided fouls. Now, he played the half of his life. He blocked a shot, hit a fifteen-foot jumper (which sent the somnambulent crowd into a fit of ecstasy), and then rebounded a Nolan miss and made the layup and the ensuing foul shot.

His play gave his teammates a jolt of adrenaline. Then Curtis Staples hit a pair of threes and Virginia went on an 11–0 run that turned a 17–15 lead into a 28–15 lead. Carolina looked dazed — again. Smith was willing to try anything — and anyone. He put his two senior walk-ons, Charlie McNairy and Webb Tyndall, into the game, hoping they might make a play and give their teammates a boost. McNairy and Tyndall tried mightily, but they didn't have any more luck than their more decorated teammates. Everything was going right for Virginia. Up 12 with 30 seconds left, Jones used a 20-second time-out to set up a final shot. The ball ended up in the hands of senior Jamal Robinson, a slasher whose favorite move was to go straight to the basket. There was no time for that. Robinson launched a three.

Swish. It was 35–20, Virginia at halftime. That meant in its most recent 34 minutes of basketball Carolina had been outscored 76–29.

Jones's major concern during the break was getting his players' feet back on the ground. They weren't accustomed to being up 15 on anyone, much less Carolina. While the players congratulated themselves, Jones walked to the board and wrote:

20 down.
20 to go.

Before he said anything, Deane jumped out of his seat. "Hey, fellas, remember Clemson. We were way up" — actually, 27–19 — "on them and didn't get it done the second twenty minutes."

Jones couldn't have written that line any better. "So the way to keep that from happening again," he said, "is to fight to the last tick of that damn clock. I guarantee you right now, down the hall, he's [Smith] mad at them for not hustling. But he's also reminding them that they were up twenty-two the other night and lost. Fifteen is less than twenty-two.

"They're going to trap and press more. They're going to be more aggressive. That's fine. Take advantage of it. Remember, we aren't content. If they try to pound it inside, that's fine. Let 'em know we're physical — not soft. Send a message that this is our place and our game."

It was their game, although Carolina did try to rally. An Ademola Okulaja three-pointer three minutes in sliced the lead to nine, but every time Carolina had a chance to get closer than that, it couldn't come up with a shot. Down 47–37 with more than 10 minutes left, the best shot they could find was a Webb Tyndall three. Tyndall was a classic Carolina walk-on: bright, personable, eager, a great cheerleader on the bench, a hard worker in practice. But he had never scored from the field in two years on the varsity. In fact, this shot was only his second attempt of the season. But with Carter still acting hobbled — he played 10 minutes and scored two points — and Cota still struggling with his shot, Smith was hunting. That's why Tyndall and McNairy were on the floor with both the Maryland and Virginia games in doubt. Tyndall's shot was woefully short.

"He makes them in practice," Smith lamented.

Virginia rebuilt the lead to 16 after that and, although Jamison tried to lead a one-man comeback late in the game, scoring five points in seven seconds to cut the margin to 66–60 with 1:55 left, it was Virginia's night. A gorgeous Deane-to-Ducharme pass made it 68–60 and then, after an exchange of free throws, Tyndall was forced to launch another three (an air ball). When Jamison fouled out trying to go over Deane's back on the rebound, it was over. The final was 75–63.

Jones knew they had caught Carolina at a perfect time. The Tar Heels were beat up both physically and emotionally. He didn't care. It was a big win, especially on a night when his two best shooters, Alexander and Staples, had been a combined 11 for 27. After staring at a possible 0–6 start four days earlier, they were 2–2. He felt badly that he hadn't been able to get the hardworking freshman Willie Dersch into the game, but the chance simply hadn't come. "That's what's tough about coaching sometimes," he said. "We win a big game and I can't help but think about Dersch. I'll sit back and enjoy this for about five minutes. Then I'll start worrying about Wake."

Smith would wait at least a day before he started worrying about NC State, Wednesday's opponent. Right now, he was worried only about his team. He actually thought he had seen some progress in the second half. He started to take one of his little shots at Virginia in his postgame press conference. "They're strong and pushy," he said. Then he stopped himself. "I mean strong. That's part of the game." He paused again. "Antawn" — Jamison, who had fouled out — "has to learn not to get frustrated."

While Smith was talking calmly about improved shot selection and patience, his players were anything but calm. As the media was being herded out of the locker room, Zwikker could be heard screaming in the shower, "When are we going to stop playing like shit!" The doors closed and loud, angry voices could be heard inside. The Tar Heels were holding a get-it-all-out players-only meeting.

That would mean more headlines back home. The 0–3 start was bad enough, but now it appeared the players were starting to lose their famous Carolina cool. One man hadn't lost his cool, though. As Dean Smith walked into the cold Charlottesville night, he had the game tape in his hand. He would watch it on the bus ride home. Walking out the door he turned to a reporter, smiled, and said, "Got any suggestions?"

If the question had been a serious one there would have been reason for the Carolina faithful to panic. It wasn't. Dean Smith never panicked.

The loss to Virginia dropped Carolina into a tie for last place with Georgia Tech. Neither team's coach — Smith or Bobby Cremins — had ever been 0–3 in conference play before. Smith's 0–3 drew headlines; Cremins's drew murmurs. One other team was winless in the league, but that was a surprise to no one: NC State.

Picked to finish ninth by everyone alive, the Wolfpack was 0–2 in the league, but had played very respectably throughout the month of December. They had beaten Penn State and Memphis (breaking a 33-game home winning streak for the Tigers) and had played very well in their league opener against Wake Forest. That game had been tied 17–17 at halftime before Wake had pulled away late for a 53–45 win.

That game was a prototype for the way Herb Sendek wanted his team to play: the pace of the game had been slow and State's aggressive defense had forced 24 turnovers, a huge number in a low-possession game. That was what Sendek wanted: fewer possessions for the opposition and more turnovers. So far, State had succeeded well. In 11 games, opponents had averaged just 50.3 points and had turned the ball over almost 23 times a game — seven more than State had forced a year ago playing at a faster tempo.

The Wolfpack had been blown out twice: 84–56 at Kansas and 71–51 at Florida State. In both those games, the other team had quick big men who got the Wolfpack into foul trouble and raced downcourt, wearing them down as the game went on. State lacked size and depth, but it did have some experience with seniors Jeremy Hyatt and Danny Strong and junior guards C. C. Harrison and Ishua Benjamin in the starting lineup. The fifth starter was a talented freshman center, Damon Thornton. As long as Sendek could keep his starters on the floor and keep the score of the game low, he felt his team could compete.

State was the kind of team no one liked to play against. It took tremendous patience to deal with their style, and their defense made the game hard work, no matter what the score. Walking into Reynolds Coliseum on a cold Sunday afternoon to play the Wolfpack, Gary Williams was even more apprehensive than usual.

"It's a no-win game," he said. "The last three days everyone in the world has been telling us how great we are. Now, we come down here against a team everyone expects us to beat and I know — I mean I know — it's going to be a bitch because playing in this place was tough when I was a player thirty years ago and it's tough now. You never walk in here and win easily. Never. But telling the players that is tough. They figure, 'Hey, we went into Carolina and won, this is a piece of cake.' Only they're wrong if they think that."

Reynolds Coliseum is one of college basketball's grand old places. When it opened in 1949, its seating capacity of 12,400 made it the largest indoor arena south of Atlantic City and north of New Orleans. It was not the most superbly constructed building in history, with almost two-thirds of the seats behind the baskets, but like Cole Field House and Cameron Indoor Stadium, it was an intimate old place with seats right on top of the floor, balcony seats that practically hung over the court, and a low ceiling that held the noise. And, like Maryland and Duke, State had always kept its students courtside. As at Cameron, they surrounded the court. They were so close to the benches that they could practically lean into time-out huddles.

Like Maryland, State was in the process of trying to build a new building. Sendek understood that a new arena would be good for the athletic department's bottom line. But he also hated the idea of leaving a building where the home court advantage was so huge. Newer buildings like the DeanDome tended to be much more antiseptic and visitor-friendly. The new building's supporters wanted a facility every bit as big and glamorous as the DeanDome. The new building would be several miles from campus and would eventually be the home for a National Hockey League team. All of that meant it would be less of a home for State. In fact, the team would still practice on campus. It would be sharing the new facility with a tenant that would use it three times as often. No matter what promises were made, the hockey team would be the building's first priority.

Sendek didn't like any of this. "But it's one of those situations where I have no say," he said. "These decisions were made before I got here at levels way above mine. All I can do is focus on coaching the basketball team."

Focus has never been a problem for Sendek, especially when it comes to basketball. Like Dean Smith and Jeff Jones, he is a coach's son who has been around basketball for as long as he can remember. His dad, Herb Sr., was a high school coach in Pittsburgh before becoming the head coach at Allegheny County Community College. The Sendek house was always full of basketball talk, and Herb Jr. constantly tagged along to practice with his dad, learning the game from him as he grew up.

He was a good high school player, never big enough or quick enough to be recruited by any Division I schools, but good enough — and smart enough — to get into Carnegie Mellon University. His grade point average in high school was 4.0. In college he faltered — making two B's in four years and finishing with a 3.95 average. "The B's were disappointing," he said, dead serious as always. "One was in microbiology, the other was in calculus. I did everything I possibly could and B was still the best I could do."

Sendek, according to Sendek, has always been a driven perfectionist. Anything he did, he wanted to do better than anybody else. "I was that way as a kid," he said. "I never wanted to disappoint my parents. I didn't get into trouble, I worked hard in school, and I tried to be well behaved."

There are no wild and crazy Herb Sendek stories. Ask friends of his if he loosens up and relaxes in private and their answer is simple: no.

"Not true," he said, almost smiling. "I think I am different when I'm around my friends and family. When I'm in public, I'm very aware of my responsibilities and of not wanting to say or do anything that's going to make anyone feel bad. But I do loosen up with the people I'm close to."

This is a controversial subject. Coaches whom Sendek worked with before he got to State love to talk about postgame Herb, standing in the corner of the locker room after a big victory, shaking his head, worrying about the next game while everyone else celebrated. Sendek insists that reputation was born in 1992 after Kentucky had beaten Massachusetts in the Sweet Sixteen of the NCAAs. Sendek was assigned to scout the next opponent: Duke. On the bus back to the hotel, Rick Pitino was still enjoying the UMass win when Sendek leaned over and said, "Coach, have you looked at Duke yet? They're awesome."

Pitino laughed and said, "We'll worry about Duke in the morning."

Which, Sendek says now, was easy for him to say. "It was my job to have the scouting report on Duke finished and ready first thing in the morning," he said. "I was the one staying up all night to get that ready. If Coach had walked in the next morning and said, 'Where's the stuff on Duke,' and I had said, 'You know, Coach, I didn't get to it last night because I was enjoying the win over UMass,' I promise you he would not have been happy."

No doubt, the truth lies somewhere in the middle. All coaches get their game face on for the next opponent about fifteen minutes after the last victory. Most will tell you they remember losses longer and more vividly than wins.

Sendek has always been a learner — a fast learner. After he played point guard at Carnegie Mellon for three years, he suffered the humiliation of being cut before his senior season. The school had hired a new coach who decided to go with younger players to rebuild. A number of the juniors and seniors, Sendek among them, were let go. "It hurt a lot," he remembered. "But it was probably a lucky break because it got me started in coaching."

He coached that year as a student assistant at Pittsburgh Central High School under Al Van Blow, an old friend of his father's. That spring, he was sitting at home reading the paper, trying to figure out exactly what he was going to do after graduation, when he saw an item about Providence naming a new coach. When he saw the name of the coach, he sat up straight in his chair: Rick Pitino.

Sendek knew Pitino — sort of. He had worked as a counselor at the Five-Star Camp outside of Pittsburgh for a couple of summers and had briefly met Pitino, who was almost as legendary a clinician at Five-Star as Valvano had been at Kennedy's camp. More important, he had become friends with camp director Howard Garfinkel, one of basketball's true characters. A lifelong New Yorker, with slick black hair, thick glasses, and an ever-present cigarette, Garfinkel had never driven a car or had a driver's license. He had been a New York bird dog for Everett Case in the 1950s when Case was at NC State and, along with Frank McGuire, one of the dominant forces in the ACC.

In 1967, Garfinkel had started the Five-Star Camp and it had grown into the first truly national basketball camp. If you wanted to show people you were a great player, you had to go to Five-Star. Every college coach not working at the camp — and, until the NCAA rewrote the rulebook to forbid it, coaches lined up for the chance to work at Five-Star because it meant you had a pipeline to the top players — came to the camp to watch. Michael Jordan's first national splash was at Five-Star in 1980, the summer before his senior year at Laney High School. But he wasn't the first or last star to attend the camp.

Garfinkel was always on the lookout for up and coming young

coaches. Pitino had been a protégé. So had Odom. And John Calipari. Earlier, Hubie Brown and Bob Knight had been Five-Star regulars. Garfinkel had noticed Sendek. He liked his work ethic and his demeanor. As serious as he was, Sendek always seemed to connect with the campers. And, when it came time for the campers to go through Garfinkel's beloved drill stations, Sendek never let anyone slack off.

Sendek knew that Garfinkel and Pitino were close. He called Garfinkel. Was there any chance, he wondered, that Garfinkel might call Pitino and ask him if he would interview Sendek for a graduate assistant's job? The call back came from Pitino, who hired Sendek over the phone, based on Garfinkel's recommendation and a vague memory he had of the hardworking kid at the camp.

And so, less than three years after being told he wasn't good enough to play point guard for Carnegie Mellon, Sendek was good enough to be on the coaching staff of a Final Four team. Providence finally lost to Syracuse in New Orleans after a run miraculous enough to land Pitino the New York Knicks job. When Gordy Chiesa moved up to replace him, Sendek became a full-time assistant coach — at the age of twenty-three. His salary jumped from expenses to $32,000. He felt like a millionaire. He worked for Chiesa for one year and for Rick Barnes for one year before Pitino called again. He was leaving the Knicks after two years for Kentucky and he wanted Sendek to go with him. Four years later, after another trip to the Final Four, Sendek was hired at Miami of Ohio. He had just turned thirty. Three straight twenty-victory seasons after that, he was moving south to NC State.

It wasn't an easy time to move. His wife, Melanie, whom he had met in Lexington through Pitino (she worked in a health club where the coaches worked out and Pitino convinced her to go out with his shy assistant) was pregnant with their second daughter. But both she and her husband knew this was not a chance they could turn down. And since she had been pregnant with their first daughter when the Miami job came up, the drill was not an unfamiliar one. It wasn't so much the money — although by making the move Sendek doubled his income to the $300,000 a year neighborhood — it was the chance to coach in the ACC.

"I understand how lucky I've been," Sendek said on the morning of the Maryland game after his team had gone through an 8:30 A.M. shoot around and practice. "I think I have a responsibility not to let people down. It's no different now than when I was a kid. Then, I didn't want to let my parents down. Now, I don't want to let my wife and kids down. Or the people here who brought me in to do a job."

The people who had brought him in to do a job were very happy with him. They liked his intense manner and the enthusiasm his team brought to the floor. It wasn't all that different than Rick Barnes's first year at Clemson. The Wolfpack — like that Clemson team — was picked to finish last in the conference. Every team it played expected to win, regardless of where the game was played. Sendek kept telling his players — as Barnes had — that they had something to prove. No one on the team had ever played in postseason or on a winning team. They could do both those things, Sendek said, if they didn't get down on themselves, if they kept coming to practice to work hard every day, whether they were winning or losing.

Sendek set the tone. Often, he would run wind sprints with the team that had lost a drill or made a mistake that caused a sprint to be run. He was a different person in practice than he was giving a speech or speaking to the media or even chatting with people in a restaurant. Gone was the super-serious, cautious demeanor. He was serious, but it was a different kind of seriousness, it was a let's-get-after-it approach. The basketball court was clearly his domain. He was completely confident, clearly enjoying himself, very much the man in charge. When he spoke to a player, he never said, "I think." It was more definitive than that. "Justin, you cannot be a good basketball player if that's the closest you can come to a defensive stance." Or, "Osh" — Ishua Benjamin's name is pronounced "Oshua" — "that's just not a good shot. We can't take shots like that and win games."

The Sendek who ran practice and in-game huddles was a lot different from the Sendek who analyzed the game for the media when it was over. The latter always had that deer-in-the-headlights look, a kid with prominent teeth and a receding hairline who someone had dressed up in a suit. The former could easily have been a young Pitino — without the histrionics and preening — a precocious leader who talked about everything from traps to body language, sometimes in the same time-out.

Williams knew exactly who Sendek was and what he brought to the table because he had once been that same young coach, supremely confident, ready to take on anyone and anybody. At fifty-one, he wasn't all that different than he had been eighteen years earlier when he was Sendek's age and a rookie head coach at American, but he had a sense now of limitations and time that he hadn't had then. As good a coach as he was, and he had no doubts about his ability, he still hadn't been to the Final Four. Doubts gnawed at him on occasion. Maybe it wasn't meant to be for him. Maybe he would just be a very good coach who had made a lot of money and won a lot of games but had never quite gotten to the promised land.

Once, he had been certain that the Final Four, a national title, were just a matter of time. Sendek felt that way now. Williams still hoped. But there were days when he wondered. "If I walked away from it without ever having gone to the Final Four, would it bother me? Yeah, it would. I don't think my life would be ruined by it, but it would bother me. At this level, that's your goal — the Final Four, the national championship. Some years, you may not be good enough to get there. Others, maybe you are. But you don't really know which is going to be the year. Did Mike [Krzyzewski] think that '91 was going to be the year he broke through? I doubt it. Did Rollie [Massimino] really think his team was good enough in '85 going in as an eighth seed to win the whole thing? Probably not. You have to be prepared every year, because you don't know which year is going to be the one when the door suddenly pops open for you."

So far, this year had been filled with open doors. The Carolina game was a perfect example. Williams kept reminding his players that they had played horrendously for 26 minutes and that most nights in the ACC you can't overcome 26 horrendous minutes with 14 good ones. He knew that with Clemson coming to Cole in three days, his players' minds were likely to be anyplace but where they needed to be: in Reynolds Coliseum on Sunday. "Half of them are still thinking about Carolina, the other half are thinking about Clemson," he said. "They can relate to 'Hey, we're going to play the number three team in the country on ESPN.' This, they can't relate to because they don't know anything about history."

History said that State had a record in their building of 557–161 through the years. History also said that Maryland was 3–4 in Reynolds under Williams. Williams remembered playing ACC tournament games in this place (the first thirteen were in Reynolds) and he still had a great feeling for what it meant to college basketball — and, more important, what it meant to be the home team.

Before they went up the steps that led from the basement locker rooms to the floor, Williams gave his team a little history lesson. "We have a chance to do something today that very few — if any — Maryland teams have ever done," he said. "We have a chance to win at Carolina and at State in the same week. That is really hard to do. We barely beat this team both times we played them last year and they have four starters back.

"They are a good shooting team and they will defend well. But they have been doubled on the boards in both their ACC games. We should kick their ass on the boards. But we can't just say, 'We're bigger so we'll do it.' We have to actually go out there and do it. Remember, fellas, you never know when the chance to win the game will come. It could be the first five minutes or the last five. But you have to be ready to win for all forty.

"This is about *today*. Not last Wednesday or next Wednesday. It's about today. That's all that matters. Our job is today, right here, right now."

They listened. They understood. But it was still tough to get wound up to play when the building was less than full and a lot of the fans seemed more focused on the updates the Wolf mascot was carrying around the floor on the Carolina Panthers–Green Bay Packers NFC championship game. "It's either a late-arriving crowd or a crowd that ain't coming," assistant coach Billy Hahn said, returning to the locker room after warm-ups. Williams was standing in the middle of the empty locker room, practicing his golf swing — without a club. "A couple more months and I'll be playing," he said. Then he sat down. "Either way, coaching or playing golf, I'll probably end up pissed." He laughed and looked at Hahn. "If this is a one o'clock game, why do I feel like it's about midnight."

Hahn was right about the crowd. All of North Carolina had been hit with Panthers fever and even the once untouchable ACC was feeling it. The announced crowd in Reynolds on this Sunday afternoon was 11,700 but it looked like less. Still, the State students were there, making suggestions to Williams during time-outs and keeping the atmosphere raucous.

"No, Gary, not that play," someone would shout. Or, "Fifty-five, they're in fifty-five," to the State players taking the court. "That's the press," someone else would say. "Yeah, but which one, they've got about four of them."

They knew their hoops. Maryland did have a lot of different presses. Both teams started everything with their defense. Maryland jumped to a quick 11–4 lead, but State began to find its range from outside. Williams keeps up a running commentary on the bench during games, most of it directed at his assistants. In truth, though, he is often talking to himself. "The only way they can beat us is hitting threes. Damn! That's a three. We can't give them that!"

His players and his coaches know that most of what he says in the heat of battle is hyperbolic. During the forty minutes of a game, Williams thinks that just about everyone and everything sucks. The refs suck. His team's defense sucks. The shot selection is worse. And each player is probably the worst player he or any coach in the history of the game has ever recruited. What's more, his assistants can't coach and neither can he. Why the hell are any of them here in the first place? Then, up ten at the break he will walk into the locker room and say, "OK, fellas, that was good work." He will mean every word.

Williams wasn't happy at halftime, even with a 27–17 lead, because his team had failed to recognize a zone defense on the last play of the half and had been in the wrong offensive set. "We're a goddamn nationally ranked team," Williams said. "We can't make mistakes like that. We've worked on that since October fifteenth."

Williams talks to his coaches during the break after a brief talk with the players. By the time he gets to the room where the coaches are waiting, they have the first half statistics written on a board. Williams will ask how the opposition did against certain defenses and will analyze the first twenty minutes. Rarely does he focus on what's going right. "That doesn't need fixing," he says. "The other stuff does."

"We should be up more than ten," he told the players. "We've given them life. They'll make a run and that's fine. Just be prepared to respond to it."

When the run came, Maryland responded. A Jeremy Hyatt follow-up put State up for the first time, 42–41, with 9:12 to go and Reynolds was rocking, Panthers or no Panthers. During a TV time-out, Williams was so calm you might have thought the game was a scrimmage. "We've put ourselves in a position where we have to work these last nine or ten minutes," he said. "That's fine. We've done it all year."

And they did it again. A drive by backup guard Matt Kovarik got them the lead back and started an 11–1 run that put them back in control of the game. Keith Booth, who had struggled all day, made a key steal and layup and a three-point play a possession later to put the Wolfpack away for good. The final was 68–59.

Williams was drained and elated. He had jumped Ekezie and Booth in a time-out and both had responded. They had fallen behind and come back. "I was more scared of this game than Carolina," Williams told his team. "I knew you'd play hard there and I know you'll play hard Wednesday. This worried me. This was a hell of a win. We didn't play our best, but that's OK. This time of year, all that matters is winning."

Sendek couldn't take that approach. He had to see progress, since he wasn't seeing wins. "At times you feel like you're running in place," he said. "I told the players even if that's exhausting, the intelligent thing is to keep running."

15

The New Kids
Take Command

"WE PLAYED WELL," Mike Krzyzewski said after his team lost to the Wake Forest Deacons for the ninth straight time, 81–69. "They were almost perfect." For Krzyzewski to say his team had played well after losing by 12 at home, the opponent had to be awfully good.

After two weeks of league play, there were three undefeated teams: Wake Forest, Clemson, and Maryland. The Deacons, who had looked superb in beating both Georgia Tech and Duke on the road to reach 4–0, were no surprise. They were supposed to be the best team in the league. Thus far, they had let no one down.

Clemson wasn't nearly as dominant, but it was 3–0. It had gotten a little bit lucky at home against Duke, then played well down the stretch to win at Florida State. Pat Kennedy's concern that his team would let down after losing to Virginia had proved true. The Seminoles dropped to 1–3 in the league, including two losses at home.

The real surprise was Maryland. The win at NC State put the Terrapins at 4–0, including two victories on Tobacco Road. The Terrapins were now

14–1 overall, the same as Clemson, which was coming to Cole Field House for an early season showdown on Wednesday night.

Behind the three unbeatens came Duke and Virginia at 2–2, followed by Florida State and the three winless teams: Georgia Tech, North Carolina, and NC State, all 0–3. State and Carolina would also play Wednesday, in the DeanDome. Given their histories, State and Carolina playing for last in the ACC was a little bit like Dan Rather and Tom Brokaw fighting over the weekend sports job at one of the Raleigh TV stations. Unthinkable. But in this case, quite real.

The league's noveau riche, the Clemson Tigers, sauntered into Cole Field House for their game-day shoot around full of bluster and confidence. Rick Barnes had just been the subject of a story in *Sports Illustrated* and the notion that they were the number three team in the country didn't seem like a big deal to any of the players.

"It's funny how things change," Barnes said, sitting on the scorer's table while his players warmed up. "Last week, Tim Bourret" — Clemson's sports information director — "called me and said someone from *Sports Illustrated* wanted to see me after practice." Barnes had said he couldn't do the interview because Nick, his twelve-year-old, had a basketball game and after that they were going home to celebrate his daughter Carlie's ninth birthday. "I said I'd be ready at nine-thirty, after the kids were in bed, but not before then."

"A few years ago, it would have been different. I'd have remade my schedule for *SI*. Not anymore."

The case could be made that when you are coaching the number three team in the country, you have more wherewithal to tell the media where and when you will make yourself available to them. "That's not it," Barnes said. "Fact is, we still haven't won a thing. Hell, I've never won an NCAA tournament game. Think about that. But I'm forty-two. My kids are going to be grown up and gone when I'm in my fifties. I'm not missing the years I've got left with them."

Barnes smiled. "Everyone's asking me about pressure. This isn't pressure. These are the games you live to coach. Pressure's working all morning on a fork lift and then trying to go coach. This is fun."

Gary Williams was having fun too. In his own way. His team was now ranked tenth in the national polls and he was being mentioned as a candidate for national coach of the year. That was all well and good. But he didn't want to feel satisfied. He wanted more. He loved the big-game feel Cole had when he walked in that afternoon. What he loved even more was the feeling he had that this wasn't like the old days when Duke or Carolina came to town ranked in the top five and everyone hoped against hope that the Terrapins could pull an upset. There was no reason, if they played their game, why Maryland couldn't win.

"One thing that helps in a game like this is the referees," Williams said. "If we were playing Duke or Carolina as the number three team in the country it would be tougher because they're used to the idea of them being ranked that high. With Clemson, it's different. They aren't as established as a top team in the refs' minds."

Every coach in the ACC is extremely ref-conscious. Because most games are close, one call or a couple of calls can be critical. The way the game is called — tight, loose, lots of travels, emphasis on hand-checking — can also be extremely important. The only two coaches in the league who don't seem to worry very much about the officials are Dave Odom and Bobby Cremins. Odom never even looks to see who is working one of his games until he walks into the building just before the game. Cremins sometimes has to check with his assistants to remember the names of the officials when he walks on the floor. Williams is just the opposite. He knows every official in the league and he can almost tell you off the top of his head every crew assigned to his games for the entire season. Fred Barakat makes the schedule in August and sends it to the coaches. Already, Williams was concerned about some of the crews scheduled to work Maryland games later in the season. "Fred scheduled us like an eighth-place team," he said. "Only now we're not. Why can't he change the schedule? Make adjustments."

Barakat was in Cole for Clemson-Maryland. The seat he was assigned to was labeled "Fred Bearcat." When Williams heard that he rolled his eyes and sent someone to change it before Barakat noticed. Barakat is a former coach who had a good deal of success at Fairfield University in the 1970s. He had come to the ACC in 1980 and upgraded the officiating considerably. At times, he was hard on the men who worked for him, hard enough that a number of very good officials had left the league.

What had really hurt was the NBA's decision in 1988 to go from two-man crews to three-man crews. Seven of his most experienced officials had left to work in the pros. Barakat wasn't afraid to fire officials, even experienced ones. He had a healthy ego and he was tough at times, but he was also an extremely hard worker who genuinely cared about the league and the quality of its officiating. He insisted on a full report whenever a technical foul was called in a game and he was constantly critiquing his guys. On occasion, he went so far as to go into the locker room at halftime if he wasn't happy with what he was seeing.

As an ex-coach, Barakat sympathized with the frustrations the coaches often felt. Calls got blown for the simple reason that basketball is an impossible game to officiate. The rules are so subjective that one man's block is another man's charge and another's no-call. Once, when there was no three-point shot and no thirty-five-second clock, officials only had to look at the play. Now, they have to check a shooter's feet whenever he is near the arc and constantly be aware of the shot clock. The athletes are bigger and faster, the coaches more demanding. It is hard work.

All the league coaches called Barakat constantly. Sometimes they sent him tapes to back their claims that calls had been blown or that certain players were getting away with things. After his team's loss to Virginia, Dean Smith had called Barakat and said, "Should I be teaching my players moving screens?"

Barakat had dealt with Smith for enough years to know what he was trying to say — that Virginia moved on its screens. He played innocent. "What you teach your players is strictly up to you, Coach," he answered.

The irony of that call was that UVA athletic director Terry Holland had been so incensed with what he thought was Antawn Jamison's dirty play inside that he had "suggested" that Jeff Jones send Barakat a tape of Jamison. Jones, who didn't have the kind of history with Smith that Holland did, decided against it.

Most coaches came away from their conversations with Barakat satisfied. If Barakat agreed that a call had been blown, he said so. He had also learned over the years how to schmooze the coaches to the point where they almost always hung up the phone convinced that he had agreed with them. "I hold their hands," Barakat said.

There were exceptions to that rule. When Williams complained on a couple of occasions about what he perceived to be weak crews for big games, Barakat told him he was dead wrong. When Barnes complained later in the season that Larry Rose had an anti-Clemson attitude, Barakat pointed out to him that Krzyzewski had complained long and loud about a couple of key calls Rose had made in the first Duke-Clemson game. And, the previous year when Smith had called to claim that the officials were picking on Jeff McInnis in the game in Durham where McInnis was ejected, Barakat had told him flatly, "Dean, I know you're loyal to your players, but this isn't loyalty. This is just wrong. The kid got what he deserved from my guys."

Barakat was doing something a little different with his officials this season. He had broken his top ten men into five two-man crews who would work together throughout the season. They would be joined each night by a third official, usually — but not always — someone less experienced who Barakat was trying to bring along. Barakat thought — hoped — the new system would bring a certain amount of consistency and continuity.

This game would be difficult to work. Both teams were very physical. Maryland constantly had its hands out reaching for the ball in its various presses. Clemson constantly put a body on the opponent. If they wanted, the officials could call a foul on every possession. What they had to do was not do that but still keep control of the game.

Ninety minutes before tip-off, Gary Williams walked onto the floor to tape his two pregame shows at the scorer's table. One was with the Maryland radio network, which paid him to do pre- and postgame shows. The other was with the student radio station, which didn't pay him. As Williams walked out, the Maryland students, already packed into the sections behind the scorer's table and the team benches, gave him a loud ovation.

Sitting in an empty section behind one of the baskets, getting ready to tape his own pregame show, Rick Barnes shook his head as he watched Williams. "I love coming to this place to play," he said. "They're crazy if they ever stop playing here."

Of course the money people in the Maryland athletic department were trying to stop playing there. Publicly, Williams was supportive of the new building. Privately, he hated the idea of playing anyplace but Cole.

Cole was old and it was cramped. When the school had raised money to build a new men's basketball locker room three years earlier by taking out press row and putting in a courtside row of $250-a-night seats, gender equity had required that an identical locker room be built for the women's team. What had been the visitors' locker room was now the expanded women's locker room. The visitors now dressed in a locker room that was smaller than the shower room in the home locker room.

In fact, when Clemson's players and coaches knelt in their pregame circle to say the Lord's Prayer, they were so cramped that Barnes almost fell backwards into the shower room. The Tigers kneel and pray both before and after every game. Barnes, who grew up Baptist, became a Lutheran when he married Candy, and now attends a Presbyterian church, is quietly devout. Often, when he needs to relax on game day, he will get into his car and drive around listening to gospel music. He likes to kid Larry Shyatt, who is Jewish, about being a nonbeliever. When the team prays, Shyatt kneels and prays too. "It's habit now," he said. "One more part of the pregame routine."

Barnes reminded his players over and over to take care of the basketball, understanding that everything Maryland did started with its pressure on defense. On the board he had written what had become his motto for this season: "It's your turn!"

Across the hall, Williams was just as convinced it was his team's turn, although he didn't put it in those words. Instead, as his fourth game key, he had written: "The Situation."

"What I mean by that, fellas, is the situation you've put yourselves in with the way you've played this season. You are a very good basketball team. You don't have to do anything different or extraordinary to win this game. Just be the team you've been for fifteen games. I expect to win this game and so should you. You've earned the right to be confident. You're a damn good team."

While Barnes worried about turnovers, Williams worried about giving up offensive rebounds. "That's their best offensive play," he said. "Deny them that and you take away a big chunk of their offense."

Cole was absolutely jumping when the teams walked from the tunnel underneath the stands to their benches. Walking to the floor, assistant coach Dennis Felton said to Barnes, "You know, we need to get this one and beat Wake once to have a chance to win the league."

Barnes looked at him as if he had lost his mind. "Win the league?" he said. "We've played three games. We still have to go to Duke, Carolina, and Wake after this and you're talking about winning the league?"

Shyatt nodded. "Let's just walk out of here with a win tonight."

For a while, it appeared as if the last team that could still stand would be the winner. Every possession seemed critical right from the start. Both coaches were on the officials almost before Mike Wood's toss to start the game was in the air. When Tom Wideman threw a poor pass against the Maryland press, Barnes yanked him. When Obinna Ekezie picked up three quick fouls, Williams was all over Wood and Sam Croft. Eight minutes into the game, his shirt was soaked. Cole was steaming.

It was 32–31 Clemson at the half, Maryland having rallied from an early nine-point deficit. As the teams left the floor, Billy Hahn, eyes wide as saucers, kept saying, "This is a war, a damn war!"

It was. Barnes was all over his players at halftime to be tougher with the ball. "Twenty-three of their thirty-one points are off our turnovers," he screamed. "Right now, I guarantee you he is in there telling his players that we're nothing but a bunch of damn phonies, that we'll fold if they get in our ass. I know you won't though. Be strong with the damn ball! I told you it would be like this. I told you the crowd would be like this. You know what, though, this is good. Because we're going to have to win games like this to be any good."

He paused. "Fellas, this is not a game for boys."

Williams wasn't calling Clemson phonies in the other locker room. He was telling his players to keep up the pressure that had worked for them the last few minutes of the half. Rebounding (18–13, Clemson) was a concern and so was his team's five of 12 free-throw shooting. "You can't give away points like that."

The second half was no different from the first. Maryland took the lead on a spectacular drive by Keith Booth. Clemson came back to lead by four on a McIntyre jumper. Maryland pulled even. They traded baskets. The clock wound down under five minutes. McIntrye hit a three to put the Tigers up 54–51 with 4:54 left. Laron Profit forced a three and Jamison scored on the break. A Booth turnover, a pretty pass from Iker Iturbe to Jamison, and it was 58–51. For the first time all night, Cole was quiet. Once again, Clemson had the answers in the endgame.

Maryland came back one more time. A Terrell Stokes three cut the lead to 65–63 with seven seconds left and Merl Code was fouled on the inbounds. Williams immediately called time to let him think about it. As they walked back to the foul line, Profit whispered in Code's ear: "No pressure, baby, no pressure."

Code laughed. Then he made both shots. That was the game: Clemson 67, Maryland 63.

The game had lived up to every bit of the pregame hype. Everyone in the building was drained. Clemson had turned the ball over twenty-three times and survived. Barnes had almost no voice left. "This is what we've been building to," he croaked to his players. "Walking into this atmosphere with everyone wanting you and walking out with a win. No Clemson team has ever been in this position before."

Williams felt his team had lost the game at the foul line, shooting nine of 18. It had done almost everything else he had asked. The rebounding had finished 33–32. Williams had thought that would be close enough to win the game. On the other hand, his team had twenty turnovers — only three fewer than Clemson. Each team had negated the other team's strength. The difference had been foul shooting and McIntyre hitting two critical threes — the first to get the lead, the second to stretch it — near the finish.

"We were in position to win, fellas," Williams said. "Remember that part. They're very good. But so are we. We'll win one of these soon."

This was a rare week in the ACC in that all four midweek games were being played on the same night. While Maryland and Clemson were pounding each other, Georgia Tech was finally getting a league win, beating Florida State at home, and Wake Forest was going to 5–0 by beating Virginia at home. But it wasn't easy. The Deacons trailed by as many as six late in the second half before they outscored the Cavaliers 10–0 during the last five minutes to pull out a 58–54 victory.

Jeff Jones had done something different, not doubling Tim Duncan when he had the ball. If Duncan scored, fine, but he wasn't going to give up open three pointers to the Wake guards. The strategy worked most of the night. Duncan scored 28 points — including 11 of the last 14 — but

Wake's five perimeter shooters — Ricky Peral, Tony Rutland, Jerry Braswell, Steven Goolsby, and Joseph Amonett — were a combined four of 17 from the floor. Duncan managed to win the game at the end, but it was without question the toughest of Wake's 13 straight victories.

The late game was the one for last place: State at Carolina. For much of the second half, it looked as if Carolina's stunning slide was going to continue. The Tar Heels led by eight at halftime, by nine early in the second half. Then came another of their mysterious nosedives. State went on a 26–9 binge and led 54–45 with 5:42 left. The DeanDome was a morgue. This was impossible. At least Maryland had been a good team. There might even have been a few boos and catcalls coming from the faithful. When C. C. Harrison hit a baseline jumper to make it 56–47 with 2:34 left, a number of those faithful, noting that it was 11 o'clock on a work night and knowing what DeanDome postgame traffic is like, headed for the exits.

They missed the two minutes that probably saved Carolina's season.

Antawn Jamison made a steal (State actually had the nine-point lead *and* the ball) and fed Shammond Williams for a layup: 56–49. Then, after a State miss, Williams hit a three: 56–52, still 1:38 left. Carolina trapped, causing a jump ball. The arrow was theirs. With 50 seconds left, Jamison powered inside: 56–54. State was now in full panic. The morgue had become about as loud as the DeanDome gets. The screaming had a pleading tone to it, but it was definitely loud. Ademola Okulaja fouled Ishua Benjamin. He missed the front end of the one-and-one. Then, Benjamin fouled Williams. But Williams only made one free throw and State still led 56–55. Thirty-one seconds were left. Sendek called time to set his spread offense. Danny Strong had fouled out, so Sendek was forced to play little-used Steve Norton. Carolina knew an Achilles' heel when it saw one. Jamison fouled Norton right away. He missed. Carolina set its offense, punched the ball in to Jamison, and he scored: 57–56, Carolina. Twelve seconds left. Plenty of time. But State turned the ball over again. Now the Wolfpack had to foul. Vince Carter made two free throws with 10 seconds remaining: 59–56. State had one last chance, but Serge Zwik-ker flew out at Benjamin as he tried to launch a desperate three and deflected the ball away.

Ball game. The students actually stormed the court, as much in disbelief as joy. The Tar Heels had outscored the Wolfpack 12–0 in the last two minutes. "Our last four possessions were our best four of the game," Smith said later.

State had given the game away. Sendek knew that. The thirty-eight superb minutes were little consolation. They had to make plays at the end to win in the ACC because there weren't going to be any blowouts. Smith knew his team had been lucky, but that didn't matter. "If we lose that one, then we're in real trouble," he said. "Until then, we'd lost at Wake and Virginia, which a lot of teams were going to do, and played fourteen very bad minutes against Maryland. We could handle that. But if we had lost that one, at home . . ." He shook his head to perish the thought.

The win didn't exactly calm down the in-state hysterics. Carolina was still 1–3 and had been lucky to beat the league's worst team at home. Clearly, Wake and Clemson were the class of the league. Maryland seemed just a little bit behind them. Where everyone else fit in was anybody's guess.

Most of the ACC spent the weekend in North Carolina. NC State, still emotionally wrung out, traveled to Clemson Saturday and played respectably before losing to the Tigers, 59–52. Clemson was 5–0, State 0–5. Florida State, needing a nonconference game, got one — at Seton Hall — and won easily. The win was a relief for Pat Kennedy, whose team had been going steadily downhill since the Virginia loss. It was also a nice homecoming weekend for him. He spent the day Sunday with his mom, who had recently turned eighty-five.

The three games in Carolina were spread out: Georgia Tech at UNC Saturday afternoon, Virginia at Duke Saturday night, and Maryland at Wake Forest late Sunday afternoon. Always eager to get his team where it was going early, Gary Williams had Maryland in Winston-Salem by noon on Saturday. That gave them plenty of time to work out and watch the two Saturday games.

There really wasn't very much to see. Bobby Cremins had changed his lineup before the Florida State game, moving Gary Saunders to point guard in Kevin Morris's place and inserting freshman John Babul in

Saunders' spot. The switch had worked. Saunders wasn't a pure point guard, but neither was Morris, and Babul gave them more defense at the two-guard.

Tech had beaten Carolina in the DeanDome in '96 in an overtime classic. This game was hardly that. Carolina led from the outset, building an early 13-point lead. But being ahead still wasn't easy for this group. Tech had it down to seven by halftime and was within four early in the second half. It was still just an eight-point game at 54–46 with nine minutes left. "Get serious and we can win this game," Cremins had said during a time-out a minute earlier. "Come on, I mean it, get serious. It's there for us!"

Not for long. Carolina reeled off 17 straight points. Tech simply ran out of gas. The final was 73–50. Cremins was baffled. He had thought his team was improving, then it had completely disappeared in the final nine minutes. Smith was delighted. "It's the best game we've played outside of Italy," he said, remembering his team's December performance against the Italian national team.

"Our game plan was to hang around and make a run at the end," Cremins told the media. "Problem was, we didn't stay wid it. Give credit to Naut Cowlina. Everybody's been puttin' 'em down. That's a joke. Stuff like that makes me laugh."

Eleven miles away Jeff Jones was walking into Cameron Indoor Stadium in a mood that wasn't likely to include laughter anytime soon. Even though his team had lost to Wake Forest on Wednesday, he had felt good about its performance. They had played well enough to win the game. Duncan had just been a little too good in the last five minutes. Duke, he knew, wasn't as good as Wake Forest. What's more, the Cavaliers had won four of their last five against the Blue Devils and should go into the game — Cameron or no Cameron — confident.

That had all changed Thursday afternoon. Jones was getting ready to go to practice when he got a phone call from Lynn Mitchell, the athletic department's compliance officer, who had just returned from the NCAA convention. Making a routine check of the basketball team's second semester registration forms, she had noticed that Harold Deane had only registered for eleven hours when classes started on Monday. That was one less than the minimum an athlete had to carry to be eligible to play. This wasn't that unusual. Students often added or dropped classes during the first week of a semester.

There was a problem, though, with Deane. The academic counselors had told him he had five days to juggle his classes so he had twelve hours. They were right — in part. Deane could practice for five days. But he couldn't play in a game until he was officially signed up for twelve hours. He had played against Wake on Wednesday while registered for eleven hours. The rule was very clear: he had played one game when he was technically ineligible, so he had to sit out one game — the next game; Duke.

Jones was angry, confused, and amazed. How could the two academic counselors not know the rule? Why would Deane, a senior, be messing around with registration? Why hadn't someone double- or triple-checked the rule before the team had left for Wake?

They were all logical questions. Unfortunately, there were no logical answers. They would have to go to Durham without Deane. "We have two choices," Jones told his players. "We can use it as an excuse. Or we can get angry and play our butts off."

Mike Krzyzewski heard the news about Deane shortly before midnight on Friday when Tommy Amaker called him. He had heard about it on the news. Krzyzewski's initial response was, "Whew, no Harold Deane to worry about." His second reaction was, "What if the players think that way and lose their edge?"

This was a critical game for Duke. The Blue Devils had two straight ACC losses, at Clemson and at home against Wake Forest, but neither was a bad loss. They had been the bye team at midweek and had played two easy nonconference games against Campbell and UNC-Greensboro. Now, they had to jump back into league play with a vengeance. They couldn't afford another home loss.

Part of Krzyzewski couldn't help but feel badly for Jones. Walking on the court before the game, he stopped to commiserate with him. Once the game began, though, there wasn't any more time for sympathy. He had read in the Virginia media guide that Jamal Robinson, Deane's replacement, had played point guard throughout Virginia's European tour the previous summer, since Deane hadn't been on the trip. He was a senior with plenty of playing experience. He warned his players to expect an emotional performance from Virginia. "Wojo," he told Steve Wojcie-chowski, "you have to be into Robinson from the start. Don't let him get comfortable."

Wojciechowski never let anyone get comfortable. He had emerged as Duke's most important player during the first half of the season, a remarkable thing for a five-ten guard who wasn't a consistent shooter or terribly quick. Wojo was fierce, an absolute pain to play against. And Krzyzewski loved him for it. So did the Duke students, who made barking sounds whenever Wojo got into his stance and harassed the opposing point guard up and down the floor. That's what Wojo was, the little terrier who got hold of your leg and wouldn't let go.

He had Robinson — and Virginia's — leg in his teeth from the first minute in this game. Virginia simply couldn't get into its offense. Down 11–2 after less than five minutes, Jones called a 20-second time-out and set a play for Courtney Alexander. It worked, Alexander got away from freshman Nate James and drilled a three. A moment later, during a TV time-out, Krzyzewski asked James why he had lost Alexander.

"My fault," James said.

"Not good enough!" Krzyzewski roared. "There are no goddamn 'my faults' tonight!"

That set the tone. Duke scored the next 12 points to lead 23–5 and was up 38–21 at the half. As always, Krzyzewski was willing to bring up a bad memory. Two years earlier, in their first home game after Krzyzewski had left the team, the Blue Devils had blown a 23-point lead in the second half against Virginia. "This is not two years ago," he said. "This is us, right here, right now. This is a chance to purge one hell of a bad memory."

They did — after a brief scare when Virginia opened the half with a 10–2 run to cut the lead to 40–31. After that, Trajan Langdon and Wojo took over. Langdon scored six straight points to up the lead to 15. He then made a gorgous feed to Carmen Wallace for a dunk and hit a three off a Wojo feed. The lead got as high as 27 before Krzyzewski called off the "dog," and Duke coasted home, 78–59. Krzyzewski was delighted with his team's play and its approach. Jones could not have felt more differently.

"People deal with success in different ways," he told his players, sitting on a chair in front of them as he always did after games. "Some want more and are tough enough to do whatever it takes to get it. Those are winners. Then, there are people who are afraid of it and just stand around waiting to fail. Those are losers. Finally, there are people who have success and forget why, who think they're good and don't keep doing the things that made them good, like playing defense and working hard for forty minutes.

"That was you guys tonight."

Jones knew Deane's absence was an easy excuse for a flat performance. He wasn't buying it.

Gary Williams knew that playing Wake Forest on the road was an easy excuse for losing. After all, the Deacons had won 25 straight games in the Joel Coliseum, dating back to a loss to Carolina in 1995. But he felt very comfortable the next afternoon. He had been pleased with the way his team had reacted to the Clemson loss. They had been angry. Close wasn't good enough, regardless of how high the opponent was ranked. This opponent was ranked number two. It was undefeated and playing at home.

On Thursday Williams had watched the tape of the Wake-Virginia game and had been impressed with what Virginia had done. He had been fiddling with the idea of guarding Duncan straight up even before he saw the Virginia game. "Even if he scores, he has to work harder than if he's just passing," Williams said. "And, he's less likely to rebound his own shot than somebody else's." After seeing the Virginia tape, he was convinced. They would make Wake's guards beat them.

Dave Odom knew that Maryland was likely to follow the same approach as Virginia. He was more concerned, though, with his own team than with the way Maryland planned to play. Odom did not think his team's flat performance against Virginia was a coincidence or merely the product of Virginia guarding Duncan one-on-one. Like Virginia, Wake had started second semester classes that week. All of a sudden, after a month of living in what amounted to a basketball cocoon, his players were free. No more two-a-day practices. No more sleeping in a hotel, living, eating, and breathing basketball. Their friends were around. There were parties to go to, women to talk to. All normal college stuff. Things Odom thought important, normal, and healthy.

But also distracting. He had decided that the Virginia game was a natural letdown. They had played so close to perfect in three straight games, then they had been shoved back into the real world and remembered there was life outside the gym. Everyone was telling them how great they were. Maybe they believed it a little bit. In any event, Odom hoped it was a cheap lesson learned. To make sure he had their attention on Thursday and Friday, he put a couple of new wrinkles into the offense.

Maryland still hadn't started back to class. Because the school took a long semester break, classes didn't start again until January 30. Williams still had his players' complete attention. No distractions. Or, as Odom put it, "Parris Island, hoops-style." When Williams mentioned to Odom before the game that his players still weren't in class, Odom felt his stomach twist just a little bit. Maybe, he thought, it won't matter. Or maybe it will be a long afternoon.

It was the latter. The first half was about as close to perfect as was possible for Maryland. The Terrapins jumped out to a 10–0 lead that quickly quieted the crowd and forced Odom to call a twenty-second time-out. He hadn't called one that early all year. "I knew," he said later, "that we couldn't play through it. We were all out of synch, out of kilter."

Things didn't get much better the next few minutes. The lead ballooned to 26–8. Odom was pleading with the officials to keep Obinna Ekezie from using his elbow to push Duncan from behind and move him away from the basket. "I realize we've done nothing to deserve any help by any means, but could you please keep Ekezie's elbow out of Duncan's back."

Dick Paparo assured Odom he would be on the alert for any elbows. A moment later, Odom spotted the evil elbow again. So did Duke Edsall, who was under the basket at the time and called the foul. Paparo, working outside, had the same angle as Odom but didn't make a call. "Dick, you've got the same angle as me," Odom said. "Why wouldn't you call that?"

Paparo — with some justification — figured if the call had been made, why was Odom unhappy? The answer was simple: Odom was unhappy with everything right then. Paparo didn't really care about Odom's troubles. He decided he'd heard enough and gave Odom a tee. Paparo is easily the fastest whistle in the ACC when it comes to technicals. It is both a strength — coaches know not to mess with him — and a weakness — sometimes his emotions override his judgment. This one was borderline, although, given the score, Odom's tone was probably more strident than he realized.

The technical seemed finally to wake up the Deacons. They rallied in the last six minutes to cut the margin to 32–20 at the break. Duncan had shot three for six; the rest of the Deacs were a cool two of 17. For the first time all year, Odom was angry at halftime. It wasn't so much the score as the attitude. "I could scream and yell at you guys, but I don't think that's the answer right now," he told them. "We're lucky to be down twelve. The game's still winnable. But you have to play with a lot more patience than what you did in the first half. Maryland isn't going away just because we want them to. You guys are going to have to pick it up and win the game. They won't give it to you."

They responded, starting the second half with a sizzling 16–0 run. Now it was Maryland that looked dazed. On one possession, Duncan blocked a Keith Booth shot, blocked a Laron Profit shot, then blocked another Booth shot. The place was going crazy. When Ricky Peral hit a short jumper to make it 36–32 with 14:40 left, all seemed well in Deacon-land.

Maryland missed again and Wake came down with a chance to go up by six or seven. Joel was rocking. Williams was standing, prepared to call time-out if Wake scored again. The ball swung to Steven Goolsby, wide open for a three. On many a Wake Forest night, Goolsby had been the other team's undertaker, nailing a big three during a Deacon run. Now, everyone in the building was on their feet as the ball sailed toward the rim and a seven-point lead. It bounced long. Goolsby hesitated for just an instant as if amazed the shot hadn't gone in. When he did, his man, Laron Profit, raced by him, took a pass from Keith Booth, and made a layup. Instead of a seven-point lead, it was two. Then Rutland threw a careless pass that Booth intercepted. He fed Stokes for another layup. In less than twenty seconds, the game had gone from Wake about to be up seven to a tie. Everyone sat down, including Williams. No need to call time-out now. His team had caught a second wind. "That sequence was key," Williams said later. "Because right there we easily could have been blown out."

They weren't, though, much to Odom's chagrin. "We had 'em," he said. "And we let 'em loose."

Like Virginia, Maryland led late: 49–42 with 5:19 to go. Like Virginia, Maryland let the lead slip away. Two turnovers, two missed free throws by Booth, and a Duncan basket cut it to 51–49 in the last minute. With 17 seconds left, Ekezie fouled Duncan to keep him from making a tying layup. Williams called time. "Duncan's not a great foul shooter," he said. "I thought he'd miss one. But I also didn't want to have to call time if they tied it. I wanted to come down and run a play."

Duncan fooled Williams, making both shots. It was tied at 51. Maryland spread the floor and ran a clear-out play for Booth on the left side. Wake had anticipated this and, as Booth drove, the entire defense collapsed on him. He was surrounded by four men. Somehow, Booth kept his head and spotted Profit standing on the three-point line across the court, wide open. Booth — who didn't yet have an assist in the game — flipped the ball crosscourt to Profit. As Profit released it, Paparo, standing across the court from him, had the responsibility for calling the shot good — before the buzzer — or no good.

It was a matter of a microsecond. As Profit released the ball, Paparo's arm was in the air, indicating the shot would count if it went. It hit the bottom of the net. Paparo's other arm went up to indicate it was a three — which was irrelevant. Profit was buried under his teammates as the referees raced off. Final: Maryland 54, Wake Forest 51.

Replays of the shot made one thing clear: it was unclear whether Profit had released the ball in time. When the Wake assistant coaches saw it, they were convinced it had come late. Dave Odom didn't want to hear about it. "I don't want to hear anyone say the shot shouldn't have counted," he told his players. "For one thing, that's not fair to Maryland. For another, *that's* not what cost us the ball game. The way we played before the shot cost us the game. That's where our focus needs to be this week."

Like his players, Odom felt ambushed by the loss. He hadn't expected an easy game with Maryland, but he hadn't expected to lose at home either. With a trip to Clemson coming up Thursday, followed by a quick

36-hour turnaround before a game with Florida State on Saturday, the cruising Deacons suddenly faced a critical week. "One minute you're 5–0," Odom said, "the next 5–3 isn't out of the question by any means."

Odom, his coaches, and Duncan had some thinking and talking to do before they made the trip to Clemson. As for Williams and Maryland, all they had to do was celebrate. At least for a day or two.

16

Scramble Time

AS SOON AS Fred Barakat saw the replay of Profit's shot in super slow motion the next morning, he groaned. The shot shouldn't have counted. It was a brutally tough call because it took slowing the tape down to one-thirtieth of a second per frame before Barakat was certain. Even so, the call was wrong.

Barakat wasn't upset with Paparo. Either way, a call that close almost amounted to guesswork. What bothered him was the way the officials were aligned on the court at the time of the shot. Paparo was in the middle position, which meant he had to turn his head to see the red light on top of the backboard that lit when the clock hit zero. If Paparo had been standing closer to midcourt, he would have had a better view of the light and backboard and might have had a better chance to make the call. "Even then, he still could have missed it because it was so close," Barakat said. "But he would have had a better chance."

Barakat apologized to Dave Odom on the phone that morning. Odom told Barakat the same thing he had told his players: "The call didn't cost us the game." He wanted to be certain that his players didn't use the call as an excuse.

Odom hadn't slept very much on Sunday night, not because of the loss, but because he was wrestling with a decision. For a month, seven-foot-one-inch freshman Loren Woods had been improving steadily. At times, he was brilliant. At other times, he made freshman mistakes. Odom thought he needed to get him into the flow of games earlier and more often.

What's more, he was convinced he had to rest Duncan more. Duncan had played forty minutes against Duke, forty minutes against Virginia, and forty minutes against Maryland. He had played thirty-nine against Georgia Tech. That meant he had missed one minute in four games. The league season wasn't yet half over. Duncan was going to have to play a lot of minutes in a lot of games in February and March. Odom was concerned that he was going to wear him out.

"I go into every game saying I'm going to rest him," he told his coaches on Monday morning. "But then I can't pull the trigger. I'm just not comfortable with him sitting next to me."

Actually, Duncan never sat next to Odom, since Odom never sat on the bench. But he wasn't sitting right behind him while Odom knelt in front of the bench nearly enough. Odom woke up Monday morning with an idea that he hoped would change that.

"If we start Loren and then sub Sean" — Allen — "for him at the first TV time-out, maybe I'll feel more comfortable putting Loren in for Tim three minutes or so after that because Loren will be in the flow of the game already." Odom said. "That way I'll be more likely to pull the trigger."

The coaches agreed. Odom's concern was Allen, who had been a two-year starter and had done nothing to deserve being benched. He had never been a scorer, but was a solid rebounder and defender. Now, no matter what Odom said about how important he would be coming off the bench, he would know his minutes were bound to go down. Odom sent out messages for Duncan, Woods, and Allen to see him before practice on Tuesday since he had given the team the day off on Monday. The NCAA requires every team to take one day off a week when school is in session and, since the game at Clemson wasn't until Thursday, Monday was the logical day to skip.

Odom wanted to see Duncan first, since he was being consulted on the change rather than being told about it. He was virtually certain Duncan would agree since the two of them tended to think alike on basketball matters. He wasn't necessarily going to change his mind if Duncan didn't agree, but he would at least listen.

Duncan agreed. He knew how talented Woods was and he also felt that Allen, who was twenty-three and a fifth-year senior, was mature enough to deal with the situation. What's more, he and Odom both remembered a play late in the Maryland game when Maryland backup center Rodney Elliott had beaten Duncan down the floor for a fast-break dunk because Duncan, after sinking a short baseline jumper, was too tired to sprint back against a fresh player. Duncan had looked over at the bench and said to Odom, "Sorry, my fault."

Odom's thought at that moment was, "*My* fault," for asking too much of Duncan. Once he had talked to Duncan, Odom delivered the news to the players affected. After that, he explained the change to the entire team. Woods was excited and nervous. This was the chance he had been waiting for. Woods was a high-strung kid who tended to get down on himself very quickly. Duncan often yelled at him for yelling at himself. Allen was just the opposite of Woods. He was competitive, but easygoing. When Odom told him what he was doing all he said was, "Whatever you think will work." That was what Odom wanted to hear.

They practiced with the new lineup Tuesday and Wednesday before the flight to Clemson. Thursday was one of those January days in the South that make winter bearable. The temperature had climbed into the sixties by lunchtime and Odom and his coaches spent some time by the hotel pool — which was covered — after their shoot around just to enjoy being outside. Odom was still fretting about the lineup change.

"Actually, winning the game isn't that important," he rationalized. "The point of the game is to get this new lineup in place because ultimately, if we want to win in March, this is the lineup we're going to have to play. We just want to break it in tonight and hope Loren can deal with this atmosphere."

"He came to Wake Forest to play games like this," Ernie Nestor said. Nestor, who had just turned fifty, was the wise old head on Odom's staff. He had coached at Wake Forest under Carl Tacy, had left to go to California, and had then been a head coach at George Mason for five years. Now he was back at Wake as Odom's right-hand man.

Every coach has one assistant he depends on most. Bill Guthridge had been with Dean Smith for so long — thirty years — that there were people who believed they had shared the same nursery as infants. After all, they were both from Kansas. For Rick Barnes, it was Larry Shyatt. For Krzyzewski, it had been Pete Gaudet for twelve years. Now, it was Tommy Amaker.

Pat Kennedy had Tom Carlsen, Jeff Jones had Tom Perrin, Gary Williams had Billy Hahn, and Bobby Cremins had Kevin Cantwell. Cremins and Cantwell were more like equal partners on the bench than boss-employee. Cantwell had full control of Tech's defense to the point where Cremins paid very little attention to what Cantwell was doing. A year earlier, late in Tech's overtime win at Carolina, Cantwell had pulled Gary Saunders aside leaving the huddle with Carolina setting up for a potential winning shot. Saunders was guarding Dante Calabria, who, as a senior, was a likely go-to guy in that situation. "He'll head-fake, take one dribble right, and go up," Cantwell said as Saunders nodded. Overhearing, Cremins looked at Cantwell, aghast. "You've got a freshman on Calabria!" he screamed. "That's crazy. He can't guard Calabria!"

"Bobby," Cantwell answered calmly, "he's had Calabria the whole second half. Calabria has one bucket."

"Really?" Cremins said. "OK then, fine."

Interestingly, the only coach in the league who didn't have a wise old head next to him was Herb Sendek — the league's youngest coach. His oldest assistant was Larry Harris, who had just turned forty, and his other two assistants, Sean Miller and John Groce, were not yet thirty. Of course the case could be made that Sendek was a very old thirty-three.

Nestor knew the league cold, knew Wake Forest inside out, and understood his boss perfectly. He was Wake's Mr. X and O. Odom was the one coach in the ACC who almost never used a playboard during the game. Once, maybe twice a year, he would grab a piece of yellow legal paper off of someone's clipboard and draw a play. Most of the time, he talked to the players individually, critiquing what they were doing on the floor. He might urge Duncan to look for his shot more or tell Rutland to run a different set or remind Braswell that passing the ball was allowed. He would normally finish a time-out with a summation of their play and a reminder about what offense and defense he wanted them in. It was decidedly untechnical stuff. Nestor, kneeling next to Odom, had the authority to break in to explain what the opposition was doing technically in a particular offense or defense and suggest how the players might adjust to it.

While Odom and his coaches sat around at the Holiday Inn worrying and killing time, Rick Barnes grabbed a hamburger at McDonald's, then ran home to pick up twelve-year-old Nick to go hit a few golf balls. Nick was rapidly becoming a good player and was probably going to be beating his father by the summer.

The Tigers were now ranked number two nationally (Wake had dropped to fourth after the Maryland loss) behind the only major unbeaten team left, Kansas. This was heady stuff in Tigertown. As hopped up as the place had been for the Duke game, it was even wilder for Wake Forest. After all, the Deacons were still the team to beat in the league even though Clemson was now on top at 5–0, followed by Wake and Maryland at 5–1. Duke, which had won a difficult game at NC State on Tuesday, was now 4–2, followed by Virginia at 3–4. The Cavaliers had squeezed out a critical 68–64 victory at home the previous night against Georgia Tech. That put them just ahead of 2–4 Florida State, which had played its best game of the year that night to beat North Carolina in Tallahassee. The Tar Heels were now 2–4 and the screams of panic could be from Asheville to Greenville. Only Dean Smith appeared unruffled. "I thought we played well against Florida State," he said later that week. "We just caught them on a night when they were all wound up emotionally and played great."

Georgia Tech was 1–5 and State 0–6. They appeared to be candidates for the Les Robinson game. "I'm just glad we played a competitive game for forty minutes," Cremins had said after the Virginia game, remembering the Carolina debacle. Cremins's team had been hurt late in the game when a Matt Harpring shot that had first been ruled a three by Dick Paparo was changed to a two by Frank Scagliotta. Cremins had spent the entire time-out — which he had called after Harpring made the shot with 22 seconds left — thinking he was down one. When Scagliotta overruled, Tech was down two. "We didn't adjust to that," Cremins said. Still, he refused to criticize the officials. "If Frank Scagliotta says it was a two, I believe it was a two," he said. "He's a great official. In fact, if it was a two, I'm proud of him for making that call."

No wonder ACC refs love Bobby Cremins.

Scagliotta was right. The shot was a two.

Walking into the bedlam that was Littlejohn Coliseum on the night of January 23, Rick Barnes sneaked up behind Dave Odom and grabbed him in a bear hug. Startled for an instant, Odom started laughing when he saw who his attacker was. Leaning up to speak into his ear, since there was no other possible way to be heard, Odom said, "You see what you've done, you've gone and messed up the whole damn league. It used to be fun to come here. Now just look at this place."

It was a compliment. Clemson had gone hoops-mad and the atmosphere in Littlejohn for this game was right up there with Cameron, Reynolds, and Cole at their best. It didn't bother Odom that much. He figured his experienced team would respond well to this atmosphere. Already, it had played great basketball at Tech and Duke, both very difficult places to play — especially Duke.

The only question mark was the new starter, Woods. The advantage the Deacons had was the element of surprise. Clemson hadn't known until a few minutes before tip-off about the switch and had built its game plan around playing against Woods in short spurts. Odom was thrilled when Woods scored six quick points, even though he didn't like seeing him muttering to himself about missing a couple of free throws.

Odom followed through on his substitution plan and Duncan actually got three minutes of first-half rest — which was two minutes more than he had gotten in the last four games combined. The pace was frenetic, the crowd frantic. When Terrell McIntyre came up with a steal from Goolsby and went the length of the floor to make a twisting layup over Duncan, the building felt as if it had been hit by an earthquake. Even so, Odom's theory about his team thriving in the atmosphere was right. Their shooting touch was back. Of course, for all of Odom's talk about just wanting to get better, his competitive juices got rolling once the game began. When Braswell was called for a charge with the Deacons up 32–22, Odom slammed the scorer's table in disgust. When Amonett got trapped on the baseline and turned the ball over, Odom was up screaming, "Joseph, you *cannot* go baseline! It's not there!"

A moment later Amonett nailed a three and Odom shook a "that's-the-way" fist at him. That shot put the Deacs up 35–22. But two Iker Iturbe free throws and a clutch three by (who else?) McIntyre cut the halftime margin to 35–27.

This was a fascinating game of contrasting styles. Wake was a finesse team, one that beat you by executing beautiful plays on offense and playing smart on defense, funneling drivers to Duncan, while getting up on shooters at the three-point line. Clemson was never pretty. It wanted contact, bodies flying, the game as physical as possible. Odom had noted that afternoon that Clemson was almost unique in college basketball: a team that could beat you from ten to eighteen feet, especially Greg Buckner. They were a mid-range team in an era when everyone obsessed about playing inside and out. Wake was a typical nineties team. It was built around Duncan inside and the perimeter people making defenses pay for doubling Duncan by hitting threes. On the Clemson scouting report, under Wake's weaknesses, assistant coach Dennis Felton had emphasized turnovers — "they struggle with turnovers but don't force them" — and "lack of mid-range game." He would get no argument on that assessment from Odom.

Odom's halftime talk focused on turnovers and toughness. He was excited about the way they had played in the first half, but disturbed with their tendency to give the ball up to pressure. "Do not let them intimidate you," he said. "Don't give them the basketball. That's the only way they can beat us."

They did as they were told for eight minutes. When Duncan — who had gotten another nineteen seconds of rest — threw a perfect pass to a wide-open Amonett after Clemson doubled him and Amonett hit a three, the Deacons were up 50–38. But Greg Buckner wasn't going to let Wake walk away with an easy win. He drove for a three-point play. Then he made a steal from Peral and a layup. During a TV time-out, Odom pleaded with his players to stop Buckner. "Help on him whenever he touches it," he said. "He ain't passing it. It's going up. But don't put him on the line!"

They listened. But they couldn't stop him. Buckner hit another drive and the lead was six. Then he pulled up for — you guessed it, Coach Odom — a mid-range jumper. By the time his teammates joined the act, Code hitting a jumper and McIntyre two free throws, it was 55–53 with six minutes left. "OK," Odom said calmly in a huddle gathered tight around him so people could hear, "they've had a run. Fine. Had to happen. Let's just relax and play."

No one was going to relax in this game. Wake clung to the lead. Rutland hit a huge three with 1:02 left from in front of the bench to make it 62–57. Andrus Jurkunus answered to make it 62–59. Rutland made one of two free throws to make it 63–59 but McIntyre, who never seemed to tire of making huge shots, nailed a three with 15 ticks left and it was 63–62. Clemson fouled Duncan. This time, he performed as Gary Williams had expected four days earlier, making one of two. It was 64–62. Plenty of time for Clemson.

But Rutland made a superb defensive play, blindsiding Jurkunus as he turned at the top of the key to put the ball on the floor. Jurkunus ran over Rutland and Zelton Steed, who almost hadn't made it to the game because of a kidney stone, made a gutsy charging call. The Clemson coaches screamed later it should have been a no-call, but Steed had no choice. Once Rutland fell, an advantage had been gained. It had to be a foul on someone. Rutland had had position. Duncan made one more free throw with three seconds left and Buckner's desperate heave was wide and short. Wake had won a great basketball game, 65–62.

Odom was buoyant. The lineup change had worked. Woods had produced nine points and nine rebounds. Duncan had gotten a little rest. Rutland had made a mammoth shot and they had won a game in as hostile arena as they would play in all year. There were now three ACC teams with one league loss. That was almost secondary to Odom. The big switch had worked. They could now progress toward March. That was what this season was all about.

Barnes was almost as happy. "If that's one of the prime contenders for the national championship, fellas, you're right there with them," he said. "There's no need to think you have to prove yourselves anymore. You *have* proved yourselves."

Both teams had. Of course, the ACC season wasn't yet half over.

17

Forty-three
and Counting

RICK BARNES walked down the ramp leading into the DeanDome with a wicked grin on his face. It was Super Bowl Sunday and all around the country millions of sports fans were eagerly awaiting the 6:20 P.M. kickoff between the Green Bay Packers and the New England Patriots.

In Chapel Hill, the Super Bowl was nothing more than a lengthy dessert, scheduled to begin shortly after the real event — the Clemson–North Carolina game — would end. "What do you think?" Barnes asked (one of his favorite questions) as he walked down the long hallway to the visitors' locker room with his arm around Nick, who had made the weekend trip. "Think they're a little nervous around here?"

A lot nervous would be more like it. The scenario for the afternoon was extraordinary: the ranked team in the building was Clemson; the team with the 5–1 conference record was Clemson; the national power was Clemson. The team that most of the national TV audience on ABC would want to get a closer look at was Clemson. The opposition currently sat in sixth place in the ACC with a 2–4 record, having moved half a game ahead of Florida State because the Seminoles had lost at Wake Forest on

Saturday. Georgia Tech was now tied with FSU at 2–5, having barely beaten NC State. The Wolfpack was doing a superb job of staying in every game it played, but an equally superb job of finding ways to lose. This time the margin had been 54–53. They were now 0–7.

The only person who savored this scenario more than Barnes, who loved the idea that his team coming to town was a big deal, was Dean Smith. It was a rare day when Smith could lay claim to the underdog role — especially at home. Actually, the bookies still weren't buying the notion that the axis of power had swung that completely. They had made Carolina a slight favorite in the game.

"How can they possibly do that?" Smith asked, sitting on his bench during warmups. "They're the number two team in the country."

They were also coming off a loss. More important than that was history. Clemson walked into Chapel Hill with a lifetime record on Carolina's home courts of 0–42. The first time the Tigers had played in Chapel Hill was in 1926. They had lost, 50–20. Seventy years later, in their forty-second appearance on the Carolina campus, the margin was 86–53. As much as things changed, they stayed the same. Overall, Clemson was 15–100 against the Tar Heels. If the law of averages meant anything, Clemson was a lock. If history was a harbinger, this would be another wasted trip.

Barnes wasn't interested in the law of averages or in history. He had watched the tape of Carolina's loss to Florida State and had drawn the same conclusion as Smith: "They're playing a lot better," he said. "[Ed] Cota's starting to look more comfortable and [Vince] Carter's healthy. We'll have to play our butts off to win in there."

They were waiting for Barnes in the DeanDome. They had been waiting a year ago, but it hadn't had the same feel. Then, Carolina was still the power, Clemson the pretender. Then, the second round of Smith-Barnes nastiness hadn't broken out yet. Now, it was all out in the open and Clemson was coming in highly ranked (the highest in school history) for a game Carolina had to have. With a trip to Duke coming up Wednesday, the thought of dropping to 2–5 in the league was unthinkable.

And so there was no doubt that the fans inching their way through the DeanDome traffic, listening to the final minutes of the Duke-Maryland game from College Park on the radio, were nervous. Maryland pulling out a 74–70 victory made them all feel a little better, but it wouldn't matter that much if they inched out of the parking lots toward their Super Bowl parties after another loss, especially to Clemson and Rick Barnes.

As the Tigers made their way into the visitors' locker room, Larry Shyatt was stopped by John Dubis, who was sitting in the hallway outside the locker room waiting for the team to arrive. Dubis had the dubious distinction of being Barnes's security escort to and from the floor. All the ACC schools supply the visiting coach with some kind of security, more to make certain nothing goes wrong at the end of a game — students storming the court, an attack after a controversial call, some nut jumping out of the stands — than anything else.

In the old days, a couple of ushers had been assigned to the visiting coach in the DeanDome. That had changed in 1993 when the two men assigned to Pat Kennedy had heckled him en route to the locker room after Carolina had come from 21 points down to beat the Seminoles. "How'd you like the wine and cheese, Coach?" they kept yelling at him. When Kennedy complained, Carolina, always image conscious, switched from ushers to a plainclothes security guard.

Clearly, Dubis considered today's assignment less fun than others. As Barnes walked into the locker room, Dubis asked Shyatt if he could have a minute with him. "Does Coach Barnes go onto the floor for warm-ups?" he asked.

Shyatt understood the question. Dubis knew that the sight of Barnes walking onto the floor was going to set the crowd off. He wanted to know if he was going to have to deal with making that walk once or twice before the game. Shyatt laughed and told Dubis, "In this place, he might not go out there for the second half."

He then walked into the locker room and told Barnes what had happened. The wicked grin returned to Barnes's face. "Guy's nervous, huh?" he asked.

"Probably with good reason," Shyatt answered.

Barnes walked back into the hallway and introduced himself to Dubis.

"You nervous about walking out there with me?" he asked Dubis, a deadpan expression on his face.

"No sir," Dubis answered.

"You think I'm going to cause trouble out there?" Barnes continued. "I mean, should I cause some? I think I probably can."

"No sir, we don't want any trouble," Dubis said, still unfailingly polite.

"Tell me the truth now, do they not like me here?"

"Well sir, I wouldn't really know. . . ."

"No, seriously, it's OK, you can tell me the truth. I'll be OK."

Dubis paused. "No, Coach, they don't like you at all."

Barnes nodded. "Is there anyone else they don't like?"

"Oh, absolutely. They can't stand Mike Krzyzewski."

Barnes was fighting a smile now. "Tell me the truth now. Do they hate me as much as they hate him?"

Dubis thought about that one for a split second. "No, Coach, they don't," he said. "But you're getting close."

Barnes patted Dubis on the back and went back into the locker room. "If we win, that poor guy's going to have a lot on his hands," he said.

Barnes doesn't go out for warm-ups. That made Dubis's life a little easier. Smith, who does, was out there (he has a security guard too, mostly to keep autograph seekers away) watching Clemson warm up. "Look at Iturbe," he said to Bill Guthridge. "He looks like he's got good spin on his shots today." He watched Terrell McIntyre for a while. "I love the way he plays," he said. "Maybe things would have been different if his stepfather hadn't died the night we were going to see him play. He's such a tough kid."

It was partly out of respect for McIntyre that Smith had decided to change his defense, putting the six-six Carter on him. Smith had noticed on tape that McIntyre was such a good leaper that he could get his jump shot off over most point guards without much trouble even though he was only five ten. "He plays more like six two or six three," he said. His point guards, Ed Cota and Shammond Williams, were smaller than that, so Smith decided to put Carter on him. If McIntyre used his quickness to go by Carter, Carolina's help defense would — Smith hoped — be waiting. The other reason for the switch was Carter. Smith was still looking for a way to get him to start living up to his endless potential. Maybe challenging him on the defensive end of the floor would do that.

While Smith was urging his team to start playing with more emotion, no doubt playing up their underdog status, Barnes was trying to take a low-key approach. He knew the players were aware of Clemson's history here. But he didn't want them coming out so wound up that they couldn't play. He thought they had been too juiced during the first half of the Wake Forest game and it had affected the way they played. "We need an even keel," he said. "You can win some games with emotion, you might win a few more with luck. You don't win championships with either."

The DeanDome was full of emotion for this game. Nerves were clearly frayed. When Clemson jumped to a quick 6–3 lead, you could almost hear murmuring from the crowd even though the game was less than four minutes old. Carolina quickly came back to lead 9–8, but when Clemson center Tom Wideman took Shammond Williams down on a breakaway, the crowd went into conniptions. Dick Paparo quickly called the foul intentional, which set Barnes off since he thought Wideman had made a play for the ball. As he argued, the booing — which had been considerable when he and Dubis made their way across the court before the game — grew loud and angry. To the crowd, this was another example of the kind of dirty play Smith had been complaining about the past two years. To Barnes, it was a hard breakaway foul and Paparo had overreacted because the crowd had overreacted. It didn't help things when Williams came up jawing at Wideman, who went right back at him.

It was a tense atmosphere. Both teams continued to struggle offensively. Carter was doing a good job on McIntyre, aided by Smith's occasional switching (15 possessions out of 71 according to the stats kept by the assistants) to a point zone defense. Clemson wasn't doing a good job of recognizing the switches and was consistently taking poor shots. Only excellent defense at the other end was keeping the game close. After almost 16 minutes, the score was 14–12, Carolina. Then Shammond Williams dropped in a three and Antawn Jamison made a steal for a layup. Another Clemson miss and a Jamison layup and suddenly Carolina had pushed the lead to 21–12. Barnes stood with hands on hips in front of the bench while the DeanDome crowd got about as loud as it ever gets. It was 23–16 at halftime.

Barnes was calm during the break, emphasizing the offense. "Our defense is good, fellas, great," he said. "Keep that up and we'll win the game because I promise you we're going to go out there and score some points this half."

Not many. Carolina continued to play suffocating defense when the second half started. Barnes was getting frustrated. He insisted that the Tar Heels were moving on their screens (maybe Smith had decided to teach that in practice after the Virginia game) and kept trying to encourage his players to hang on.

"Work the game," he said during one time-out. "They don't want us around late in this game. The last six minutes, our pressure will take its toll on them."

Getting to the last six minutes was the problem. A Serge Zwikker jump shot with 6:51 left extended the Carolina lead to 48–33. A three-point play by Buckner and a three-point shot by Code made it 48–39 and Smith, remembering Maryland, called a quick twenty-second time-out. Clemson had one chance to make it interesting, but Andrus Jurkunus missed an open three that could have cut the margin to six with just under five minutes to go. Zwikker scored twelve seconds later to push the lead to 11.

Clemson didn't die. It fought back to within seven at 52–45, but that was as close as it got. As the final seconds ticked down the Carolina fans, relieved and giddy at the same time, began chanting, "Overrated, overrated" at the Tigers. When the game ended, the final margin was 61–48 and some of the students saw fit to storm the court. Barnes couldn't help but smile as Dubis made certain he got to the tunnel unimpeded. "Can you believe this?" he said. "They're storming the floor because they beat Clemson!"

He was still disappointed. Carolina had played well — especially on defense — but he knew his team had not played well. Specifically, they had shot the ball horrendously: 18 for 66 from the field. Amazingly, they had gotten off 34 more field goal attempts than Carolina, in large part because of 25 offensive rebounds.

"We missed so many shots, we were bound to get some rebounds," Barnes said.

Shyatt, staring at the stat sheet, shook his head. "The bottom line is the effort was fine, but the product stunk. We got what we deserved."

"Actually, we're improving," Barnes said. "The last two years in here they beat us by thirty."

He was searching for good news. One statistic troubled him more than any other: Wideman and Harold Jamison, his two inside players, had shot a combined one of seven from the field and scored a total of three points. "We're becoming a two-man offense," he said. "Buck and Boogie [McIntyre] are it and teams know it. Carolina forced us to set up way outside all day because we had no inside threat."

Barnes had changed from his TV suit into sweats for the flight home. "Carolina fans yelling 'Overrated' at Clemson," he said. "We've come a long, long way."

The lesson of the day, though, was clear: there was still a long way to go.

While Carolina was purging a month of frustrations against Clemson, Mike Krzyzewski was sitting in the front row of Duke's charter en route home after his team's loss to Maryland. Watching him, Tommy Amaker was worried. Krzyzewski's face was blank. He sat, a blanket across his lap, staring into space.

"He looked awful," Amaker said the next day.

He felt worse. "I just felt completely alone on that flight," he said later. "I know how hard my assistants work and I knew they felt badly, but ultimately the program is my responsibility and I just felt as if our standards had slipped to a point where I didn't know what the hell I could do to get them back to where they'd been."

It wasn't as if losing to Maryland in Cole Field House was an embarrassment. Not only were the Terrapins a red-hot club, they were lying in wait for Duke. No team had been tougher on Maryland during Gary Williams's eight years at Maryland than Duke. During Williams's first season, the Terrapins had swept North Carolina. That same season, they lost three times to Duke. There had been close losses, not-so-close losses, and losses that should have been wins. For five years, though, there hadn't been a win, just twelve straight aggravating defeats. Then, when the Terrapins did finally break through in 1995 and beat the Blue Devils twice, Krzyzewski wasn't there. In fact, Williams wasn't there either for the second game that season because of his bout with pneumonia.

Krzyzewski had come back in '96 and picked up right where he left off: Duke won easily in Cameron, then stole another game in Cole when

Ricky Price hit a three-point shot at the buzzer. That made Krzyzewski's head-to-head record against Williams 14–1 — the one win in the 1985 NCAA tournament when Williams's third Boston College team had upset Krzyzewski's second good Duke team in the second round.

Williams finally ended the streak in the '96 ACC tournament. Even then, Duke people pointed out that Chris Collins, the team's leading scorer, was out with an injury. Williams didn't really give a damn. He was just happy to win the game.

There were no injuries and no excuses on Super Sunday in Cole. Both teams were healthy. Maryland, which had played (and easily defeated) Penn with the midweek bye, was 5–1 in the league. Duke was 4–2. Cole was just as packed and just as wired as it had been for Clemson — perhaps more so. Duke had won 12 of the previous 14 games in Cole, a remarkable record for any team in someone else's gym, and the Maryland fans, remembering the heartbreaking ending a year earlier, came loaded for bear.

So did Williams. He respected Krzyzewski and the program that he had built, but in many ways it was tougher for him to lose to him than to Smith. (He also had a respectable 6–11 record against Smith). Smith was of a different generation than Williams. He had *played* against Smith-coached teams. With Krzyzewski it was another story. They were peers — two years apart in age (Williams would turn fifty-two on March 4, nineteen days after Krzyzewski turned fifty), three years apart in head-coaching experience (Krzyzewski twenty-two, Williams nineteen), and strikingly similar in their strident approach to competition. Away from the court, they were friends. On the court, each hated losing to the other.

And Williams had done the losing in recent years. Another loss in Cole simply wouldn't be tolerable.

Avoiding it wasn't easy. Maryland led 33–29 after a seesaw first half. The Terrapins built the lead to 53–45 before Duke came back, led by Roshown McLeod, the six-eight transfer from St. John's, who was playing his best game of the season. A Jeff Capel three pointer tied the game at 56 with 7:52 left. They seesawed some more before two straight Laron Profit dunks off lob passes gave Maryland a 68–66 lead.

On the next play, Jeff Capel was fouled. He went to the line to shoot two. The first shot rimmed out. As Capel stepped back from the line to gather himself, both Profit and Sarunas Jasikevicius left their spots on the lane and took a step or two in his direction, clapping their hands, telling him he was going to miss the second one too.

As they did, referee Zelton Steed warned them to stop, that they could be called for a technical for taunting. That wasn't good enough for Krzyzewski. "There's nothing in the rules about a warning," he screamed at Steed. "That's a technical foul for taunting! You have to call it!"

Hearing Krzyzewski, Williams jumped out of his perpetual in-game crouch and started waving his arms, indicating that the Duke players had been moving their arms when Maryland was shooting free throws — also a violation.

Steed decided he needed to explain what he had done to both coaches, so he called them to the scorer's table. Krzyzewski was still screaming for a taunting technical. Williams was screaming about the Duke players waving their arms. "That's bullshit, Gary," Krzyzewski said.

"It's only bullshit when your guys do it, right, Mike?"

Steed had heard enough. He sent the two bickering coaches back to their benches and gave Capel the ball to shoot the second free throw. Capel, who hadn't been the least bit bothered by the alleged taunting, made the second free throw to make it 68–67. Keith Booth hit a jumper to make it 70–67 and Terrell Stokes extended it to 72–67 with two free throws. There was less than a minute left. The celebration was starting.

Too soon. Capel nailed a three to make it 72–70 with 54 seconds to go. Maryland tried to run the clock down as far as it could, but didn't get off a good shot. Duke came down with the clock under 20 and a chance to tie or win. The ball swung to Wojciechowski in the corner. He was standing on almost the same spot where Price had been a year earlier when he had broken Maryland's heart.

"Shoot it, Woj, please shoot it," Krzyzewski said from a few feet away, but not loudly enough to be heard over the screaming crowd.

Wojciechowski is a driver by instinct. He thought he saw an opening to the basket and he drove toward the middle. Obinna Ekezie cut him off. The two players went to the floor as the whistle blew with 2.2 seconds left. Everyone waited. It was a charge on Wojciechowski. Krzyzewski had no argument with the call, just with Wojo's play selection. Profit made two free throws in the last second to make the final 74–70.

Williams and Krzyzewski shook hands cordially. Krzyzewski was still angry about the taunting no-call, but not with Williams. He knew he had just been standing up for his team. Williams knew Krzyzewski had been doing the same thing. No hard feelings.

Williams was elated. It had been exactly the kind of game he had expected and his team had made just enough plays to beat a good team. The Terrapins were now 6–1 in the ACC and 17–2 overall. That equalled their victory total for the entire '96 season. They would rise to number five in the national rankings the next morning.

Duke was now 4–3 in the league, still sitting fourth behind the Big Three (Wake and Maryland 6–1, Clemson 5–2) and 15–5 overall. But Krzyzewski was angry and miserable on the plane ride home. He hadn't felt any anger from his players in the postgame locker room and that upset him. "It was almost as if it was OK to lose because it had been a good ball game," he said. "I sure as hell didn't feel OK about it. We had gotten to the point where we were willing to settle for being a decent team. The more I thought about that, the angrier I got."

He went to bed that night still angry. And when he woke up the next morning after a fitful night of sleep, he had decided that changes had to be made. If the ship was going down, it was going down his way.

18

We're Winning
on Wednesday

"GERRY, YOU MIGHT NOT want to stay for this."

Mike Krzyzewski felt that Gerry Brown, his administrative assistant, deserved fair warning. It was 11 o'clock on Monday morning and Krzyzewski and his coaches were convening for their daily morning meeting. Brown was always part of the meeting. She had worked for Krzyzewski for enough years to know that he was capable of blistering the paint off the walls in certain moods.

The walls had no chance this morning.

"Maybe I'll just stay for the first few minutes," she said.

She was as good as her word. As soon as Krzyzewski had dispensed with the office business, Brown left the room. Krzyzewski sat silently for a moment as if deciding where to begin.

"Yesterday was completely unacceptable," he said finally. "I can't begin to tell you how tired I am of this kind of shit. Watching Greg Newton on the tape last night made me want to break four televisions. All at once."

He shook his head. "This is all about standards. We've let the standards around here slip. I've let them slip. Well, not anymore. These guys are going to play the game to my fucking standards or they're not going to play. Period. I'm telling you right now there is no way I'm starting Newton against Carolina. No way. If we had yanked him earlier yesterday, we would have won the game. That's my goddamn fault for staying with him for too long.

"I'm fed up with babying these guys. That's what we've done around here for three years and look at the results it's produced. These guys think because we're 15–5 we're in the tournament. That's fool's gold. We've beaten one good team — Villanova — and I'm not so sure they're any damn good. These guys think that 18–12 is OK because it will get us in the tournament. 18–12! Are you fucking kidding me?"

He looked at his assistants — Tommy Amaker, Quin Snyder, Tim O'Toole, and Jeff La Mere — for a response. Amaker, as the number one assistant, was expected to respond first. The others would take their cue from him. "If you don't start Newt," he asked quietly, "who do you start?"

"Chris [Carrawell]," Krzyzewski answered. "At least he'll rebound and screen. He'll also make us quicker. We can put a lot more pressure on defensively with him in the game. The last two games we've played we've let the other team shoot fifty percent. Our defense sucked yesterday. We need to get back to being a full-court-pressure team on offense and defense. We've gotten away from that."

They talked a while longer about what they would tell the players when they came in later and about practice plans. Finally, Amaker cleared his throat and said quietly, "I think we need Newt to beat Carolina."

For a second Krzyzewski didn't answer. Then he stood up to indicate the meeting was over and said, "I hope you're wrong about that, Tommy."

Amaker and Snyder had been teammates in the eighties. Snyder had been Amaker's backup at the point guard spot for two years and then become the starter when Amaker graduated in 1987. They both knew their boss well enough to understand that he meant every word he had said about Newton in the morning meeting. They also knew he was speaking emotionally rather than practically. They went to eat lunch while Krzyzewski went to play racquetball. Since the back surgery, Krzyzewski has played less racquetball because his back can no longer take it five days a week. But when he feels stressed on a particular day, he tries to get in a workout because it calms him down.

"He'll come back after racquetball feeling better," Amaker said. "He knows we need Newt against Carolina."

"You think he's wrong about him?" Snyder asked.

"Absolutely not. Newt thinks because we haven't got anybody else who can play the low post that we have to play him no matter what. At least that's the way he played yesterday."

They returned to the meeting room for their prepractice session. "Coach, did you think about Newt any more during your workout?" Amaker asked when they had all sat down around the conference table.

"Yeah, I did."

"So where do you stand on starting him Wednesday?"

Krzyzewski leaned forward in his chair. "I can answer that question in three words," he said. "No fucking way."

Before Duke practices each day, the team gathers in the locker room. Sometimes the coaches show them a tape, either of a prior game or an upcoming opponent. Sometimes Krzyzewski will go over the things he thinks need to be worked on most that day. Occasionally, he will just walk in and say, "Let's go."

And every once in a while the meeting will last almost as long as practice. This was one of those days.

Krzyzewski didn't rant or rave as he spoke to his players. He didn't even raise his voice very much. He didn't need to. His words and tone sent his message quite clearly.

"Yesterday was a bad day," he said, standing in the middle of the locker room. There are lockers along each wall and the players were seated on chairs in front of their lockers, fanning out on either side of Krzyzewski as he spoke. The assistants and the managers stood in the back of the room. "It wasn't a bad day just because we lost but because of the way we lost. Now, I know you guys will say, 'Hey, we were one play away from winning the game.' That's right, you were. But what you don't understand is there were twenty-five times during the game when you could have made that one play. Everyone remembers the last one, but there were twenty-five others. If you make one, we win. But what if you make ten? Or twelve? Then we kick Maryland's ass.

"Steve, I wish you had taken that last shot. But I don't have a problem with what you did. You thought you had an opening and you went to the basket. Here's what I have a problem with, fellas: we're up 64–61 and Terrell Stokes gets a wide-open three. How does that happen? Right there, that's the one play. Make a stop there and maybe we take control of the game. You think we're close to where we want to be. We're not. We have a long way to go to being a good team."

He dealt with each player individually. Wojciechowski needed to communicate better with him from the floor. Trajan Langdon needed to work harder to get open shots. Carmen Wallace needed to be a more assertive senior leader. They all needed to help each other out more on the court. He saved Newton for last.

"You know Greg if I'd been smart enough to get you out of the game sooner yesterday, we'd have won," he said. "You were awful. We've now played seven ACC games and you've played well in one of them — the first one. Do you know how many blocked shots you have in seven games? Five. Five! How is that possible? The way we play defense you should have five in a game. You never screen. You don't rebound. And yesterday, at the start of the second half, we give you the ball four times and you're shooting fadeaways. What the hell was that?

"I'm telling you right now, no way am I starting you Wednesday. No way. Now, if there's any of you in here who think I'm wrong or being unfair to Newt, you tell me. I'll respect you for it." He paused long enough to give anyone crazy enough to speak up the opportunity. "Newt, you're such a disappointment to me. I've stood behind you for four years; tried to work with you; tried to help you and you don't want to help anybody but you. You just don't want to be a man. You'd rather be a little boy and go out and get your head shaved and put things in your body and get tattoos. You know, I don't care if you do all that as long as you act like a man after you do it. That means doing what you're supposed to do, when you're supposed to do it. You haven't done that."

He stared at Newton for a second to see if there would be a response. There was none. He went on. "See, fellas, here's the problem: we've learned how to accept not being very good. We go around saying, 'Hey, we've been close.' Right. We were close against Clemson and close against Maryland and we beat the hell out of Michigan for thirty minutes and we were right there with Wake Forest until they hit all those shots.

"Close isn't good enough! It's just not good enough. What you guys don't understand is that one of my strengths as a coach is that I hate to lose. *I hate it.* When I was a kid I got into all sorts of trouble because I had such a bad temper when I lost at something. I'd go crazy. I don't think any of you is like that."

He turned around, took a blue Magic Marker and drew a line across the marking board on the wall. "This is what I'm talking about," he said, pointing to the line. "None of you has ever drawn this line and said, 'That's it. That's as far as you go. You will have to kill me to cross this line. I mean kill me. North Carolina, you want to cross this line, no fucking way!' You guys have never done that. We haven't done that this year, we didn't do it last year, we certainly didn't do it the year before that."

He pointed to the blue line again. "This is it, right now. This is the turning point of our season. We have to draw the line right here, right now. We have to go out there with the idea that there's only one alternative on Wednesday: winning the game. That's it. We're winning on Wednesday. I'm going to find the guys in this room who will draw that line. I don't care who they are, but I'm going to find them. Because one way or the other, we're winning on Wednesday. There's no alternative. None."

The practice that followed was as intense as any all year. Krzyzewski put in some loose-ball drills, the ones where a coach rolls the ball onto the floor and two players have to dive for it. It is a punishment drill, usually reserved for preseason. There wasn't a single word about game preparation. Everything was about getting the players into another gear emotionally. Everyone seemed to understand what Krzyzewski wanted.

Everyone but Greg Newton.

From the beginning, it was clear he was unhappy with playing with the second team. He was the only player on the court not talking during drills, not encouraging teammates. Everything he did was with a poker face. Krzyzewski got angrier and angrier. Finally, near the end of the workout, when the second team was lining up for a sprint, Krzyzewski went off on Newton for not concentrating on his foul shooting. Newton rolled his eyes — just barely — but just enough.

"Don't you ever roll your eyes at me like that again!" Krzyzewski barked. "Get out of here."

"No," Newton said. "I want to run."

It was the first thing he had done right all day. He was saying he wanted to work, wanted to keep trying. But it was too late.

"I told you get out, you get the hell out of here right now," Krzyzewski said, marching at Newton with a menacing look on his face.

Newton tried one more time. "I want to stay."

Krzyzewski was now right in front of Newton, staring up at him. If the forty-nine-year-old six-one, 190-pound coach had decided to take on the twenty-one-year-old, six-ten, 225-pound player at that moment, there wasn't a soul in the gym who would have bet a nickel on the player. "I don't want you in here," Krzyzewski screamed in Newton's face. "Get out. Now!"

Newton knew he had no chance. He turned and ran out of the gym.

Practice ended a few minutes later. When it did, as is always the case, most of the players lingered on the court to talk, shoot some extra free throws, listen to a final point from the coaches. One player made a beeline for the locker room: Jeff Capel. Which was exactly what Krzyzewski wanted.

"If anyone can say to him, 'Look, I've been where you are and there's no reason why you can't fight your way back,' it's Jeff," Krzyzewski said. "The only problem is they have different attitudes. Jeff's a fighter. He never gave up on himself. Newt's not a fighter. I guarantee you he's in there right now crying his eyes out."

He was right. Capel returned to the floor a few minutes later. "How is he?" Krzyzewski asked.

"Crying, still," Capel said. "I tried to tell him the only reason you were on him is because he's letting himself down the way he's approaching things. I said that I know what it's like to be benched and to feel like you're failing. I was there a few weeks ago. Turning it around is just a matter of listening to what you're trying to tell him. I told him if he thinks you're picking on him, he should think again because we all agree with you. But that we're just like you; if he wants to work and get better, we'll try to help."

Carmen Wallace, the third senior on the team, also went in to talk to Newton. Krzyzewski sat on the scorer's table watching Capel leave. "Coaching a kid like that," he said, "is the reason I still coach."

Before he left that night, Krzyzewski made a prediction to the coaches: "Newt's response to all this will be another tattoo."

He was right — on his stomach.

When Quin Snyder delivered the news of the new tattoo the next day, Krzyzewski laughed. Snyder shrugged. "At least he's still here," he said. "I was afraid he might be halfway across the country by now."

Krzyzewski didn't want that. He honestly didn't know at that point how much Newton was going to contribute for the rest of the season. But he felt he owed it to Newton to push him as hard as he could — as a basketball player and as a person. Newton had missed a semester of school as a sophomore after being found guilty of cheating on a test. There had been some feeling that Krzyzewski should encourage him to transfer at that point. Duke had just recruited Taymon Domzalski, another highly touted inside player and McLeod had transferred from St. John's, meaning Duke would add a six-ten player one year and a six-eight player the next. Newton was probably expendable and, under the circumstances, asking him not to return was probably not unreasonable.

Krzyzewski wanted him back. Part of it was because he still thought Newton could become a good player. But beyond that, he thought he owed it to him. Newton's dad had died very suddenly the summer after his junior year of high school and Duke had been a struggle for him academically from day one. Probably, Newton should have gone to college someplace else. That didn't matter. Krzyzewski had recruited him. If a mistake had been made it was his mistake and running Newton off would be a cop out. Newton had become a father the previous summer and was clearly worried about his future, since it was very unlikely that any NBA team was going to take a serious look at him. Krzyzewski had told Newton at the start of the season that he would do whatever he could to find him a place to play overseas the next year but he wanted him to stay at Duke for summer school so he could graduate. Newton had told him he would do so. Krzyzewski would believe that when he saw it.

Newton's attitude at practice on Tuesday was better. Not so much better that Krzyzewski reconsidered his decision not to start him, but good enough that he was at least back in the playing rotation. He had decided to put Capel back in to the starting lineup. "He's earned it," Krzyzewski said. "He's been as good a kid as we've ever had here. And this is his last home game against Carolina."

More specifically, it was his last chance to win a home game against

Carolina. The Duke seniors were 0–3 against the Tar Heels in Cameron, the three losses part of a seven-game losing streak that stretched back to 1993. When Krzyzewski thought about the streak, he didn't just think about the three senior players, he thought about the entire senior class.

Krzyzewski has always had a special relationship with the Duke student body. The only other coach in the ACC who has a similar relationship with his students is Gary Williams. Krzyzewski talks often about Duke's "sixth man," and when he does he means it. In private, he tells the players how important the students are to them and how lucky they are to be appreciated by their fellow students and supported the way they are. When Duke won its first national championship, Krzyzewski's happiest moment of the entire experience came when he walked into Cameron and looked out at the student body, which had gathered en masse to greet the team, and said simply, "So, where should we put the banner?" He wanted them to know that the banner was theirs, not just the team's.

Krzyzewski didn't want the senior class to graduate without a win in Cameron over Carolina. On Tuesday night, he brought the students in to Cameron as he always did the night before the Carolina game. They had been camping — in shifts — outside Cameron in what has come to be known as "Krzyzewskiville," for a week in anticipation of this game. Pizzas were ordered and Wojciechowski spoke to the students on behalf of the team. Then it was Krzyzewski's turn.

He spoke for almost an hour. He talked about how much their support meant to him and to the team. "You know, I always hope there will be a Krzyzewskiville," he said. "Because of all the things I've been a part of and all the honors I've received, that's the best honor I've had. To have your name on something so living and so vibrant, makes me feel so good I can't tell you.

"We need you tomorrow night like we've never needed you before. Believe me when I say that. We need you loud all the time. We need you screaming for defense. We need to feel you the whole night. Check out the lobby on your way out tonight. On the wall, with all our trophies and pictures of championship teams, is a picture of you — the Cameron Crazies. Because you're a part of this. There's another picture in the locker room. You're what makes Duke a special place to play. We've had good teams, great teams, but they wouldn't have felt special without our students.

"We haven't been as good the last couple of years as I'd have liked. We're still working to get back to where we were. Tomorrow night, we can start something. We're going to do something special. We're going to win this game for all of you because we owe it to you. I can't tell you how lucky I feel to be the coach at Duke, to be a part of this."

He paused and added a final thought. "I'll tell you guys the same thing I told the team: We're winning on Wednesday."

Eleven miles away in Chapel Hill, there weren't any speeches being made about drawing lines or turning points. For one thing, Carolina hadn't lost seven in a row to Duke. For another, the Tar Heels were coming off their best win of the season. They also weren't playing at home. But the game was just as important to Carolina in the grand scheme of things as it was to Duke. After all, a win would leave them 4–4 at the halfway point of the conference season after the awful 0–3 start. What's more, with three straight home games coming up, the chance to get on a roll was quite real.

And there was one other thing: it was Duke at Duke. If Dean Smith had been candid on one subject over the years it was the fact that he enjoyed nothing more than beating Duke at Duke. He had never liked the irreverent atmosphere of Cameron; Duke was the archrival and the greatest threat — long term — to Carolina's mastery over the ACC. Krzyzewski's presence over the years had made it more personal. Smith always had his team ready for Cameron. He was 18–17 throughout his lengthy career there and there is little doubt that each of the 18 ranked high on his list of satisfying wins.

Smith was probably feeling as good about his team's progress as Krzyzewski was feeling frustrated by his team's lack thereof. Since the escape from NC State, the Tar Heels had played better and better. Even the loss to Florida State hadn't bothered Smith that much because he thought the Seminoles had one of those nights. "We played well enough to beat most teams that night," he said.

The Tar Heels were 3–4 in the league. A year earlier at the halfway mark, Carolina had been 7–1. But Smith felt better about this team than the '96 team. Although he would never admit it publicly, coaching the high-strung, temperamental Jeff McInnis had not been fun. He had not enjoyed relying on a freshman — no matter how superb Antawn Jamison had been — as his best player and Vince Carter had been a handful from day one. This team was a long way from being perfect. He was again dependent on a freshman, in this case point guard Ed Cota, in a key role, and Carter was still a lot of work. But this group had worked hard in practice from the start and Smith was starting to see the fruits of that labor.

"Right now, I'm enjoying this team a lot," he said on the afternoon of the Duke game. "I enjoy coming to practice every day. There have been years when, this time of year, I would have had trouble saying that. Not this year."

One of those years had been 1996. "If you had asked me in February of last year when I was retiring, I'd have probably told you this is it," he admitted.

And so while all of North Carolina wondered if Smith was contemplating retirement this year, he had probably been a lot closer to it a year earlier when, at least in terms of wins and losses, the first half of the season had been far more promising.

The differences between Smith and Krzyzewski are never more apparent than on game day. Krzyzewski is an early riser. He will come into the office, meet with his coaches, get some work done, then bring the team in for a walk-through. After that he goes home and takes a nap. Smith has never been an early riser. He doesn't like to be in the office before 11. To him, game day is for catching up on mail and phone calls. Rarely does he bring the team in for a walk-through. Almost every ACC team will go to a road gym to shoot on the day of a game. Carolina almost never does. When the Tar Heels play in North Carolina, they get on their bus twice: to go to the game and to leave the game. Their coach drives in his BMW — "the only reason I drive one is because one of my former managers has a dealership" — and meets them at the game site.

This was a 9 o'clock game, meaning the day stretched on forever for both coaches. For Krzyzewski, it was even longer than usual for reasons that had almost nothing to do with the game.

Throughout the season, Krzyzewski had wrestled with the loss of his mother. Emily Krzyzewski had made herself into a basketball fan because of her son. It had become a part of his postgame routine throughout his years as a coach to call his mom before he left the locker room to give her a report on the game. She always knew the final score before he called, whether the game was on TV or not. On the night that he won his first national championship, Krzyzewski had excused himself from a raucous victory party to spend some time alone with his mom. There were few things in life that made Emily Krzyzewski happier than a Duke win over Carolina.

It was only natural, then, that on several game nights, Krzyzewski had come back into the coaches' dressing area in the back of the Duke locker room, sat down at his desk, looked at the picture sitting there of him and his mom dancing, and reached for the phone. It was just as natural that when it occurred to him that she wouldn't be there to answer the call, that he started to cry. As much as he craved a win over Carolina, Krzyzewski knew it wouldn't feel the same without a call to his mom. Her birthday would have been on Saturday.

She was on his mind all day. As he left the house for the game, he pulled out a pin that he had given her years ago. It was the West Point A-Pin, which each Cadet receives to give to his best girl (or, nowadays, her best boy). Years ago Krzyzewski had given one to his mother and one to Mickie. Now, he took his mom's and put it in his pocket.

By the time he got to Cameron, the place was jumping. He had lectured his team during the shoot around about three things: not giving Shammond Williams any open shots; forcing the Tar Heels to dribble the ball rather than move the ball by way of their crisp passing game, and, most important, keeping Jamison off the boards. Rebounding would be critical in this game. With Newton, Duke was not a good rebounding team and Carolina — especially Jamison — was excellent. Without Newton, they could get hammered inside. "Keep the ball alive any way you can," he had told his players. "If you can tip the ball to someone three times in this game, we might get three threes out of that. How big a difference do you think nine extra points will make in this game?"

The locker room was more crowded than normal prior to the game. Howard Garfinkel, the Five-Star guru, was making the first of his two winter trips to North Carolina along with his friend Bill Pollock, an agent who lived in Washington. They had spent the previous day at Wake Forest with Dave Odom before making the seventy-five-minute drive to Durham.

Krzyzewski was killing time watching the Indiana-Purdue game in the coaches' lounge when Garfinkel and Pollock came in. Garfinkel launched into a treatise on why Indiana was having a tough time winning games in the Big Ten. Krzyzewski listened for a while, then left to return to the sanctuary of the coaches' dressing area. He was looking at the Carolina scouting report one last time when Dick Vitale bounded up the steps.

"Hey, Mike, everywhere I go people are saying, 'What's with Duke,' I tell 'em, 'Hey, they're 15–5, they'll get their twenty, be back in the tournament, then next year, watch out, baby.' "

Vitale was like a runaway train, especially on a game night, especially on a night when it was Duke-Carolina in Cameron and a coterie of ESPN bigwigs had flown down for the game. One minute he was telling people how strange it felt to have these two teams sitting fourth and tied for sixth in the ACC instead of one, two in the country, the next he was saying there was still nothing like this rivalry.

Once he finished his opening monologue, Vitale came to the real reason for his visit. "What's the story with Newton?" he said. "The real story."

Krzyzewski took off his reading glasses. "The real story is that he's not playing well enough to deserve to start."

"I heard you threw him out of practice Monday."

"Dick, if I didn't start every player who ever got thrown out of practice, we'd have no starters."

Vitale nodded. He still didn't have the answer he wanted, something he could use on the air, like Newton having so many tattoos he couldn't jump high enough to rebound. "You know," he said, zigging and zagging, "I keep telling people you guys are three plays from being 18–2."

"We're also three plays from being 12–8. That's the way the league is this year. You've got no margin for error."

Vitale wasn't listening. "Well, you'll get your twenty. You think Wake's a Final Four team?"

"There are a lot of teams with Final Four potential. They're one of them."

Vitale could tell Krzyzewski wasn't in a kibitzing mood. He shook hands and headed out of the locker room. Krzyzewski sat back in his chair. "I like Dick, I really do," he said. "But sometimes, unless you tell him that you're recruiting a player from Mars, he doesn't listen to a word you're saying."

He was quiet for a while, unusual for pregame. Most of the time, he made nervous chatter, wondering about who was ready and who wasn't. He would ask Amaker and Snyder over and over, "How are we? Are we OK? How's Wojo? Trajan?"

Now, he was silent for a long time. He stared at the picture of his mother. "I can't tell you," he said, "how much I miss my mom right now."

Amaker walked in. "What do you think?" Krzyzewski asked.

"Not sure," Amaker said.

"I think I've done enough talking, don't you?" Krzyzewski said.

"Let me put it this way," Amaker said. "If they haven't figured it out by now, they're not going to."

Krzyzewski nodded. He walked down the hall to the players' dressing area. They sat in front of their lockers in their warm-ups, leaning forward, ready to explode through the door. Krzyzewski looked at them briefly, then turned to the marking board and picked up the blue pen. He drew a line across the board. Then he walked to the middle of the room and put his hand out. "Let's go," he said. They were around him in a split second. Krzyzewski's instinct had been right. He didn't need to say another word.

The atmosphere in Cameron for any big game is always electric. With the students surrounding the court on all four sides, one has the feeling walking onto the floor of being a gladiator. Even the visitors love the way it feels. For Duke-Carolina, all of that feeling goes up a notch. Or two. Or eight. Dean Smith loved telling his team that there was no better feeling than to silence the crowd in Cameron.

There would be no lulls in this game. The students had made a pledge to Krzyzewski and they weren't going to let him down. Duke was flying at the start. Carolina couldn't get a shot off on its first five possessions.

McLeod hit a jumper and Capel a three for a quick 5–0 start and it felt as if the roof would come off the place.

Of course emotion only lasts a few minutes in a basketball game. Then everyone settles down and the game is ultimately decided in the 94-foot by 50-foot rectangle of the court. ACC teams are used to hostile atmospheres, no one more so than the Tar Heels. Once they caught their breath, the game settled into the kind of up-and-down duel that most Duke-Carolina games ultimately become.

Duke was hot from outside early. During one stretch, Langdon, Wojciechowski, and freshman Mike Chappell hit consecutive threes. Duke led 21–15 at the second TV time-out. The pace was frantic. That was what Krzyzewski wanted. Smith wanted to get a hold of the game, slow it to a half-court tempo so his team could assert its strength inside and on the boards. The freshman Ed Cota had looked frightened at the start. Now, he settled down and made two straight buckets, then fed Ademola Okulaja for a three. Suddenly, Carolina had the lead, 24–21.

The Tar Heels listened eagerly for the silence. There was none. The students weren't backing down. Not on this night. The teams scratched to half-time. Duke took the lead into the locker room on a Capel jumper, 33–31.

Krzyzewski was clinical at halftime. They had to do a better job of handling the ball. Carter, Zwikker, and Cota had hurt them but they had done a good job on Jamison (two points) and Williams (three). That was the tough thing about playing Carolina: if you focused on cutting off one player, another would hurt you. Everyone on the floor could score. They had done a great job on the boards: 15–12 in their favor. That would have to continue.

Smith was very happy with where the game was. They had weathered the early emotion and come back to lead. If they got a good start in the second half, they could knock Duke backwards emotionally, quiet the crowd, and take control. After all, the pressure was on Duke. It was their home game. Remember, he told his players, they're supposed to win.

The start of the second half couldn't have been better for Carolina if Smith had scripted it himself. Okulaja hit a three right away and Zwikker hit a baby hook and got a rebound basket. It was 38–33, Carolina. Still, the crowd wouldn't go away. Neither would the crowd's team. Langdon hit back-to-back threes. Then Wojo dove on the floor for a steal, fed

Capel, who beat the defense on the baseline and dunked. Duke was up 43–40.

Back and forth they went, each team making plays. Wojo picked up his fourth foul with 13:08 left and Krzyzewski was up screaming at Larry Rose. All game long, the Carolina coaches had been screaming for hand-check calls on Wojo. When they finally got one, they were ecstatic. As soon as Wojo left, Cota made a steal and fed Okulaja. Carolina was up, 54–48. TV time-out.

"Hey, fellas, our defense sucks right now," Krzyzewski said in the huddle. "We need our defense to set up our offense. You've got to pick that up right away."

This was a critical juncture. If Carolina built a big lead, rallying would be difficult. They ran a play for Langdon, whose jumper hit the rim. From out of nowhere came Ricky Price, a forgotten man for most of January. He skied over the Carolina big men, grabbed the rebound with one hand, and put it back as Okulaja fouled him. It was a gigantic play. It became even bigger when Price missed the free throw and Carrawell got his hand on it to back-tap it. (*We'll get threes if you get a hand on the ball . . .*) Langdon grabbed it, fired a three and — swish. It was a five-point swing. Carolina's lead was 54–53. A minute later, Jamison picked up *his* fourth foul on a charging call and Smith called a twenty-second time-out for the express purpose of screaming about the call.

Nerves were frayed on both benches by now. Capel made a steal to put Duke back ahead 56–54. No one could take control of the game. Carolina was pounding the offensive boards (the second half rebounding margin would be 23–10) but Duke's defense was now doing what it was supposed to: creating turnovers and denying open shots. Carolina's best offense was to get the ball on the glass and go after it.

Williams put Carolina ahead; McLeod answered. Langdon put Duke on top; Williams hit again. McLeod hit a three and Duke was up two. Williams came up with a driving three-point play. Carolina led 66–65. The clock was under four minutes. The quality of play was so good that every possession felt like the last seconds of a championship game.

Jeff Capel had been superb all night. Every time Duke had had to have a play, he had come up with one. Now, he head-faked and drove the left side, floating the ball over the seven-three Zwikker into the hoop. Duke up again, 67–66. Krzyzewski was on his knees in front of the bench, pounding the floor with his hands, screaming for them to get down and play defense. He had to show them what he wanted because there was no way possible to hear anything. They dug in. The ball swung to Okulaja. The scouting report had noted that he was an effective three-point shooter but that his release was slow. Capel flew at him and cleanly blocked the shot. Before Okulaja could react, Capel had the ball and was flying the other way. Layup; 69–66. Pandemonium. Smith used his last twenty-second time-out to calm his team. Calming the crowd was now out of the question.

Jamison used all his strength to get inside for a layup. Now it was Krzyzewski's turn to call time. The clock was down to 2:23. This was the time of the game when one play could win it — or lose it. Now, not on the last play. Calmly, he drew the play to isolate Capel. "We're in better shape than they are," he said. "This is our time of the game."

The ball swung to Capel on the left side. He had been going baseline all night. This time, he faked that way and drove toward the middle. Zwikker had no choice but to come out to help on him. Capel waited until the last possible second, then swung the ball around Zwikker to Newton — left wide open by Zwikker. Newton had played hard all night but hadn't scored. He had missed four shots inside and two free throws. This time, he made sure he didn't miss, catching the ball cleanly and dunking as Carter, flying in from the weak side a split second late, fouled him.

Capel, knocked to the floor by Zwikker's momentum, lay on his back, joyously kicking his feet and arms. The clock was under two minutes. Newton made the free throw: 72–68, Duke. Carolina wouldn't go away, though. Cota, maturing with each passing minute, it seemed, hit a tough jumper to make it 72–70. With sixty-one seconds left, Krzyzewski called time to set up the most critical possession of the season.

Again, he wanted the ball in Capel's hands. He would be the decision maker. But there were other options, including Langdon coming off a screen away from the ball. They reset. Wojo got the ball to Capel on the left side. Everyone waited for him to shoot or drive again. He faked left, then swung the ball across the key to Langdon, who had come off a McLeod screen. Langdon was in the air to shoot almost before he caught the ball.

Swish. For three. Forty seconds left and the lead was 75–70. On the Carolina scouting reports, players are given either a plus or a minus as three-point shooters. A plus means don't give him an open shot. Langdon was marked double plus on the scouting report. He had still managed to get open for seven threes. The seventh was the most important.

Finally, Carolina had no answers left. A couple of Duke steals and free throws down the stretch and the final was 80–73. As the last seconds ticked off, Krzyzewski was out on the court, pointing into the stands at the students. "You did this," he kept mouthing. "You did this."

They knew. As soon as the buzzer sounded, they were coming over the scorer's table and the benches and the press table. They didn't want to hurt anybody, but it was a dangerous situation anyway, bodies flying from the stands toward the floor. Somehow, everyone on both teams got out unharmed. Smith was almost smiling after shaking Krzyzewski's hand. It had taken every bit of moxie and guts Duke had to beat his team in Cameron. In losing, his team had played its best game of the year. There was no doubt in his mind that they were now a good team. If he couldn't silence the Cameron crowd, the second best thing was knowing that beating his team meant so much to them.

The Duke players were in full celebration when they reached the safety of their locker room. There were heartfelt hugs all around the room. The only person not celebrating was Krzyzewski. Throughout the final minutes of the game, he had kept his mother's A-pin in his shirt pocket. On every big play, he had reached for it, clutching it. When he reached the locker room, rather than go directly to the player's locker area as he normally did, he walked back to the coaches' lounge, clutching the pin in his right hand.

As soon as he was out of sight, he broke down. He knelt in the middle of the room, on the carpet that said, "Duke University, National Champions 1991–92," and cried for a couple of minutes. Then he gathered himself and went in to talk to his team.

"That was drawing the line, fellas," he said. "That was a great, gutsy win because, let me tell you something, you beat a hell of a basketball team. I guarantee you that team isn't going to lose very often the rest of the season. Every one of you was part of this. Ricky, your rebound bucket was huge. Absolutely huge. Newt, you worked your ass off all night. That's all I want from you. You were terrific. Trajan, you can take a big shot for me anytime. Wojo, you were great playing with foul trouble." He looked at Capel. "Jeff, wow. That's all I can say. Wow. And I want to tell you one more thing: when the press comes in here, you be sure and talk about your fellow students and what they did tonight. Because they were great. I've been here seventeen years and I've never heard Cameron louder than tonight. Never."

They cheered for each player as Krzyzewski went down the list. He stopped and took a deep breath. "There's one other thing I want to tell you," he said, his voice becoming very soft. "This has been a tough week for me. My mom's birthday would have been this Saturday. I've cried a lot."

He opened up his hand, so they could see the A-pin. "This pin was hers. I took it with me tonight, so I could have something of hers with me. I needed that. Every big play, down the stretch, I was clutching it, holding on for dear life." He was losing it now, but he plowed on. "Fellas, my mom was here tonight. She was. And you made her proud. I just want to thank you for that."

He was crying by the time he was finished. He wasn't alone.

19

Round Two

THE DUKE-CAROLINA EPIC was the last game of round one in the ACC season. Everyone had played everyone else once. Wake Forest was alone in first place at 7–1 because Maryland had lost its last game of the first round at Florida State. That left the Terrapins tied with Clemson at 6–2. Duke was next at 5–3 — the three losses to the teams ahead of it — followed by Virginia at 4–4. Carolina and Florida State were at 3–5, Georgia Tech was 2–6, and NC State was 0–8.

The second half would begin on February's first weekend and the opening game on Saturday afternoon was Clemson at NC State. Rick Barnes was terrified. "I'm going to tell you something right now," he said. "State's going to beat some people. They've been in every game but one and had four or five real chances to win. They aren't just going to win one, they're going to win three or four."

Herb Sendek would have loved hearing that the morning after his team had finished the first round with a 69–64 loss at Virginia. The game had followed a script Sendek was becoming familiar with: the Wolfpack had led late, failed to make plays, and walked off with another loss. "It's one thing to be told you face a challenging season," Sendek said, his eyes bleary from lack of sleep. "The reality of going through it is entirely different."

Sendek had gotten angry with his team after the Virginia game, something he hadn't done very often. He knew he was walking a fine line. He didn't want to beat them down to the point where they lost their competitiveness, but he also didn't want them thinking that being competitive was enough. The game had been there to be won. They had lost it as much as Virginia had won it and that's what disturbed him. "You just can't stop playing when things are tight at the end," he told the players.

He had told them to shower and think about what had happened and then they would talk some more. He was gentler the second time around, telling them they had done everything he had asked them to do from day one and that there was no other team he would rather be coaching. But 0–8 was 0–8 and they had to look in the mirror and figure out how to get better because there was no one on the ACC schedule they could point to and say, "There's a win."

Sendek's lengthy postgame session with his team did nothing for his relationship with the local media. Already frustrated by his policy of bringing players out of the locker room rather than simply opening it, they were less than happy when they had to wait twenty minutes after a 9 o'clock game and then had to chase the already-dressed players out to the bus to get any comments from them.

That, of course, was the least of Sendek's worries. "We're better now than we were four weeks ago," he said. "That's the good news. I want to keep the big picture in mind here and I don't want winning to become our sole measuring stick. But I had to make the point to them that they can be better. If I didn't think so, there would be no point in all of us putting this effort in. They need some balls and some courage right now to keep on going."

Sendek spent a good deal of time that next morning on the phone with his old friend Billy Donovan, who was going through a similarly difficult first year at Florida. The difference was that the SEC had some teams that were beatable without a superhuman effort. Donovan wasn't facing the possibility of 0–16. Sendek hadn't even thought about 0–16 until now.

"We've had chances to win, but we haven't won," he said. "Until we win a game, it's something that's not out of the question." He would never voice that to the team. But with the first round over, he couldn't help but wonder where — and when — the first victory would come.

It came, three days later — against Rick Barnes and Clemson. Still struggling to find inside offense, the Tigers came into Reynolds Coliseum and lost 68–65. State played well and finally made some big plays at the finish. But it still took a bad call to clinch the game for the Wolfpack. State was up one with under ten seconds left when Terrell McIntyre raced into the frontcourt with the ball. He was trapped near the baseline and the ball came loose. One official, Steve Gordon, was blocked and couldn't see who the ball had gone off. He asked for help and Frank Scagliotta, in the trail position, came in and said the ball had gone off McIntyre. Barnes saw it differently.

"Frank, there's no way," he said. "The ball was off them."

Scagliotta shook his head. "Sorry, Rick, I saw it go off your guy's foot."

It hadn't gone off his guy's foot; it had gone off not one, but two State players. Scagliotta, one of the country's top officials, was horrified when he saw the replay. So was Gordon, who felt responsible since he had allowed himself to be blocked and put Scagliotta in the awkward position of having to make a call that should have been his.

Twelve days later, when Scagliotta and Gordon worked the Clemson–Wake Forest game, both made a point of apologizing to Barnes before the game. "We blew it," Scagliotta said. "I feel awful. All I can tell you is we'll work our butts off for you for the rest of the season."

Barnes appreciated that. He would rather have had the basketball with seven seconds left at State. It wasn't a good way to start February for Barnes — or for the league's officials. Unfortunately for both, there was more to come.

The win was a huge relief for everyone from State. There was much hugging in the locker room. Sendek felt as if a giant weight had been removed from his shoulders. A number of his friends from college had come to town for the weekend and they had a great celebration dinner that night — with Melanie Sendek. Herb was out eating with a recruit. He came home, relieved the baby-sitter, and waited for everyone else to come home. He was up early the next morning. "If winning one told me anything, it was that we had to find a way to get another," he said.

*   *   *

The glamour game of the weekend was in College Park: Wake Forest–Maryland, The Rematch. The loss to Maryland was still the only blemish on Wake's 17–1 record. Maryland was 17–3 after the defeat at Florida State and Gary Williams wanted to make sure his team bounced back quickly after the loss.

Losing the game had bothered him because his team had come from way behind, weathering a very hot FSU start, and then had made key mistakes at the finish. "First time all year we've done that," he said. "The Clemson game, they made plays at the end. This game, we could have made plays and didn't."

The other disturbing thing about the game had been Williams's ejection in the final seconds by Dick Paparo. For all of his sideline gyrations and machinations, Williams had never been ejected from a game. He was embarrassed and disturbed about it, especially since his second technical had come when he was yelling something at Laron Profit and Paparo thought it was directed at him.

"If what I said had been directed at him, he would have been right to toss me," Williams said. "But it wasn't. I was talking to Laron."

Williams knew that Paparo had genuinely misunderstood. "All the years I've coached in games that he's reffed, I would hope he'd know me well enough to give me the benefit of the doubt on something like that," he said. "No hard feelings, though. Stuff happens."

His major concern now was Wake Forest. He expected Wake to come into Cole extremely ready to play after what had happened in the first game. It would be another hot, sweaty day indoors. With the temperature outside climbing into the sixties, the building was already steamy even before the crowd began to fill it up.

Odom was tight before the game. His team had played Virginia Tech and Wofford back to back at midweek with the league bye and, although it had won both games easily, Odom had sensed that his players were on cruise control. Throughout the Tech game he had pushed them to work harder, to keep attacking and working, to use the game to get better. He had even invoked his Precious Present speech during a time-out huddle. "Once tonight is over, we can't get it back, fellas," he said. "We've got to work through this."

They worked hard enough never to be threatened. That wasn't what Odom wanted; but it was what he got. The only light moment had come when he lifted Duncan with five minutes left in the Virginia Tech game. Bill Old, the administrative assistant, who sat on the end of the bench and kept statistics, noticed that Duncan had 10 points and eight rebounds. He had been in double figures in points and rebounds for 25 straight games. During a time-out, Old pointed out to Ernie Nestor that Duncan needed two rebounds to continue the streak. If the game had been close, Nestor never would have brought it up. Of course if the game had been close, Duncan wouldn't have been on the bench. So, Nestor pointed it out to Odom.

Odom knew that Duncan was not a stat hog like some players. "Timmy, if I put you back in with this kind of lead it might look bad," he said.

"I understand, Coach."

"Listen, how long will it take you to get two rebounds?"

"Two possessions."

"Get back in."

The crowd knew just what was going on and it cheered lustily when Duncan came back into the game. It took Duncan *one* possession to get the rebounds because he got some help from his teammates, who missed two shots. Duncan rebounded them both, then indicated to Odom that he had two rebounds in case he hadn't noticed. Odom got him right out of the game.

"Good night for Tim," Old said to Odom as Duncan sat down again. "Nine points, ten rebounds."

Odom wheeled around, eyes bugging out until he saw everyone on the bench cracking up.

There wouldn't be much laughter on the Wake bench at Cole. Odom did joke with Williams about the lengthy — two minutes and 15 seconds — ABC time-outs. "You'd think they'd let us have another warm-up after each one of those."

"I know," Williams said. "I usually run out of things to say after about thirty seconds."

He had reemphasized to his players before the game the notion of enjoying where they were and how much they had accomplished. He didn't want them to think that a road loss to Florida State diminished what they had already achieved. "Florida State is not going to lose at home again this season if they keep playing that way," he told the players. "You guys know how talented they are. Ask North Carolina. They lost down there too."

He had written on the board as the fourth key to the game: Enjoy the Moment.

"Look around you when you walk out there today. We're playing in as big a game as there is in the country today. They're ranked number two; we're ranked number five and we both deserve those rankings. We're on national TV. This place is packed. It's going to be hot and sweaty and that's fine with us. Enjoy this. You deserve it."

Williams only wished he could enjoy it more. He had noticed a quote in the paper that morning from starting wing guard Sarunas Jasikevicius on the subject of how much he sweated during a game. "He still wants to play," Jasikevicius had said. "He's just too old."

Williams laughed when he read the line. "He's right. I would like to play. I hate coaching."

Especially during the twenty minutes before tip-off. Billy Hahn came in from the court to report that the Wake Forest team warming up right now was in a lot more serious mood than the one he had watched warm up in Winston-Salem. That was no surprise. What was a surprise was the first half. Except for Wake jumping to a 6–2 lead, it wasn't very different from the first half two weeks earlier. Maryland's pressure was getting to Wake, just as it had the first time. And his team's sloppy play was getting to Odom — even more so than the first time.

"They don't like the pressure," Williams said with his team up 25–19. "They don't like to run back either. Pressure them, make them run back. Make it hard for them."

They did. Two minutes later, Odom erupted when the officials missed an apparent double dribble on Keith Booth. He came out of the box screaming and Sam Croft teed him up immediately. Odom was genuinely angry. He even shoved Nestor away when he came to try and pull him back. The call angered him, but what was really bothering him was his team's play. How could they come in to play the one team that had beaten them all year and let the same things happen all over again? Maryland came at them and they had taken a step back. Inexcusable.

It didn't get any better after the technical. Booth cleanly stripped

Duncan and went the length of the court for a dunk. Odom called a twenty-second time-out. No use. Matt Kovarik split the defense for a layup. Jasikevicius hit a baseline jumper. Steve Goolsby finally stopped the bleeding with a pair of critical three pointers that cut the margin to 41–31. Maryland held for the last shot. As Terrell Stokes dribbled at the top of the key, the entire Wake bench was screaming at Jerry Braswell to cheat left because Stokes will always drive right. It was written plain as day on the scouting report.

Braswell didn't remember and he didn't hear. Stokes zoomed past him on the right, the help came late, and he laid the ball in easily as the half ended. It was 43–31 and Cole was crazed. So were the Deacons, who were yelling angrily at one another as they ran down the tunnel to the locker room.

"They look like us last year," Williams said to his coaches.

"At least we're showing some emotion," Nestor said to Odom.

Odom didn't want to hear it. Not at that moment. He was hotter than he had been all season — literally and figuratively. He took his coat off before he was inside the locker room and then ripped into his players as soon as the door was shut.

"You are playing right now exactly the way people think you will play under pressure," he said. "Like a bunch of talented pussies. That's what that first half was all about. You cannot be champions if you back off and are intimidated whenever someone gets in your face. It doesn't work that way."

He was angry because they weren't paying attention to the bench, to the scouting report, or to each other. "Jerry, you let Stokes beat you to the right not once but *twice*," he said. "What are you thinking about? That's the trouble — you're not thinking. You have to get your thinking caps on now, guys. And you are going to have to be tougher this second half, tougher in every possible way.

"I really don't care about the score right now. That's not my concern. But you had better play better and you had better play tougher. The way you played that first half is unacceptable. Completely unacceptable."

The players knew that Odom's anger was genuine. He rarely ripped into them at halftime — especially when they were losing or in a tight game. He was most likely to go off at halftime if they were playing flat against an outmatched oppponent. Now, he was clearly pissed off. Odom doesn't throw profanity around that often. Some coaches call their players pussies as often as they call them by their names. Not Odom. When he invoked that term, everybody noticed.

Odom meant what he said about not being that concerned with the score. He wanted to win the game, but he was thinking beyond that. In the back of his mind was the memory of the Kentucky game in the regional final, his team's offense breaking down in the face of Kentucky's pressure, his players taking enough of a step back to be off-balance, playing right into Kentucky's hands. He knew that Kentucky and other teams would bring that kind of pressure to bear on his team in March. A year ago, Rutland's knee injury had been an easy excuse — although Odom had never used it publicly — for ballhandling troubles. Now, there were no excuses.

Odom's concerns had been summed up in the Clemson scouting report: "They will turn it over under pressure." You didn't get to the Final Four or win a national championship if that was true of your team. They had gotten away with it at Clemson only because Clemson didn't have enough offense to close the deal in the second half. Now, he wanted to find out if they had the guts to respond to his angry challenge.

They did — with some help. Their first break came early, when Obinna Ekezie picked up his fourth foul putting his elbow into Duncan's back. Williams had warned Ekezie during halftime to be careful about not picking up a quick foul that way because he knew Odom had been pleading with the officials for two games to be on the alert for that move. Ekezie may be the smartest player on the Maryland team. He is an engineering major who put in so many hours studying that Williams thought it sometimes affected his basketball. That was why the quick foul baffled and frustrated Williams. "That may be the dumbest thing I've seen you do in two years," he told Ekezie as Rodney Elliott, two inches shorter and thirty pounds lighter, reported into the game to try and guard Duncan.

With Ekezie out, Maryland looked like a high school team inside compared to Duncan and Woods. Odom went right at them. Duncan scored twice and Woods scored twice in less than three minutes. Just like that the 12-point lead was a three-point lead and Williams had to spend a time-out. "Hey, fellas, forget about what I think," Williams said, "don't you think you owe it to all these people in here to at least *work*. You've stopped working the game. Now come on!"

Williams never stops working a game. Coming out of the huddle, he yelled at referee Curtis Shaw about the fact that there had been five Maryland fouls to none for Wake Forest. Any coach whose team has been called for a bunch of quick fouls early in a half will point out the foul disparity, whether that disparity is legitimate or not. Dean Smith is famous for standing in front of his bench and just pointing at the scoreboard as if to say, 'How could you?' Shaw wasn't buying. "Coach, don't say that," he said. "You know that has nothing to do with what's happening."

Williams knew that. But he had to try. Maryland managed to stretch the lead back to eight, but Wake promptly scored the next eight to tie. Maryland crept ahead again, Wake hung close. Maryland was in foul trouble. Williams went deep into his bench for freshman Kelly Hite and he responded with a good defensive play and a fast-break layup. Cole was rocking. The lead was five again. But Duncan wasn't going to lose this game. He had that look that a great player gets when it is serious buckle-down time. He hit twice, then reacted to a double-team to pitch the ball to Peral for an open three. When the ball hit the net, Wake had the lead for the first time since the opening minutes, 66–65, with 4:45 left.

The rest was just wickedly intense basketball. Duncan scored with a little more than a minute to go to put Wake up, 70–67, but Ekezie answered with forty-one seconds left. It was 70–69. Williams was screaming at his players not to foul, to just dig in and play thirty-five seconds of defense. But it was so loud that all Laron Profit heard was "foul." He grabbed Duncan with thirty-six seconds to go. Duncan made one, but missed the second. Maryland was down two with the ball and plenty of time left to set up for a shot.

Just as in the first game, Maryland cleared a side for Booth. Odom had been upset looking at the tape of the first game because too many people — three — had come to help on the last play, which was why Profit had been so wide-open. Booth faced up with the clock ticking toward ten and found Duncan in front of him. Quicker than Duncan, he took a giant step toward the lane. But Peral came to help at just the right moment and Booth had to try to shoot over his six-ten reach. The ball went over the rim and Duncan grabbed it as Ekezie fouled him with eight seconds left. This time he made both foul shots. It was over. Wake had outscored the Terrapins 43–26 in the second half for a 74–69 win. The Deacons had given Odom the toughness he had demanded at halftime. Duncan had scored 25 points in the second half. No other Deacon had scored in double figures for the ball game.

Williams was incensed. Knowing that the Deacons were going to come out full bore in the second half, his players hadn't been ready. "You did not lose that game in the last minute fellas," he said. "You lost it in the first five minutes of the second half. How in the world could you come out like that? Obinna, I have no idea what you were thinking when you committed your fourth foul. What did you think, that I was joking about them watching you?"

He paced around the middle of the locker room for a moment as if trying to decide just how angry to get. They had done a lot of things well in the game. And they had been beaten by a fabulous performance by the country's best player. Still, they had been in control and given up that control. "You guys have to decide how good you want to be," he said finally. "You can have a nice season, win twenty games, and go to the NCAAs and let that be enough for you. Or, you can be a special team. Special teams win this game. You didn't do that today."

He was angry and drained. He was also convinced that the officials had let Duncan get away with traveling and backing in on the defense in the low post. There's no doubt that seniors (especially these days when there are so few) get a break from referees, and star seniors even more of a break. If a call is close, they're likely to get it. When Williams called Fred Barakat on Monday to complain, Barakat wasn't buying. "They called an offensive foul on Duncan in the first half, they called him for walking, and they called him for three seconds," he said. "You've got no case, Gary."

Williams thought Barakat was wrong. But there wasn't much he could do except get ready to play NC State. And toss and turn each night.

Maryland was the only home team that didn't win over the weekend. Virginia continued Florida State's road miseries with a victory in Charlottesville, and Duke easily beat Georgia Tech in Cameron. After the game, Mike Krzyzewski asked Bobby Cremins if he was holding up all right with a 2–7 conference record. Cremins insisted he was fine. "I'm not going to have a midlife crisis, Mike," he told him. "I already did that once."

All the midweek games were on Wednesday and Thursday. Again, the home teams dominated: North Carolina, gaining in confidence with each game, embarrassed Florida State, 90–62. The score was impressive if you were Dean Smith and disappointing if you were Pat Kennedy, since FSU had traditionally played very well in front of the wine-and-cheese crowd. The Seminoles dropped to 0–5 on the road. "We can't get into the NCAA tournament without winning on the road," Kennedy told his coaches afterward. "We already have two losses at home" — Virginia and Clemson. "We won't get in at 6–10, that's for sure. We have to stop folding on the road."

Jeff Jones was thinking the same thing that night. His team had gotten through a key four-game home stretch with four absolute-must wins. That put the Cavaliers at 5–4 in the league and 15–6 overall. Like Kennedy — and most coaches across the country — Jones was starting to think about postseason even though there were four weeks left in the regular season. He knew that eight ACC wins would lock up an NCAA bid for his team. He also knew, looking at the schedule, that eight ACC wins were far from a lock. The three remaining home games were against Duke, Wake Forest, and Maryland. None of those games was a gimme. Road games in the ACC are never gimmes. Realistically, the Cavaliers' best chances were at Georgia Tech and NC State.

Which was why losing at Georgia Tech that Thursday — losing convincingly, 66–53, while shooting one-for-12 from beyond the three-point line — was so galling. "It had to be biorhythms," Tom Perrin said later. "It was as if everyone in our locker room, coaches included, had bad biorhythms that night. Either that or it was bad karma. We should all have been home in bed that night."

In any event, it was a bad loss. Maryland had also won at home, bouncing back from the Wake Forest loss to coast to a 66–55 victory over NC State. Herb Sendek's campaign for ACC win number two was set back severely when his best player, C. C. Harrison, hurt his foot stepping off a step while walking across campus, and, although he played twenty-four minutes, could produce only two points. Sendek spent the whole game imploring his players to play with more emotion. They were trying, but without Harrison, they had little chance to beat a Maryland team playing at home that badly needed a win.

Sendek was frustrated enough that he picked up a rare technical — his second of the season and the second of his head coaching career — for stomping in anger when Larry Rose didn't call a foul after Sendek thought Rodney Elliott had hammered his freshman center, Damon Thornton. Rose had given Sendek his first tee (at Kansas) and now he gave him his second one. "Larry, you have to call that foul," Sendek said, getting in his money's worth as Rose informed the scorer's table about the technical. "What do we have to do to get a foul. Elliott hit him three times!"

The Wolfpack did cut an 11-point lead to five after that, but never got any closer. "They were never in danger of losing the game," Sendek said later. "They played as well as they needed to."

That wasn't good enough for Williams, who blistered his team in the locker room after the game. He didn't like what he was seeing. He was starting to notice a different attitude in practice and he thought he knew why: classes had finally started a week earlier. Like Odom — and a lot of other coaches — Williams saw the time in between semesters as ideal for basketball. There were no distractions. In a way, it was like running a pro basketball team. Everything was built around two practices a day. The players bonded because they were together all the time, and, if the coaches didn't like what they were seeing they could use the extra time they had any way they pleased: individual meetings, film sessions, more practice. The NCAA's twenty-hour rule wasn't in effect and the players knew it. That meant they came to practice each day wanting to do well so they wouldn't have to stay any longer than necessary.

Maryland had been fortunate that its schedule kept the players out of class for the entire first round of ACC play. Now, classes and the normal distractions that came with them were back. Williams knew that was part of the deal and simply leveled the playing field between him and the other eight coaches who had been back in class since early or mid-January.

But something else was bothering him. When the students had left in mid-December, the Terrapins had been an unranked team whose most impressive victories were over California and Georgia Tech. There had been murmurings around campus that maybe the team was going to be better than people had thought. By the time they got back, the team was ranked fifth in the nation; it was in second place in the ACC; it had wins over Wake Forest, North Carolina, and Duke; and ESPN was running graphics comparing Laron Profit's statistics as a sophomore to Michael Jordan's statistics as a sophomore.

The world had changed considerably in six weeks. "Now, everywhere they go, they have people telling them how great they are," Williams said before the State game. "It's great to be a winner around here because you get a lot of attention, it's a major media center and people notice you. But it can also be a problem. I have to make them understand that, in the grand scheme of things, we haven't done a damn thing yet. We haven't won an ACC title; we haven't even won twenty games yet. They don't want to hear that though. They just want to hear how good they are. It's human nature."

And so, after the State game was over, Williams let his players know that although they had done their job for that night, they had a lot of work to do. He has always believed that the best time to yell is after a win because no one is sulking.

"Fellas, you don't understand," he said. "My goal isn't to win twenty games. It isn't to win the goddamn ACC either. It's to win the national championship.

"A couple weeks ago, we were playing as well as anybody in the country. Anybody. Now, we're not. Think about it, fellas. Think about it."

The only home loser of the midweek was a shock: Wake Forest. The Demon Deacons now had two losses all season and both had been at the Joel Coliseum. This time, the perpetrator was Duke.

Maybe it was inevitable. After all, the Deacons hadn't lost to the Blue Devils since 1993 — nine straight games — and Duke seemed to be on a roll when it came to exorcising recent ghosts. Mike Krzyzewski had restored Greg Newton to the starting lineup against Georgia Tech as a reward for playing hard against North Carolina, but Newton had again been ineffective — six points in twenty-four minutes. As a result, Krzyzewski went back to his small lineup against Wake, a curious move — or so it would seem — against a team that was seven one, six ten, six ten across the front line. Duke countered that with six eight, six eight, and six four.

"It was a good move," Odom said later. "I know we hurt them on the boards, but they hurt us in other ways with their quickness. What's more, it was a new look, something we weren't used to, and we had trouble adjusting to it."

Even without his close friend Newton to push around, Duncan was dominant inside, shooting 11 for 13. But again his pals on the perimeter failed him. Only Steve Goolsby, who made two NBA-length threes when Wake was rallying late, produced any outside shooting worth discussing. Rutland, Braswell, Amonett, and Peral produced two three pointers in a combined 112 minutes of basketball.

It was Duke's shooting — and, once again, Capel's toughness down the stretch — that won the game. The Blue Devils shot 46 percent from the field, not an overwhelming figure, except when you realize that no one had shot better than 38 percent against Wake all season. Every time they needed a big shot, they got one, and they were nine of 22 from outside the three-point arc.

All of that said, it still looked like the Deacons' game when a Goolsby bomb from about halfway down I-40 to Greensboro tied the score at 60 with 4:35 left after Duke had led by 11. The Deacons even took the lead on a Peral jumper, but Wojciechowski promptly answered with a jumper and then Roshown McLeod took a feed from (who else?) Capel and drilled a three to put Duke up 65–62. Wake never got even again. Capel and Langdon made their free throws down the stretch; Duncan didn't. Teams were now fouling Duncan in the endgame, figuring they had a better chance with him shooting from fifteen feet than from three feet. Duncan was two for six in the last seven minutes of the game, including two missed one-and-ones. That and Duke's consistency at the other end doomed Wake.

As disappointed as he was, Odom wasn't that upset. Like Smith a week earlier, he understood how much the game meant to Duke and he also knew that the Blue Devils had played brilliantly. "It was a great basketball game," he said. "We could have won, had chances to win, but didn't. We go on."

He was concerned, but not overly concerned. Wake had a non-league road game at Missouri on Sunday. That, Odom thought, would be a good break for his team. See some fresh faces, get away from the trials of league play. Kansas had lost to Missouri on Monday night. That meant Wake could have been number one if it had won twice during the week, but Odom didn't care about that. It also meant Missouri would be hyped to beat number one and number two in the same week when the Deacons rolled into Columbia. *That* Odom cared about.

Duke now had a three-game winning streak and a monumental road victory. Wake was 8–2 and still leading the league. All of a sudden, second place was a three-way tie: Clemson, Maryland, and Duke at 7–3. "We now have a chance to win the league," Krzyzewski told his coaches.

They all agreed it was too soon to think in those terms. "No," Krzyzewski said. "It's not too early to think in those terms. It's been too damn long since we thought in those terms around here. We need something to shoot for. That's as good as anything I can think of."

They had come a long way in the ten days since Krzyzewski had drawn the blue line on the marking board.

20

Nightmare in Stripes

THE WEATHER up and down the East coast on Saturday, February 8 was awful. It was windy and raining in Clemson, South Carolina; frigid and raining in Chapel Hill and in Durham, North Carolina.

The bleak, rainy afternoon fit the mood in the Virginia locker room before their game in the DeanDome. The Cavaliers had spent two days in North Carolina after the debacle at Georgia Tech, since it was pointless to get home to Charlottesville in the wee hours of Friday and then turn around and travel again that night.

Tip-off of the UNC-Virginia game was shortly after 2 o'clock. By then, Clemson had finished off a critical 80–68 win over Maryland. Gary Williams's concerns over his team's emotional malaise had proven correct. After playing the Tigers even for twenty-one minutes, the Terrapins were blitzed 16–1 during a three-minute stretch early in the second half. As usual, Greg Buckner and Terrell McIntyre were the catalysts for Clemson. Williams called two time-outs during the run, to no avail. It was as if his players had decided that winning at Clemson was just a little too tough, and once Clemson asserted itself the game was over.

The only good news, Williams figured, was that with a noon tip-off, they would be able to get home at a reasonable hour and get some rest. It didn't happen that way. Fog and rain delayed them when they got to the airport in Anderson, about thirty minutes from Clemson. They finally took off after a two-hour delay, but en route, the pilot learned that the airport in Baltimore was closed. The only choice was to go to Atlantic City. There, they waited for the fog to clear. It didn't. They ended up busing back to College Park. The bus pulled up to the back door of Cole at 11:30 — eight-and-a-half hours after they had left Clemson.

The other teams playing on the road that day — Virginia and NC State — didn't have the same travel problems, but they didn't have any more fun on the court than the Terrapins. North Carolina and Duke were both hot teams. Each of them had come out of the classic in Cameron eleven days earlier brimming with confidence and it showed.

Even the orb couldn't help Virginia in this game. The orb was a ball of masking tape that had been wound and wound to the point where it was the size of a large softball. Several years earlier, when Chris Havlicek, son of the immortal John Havlicek, had been a backup guard at UVA, he had started the orb tradition, bringing it on the road and passing it around the room before the game started. Jeff Jones would start the orb around the room and it would always end up with him after everyone had touched it, made a comment, and then passed it on to someone else. Players, coaches, managers, trainers. Everyone touched the orb. Then Jones put it in the middle of the room, where it was supposed to stay until the job was done.

The job hadn't gotten done at Georgia Tech. Jones had hoped that his team would respond to the embarrassment there with a superior performance at Carolina. Virginia hadn't won in Chapel Hill since 1981 — Jones's sophomore year — and he didn't hesitate to remind his players about that streak. "Seniors, this is your last chance to win in this place," he said. "All you guys, think about this: no Virginia team has ever won in this building. We're 0–11 in the DeanDome. Right now, you guys are forty minutes away from ending that streak."

Forty minutes later, they were still forty minutes away from ending the streak. The game was close for eighteen minutes. Carolina couldn't hit from the perimeter but was burying the Cavaliers on the boards. Every time Carolina missed a free throw, it somehow came away with the rebound.

Even so, the lead was only 33–30 with two minutes to go when Harold Deane went up for an open three pointer. It rimmed out. After that, all hell broke loose. Carolina scored the last nine points of the half to go up 42–30. Jones was beside himself at halftime because he felt as if the deficit had been caused by nothing more than careless basketball. "Basketball's a funny game," he said finally after a mini tirade. "The funny thing is if we play smart and play hard in this half, we can still win the game because we're obviously good enough to beat these guys."

"This is the same team we beat last month," Deane added.

He was wrong about that. Carolina was a much better team than it had been in Charlottesville. Vince Carter (16 points, six rebounds) was healthy and playing better almost every time out. So was Ed Cota, who was getting more and more minutes at the point, which freed Shammond Williams to roam the perimeter and shoot jump shots instead of having to worry about running the team. Cota's ability to penetrate opened things up inside for Antawn Jamison and Serge Zwikker. The Tar Heels weren't even close to being the same team that the Cavaliers had beaten.

They erased any hope that Jones's halftime pleading would have any meaning by scoring the first eight points of the second half. That made the run 17–0 and the lead 50–30. The rest was just a race to get the clock to zero except when Frank Scagliotta came over to officially inform Jones that Colin Ducharme had fouled out with 8:39 left and Carolina leading 65–43.

Jones was squatting in front of his bench and when Scagliotta came toward him holding up five fingers to let him know that Ducharme had committed five fouls, Jones didn't move. But he had plenty to say. "Frank, I'm telling you right now that if you guys keep letting Jamison get away with all this shit, I'm going to embarrass you, I'm going to embarrass me, I'm going to embarrass everyone in here."

Scagliotta didn't answer for a moment. He walked right up to Jones and leaned down. "What shit, Jeff?" he asked.

"Holding, pushing, shoving, talking trash. You want me to go on?" Scagliotta stood up. "I'll take care of it," he said.

The game wasn't in doubt and Jones was clearly frustrated. Jamison,

Carter, and Zwikker had been killing his team inside all game. Jamison had picked up some of Carter's swagger and Jones didn't like it one bit. Especially down 22. Things were so bad for Virginia at that point that senior manager Kieran Donahue, whose efficiency was legendary, spilled a cup of Gatorade all over Jamal Robinson during a time-out. Scagliotta had no further trouble with Jones. With the game a rout, Jamison came out seconds later.

The end finally came at 81–57. Jones felt as if his team had slipped back to where it had been in early January. Once again, a minor injury to Courtney Alexander (he had twisted the ankle again) was part of the problem. Jones had tried not starting him because he felt he hadn't been working hard enough in practice to merit starting. Robinson, his replacement, had gone two for nine. Alexander had come in and been four for 12. Everyone had been lousy. They had shot 29 percent in the second half and been outrebounded by an embarrassing 48–27 margin. Their ACC record was now 5–6. Their margin for error — NCAA tournament–wise — was about zero. Now, Duke would come to Charlottesville in three days on a hot streak for a game Virginia felt it absolutely had to win.

Jones didn't feel as if he could wait until the next day to start preparing. He spent almost twenty minutes in the locker room lecturing them. Not screaming or yelling. He had tried that at halftime and it hadn't worked. Instead, he just laid out the facts for them.

"I had hoped you were upset enough after Georgia Tech to come back and play well today," he said. "I was wrong. Well, let me tell you something, fellas, we're back to square one right now. We're back to the point where you guys can't even look me in the eye on the bench. That's how bad it is. Some of you don't like your roles. Well, I'm sorry. I wish we could have a team where everyone liked their roles, but that's not the way it works. You think everyone playing for North Carolina is happy with his role? For Duke? For Wake Forest? No. Of course not. But they're still ready to go in the goddamn ball game when they're needed.

"I don't know what you guys are thinking. Maybe you've been reading all that BS that if we win three more games we're in the tournament or whatever. Well, forget that! Because I'm gonna tell you right now, you play like today and we aren't winning again this season. How many games have we got left — seven? We're 0 for seven, we play like this, guaranteed. I mean it; 0-fer.

"If this was the old days and the rules didn't prevent it, we'd be practicing tonight as soon as we got back to Charlottesville. That's how urgent it is. But we can't do that. And we haven't got much time to regroup before Duke on Tuesday. So what we've got to do is come in tomorrow with a new attitude; with the attitude that we're going to do whatever it takes to win that game. Whatever it takes. Because it won't be easy. Duke ain't going to come in there feeling sorry for you guys.

"You better understand where we are, fellas. We've still got a lot of time left to get this right and there's no doubt the talent is in this room to win these games. But we can't win 'em like this. No way. I want you to understand that our season is hanging in the balance right now. If that scares some of you, I'm sorry, but that's the way it is."

He looked around the room. "NCAA tournament. You guys want to go or you want to watch like last year? It's up to you."

Watching Duke play NC State that night couldn't have been comforting for Jones. The Blue Devils were in a zone, one in which they could do almost nothing wrong. For the second time all season (Kansas had been the first) Herb Sendek felt as if his team had no chance to compete. C. C. Harrison didn't even suit up because of his foot injury but, as Sendek said after the 83–53 shellacking, "It wouldn't have made a bit of difference. Not tonight."

Krzyzewski had decided that bringing up the ACC regular season title to his team was the right way to go. When he arrived in the locker room ninety minutes before tip-off, it was still empty. Krzyzewski tells his players to be in the building at least an hour before game time but no more than ninety minutes beforehand. He walked to the marking board where he had drawn the now-famous blue line and wrote a different message:

Wake . . . 8–2

Clemson 7–3

Maryland 7–4

Duke?

Krzyzewski writes words on the board so rarely and his handwriting is so scratchy looking that manager Lee Rashman, thinking the chicken scratches belonged to someone else, was about to erase them when Kiersten Green, the other senior manager, stopped him.

That was about the most suspenseful moment of the evening. Duke led 39–21 at the half and Krzyzewski's only complaint was Chris Carrawell's failure to recognize a play call on the last possession of the half. The carnage continued after the intermission, Duke raining threes on the Wolfpack. By the time it was over, the Blue Devils had hit 15 of 23 from beyond the line. "You wouldn't expect to shoot that well in an empty gym," Sendek commented.

And so the answer to the question Krzyzewski had written on the board before the game was 8–3. Duke had won three home games — Carolina, Georgia Tech, and State — and one critical road game — Wake — to move into second place. Now, though, came a week on the road: Tuesday at Virginia, Saturday at Florida State. Both teams were fighting for NCAA survival and felt they couldn't afford to lose another home game. Krzyzewski knew both would be difficult. But with his team now 19–5, he felt a sense of relief.

"Now I know we're in the tournament," he said. "Nineteen wins overall, eight in the conference, we're definitely in. I feel like I can take a deep breath, at least for a minute." As for the week to come, he shook his head and looked at his coaches. "We have a chance," he said, "to do something really special."

The atmosphere in University Hall three nights later wasn't exactly what Jeff Jones was hoping for. Not all the Virginia student tickets had been picked up, so they had been put on sale to the public. Quite a few of them had been snatched up by UVA graduate students who had done their undergraduate work at Duke. As a result, smack in the middle of the Virginia students were three solid rows of Dukies, all outfitted in Duke shirts, all of them trying to make as much noise as their Virginia counterparts. What's more, even with the student tickets on sale, the building was less than sold out. Duke's four-game winning streak had moved it to number seven in the national polls, and it was one of Virginia's great traditional rivals. The game was absolutely critical to the Cavaliers. And still, no sellout.

Jones couldn't spend a lot of time worrying about that. His team had practiced very well for two days following the Carolina debacle and he was confident they would be ready to play. But Harold Deane had practiced very little and, as the team went through its afternoon shoot around, he sat on the bench with ice on his ankle and foot. Deane had suffered a small stress fracture in his right ankle a month earlier. It wasn't bad enough to stop him from playing, but the more he ran on it and pushed off on it, the worse it got. It wasn't going to get better until he had a lengthy rest, and that wasn't going to come until the season was over. As time went by, Deane practiced less and less in order to save himself for the games.

That wasn't exactly ideal, but Jones had no choice. He had pulled Deane early in both the Georgia Tech and North Carolina games to save the ankle. There would be no saving anything this evening. As if that wasn't enough, Norman Nolan and Jones were both fighting the flu. Jones didn't really care if he felt sick, but he couldn't afford to have his best inside player feeling weak.

"How do you feel, Norman?" Jones asked as Nolan popped a couple of pills given to him by trainer Ethan Saliba before the game.

"OK, Coach," Nolan answered.

"That's not the right answer," Jones said. "The right answer is, 'Great, Coach. I'm ready to go out and kick someone's butt.' "

Nolan forced a smile. "If you say so, Coach."

The two coaches were taking entirely different approaches to this game. Krzyzewski, feeling his team was safely in the NCAAs, kept reminding his team of the golden opportunity it had. They had to expect Virginia's best shot, he told them, because Virginia was a desperate team.

"I feel a little bit like a jockey tonight," he said before the game. "I know the other guy" — Jones — "is going to his whip because he really needs to. But I don't want to go to my whip yet. I've got a longer race to run. It's a calculated risk."

His analysis of jockey Jones was right. During pregame meal, Pete Herrmann began his scouting report by pointing out to the players that they were listed in that day's newspaper as three-point underdogs. "We've won ten in a row in here, four in a row in the ACC, and we're underdogs?" he said. "Why? I'll tell you why, because we went to their place and were awful last month. Well, this is our place. We have to make that clear right from the beginning."

Krzyzewski drew lines, Jones talked about walls. "We're up against the wall tonight," he said. "We have to defend the wall to the death if need be. You've done a great job the last two days getting ready to play this game. You know exactly what's at stake. We cannot rest, not for one single second, until we get this job done."

Greg Newton, who had played very little in the NC State game, hadn't even made the trip to Charlottesville. He had hyperextended his back late in that game and the doctors had told Krzyzewski he needed a week to rest. Krzyzewski was hoping the break might turn his attitude around. When the Virginia coaches heard about the injury, they shrugged.

"His real problem is a hyperextended atttude," Tom Perrin said.

"They don't really need him," Jones added. "They're better with the small lineup."

The Virginia scouting report was built around playing the smaller team anyway. The emphasis was on guarding the perimeter and taking care of the ball against Duke's ball-hawking defense.

"What does that sign we have in the locker room say?" Jones asked rhetorically. " 'Who will be left standing at the end?' Let's make sure it's us."

There was very little standing around during the first half, just a lot of bodies flying in different directions. University Hall has a reputation around the ACC as being the worst arena to shoot in among the nine schools. The building, first opened in 1965, is a round mini-dome and some people say the lighting and the backgrounds behind the baskets make for poor shooting. The other theory — more plausible — is that Virginia always plays good defense and rarely shoots the ball well. A home team that shoots poorly but plays good defense will likely combine to produce games with a lot of missed shots.

That was the case in this game. Virginia shot 13 of 30 in the first half — and led by six because Duke was even worse, nine for 35. The same team that couldn't miss against NC State couldn't buy a jump shot against Virginia. A basket by Jamal Robinson, on a third put-back attempt, built the 31–25 halftime margin and symbolized Virginia's effort, as did a 27–18 rebounding margin.

"That's the way we need to play," Jones said. "We need to go after every loose ball and rebound. We need to keep challenging every damn shot they take, and as good as the effort was the first half, it has to be *better* in the second. Because I guarantee you right now, he [Krzyzewski] is all over their ass for being outhustled and outplayed. You know what? He's right about that. Let's make absolutely certain we do that again. The rest will take care of itself."

Krzyzewski hadn't gone off on his team. He had counseled them to be more patient and wait for better shots and he had told them that they were fortunate to be down only six, considering the way they had shot the ball. "Stop taking *your* shots," he told them. "Look for a good shot for *Duke*, not for you. You got here by playing together. You haven't played together for a half. Let's play together this half and see what happens."

What happened was as bizarre an ending as anyone in the building had ever witnessed. Predictably, neither team could get control of the game. Duke came out hot and took a 41–37 lead with a 16–6 burst. Jones thought about a time-out but opted instead simply to remind his players to "compete . . . run your stuff and we're fine."

They were. A 10–0 run, capped by back-to-back threes by Curtis Staples, who had been blanketed all night until that point, and Deane, put them back on top, 47–41. Krzyzewski called time because now, for the first time all night, the crowd was genuinely into the game. Methodically, Duke came back. It wasn't easy for the Blue Devils because Langdon, their best shooter, was having an awful (two-of-11) shooting night, and every time he popped open for what might have been a key three he was drawing iron. Still, a drive by Roshown McLeod with 6:07 left put Duke back up, 52–51.

Staples made another three. Then Willie Dersch, the freshman whom Jones had worried about not getting enough playing time in January, made a huge play, posting up, scoring, and getting fouled with 2:11 left. The free throw made it 60–56, Cavaliers. Langdon missed another critical three, but Jeff Capel somehow got to the rebound and got fouled. He made both free throws with Jones screaming that Capel had been on Dersch's back when he had rebounded the ball.

With fifty-three seconds left and the lead at 60–59, Jones called time to set a play. They screened for Courtney Alexander because Deane's ankle was so bad that there was no way he could possibly drive the lane and stop the way he normally would in an endgame situation. Alexander was open, but the shot hit the back rim. The littlest guy on the court, Steve Wojciechowski, rebounded with twenty-six seconds left and Duke called time to set up a play of its own.

The ball swung to Wojo, who was open for a three. He missed. The rebound — and the game — were on the glass for someone from Virginia to grab. But the ball ended up — again — in the hands of Capel. Staples had no choice but to foul him to prevent a layup with eleven seconds to go. Virginia called time to let him think it over. The ploy half-worked. Capel swished the first shot, but was way short on the second.

It was 60–60. Deane raced the ball downcourt and found Nolan open under the basket. Langdon hammered him, rather than allow him to go up and dunk. The clock was down to five seconds. Nolan would shoot two. He had played a superb game to that point, with 15 points and six rebounds. But he had only shot one free throw and that had come with 17:28 left in the game.

Knowing that Krzyzewski didn't like to call time-out in situations like this so his team could rush the ball downcourt against a defense scrambling to get back, Jones sent Dersch to the scorer's table. He would report in for Nolan if Nolan made the second shot. That would stop the game long enough for Virginia to set up its defense. Normally, Jones would have told one of his players to let the officials know that Virginia was going to call time-out if the second free throw went in. But Virginia was out of time-outs. The only way to stop the game was to substitute for the free-throw shooter.

With Dersch kneeling at the scorer's table, Nolan's first free throw hit the back rim. Both benches were standing. Rick Hartzell, the lead official for the game, was standing at center court. He saw Dersch and waved him into the game. Dersch responded by making a shooting motion with his hand to indicate he was coming in for the shooter. Hartzell nodded.

In the meantime, Wojciechowski stepped back from his spot on the lane for a moment and signaled to Krzyzewski to see if he wanted a time-out if Nolan missed the second shot and the score was tied. Krzyzewski shook his head vehemently and waved his arm to indicate he wanted the ball pushed up court in a hurry, whether the next shot was a make or a miss. Seeing this, Hartzell knew the ball would be coming at him very quickly if Nolan missed. Officials always try to anticipate what will happen next in a game so they can get themselves into position. Hartzell didn't want to be caught lingering near center court while a critical play was occurring near the Duke basket.

Zelton Steed handed the ball to Nolan. The third official was not one of Fred Barakat's up-and-coming kids but Tim Higgins, who normally worked the Big East but also did several ACC games each season. Higgins is one of the best-liked and most respected officials in the country. He would work the national championship game for the second time in March. Now, he was under the basket.

Nolan eyed the rim and shot. The ball hit the rim, bounded into the air, rolled around the rim and looked as if it would fall off. All three officials girded for the scramble that was coming. But the ball spun around the rim one more time and dropped through. U-Hall was bedlam. Virginia was up, 61–60.

As soon as the ball went through, Capel grabbed it, stepped out-of-bounds, and threw it inbounds to Wojciechowski, who took off down-court under a full head of steam. At the scorer's table, they were sitting on the substitution horn to try and get Hartzell's attention.

He had forgotten to let Dersch come into the game.

Hartzell, scrambling to get into position, didn't hear the horn over the din. Neither Higgins nor Steed stopped Capel or Wojo. Because Dick Engel, who was in charge of subs, was trying to get Hartzell's attention, timekeeper Cy Weaver didn't start the clock when the ball came inbounds.

As Wojo flew across midcourt, the Virginia players realized the clock hadn't started. Harold Deane stopped and began pointing at the scoreboard screaming, "Start the clock, start the clock!" At that point, Weaver, nonplussed, started the clock. Wojo, left unguarded by the screaming Deane, kept on going, right to the basket. Nolan had hustled back and as

Wojo went up, he went up with him. Hartzell's whistle blew. He called a foul on Nolan. Later, the Virginia coaches would insist that, in addition to everything else, Hartzell had called a foul that wasn't a foul.

The scoreboard clock said there were 2.7 seconds left. Wojo had caught the inbounds at least seventy-five feet from the basket. There was no way he had gone that far in 2.3 seconds. Everyone on the Virginia bench was screaming that the game was over, that if the clock had started on time, the foul would have come after time had expired. Hartzell, his face white as a ghost, came to the scorer's table to confer with the officials there and with Steed and Higgins.

"I think we got two mistakes here," he said. "But only one of them is correctible."

A correctible error, according to the rules, occurs when a mistake is made and no time has gone off the clock. If the wrong free-throw shooter takes a shot, that's correctible. If someone has subbed into the game incorrectly and play hasn't started, that's correctible. But if the clock has started, there are no do-overs. Nolan had fouled Wojciechowski. If time had not run out, that could not be replayed.

What was correctible was the incorrect starting of the clock. By rule, there are two circumstances in which the officials may use TV replay. One is to determine which players may have left the bench during a fight. The other is if they suspect there has been a clock malfunction of some kind. Hartzell asked the producers in the Jefferson-Pilot truck to bring up the last five seconds on the TV monitor at the scorer's table. He also asked for a stopwatch.

"The game's over," Jones said. "It was more than five seconds."

Krzyzewski stood a few feet away, arms folded. "You replay it," Krzyzewski said, as calmly as if it were October 15 in the practice gym, "and there's going to be about a second left."

"Game's over," Jones said.

While the crowd murmured and hollered, many screaming, "The game's over," Craig Littlepage, Virginia's assistant athletic director, came out of the stands. Littlepage had been a great player at Penn in the 1970s and had been a Terry Holland assistant before becoming the head coach at Penn and then Rutgers. He was now back at Virginia as an administrator. But he still had a player and coach's feel for the rhythm of a game.

He grabbed Perrin and Anthony Solomon, the other full-time assistant. "Tell J.J. I think the play will count," he said. "I think you guys are going to get screwed if they call up the replay. You'll have less than a second."

Perrin and Solomon looked at each other. Perrin started to take a step toward the scorer's table, then stopped. It was too late anyway. The replay was on the screen and Hartzell and Higgins had the stopwatch on it. They ran it once: 4.7 seconds. They ran it again: 4.6. Hartzell shrugged helplessly. Higgins said, "Let's do it one more time Rick, just to be sure." They ran it one more time: 4.6 seconds.

"We'll put 0.7 seconds on the clock," Hartzell said. "We'll add three-tenths to allow for lag time."

"Wait a minute," Jones said. "If the game isn't over, we should replay the last five seconds because we didn't get our sub in."

"Can't do that," Higgins answered. "That's not correctible. What if they had run the play, Wojo missed, and there was no foul? Would you want to replay the five seconds then?"

Jones was trapped. At that moment, he and everyone else in the building thought the screwup had been at the scorer's table, that Weaver's failure to start the clock was the major crime that had been committed against his team. Deane had made a huge mistake by not playing until the whistle, but his reaction was both instinctive and understandable.

By now, ten minutes had gone by. Wojciechowski still had to go to the line and shoot two free throws with his team trailing by one and all hell breaking loose in the gym. "No one has ever been frozen for longer in the history of the game," Krzyzewski said.

Wojo was cool, not cold. He swished the first to tie the game. He swished the second. Duke was up 62–61. Nolan's heave from seventy feet was short and wide as the buzzer sounded.

In almost any other ACC arena, there might have been a riot. The Virginia fans were angry — justifiably — and confused and disbelieving. They booed and hollered as loudly as they could. Krzyzewski shook hands with Jones and said, "That's no way for a game to end." Deane was sitting on the bench with his head in his hands. Krzyzewski stopped and patted him gently, saying, "I'm sorry." Deane had played all forty minutes even though the ankle had been so sore down the stretch he could barely push off. Krzyzewski also tried to console Nolan, who wanted no part of it. "That's bullshit, Coach," he said, pushing Krzyzewski's outstretched hand away. Krzyzewski understood.

Duke's win was clearly tainted. It was certainly possible that the Blue Devils could have scored in the final five seconds and won the game anyway, but those five seconds had not been played the way they should have been under the rules. Duke had been given an unfair advantage by Hartzell. What wasn't tainted was the play Wojciechowski had made: he had played to the whistle and then, after the lengthy delay, calmly made both free throws.

"Whatever else happened," Krzyzewski said, "the little kid made a bigtime play. Big-time."

There was little talk about Wojo's big-time play in the the Virginia locker room. Just tears and anguished cries. Deane, who had ripped his uniform off leaving the floor, kept saying, "How can that be?" Jones had a hard time finding anything to say to his heartbroken team. "You gave the effort we asked of you," he said. "You deserved to win the game. We got fucked by our own people."

That part, as it turned out, wasn't true. The men on the scorer's table had done what they were supposed to. They had blown the horn to signal for the substitute. When Hartzell didn't wave Dersch in, they had continued blowing the horn and had even stood waving their arms to try and get someone — anyone's — attention.

Rich Murray, the Virginia sports information director, went to the officials' locker room to get a statement from Hartzell. He said he had not been aware of the sub at the table and hadn't heard the horn. When Murray handed Jones the statement, he looked at it, then threw it on the ground in disgust. "He's a goddamn liar," he said. "He tried to wave Willie in after the first shot. How can he say he didn't know there was a sub there?"

The answer — as it turned out — was brain lock. In his official report to Barakat, written the next morning, Hartzell took the blame for the screwup, but said again that he had never seen the sub.

"Fred," he wrote, "if you need me to write or call Jeff Jones, I will. If there was a sub or horn then I owe him, his team and UVA an apology. I honestly can tell you that I did not see any sub, or hear a horn."

Later that day, Hartzell saw a replay of the final seconds. He saw Dersch at the table and he saw his attempt to wave him in. His heart sank. He had been so intent on preparing for the next play that he had totally blocked out Dersch's presence at the table. Even after the game, even the next morning, he hadn't remembered that Dersch was there. "It was a sick feeling," he said later. "The whole thing was so unfair to everyone and it was my fault."

The following day, Hartzell wrote a letter to Jones and Holland. "Please accept this letter with my most sincere and heartfelt apology . . ." he wrote. "I cannot possibly express to you in words my regret over my mistake. I apologize to your fine university and its community and supporters, to your student body and fellow administrators; most of all I apologize to your team and to each of you. . . . Further, I would appreciate it if you would pass on my apology to Dick Engel and Cy Weaver. I am sure they have been put in a very bad situation given my error. . . . I simply did not recognize the substitute nor did I hear the horn as the inbounds play began."

The letter went on at length about how thankful he was that Virginia had handled the situation with such dignity. The next day Holland wrote back to Hartzell, who in real life is the athletic director at Bucknell. "[Your letter] meant a lot to both Jeff and me . . ." he wrote. "It was very difficult for us since the game was so important for the NCAA tournament and for each of us personally.

"As I watched the replay, it looked like the ball was not going to go in on the free throw and maybe as all of you geared up for what was likely to happen, you were so focused on officiating the last five seconds that everything else became irrelevant. Thank goodness that the crew was composed of people that we all respect personally and professionally. . . ."

That was the sad irony of the situation. The crew on the game was a strong one, three experienced, respected officials. Some ACC coaches consider Hartzell the league's best referee. Almost all of them would rank him among the top three or four. Because of the furor, ACC Commissioner Gene Corrigan took the unprecedented step of announcing that all three officials would be suspended from one ACC assignment before the end of the season. All three had to be held responsible, he said, because the mistake had been one not of judgment but of game administration.

"I hope," Barakat said after the suspensions had been announced, "that we can try and put this behind us now."

It would not be nearly that simple.

21

Dog Days

THE DUKE-VIRGINIA GAME was the talk of the ACC for the rest of that week. Since the game had been the only one played on Tuesday, everyone in the league had watched. Making matters worse for Hartzell, Barakat, and the officiating corps was the fact that ESPN had switched over to the final minutes of the game, meaning that the entire country had watched the final-seconds fiasco.

"What's the lesson out of that game?" Dave Odom asked his team the next afternoon. Wake Forest was about to go through its walk-through prior to playing Clemson, but Odom wanted to make a point. He and his players had watched the last couple of minutes together after their 10 o'clock meeting the previous night. Odom felt terrible for Virginia because he was still close to Terry Holland and Jeff Jones. What's more, from a selfish standpoint, he was now aware of Duke breathing down his team's neck for first place.

"You saw what happened," Odom said. "What did Virginia do wrong on that play?"

"Stopped playing," Tim Duncan said.

"Exactly. Doesn't matter what's going on, what the clock is doing, you have to keep playing till you hear a whistle. That's what Wojo did and he won the game for Duke."

Odom was feeling a lot more comfortable than he had a week earlier. His instincts about a nonleague game had been right. The Deacons had gone to Missouri and found their shooting touch in the second half, making 12 of 15 shots including four of four from beyond the three-point arc. Ricky Peral's jump shot, missing in action for almost a month, had returned. Odom was hoping that his team had been through an inevitable lull and was about to get a second wind.

"This time of year the hardest thing is figuring out how hard you can push your team," he said. "Everyone's a little tired. You want to work on things, but you don't want them worn out for the games."

Every coach worries about his team's mental and physical state in February. Dean Smith often says that if you ask almost any coach during February if he'll be back the next year, he's apt to tell you, "No way." Mike Krzyzewski — for once — agrees with Smith. "You get to this time of year," he said, "and you start to think the season will never end."

In college basketball, the dog days come in February. Everyone is sick of bad weather. A lot of people are just sick. Travel is often difficult. Postseason is still to come, but March seems a long way off. Rick Barnes had been pushing his team all season. Now, he felt the need to back off a little, to offer encouragement, to let his players know that they were making progress, that, even after a few losses, the goals they had set for themselves in the fall were still very realistic.

Odom always worried about keeping his players interested. He was happy when he heard that the wrestler Rick Flair had asked for tickets to the Clemson game. A lot of his players, most notably Duncan, were big wrestling fans and having Flair in the building would be something different. Flair no doubt would have been delighted to talk to Odom's team that day if he had been asked. That wasn't going to happen. But Odom, searching for a different voice for the players to hear, did bring in a guest speaker for the afternoon: Howard Garfinkel.

Most of the players knew Garfinkel, having attended his camp. "I said last summer that Wake Forest was the best team in the country and people laughed at me," Garfinkel roared. "I said that Tim Duncan was the best college center since Bill Walton and people laughed." (Actually, no one would have seriously argued with either statement but Garf was nothing if he wasn't full of hyperbole.) "Well, let me tell you something. Now, everyone is raving about Duncan. Well, I'm going to tell you, come the end of March in Indy, you guys are gonna be the Main Men. You're winning the whole thing just like I said. You're winning the NCAA. You got it. Book that and book 'em, Danno."

Normally, the last thing Odom wanted was someone talking to them about March and Indianapolis, especially on game day. But it was different with Garfinkel. The players knew that was the way he talked.

No one playing in the ACC that night looked ready for Indianapolis, except maybe to work at the Indianapolis Motor Speedway — also known as the Brickyard. Bricks were flying everywhere. Wake Forest shot 32 percent against Clemson — and won. In Raleigh, North Carolina shot 37.7 percent against NC State — and won. Both scores reflected the ugliness of the games: Wake 55–49 over Clemson; Carolina 45–44 over State as the Wolfpack again couldn't hang on to a second-half lead against the Tar Heels.

All four coaches felt their teams had played hard. They were right. But both games were a reflection of February fatigue. The defenses were ahead of the offenses. What's more, when ACC teams play each other a second time, they are so familiar with each other through competition and TV and scouting reports, they often know each other's plays by heart. That means offenses have to hit tough shots to be effective. On Abraham Lincoln's 188th birthday, no one in the South could shoot straight.

Wake's victory made the Deacons 9–2 in conference play, putting them half a game up on Duke. Clemson dropped back to 7–4. Amazingly, that meant the Tigers were now just a game ahead of Carolina, which was 3–0 in the second round and 6–5 overall. Barnes refused to be discouraged. "If you guys keep playing defense the way you did tonight," he said after the Wake game, "we're going to win a lot more games before this is over. Our shots didn't fall. That's fine. They will. Don't worry about it for a minute."

He would do the worrying for all of them.

*   *   *

Maryland was also 7–4 in league play and had the Thursday night game, at home, against Florida State. Gary Williams was wound tighter than Virginia's orb by the time the Seminoles arrived at Cole Field House. The Terrapins had lost their first game with Florida State, which, Williams knew, would give Pat Kennedy's team confidence. FSU had been a poor road team thus far, but with the season winding down, Kennedy would be going to the whip to try and get a road win, knowing he had to have at least one to have a chance to make the NCAAs. Making Williams even less happy was the prospect of having to travel to Worcester, Massachusetts, on Friday for a Saturday afternoon game against UMass. Williams knew everyone in the league had a Thursday-Saturday on their schedule, but that didn't mean he was happy about his, especially since Massachusetts, after a slow start, was now making an NCAA-bid drive of its own.

"Two games in thirty-six hours against desperate teams," he said. "Not exactly ideal."

He was certainly right about Florida State being desperate. The Seminoles had been the ACC's most up-and-down team all winter. One minute they were beating Maryland or North Carolina, the next they were losing at Georgia Tech or to Virginia at home. The previous Sunday they had blown a 12-point lead at home against Georgia Tech only to be bailed out by point guard Kerry Thompson's game-winning jumper with 2.5 seconds left. It was the second time (the first being against Maryland) that Thompson had hit a big shot to rescue his team.

"I've told the kids that seventeen is the magic number," Kennedy said after his team had practiced in Cole before the Maryland game. "We've got thirteen now and one nonconference game we should win [Alabama State] left. That means we need to win three more conference games. Anything beyond that is gravy."

FSU was 4–7 in ACC play. That meant Kennedy was figuring a 7–9 record would get his team into the tournament. He was probably right, since the ACC was clearly rated as the top league in the country by computers, pundits, and media everywhere. But the league had never gotten seven tournament bids before. Kennedy figured if there was a year when it could happen, this was it.

"Let's face it," he said. "You put any ACC team in the Big East, including NC State or Georgia Tech, they finish in the top half. We go up and play at Seton Hall when we're reeling last month and we win easily. If the committee's being fair, they have no problem taking seven from our league and probably no more than four from the Big East."

Perhaps. Politics tended to get in the way of fairness once the nine-man basketball committee got behind closed doors in a Kansas City hotel the second weekend in March. Kennedy knew that. "The best thing for us to do is get some impressive wins," he said. "We've got two — Maryland and North Carolina. We could use a couple more."

This was a week that presented that opportunity. FSU also had to go Thursday-Saturday, but at least its Saturday game was at home and it was at night. It was also against Duke. "We can't lose another home game," Kennedy said. "That's a given. But we also need to steal one or two on the road."

Maryland appeared ripe for that. Since their win over Duke that had pushed them to 6–1 in league play, the Terrapins had lost three of four. Williams was searching for a message that would get through to his players. He could no longer tell them that no one thought they were any good because they had spent close to a month ranked in the top ten. The notion of winning the ACC regular season was far-fetched now because they were two games behind Wake Forest with five to play. It seemed unlikely that the Deacons would lose two more and, even if they did, Maryland would have to go undefeated just to tie.

For this game, his message was simple: we owe these guys one. By winning on Saturday, Clemson had swept the Terrapins in the regular season series. FSU was the only other team that had a chance to do that. Don't let them, Williams told his players.

Kennedy's pregame speech was much longer and more emotional than the one Williams was giving. "Close your eyes," he told his players once he had finished his X's and O's chalk talk. "I want you to close your eyes and picture yourselves in a fistfight. You're fighting someone who wants to knock you down so they can get to your mom. Picture that. You have to protect your mom. What will you do to protect her? Absolutely anything, right? But here comes this guy and he wants to go through you to get to your mom. NO! You won't let it happen. Not ever!

"Fellas, that's the way we have to play tonight. Keep your eyes closed. Now, picture yourself on the court. Here comes Maryland. What do they want to take from you? The NCAA tournament! And your integrity and your pride! Are you going to let them do that? NO! You are going to go out there and bust your tails on every single play for the entire forty minutes so we can walk in here with our integrity and our pride and one step closer to the tournament! I want you to think about Sam Cassell, running out of here, his arms in the air, 15,000 people watching with nothing to say because we had kicked their tails in here, not once, but twice in a row! Picture that! Now picture us doing that same thing in here tonight! That's what this is about. Win tonight, beat Duke on Saturday, and where are we? We're right on the doorstep! That would give us sixteen, and seventeen is the magic number!

"Do you understand me?"

"YES!"

Like most coaches, Kennedy spices his pregame talks with the occasional profanity. One adjustment he had been forced to make when he had come south from New York was the way he used language. In the South, a lot of people take offense to words like "damn" and "hell."

Kennedy's biggest shock had come when Charlie Ward, the Heisman Trophy–winning quarterback, had joined the basketball team in 1990 after completing football his freshman year. Kennedy gave one of his patented stem-winding pregame talks. After the game, Ward asked if he could see Kennedy in private for a minute. Kennedy was afraid that Ward was going to tell him that trying to play football and basketball was just too much for him.

"Coach, it's about your language," Ward said.

"My language?" Kennedy was confused.

"I'm a Christian, Coach. I don't like profanity."

Kennedy knew that Ward was sincere. "Charlie, I'm sorry," he said. "I'll do my best to control it."

Sometimes, he did control it. Other times, he didn't.

It didn't help Florida State's cause to be playing this game without sixten Randell Jackson. He had suffered a hip pointer in practice on Tuesday and wasn't ready to play. Kennedy was hoping that, with rest, he could play against Duke.

Kennedy was almost obsessed with making it to the NCAAs. He had studied all the power ratings and knew by heart the record of almost every so-called "bubble" team around the country. FSU was sitting right on the bubble and could fall in either direction. Kennedy believed that making the NCAAs out of a league as tough as the ACC in 1997 would strengthen his position either to renegotiate with Dave Hart or to move elsewhere. He knew that the most likely scenario at the end of the season was another nonrollover, meaning he would have three years left on his contract.

The local papers were always full of speculation about his future at Florida State. At times, he wondered if eleven years in one place was enough. His son, Joey, was thirteen now and understood what people were saying about his dad. Kennedy felt the program was back on solid ground and that the recruiting class he and his staff had signed in November was a good one. He had hoped to make a big splash by signing Tracy McGrady, a six-eight phenom from Florida whom he had been following for most of four years. But McGrady had gone away to school for his senior year, transferring to Mt. Zion, a tiny Christian school/basketball factory in Durham, and now it was a virtual lock that he was going to skip college and turn pro.

Signing a McGrady or making the tournament were the two best ways to make it clear to people in Tallahassee that the program was progressing, that it was on the way back. McGrady wasn't going to happen; the tournament was the best option left.

For ten minutes, the Seminoles played the way Kennedy had asked them to envision playing. They got back on defense — the major point of emphasis on the scouting report — so Maryland would have to run a half-court offense. They hit their shots. And they led 18–11 after freshman Ron Hale, starting in Jackson's place, made a pretty post-up move.

But things went downhill rapidly after that. Kirk Luchman picked up his third foul on Maryland's next possession. That meant Kennedy was without two-thirds of his frontcourt — Jackson because of the hip, Luchman because of the fouls. Kennedy stood with arms folded in front of the bench as Luchman came out. "You would think," he said to assistant Tom Carlsen, "that a senior could play with two fouls, knowing he can't afford to commit a third."

"You would think," Carlsen answered, helplessly.

Whether it was Luchman's absence or fate, Maryland scored the next 16 points to take control of the game. Kennedy was pleading with his players to hold the fort until halftime, but Maryland was coming at them in waves, sensing the kill. A vicious dunk on a rebound by Obinna Ekezie just before halftime made it 38–27.

The game never really got close in the second half. The closest FSU got was 55–47 with 12:20 left. Maryland promptly went on an 11–1 run and Kennedy was reduced the last few minutes to asking his players not to quit and get blown out by an embarrassing score. "Don't do this to your-selves," he said. "Keep playing hard. Do not let this become a 20-point game."

It did, briefly, at 70–50, but Williams pulled his starters late. Even the officials took some mercy on the struggling Seminoles. When freshman Devonaire Deas fouled out, he angrily yelled, "Fuck!" right in Mike Wood's face. "I'm not gonna tee you up," Wood told him, "because of the score."

The final was 73–57. Kennedy was genuinely discouraged. "We got manhandled," he said to his coaches before he went in to talk to the players. "Why does that happen to us? Kirk gets his third foul and we fall apart. Why?"

He leaned against a wall. "What should I talk to them about?" he asked.

"Duke," Carlsen answered. "That's all we can do. Go on from here."

Kennedy nodded. "We can't practice tomorrow," he said. "That will wear them out. I want to meet individually with each kid after we get back."

Kennedy had brought several key players to his hotel room on the Seton Hall trip to ask them what they thought was wrong with the team. He had asked each of them to take on more responsibility on the floor, to play more as a unit than as talented individuals. They had responded to that. Maybe they would respond to individual meetings again now.

"That was embarrassing," Kennedy told the team. "I don't understand how we can come in here, ready to play, with a good game plan and let that happen to us. We were down twenty in this game. You should be disgusted by that. I know I am.

"We're running out of opportunities here, fellas. We're running out of chances to show people that all I've been saying about you all year is true. Do you know what kind of effort it's going to take to beat Duke? Do you know how well they're playing? But you know what, if we beat Duke, we're 5–8 in the league. We *still* have to win a road game. We have to. But we can't even begin to worry about that until we win on Saturday. But I can't even begin to tell you what kind of an effort you're going to need to win that game. What you gave here tonight, I guarantee, will not get it done."

The effort was better two nights later. But it was still not enough to get it done. Duke started the game hot and stayed hot all night. The Civic Center was close to full and — for the Civic Center — hopped up. But having played at Clemson, Maryland, and NC State, the Blue Devils barely noticed. Every time FSU made a run, one of them came up with a big shot. It was never really close. Duke won 89–79 for its sixth straight win since Krzyzewski had drawn the line. Newton again missed the trip. Again, almost no one noticed. The win moved their conference record to 10–3. Florida State fell to 4–9, meaning its only realistic chance to get into the NCAAs was to sweep their last three league games — at Clemson and NC State and at home against Wake Forest. That hardly seemed likely.

That same day, North Carolina pulled off yet another miracle comeback at Georgia Tech, coming from 16 points down in the last nine minutes — and nine down in the last three — to win, 72–68. That game proved to be Tech's last gasp. Bobby Cremins had hoped that a victory over the Tar Heels would be a springboard for his team to finish strong. They would have been 10–12 at that stage and in position to at least salvage an NIT bid. But nine-of-30 three-point shooting and careless ballhandling doomed them. Clemson also won that afternoon, holding off a Virginia team that kept falling behind and coming back, for a 71–65 victory. Jeff Jones's unhappiness with ACC officials continued when Sam Croft teed him up less than four minutes into the game.

"If coaches were given technicals every time they said what I said, none of us would make it through a game," Jones said afterward. Barakat apparently agreed with him. After Croft filed his report, Barakat reprimanded him privately for giving Jones an unwarranted technical. None of that changed the outcome of the game. Clemson was 8–4, still a game ahead of North Carolina, and Virginia was 5–8, the losing streak that had started at Georgia Tech now reaching four.

Sunday was February 16, the only game NC State at Wake Forest. With the end of the regular season exactly two weeks away, the Demon Deacons needed a win to maintain their half-game lead on Duke. There was no reason to believe they would have any trouble getting it. State was now 1–11 in the league and was reeling from a second straight giveaway to North Carolina. Losing to Carolina under any circumstances is painful for State. To snatch defeat from the jaws of victory twice in five weeks was painful and demoralizing.

Dave Odom's concern going into the game was that his team might overlook the Wolfpack for all the logical reasons that a 1–11 team could be overlooked. He pointed out to his players repeatedly how well State had played against them in December and how close it had been to having four or five more victories. "They were listening," Odom said, "but I don't think they heard."

As with Maryland four Sundays earlier, Odom had a bad feeling from the minute the game started. State wasn't capable of getting 19 points ahead of anyone, but it looked like the better prepared team from the beginning, the team with more purpose. That shouldn't have been the case given that Wake was playing not only to hang on to first place in the ACC but to solidify its position as a number one seed in the NCAA tournament. State led most of the first half, but the Deacons finished strong. Steve Goolsby hit a three to tie the score at 23–23, Tim Duncan produced a three-point play, and Goolsby made two free throws with a second to play for a 28–23 lead. Given State's inability to score — even with C. C. Harrison back in the lineup — that looked like an insurmountable lead.

It wasn't. Even though Odom pleaded with his players to come out strong and put the game away, they didn't. Or couldn't. Jerry Braswell threw away the inbounds pass to start the half and State tied the game soon after that. Wake took a deep breath and built a nine-point lead with 12:47 left. Now, at last, State was dead. Wrong again. The Wolfpack kept clawing back and finally took a 48–47 lead with 4:20 left on a Harrison three.

Odom had tried just about everything. He had changed defenses. He had changed the lineup. He had played big and he had played small. He had demanded that they push the ball up the floor. He had screamed, he had cajoled. He had done everything but dance the macarena. Duncan tied the score with a free throw. Then Braswell made two more and Wake led again, 50–48, with 3:12 left. Then, no one could score. State missed; Wake missed. Danny Strong missed for State with under a minute to go and Tony Rutland walked the ball up the floor. The plan was to spread the court, work the clock down, and let Duncan shoot with less than twenty seconds on the game clock.

As Rutland worked his way across midcourt, he was guarded by State freshman Justin Gainey. Earlier in the season, Gainey had been completely overwhelmed by playing in the ACC. At Florida State in early January, he had been incapable of touching the ball without turning it over. He was so bad that when Maryland prepared to play State the following week, Gary Williams wouldn't show his players any tape of Gainey. "I was afraid they might laugh," he said.

Gainey had steadily improved since then. Now, as Rutland turned his back to keep him away from the ball, Gainey made a quick move to his right, got a hand on the ball and knocked it away. Before Rutland had a chance to recover, Gainey leaped past him, scooped the ball up, and was gone for a tying layup. Joel Coliseum was almost silent except for the cheering coming from the tiny section of State fans behind the visiting bench. Rutland was stunned. Odom called time. There were still thirty-five seconds left and the score was tied at 50. That meant his team would get the last shot. So, guys, he said, let's score, win the game, and get out of here.

It made sense. The ball went to Duncan, who had position inside on State freshman Damon Thornton. Duncan went up for a short runner with two seconds left. The ball rimmed out. Duncan, who would finish with 25 points and 18 rebounds, stared in disbelief. Overtime.

One more time, Odom tried to calm his rattled troops. The overtime seesawed just as the game had. State led 57–55 when Rutland coolly made two free throws with 54.7 seconds left. Then, after a State miss, Rutland got redemption for his regulation miscue, drilling a 15 footer with 3.7 seconds left to put the Deacons up, 59–57. All they had to do now was keep State from going ninety-four feet in less than four seconds and their long Sunday afternoon nightmare would be over.

Unlike Virginia five days earlier, the Deacons had plenty of time to set their defense. State called time. Sendek's strategy was to try and throw one quick pass near midcourt, call time again, and try to set a play from there. The first part of the plan worked. State called time with 3.2 seconds left after inbounding. The Wolfpack was still fifty feet from the basket.

With the ball coming in on a side out-of-bounds play, Odom inserted seven-one Loren Woods to guard the inbounder and make it difficult to throw a long pass. The strategy paid off. State had to call its last time-out — a twenty — to adjust the play one more time. By now, almost five minutes had gone by since Rutland had made his shot. In fact, the overtime had lasted more than twenty minutes. Odom glanced at his watch and saw that it was almost 6:20. "This game may never end," he muttered to Nestor.

State finally got the ball inbounds. C. C. Harrison came to meet Gainey's pass and, with Goolsby draped on him, dribbled frantically toward the top of the key. Just before the clock hit zero, he leaned in on Goolsby and tossed a prayer in the direction of the hoop. Mike Wood, standing to the left of Harrison in almost the same position Paparo had been in four weeks earlier in the Maryland game, saw the ball leave Harrison's hand just before the buzzer sounded. In the same instant, he had to make certain that the contact between Harrison and Goolsby wasn't a foul.

Wood was standing a little bit deeper as the ball went up than Paparo had been, adhering to Barakat's request that the center official give himself a better angle to see the red light that lit as soon as the buzzer sounded. His view of the light was better than Paparo's had been and he got that part of the call right.

The ball hung in the air for what seemed like days. Finally, it hit the glass and banked in. Double overtime! Harrison had tied the game again. Odom was right. The game was never going to end.

Only it was going to end — on that play. Because he was standing a little deeper than Paparo, Wood's view of Harrison's feet wasn't as good as it would have been if he had been looking at the play from a sharper angle. In fact, the only one of the three officials who might have had an angle to make the call was Raymie Styons, who was under the basket. Duke Edsall, in the trail position on the far side of the court, had no chance. Wood had to make the call on whether the shot was a two or a three. His arms went up in the air in the touchdown — three-point — signal. Because Harrison had been leaning in as he shot the ball, it appeared from Wood's angle to be a three. But he was wrong. Harrison's foot was clearly on the line, halfway across it in fact. Wood's arms went up and the State bench went into compete delirium, everyone pouring onto the floor to mob Harrison. They had won the game, 61–60.

No one on the Wake bench had been able to see Harrison's foot since they were at the far end of the court. Like everyone else in the building, the players and coaches stood where they were for a moment, watching State celebrate. They couldn't believe the game was finally over — and they had lost. Odom shook hands with Sendek and his assistants while the players began walking up the runway that led to their locker room.

At the end of the runway is a TV monitor. As they reached the end of the runway, several players stopped to stare at the monitor. Jefferson-Pilot was replaying the final shot from every possible angle. Initially, the players stopped just to make sure Harrison had released the shot in time. Of that there was no doubt. But then they saw Harrison's foot, plain as day, clearly over the line.

As Odom came trudging up the runway, he heard shouting coming from the hallway. "Coach, Coach, look at this, look at this." They were animated, yelling, thinking that perhaps replay could be used to show that the shot should have only counted for two points. Odom knew that wasn't the case. He looked at the replay once. Sure enough, Harrison's foot was on the line. He felt sick to his stomach.

"Come on," he said. "Everyone inside. There's no point looking at this."

He had to admit that this wasn't quite the same as the Maryland game. That call had been so close, you couldn't be sure even watching replay. On this one, there was no doubt. The game should have been in a second overtime. Still, he felt compelled to tell the players the same thing he had told them after Maryland.

"That call did not lose us the ball game, guys," he said. "We lost it a lot earlier than that. We did not play good basketball. We didn't play winning basketball. Now, I know how much this hurts, but we have got to regroup and find a way to play better by Wednesday. We still have a lot of basketball to play and we have got to play better than we did here today."

Odom was confused and mystified. The Deacons now had a grand total of three losses — all of them at home — two of them on blown calls at the end of the game. And yet, he sensed his team slipping. This wasn't the same confident group that had blown North Carolina and Duke away in January. The perimeter people had been awful again: nine-of-29, not to mention Rutland's killing turnover. They had turned it over 14 times, a very high number for such a low-possession game. Only Duncan's consistent brilliance was keeping their heads above water, and Odom knew that wasn't going to be enough in March.

Right now though, he had to worry about February. Duke was now in first place by a half game in the ACC. The number one NCAA tournament seed, which had seemed like a lock all season, was suddenly in jeopardy. Odom breathed a deep sigh, told his players to keep their heads up and take the loss like men when the media came into the locker room. Then he walked into the hallway to go to the interview room. He took two steps out the door and almost bumped head on into Mike Wood, who was leaving the referees' room directly across the hall from the Wake locker room.

Wood had seen the replay on the monitor inside. He looked almost as pale as Odom. "Dave, I'm so sorry," Wood said. "I just missed it."

Odom put up a hand. "Don't think about it for a minute, Mike. I know you did your best. That's all I ask."

Wood still felt sick, but he was grateful that Odom could be so gracious at such a difficult moment.

The next morning, the entire phone system in the ACC offices went down. Fred Barakat's voice mail was so overloaded with messages and people trying to get through that the system couldn't stand the strain.

22

Rise of the Icons

THE PUBLIC ADDRESS announcer at Cameron Indoor Stadium for the last twenty-five years has been Dr. Art Chandler, an eye doctor in real life, who last missed a game in 1991 when, as a member of the Air Force reserve, he was sent to Saudi Arabia during Operation Desert Storm. His years in the military have taught Chandler how to take orders, even though he's old enough now that he might occasionally snicker quietly when he hears them.

On the night of February 18, when Clemson came to Cameron, Chandler received orders that had never before been sent out from the ACC office. They were brief but direct: "Do not introduce tonight's referees."

And so, after introducing Duke's starting lineup and telling the crowd that Duke's coach was "Mr. Mike Krzyzewski," Chandler did not add, as he normally would have, "Tonight's officials, Messrs. Duke Edsall, Dick Paparo, and Larry Rose." Edsall, Paparo, and Rose were standing right there, but Chandler was under orders to pretend he had no idea who they were.

"Funny thing about that," Dave Odom joked the next day, "is that

Duke's the one place in the league where they might have gotten a standing ovation."

Rick Hartzell's mistake at Virginia had benefited Duke and Mike Wood's miscall two days earlier at Wake Forest had put the Blue Devils in first place. Of course the non-intro orders had gone to all nine schools. Fred Barakat and his officials were under siege and he had decided that the less attention the referees called to themselves, the better.

"We're getting killed," Barakat said. "ESPN won't let us up."

The replay of Harrison's shot and Wood's call had been on the air several dozen times by now. ESPN's most popular show was *Sportscenter*, which aired at 6:30 P.M., 11:30 P.M., and 2:30 A.M., and the 2:30 show was rerun all morning long, from 7 until noon. Making matters worse, each time the replay was shown, the ESPN anchor would come up with a new way of retelling the story. At one point Barakat saw tape of someone hitting a long three-pointer in an NBA game. "Gee, if he'd made that in the ACC, they'd have probably given him seven points," Keith Olbermann said over the tape.

To say that it had been a brutal week for ACC officials would be like saying Bob Dole hadn't enjoyed Election Day. They were having a tough year, one made more difficult by the fact that there had been so many games in the league that had been decided in the last minute or on the final play. The previous week had been typical: eight games, four decided in the last 10 seconds, three by one point on the last play.

When Odom arrived home after the NC State game, one of his first phone calls came from his ex-boss and close friend Terry Holland. "Believe me," Holland said, "I know how you feel."

Clemson-Duke was another one of those 9 o'clock TV games that coaches dread, but the day was beautiful, the temperatures climbing into the sixties. "Ten days till March," Rick Barnes said, walking into the mild afternoon. "Think there's anybody in this league who can't wait for that?"

Barnes and his coaches had finally changed their pregame movie after the loss at Wake Forest. Mel Gibson and *Braveheart* had been retired in favor of a Sean Connery movie called *The Rock*. For inspiration the coaches had latched on to the Connery character, who always gets his way.

Barnes was more than willing to settle for winning a basketball game. It had been six weeks since his team and Duke had played their epic overtime game at Clemson. Things had changed considerably in the league since then. In January, it had appeared that this was a season destined to belong to Wake Forest and Clemson, with Maryland in the role of challenging upstart. Duke and North Carolina had looked like little more than bit players, their two coaching icons reduced to answering questions about their glorious pasts and questionable futures.

Then Mike Krzyzewski had drawn his line and Dean Smith had figured out a way to get inside Vince Carter's head. Duke had now won six in a row and Carolina had won five in a row and six out of seven. Duke had jumped from fourth to first in the conference standings and Carolina had gone from seventh to fifth — but just a game out of third. A Clemson victory in Cameron would put Wake back into first place and leave Maryland, Clemson, and Duke in a virtual tie with Carolina right behind. But if Duke won and Carolina continued hot the next night at home against Wake Forest, the Blue Devils would suddenly be one victory from clinching a tie for first place.

"We're in a neighborhood I can honestly say I never expected to be in this season," Krzyzewski said before the game. "That's why this game makes me so nervous."

It made him nervous because, for the first time all season, people were starting to talk about Duke nationally again. They were up to number six in the polls (Clemson was at eight) and there were even some murmurs around about nosing Wake out not just for the regular season title but for a number one NCAA seed. Naturally, Kryzewski didn't want to talk about that. He didn't mind being in the role of the hunted, but he knew this particular team wasn't accustomed to that. He wasn't sure how it would respond. His emphasis in pregame was on staying composed and attacking. He knew Clemson would come out in an attack mode; that was the way the Tigers played. He wanted to be certain his team was prepared to attack right back; that was the way it played most effectively.

Both coaches were tight and hyper from the start. Krzyzewski was screaming at the officials to get Clemson's hands off his players while the early fouls mounted on his team. "Call a hand check, Duke," he yelled at Edsall at one point. "The fouls are 5–2; that's ridiculous."

"They're playing the same way you're playing, Mike," Edsall replied as he ran past the Duke bench.

"What!" Krzyzewski yelled. "Don't insult me by saying we're playing the same way they play."

They *were* playing the same way in one sense: both were very aggressive defensive teams, overplaying passes and pressuring the basketball every chance they got. Clemson was a bigger team — wider more than taller — and stronger, more likely to send bodies flying than Duke. It wasn't that the Tigers committed more fouls, they just got more for their money because of their size. "You go up for a shot against Clemson," Gary Williams had said, "and you expect to come down a few feet away because they're strong enough to move you every time."

The perceived injustices against Krzyzewski's team didn't seem to bother the Blue Devils during the first twelve minutes. Trajan Langdon was making every shot he looked at and Ricky Price also started the game hot. A spectacular off-balance bank shot by Langdon put Duke up 29–19. Then things soured for Duke. Steve Wojciechowski picked up his second and third fouls in quick succession, the third on a charge with 5:43 left. That call, by Dick Paparo, made Krzyzewski crazy and he picked up a technical that was both inevitable and predictable.

Once Krzyzewski had the tee out of his system, he calmed down. Wojo's foul trouble, the technical, and Clemson's ability to get into the lane helped the Tigers climb back to a 32–32 tie. Krzyzewski was still discussing hand checks with Paparo, but now he was being diplomatic. "One of the reasons you're a good official is that you're so consistent," he told Paparo. "You have to get the other guys to call the hand check consistently."

"I'll work on it," Paparo said dryly.

No one in the building could check Trajan Langdon, whether they tried hands, feet, or a gun. He drilled a three to put Duke back on top and the Blue Devils made it to halftime up 37–33.

Krzyzewski was concerned with the foul trouble his team was in — especially Wojciechowski. He even considered not starting him in the second half, but abandoned that idea. He had to be out there, as much to keep Terrell McIntyre from going off as anything else. Krzyzewski didn't know that McIntyre was fighting the flu and feeling weak. What he did know was that a player that good wasn't likely to go zero for six in two straight halves. "That's what's scary," he said. "McIntyre hasn't made a shot and they're only down four."

Krzyzewski felt his team was playing tight, that it wasn't fluid the way it had been against Florida State. As much as he had complained to the officials, he knew the foul trouble was connected to that: when you are a step slow or just a little out of synch you arrive at places late. That causes fouls.

He walked back into the locker room and calmly went through what he wanted to do offensively and defensively. He reminded everyone that Wojo had three fouls and had to be protected as much as possible on the defensive end. "They screen for McIntyre," Krzyzewski said, "Someone better call out the goddamn screen."

He took a deep breath. "Rebounds, fellas," he said. "Loose balls." He picked up a basketball that he had carried into the room with him. Then he rolled it along the carpet in the middle of the room. "You see a loose ball," he said . . . And then, surgical back be damned, he *dove* on the basketball, rolling along the carpet to get it under control . . . "You go after it! You say, 'That's my damn ball; that's Duke's ball and this is Duke's game!' Now come on!"

That got their attention. The second half was played at a quicker, looser pace by both teams. McIntyre's poor shooting continued and so did Langdon's brilliance. Duke's lead kept vacillating — it would jump to 10, then slide to four. With under nine minutes left, it was 55–51 and there was a sense in the building that the game was going to the wire. Less than ninety seconds later, that feeling vanished.

First, Carmen Wallace, the oft-injured senior, took a crisp Wojciechowski pass and, with Wojo screaming, "Nail it, Carmen," he did just that — for three. Then, Roshown McLeod jumped into a passing lane and knocked the ball loose from Tom Wideman at the top of the key. He took off with Wideman in pursuit. Wideman had a choice: give up a dunk or wrap him up. He opted for the latter. Intentional foul.

Now, it was Barnes's turn to be furious. The steal had been right in front of him and he was convinced McLeod had fouled Wideman. The intentional foul just made it worse. McLeod made both free throws for a 60–51 lead. Then, on the possession created by the intentional call, Jeff Capel hit a circus shot as he was going down. The free throw made it 63–51. Finally, Langdon drained another three to make it 66–51. Disgusted and angry, Barnes called a twenty-second time-out. It was too late.

Clemson didn't give up until the final buzzer, scoring 14 points in the last minute of the game. But that just made the final a respectable 84–77. Larry Shyatt was so upset with Larry Rose that he chased Paparo down to tell him that. Barnes was angry too, especially about the noncall on McLeod, although when he looked at the tape he decided the noncall was probably correct. The next morning he flew to Greensboro to look at tape with Barakat, trying to prove that Clemson still wasn't getting the respect it deserved from the league's officials. Barakat, who had plenty on his mind already, picked him up at the airport, spent a couple of hours with him, and told him he understood his frustration. He also told him categorically that he and Shyatt were wrong about Larry Rose having an attitude about Clemson.

"I had Mike complaining about Larry in January and Rick complaining about him in February," Barakat said later. "What that said to me was that the guy was doing a pretty good job being balanced."

Krzyzewski wasn't concerned with Rose after the Clemson victory. His team had now won seven straight ACC games to be 11–3 in the league. It had the weekend bye — which would be used to play a game at UCLA — and didn't play another conference game until the following Thursday when Maryland came to Cameron.

Langdon had finished with 34 points, making every kind of shot there was to make. Late in the game, he had started a drive from the left-hand side, run into two Clemson defenders, twisted underneath them, and laid the ball in from the reverse side. It was the kind of play that made you blink in disbelief. "Did you see that move?" Barnes said to Shyatt.

"I think so," Shyatt answered. "But I'm not really sure."

Krzyzewski was so excited he asked Paparo during the next break if he believed what he had seen. "I'll tell you what, Dick," he said. "That was as good as you're going to see all season."

Tommy Amaker, not a man given to hyperbole, summed the performance up best: "That kid," he said, "is an assassin. He just shoots you down."

Barnes and his team could relate to that comment.

"Let's just sit back for a few days," Krzyzewski told his players, "and let everyone else fight it out."

*   *   *

No one was more ready for a fight the next night — February 19 — than North Carolina. This was revenge week for the Tar Heels. The two teams that had caused them the most misery in January — Wake Forest and Maryland — were on the schedule, Wake in the DeanDome followed by Maryland in Cole on Saturday afternoon. No one in the world was better than Dean Smith at reminding his players of past slights. Wake had humiliated them by 24 points in Winston-Salem, showing them no mercy. This was their chance to even the score.

Wake was hobbling when it arrived at the DeanDome — in more ways than one. Dave Odom was limping and was told again by his doctor that he needed surgery on the second toe on his right foot as soon as the season was over. His team was physically healthy, but still limping emotionally after the NC State game. Odom had been as angry and frustrated after that game as he could remember being in a long time. He was most upset with Ricky Peral, the six-ten senior whose play had been a key to Wake's success the previous two years. Peral was a superb shooter and had become a good rebounder. Against State, he had made one shot and gotten three rebounds. Odom sat down with him the next day and said bluntly, "Ricky, the only one who would have played worse than you did was a dead man."

He knew Peral was trying. He was a bright, hardworking kid. But somewhere, he had misplaced his confidence. Of course he wasn't alone. Watching tape of Carolina on Monday and Tuesday, Odom was struck by how different the Tar Heels looked from his own team. They were loose and free; they looked comfortable. "You watch them," he said, "everything looks easy. That doesn't mean they score every time or stop the other guy every time. But they look like a team that's playing together, being on the court is a pleasure. My team doesn't look that way. Everything is work for us right now. Everything's hard."

Odom thought the team had become too Tim Duncan–dependent. When things weren't going well, Duncan took over. Teams were pounding on him and he wasn't getting enough help to get people to lay off him. "We're staying in games by the force of Tim's will," Odom said. "That's not good. If you look at our three losses, he had at least 25 points and 18 rebounds in all three of them. That means he's trying to do everything. We can't win that way."

To try and get his players out of the Tim-will-do-it-all mode, Odom played Duncan with the second team in practice on Monday and Tuesday. That meant the other four starters — plus Steve Goolsby — had to figure out ways to score without Duncan. They had to stop the second team with Duncan. Odom had called Duncan in on Monday and told him about something he had done two years earlier.

"Our best player was Randolph [Childress]," he said. "Randolph could get any shot he wanted in practice. You hadn't become a scorer yet. We needed you to score inside to balance Randolph outside. I called Randolph in and asked him to stop shooting in practice for a while. I told him I wanted him to give you the ball every time he could and demand that you shoot. But we never told you what we were doing.

"I need you to do the same thing now. When I put you back with the first team in a couple of days, I want you to shoot less. Get the other guys shots. MAKE them take shots. I know you can get your shots. I need them to know they can get theirs."

Duncan smiled. "Coach, what did you major in in college?" he asked.

"Phys ed and psychology," Odom answered.

Duncan, a psychology major, nodded. "That's what I figured."

He understood. So did his teammates. They worked hard for two days in practice. Still, Odom admitted en route to Chapel Hill on Wednesday, he had no feel for how his team would play. "I never thought this would be a team that would back off mentally in tough situations," he said. "I thought we might have nights where we wouldn't shoot or nights where we might not handle the ball well. But back off when a play needed to be made — no. That's what we need to get back to, making big plays. That's what's made us a good team the last couple of years."

The players understood what Odom was trying to do. But they were still clearly struggling. If Odom wasn't sure what to expect from his team against Carolina, he was more certain about what to expect from the Tar Heels.

"They're very confident right now," he told his players in the locker room. "Almost cocky. Vince Carter is a talker. He will come out and try to make great plays. If we don't let him do that, he will make bad plays, because he will keep trying to be spectacular. Don't let him be spectacular."

He was speaking directly to Tony Rutland about Carter. This was a serious matchup problem. Odom's three big men couldn't possibly play Carter on the perimeter, so either Rutland, Braswell, or Goolsby had to do it. None of them had Carter's size or strength. In January, when Carter had been tentative and uncertain about his role, it hadn't been a problem. Now, it had the potential to be a serious problem.

Odom had written four keys to the game on the board. One said simply "3/33" — that was Shammond Williams (3) and Antawn Jamison (33). Just like Krzyzewski, Odom was convinced that Williams's shooting and Jamison's rebounding were the heart and soul of Carolina's team. His fourth key had nothing to do with the Tar Heels. "Poise/confidence — WF basketball," it said. That was what they had to get back in this game. First their poise and then their confidence. That was what Odom thought Wake Forest basketball should be — and had been for the past four years.

Walking down the long hallway that leads to the DeanDome court, Odom bumped smack into Roy Williams. The Kansas coach had flown in on an off night to watch his son play for the Carolina JV team.

"Look at you," Odom said. "Your team is so good, it should be illegal."

Williams laughed. "Listen, nothing's really changed," he said. "Ten years ago I spent a lot of time in that JV locker room and now I'm still spending time in the JV locker room."

Once upon a time, Williams had coached the Carolina JV team. He had come a long way since then, even if he was still visiting that same locker room. "I'd wish you luck," Williams said, "but you'd know I'm lying."

"I understand," Odom said.

"See you in March?" Williams asked.

Odom rolled his eyes. "Right now, I'm just trying to get out of February alive."

This was not going to be a night that would make the month feel any shorter. Odom's instincts about Carolina and Carter were completely accurate. Carter, smelling blood the minute he saw Rutland matched up with him, went right to work. He had seven of Carolina's first nine points on a jumper, a hook, and a three. Then he went over everyone to take a lob pass for a dunk. He rebounded a miss. That gave him 11 of the first 16. The good news was that Rutland hit his first two shots, one of them a three, in response. But Carolina simply wouldn't miss. Carter bombed a second three, then a third.

Odom was almost speechless at the next TV time-out. It was 24–11 and Carter had scored 17 points in less than 13 minutes. "Carter's annihilating us!" he screamed. "We've got no pace at either end of the floor, guys. I mean . . ." He stopped, looking for something to say. "I mean, jeepers creepers!"

If jeepers creepers didn't snap them out of it, nothing would. The carnage continued. Wake's defense pushed out to deny Carter room, so Serge Zwikker went to work for three quick baskets. The very balance Odom was searching for was right there — in Carolina blue. There was no one on the floor you could lay off of, no weak link. It was 38–18 at halftime. Carter had 21 on nine-of-ten shooting.

Odom didn't rant during the break. He was searching for something — anything — to get his team going. He decided to play small, taking Loren Woods out for Goolsby, and pressure full-court. There was really nothing to lose, down 20. "I want to see you fight," he told them. "Forget the score. Fight your way back. Be aggressive. Don't worry about making mistakes. Just *play.*"

The second half didn't start off any better than the first. Carter took the ball on Carolina's first possession, swooped past everyone and delivered a monster dunk. The players on the Carolina bench were so delighted that they jumped up en masse, spilling the drinks that had just been passed out by the managers all over their sweats and the floor. The lead grew to 23 before the Deacons began to come back. Finally, they hit some shots from the perimeter. They cut the lead to 15. "Get it to single digits with eight minutes to go," Odom asked. They did just that, a Rutland three cutting the margin to 54–47 with 8:23 left. The giddiness was gone on the Carolina bench and in the crowd. Everyone remembered Maryland. Smith called time-out — a full time-out — something that happened before the game's last two minutes almost as often as leap year.

It was the right move. He convinced his players that spectacular plays weren't needed or appropriate. Ed Cota hit on a drive, Jamison hit a layup, and Shammond Williams buried a three. The lead jumped back to 61–49. The Deacons had tried. They hadn't given up when they easily could have. That pleased Odom. Little else did. The final was 74–60.

"Right now," Odom said to his coaches. "They're better than us. A lot better than us."

Odom stood in the middle of the locker room and ordered his players to stand up and form a tight circle around him. "I want to feel you," he said. He looked around at their sad faces. "Hey, listen," he said. "The second half, that was more like us. That's the way we need to get back to playing. The good news is, we know it's still there. Now, we've got to figure out how to do it consistently." He looked at them again. "We'll do it, guys. Don't worry. We'll do it."

Carolina's performance against Wake confirmed what most people around the league had begun to suspect much earlier in the month: the Tar Heels were on a roll. That, of course, was the last thing Gary Williams wanted to hear, with Carolina coming into Cole for Maryland's last home game of the season. The Terrapins had won at Georgia Tech on Wednesday to up their conference record to 9–4. It was also their twentieth win of the season, an important milestone for Williams because it was only the second time in his eight years at Maryland that his team had won twenty games.

Like Odom, Williams felt as if he were searching for the key that would unlock the kind of play his team had produced throughout January, but had been unable to produce with any consistency in February. And like Odom he didn't feel as if his team was all that far away from being very good again. "The problem in this league is that there's no margin for error," he said. "Even against Georgia Tech, we played pretty well and it still wasn't an easy game."

Tech was in a free fall at 3–10, leading only NC State (2–11). Those two teams were now virtual locks to play in the Les Robinson game. The difference was that State — in spite of a loss to Virginia — seemed to be improving each week while Tech was regressing. That was never more apparent than early on Saturday, when the Wolfpack demolished Tech, 72–51. Bobby Cremins was embarrassed and humiliated. After the game, he told his coaches they needed to meet on Monday to discuss the future of the program.

A few hours later, Williams was interested only in the present. He had watched the Wake Forest–Virginia game almost from beginning to end, fascinated that Odom had taken the drastic step of benching Ricky Peral in favor of sophomore shooting specialist Joseph Amonett. "I guess he figures he has to do something to get Peral's attention before the tournament starts," Williams said. On this day, the move worked. Peral played well off the bench and Wake pulled out a close game down the stretch. The loss put Virginia at 6–9 in the league. Since the Cavaliers had the midweek bye (they would play in-state rival Virginia Tech) they had just one league game left: at home the following Sunday against Maryland.

Knowing that, Williams pulled hard for Virginia to beat Wake. "If they have seven league wins and eighteen overall coming into our game, they'll feel like they're in [the NCAAs] already," he said. "If they only have six wins, our game becomes do or die. I don't like playing teams in a do or die situation for them, but not for us. No matter what you say to your players, there's a difference in emotion."

On this day, the emotional edge should have been with Maryland. It was Keith Booth's last home game and his number was being raised to the rafters in Cole in a pregame ceremony. Senior day, invented by Dean Smith in 1962, had now become a tradition at virtually every basketball-playing school in the country. Of course Smith was in his locker room telling his players how much fun it would be to ruin senior day for Maryland.

Although Duke is North Carolina's archrival, Smith has some fond memories of Cole Field House down through the years. In 1985, Carolina had come into Cole on a night when Lefty Driesell was going for his five hundredth win as a coach. Before the game, Smith promised his players that he would sing the Maryland fight song afterward if they won the game. They won, Smith sang, and Driesell ended up winning number five hundred against Towson State — not quite the same as getting it against Carolina and Smith.

"Some of my most enjoyable wins came in here," he said prior to the game. He was standing in the tunnel between the locker rooms killing time talking to Digger Phelps, the ex–Notre Dame coach turned ESPN broadcaster. Phelps wanted to talk about Carolina's resurgence, what had been the key, what Dean had done to get the team going. Smith wanted to talk golf. Ironically, another of Smith's fondest Cole memories involved

Phelps: in 1977, Carolina had come from 16 points down in the second half to beat Phelps and Notre Dame in an Eastern Regional semifinal game.

"We had it won," Phelps said.

"On St. Patty's day too," Smith said, grinning. "Can you imagine that? Notre Dame losing on St. Patty's day."

Now *Phelps* wanted to talk golf.

Inside the Maryland locker room, Williams was writing his four keys on the board. The last one said, "Physical-40." Williams had noticed that Carolina had become a team that liked to bump and use its size and that it had become — very out of character for Smith-coached teams — a talking team.

"Vince Carter's a woofer," he said. "Last year, McInnis was a woofer. So was Rasheed [Wallace]. Ten years ago, I don't think Dean would have put up with some of that stuff. Now, he does. Which is probably smart. The hardest thing about coaching as you get older is thinking the players always have to live up to your standards. In some things, they do. In others, you have to leave them alone."

The Maryland players always walked from the locker room to the court clapping their hands in unison while Rodney Elliott led them in a rap chant called "Crunch Time." Williams would no more participate in a rap chant than fly to the moon, but if that was what the players enjoyed, it was fine with him. Like most coaches, Williams and Smith had both accepted the fact that some of their players wore earrings around campus. They did not, however, wear them in the locker room or on the court or when traveling with the team.

Williams's pregame emphasis did not just focus on Carolina. He wanted the players to understand that, this being their last home game, they were now entering the portion of the season that would ultimately decide how they would be judged. "Twenty wins is a great thing, fellas," he said. "But it isn't that great if you get there and stop. Let's make sure we keep on going."

To be fair, it would have been difficult for almost anyone to stop the Carolina team that rolled into Cole that day. Maryland didn't play poorly in the first half — especially at the offensive end — but still trailed 48–37 at the break. Carolina was running its offense almost perfectly. If Serge

Zwikker didn't have an open jump shot, Antawn Jamison was powering past the Maryland defense. The two of them were 16 for 20 from the field the first 20 minutes. Jamison had 21 points, Zwikker 15. Williams was so angry he almost couldn't see.

"How can you let a team come in here in our last home game and give them forty-eight points in a half?" he screamed. "How can you let that happen? I mean, Jesus Christ, fellas, what's going on here? Are you telling me you don't have the guts to outrun these guys for twenty minutes? Are you going to let them walk in here and kick your ass this way? Think about it for a few minutes, just think about it!"

Williams was so angry that he screamed at assistant coach Dave Dickerson for not sweating enough. "If you really cared," he yelled, "you'd be sweating!"

Williams was sweating profusely. He wanted so much to see his team get better and it wasn't. Why not? Why was Carolina so much better in February than it had been in January and his team wasn't?

The answer, of course, was the improvement of Cota and Carter. Maryland had been playing about as well as it could hope to in January. Carolina hadn't been close to that level. Now, the Tar Heels were getting closer with each game. Williams felt like he was flailing at a target he couldn't touch.

His team felt the same way throughout the second half. Every time the Terrapins made a run, the Tar Heels had an answer. They cut the lead to five and Carolina pushed it back to 11. Then Carter and Cota, who had been quiet during the Jamison/Zwikker outburst, got hot, using Maryland misses to set up the fast break, and the lead ballooned to 18. Williams was so angry during a time-out that he threatened to hold a practice after the game if the Terrapins gave up another layup. After that, the defense got back and they cut the margin to seven several times but never got closer. Carolina won 93–81 and Smith was no doubt humming the Maryland fight song leaving the court. The winning streak was now seven and the two teams were tied in the ACC at 9–5.

Williams was so angry in the locker room that he kicked over, then heaved, a heavy stationary bicycle — no mean feat. When he walked in and saw the players sitting in front of their lockers with their heads down, he went off. "Don't put your heads down *now*," he said. "*Now* is too fucking late. Where was that emotion before the game? During the game? Don't sit there now and tell me how sorry you are that we lost. The hell with that."

He stalked around the room like a caged animal. "You see, what you don't understand is that I'm not in this for twenty wins or to make the NCAAs or whatever the hell else you guys want to talk about. I want to win the *national championship!* That's my goal! And you know what? We can do that. There are a lot of teams out there that can do that and we're one of them. You guys think Carolina's good enough to win it? I do. Do you think they're better than we are? Today, yes, because you guys won't guard anybody."

He paused again, then came back for one last swipe. "The problem is, you guys go around and everybody here is kissing your ass telling you how great you are because you've won twenty games or whatever. Well fuck that! That's done. That's over. All that is just to get us into position to win games in March. You understand that! March! That's next week, fellas! We're going to Duke on Thursday, and you know what? Believe it or not, we can still win the conference championship. But not like this. Think about it. Think about that tonight while you're out with your buddies and they're telling you it's no big deal that you lost today."

Chuck Walsh, the Maryland sports information director, walked in with the game stats. Williams swiped at them once and dropped them, then, after Walsh picked them up, swiped at them twice — and dropped them again. When he finally got hold of them, he shook his head again. "They shot fifty-six percent, fellas. Need I say more?"

Two minutes later, when the media was allowed into the interview room, they were greeted by a soaking-wet but calm as can be Gary Williams. "Carolina's playing very well," he said quietly. "We were just a little slow today."

He had been planning to drive to Baltimore that night to watch a high school senior play. He canceled the trip. He couldn't bear to be around a festive crowd. He wanted to go home and sulk.

23

Jockeying

WITH ONE WEEK left in the regular season, four ACC teams still had a mathematical chance to tie for first place — Duke (11–3), Wake Forest (11–3), North Carolina (9–5), and Maryland (9–5). Clemson (8–6) couldn't finish first, but, like the top four, the Tigers had locked up an NCAA tournament bid. Virginia (6–9) had to beat Maryland on Sunday to feel confident it would get a berth. Florida State (5–9), which had finally gotten the road win Pat Kennedy had been pleading for by beating Clemson on Sunday at the buzzer, could also put itself in strong position if it won at NC State and at home against Wake Forest. If Virginia and FSU tied at 7–9 and the committee decided to take only six ACC teams, the advantage would go to Virginia, since it had beaten the Seminoles twice.

Georgia Tech was 3–11 and NC State 3–12. The difference was, State was still playing with enthusiasm and hope. The Wolfpack believed that if it could beat Florida State at home, win its easy nonleague finisher against Wofford, and then beat Tech in the Les Robinson game, it would get an NIT bid because that would clinch a record of no worse than 14–14 overall. Since no one on State's team had ever been in postseason, this would be a great achievement for Herb Sendek's first team.

Georgia Tech was going no place after the ACC tournament. The Yellow Jackets had to play at Wake Forest on Tuesday and host Clemson Saturday. Then would come the Les Robinson game and, in all likelihood, packing up the uniforms. Bobby Cremins kept saying that he wasn't giving up on the season, that he still thought something might be salvaged, but he didn't really believe it. Kevin Cantwell had given him a new nickname: Mr. Gloom and Doom.

Mr. G&D had called his staff in for a long meeting after the embarrassing loss at NC State. Tough decisions had to be made. Only one senior — Eddie Elisma — would be gone next season, but Cremins didn't feel comfortable with the players who were scheduled to return. Specifically, he didn't feel comfortable with his guards, freshman Kevin Morris and sophomore Gary Saunders.

Morris had never been comfortable running the team. Even though he was point-guard size, his skills were really more suited to the shooting-guard spot. Saunders had played well at times but Cremins was convinced that a lot of the team's "chemistry," problems started with Saunders. What's more, he had struggled academically from the start.

On the day before the Yellow Jackets left to play at Wake Forest, Cremins made a tough decision: Morris and Saunders would not be asked back.

This was a perfect example of the arbitrariness of the NCAA's one-year scholarship rule. Because athletic scholarships are renewable each year, any coach can pull a scholarship for any reason at all. Or for no reason. The player has no recourse. He might be a straight-A student who worked as hard as possible every single day in practice, and if the coach decided he wasn't good enough, he was gone.

Running players off was far more common in football than in basketball. Because schools are allowed to recruit up to twenty-five players a year, but can only have a total of eighty-five on scholarship at any one time, football coaches must have attrition. If it doesn't come about through injuries or grade problems, they simply cut the weakest players. Basketball teams rarely have that kind of numbers problem because most coaches carry fewer than the allowable thirteen scholarship players.

Cremins always carried less than thirteen. He could have kept Morris and Saunders on scholarship and told them they weren't going to play. But he didn't want to do that. He wanted to start with a clean slate, for him and for them.

"Gary's had some problems," he said. "And I don't think Kevin would adjust well to being a backup."

Translation: I want them gone.

Cremins would take some heat in the Atlanta papers for this decision. He knew that, and was prepared for it. Tech's season would bring heat down on him anyway so he figured why not take it all at once and hope to bounce back next season with a new set of guards. He and his assistants would begin feverishly recruiting every available guard in the country the minute the season was over.

There was still the matter of playing out the string. Cremins wasn't at all pleased to find himself in the Lawrence Joel Coliseum for Tim Duncan's last home game. Not only was it Senior Night for a class that had won two ACC tournament titles and was about to go to a fourth straight NCAA tournament, it was the last home appearance for the player certain to be named national player of the year and, arguably, Wake Forest's greatest player ever. Duncan wasn't an emotional person, but with his family in the building and a postgame ceremony scheduled to retire his number, it would be an emotional night.

"Now I know how the Christians felt going in to face the lions," Cremins joked before the game.

He was sitting in a meeting room at the Adams-Mark Hotel waiting to eat pregame meal. March was three days away, but it could not come soon enough. As if to remind him how miserable the season had been, Elisma and Saunders were both late. As punishment they had to wait outside the room until someone on the team had finished eating. Then they were allowed to come in. Another glitch in a glitch-filled season.

Cremins didn't want to see his players quit. Before the game, he implored them to come up with an effort that would give them something to feel good about before the season was over. "With all we've been through," he said, "there's no place I'd rather be tonight than right here, in this building, coaching you guys."

Maybe Cremins really felt that way. In all likelihood, he was trying to convince himself that he felt that way. His players, clearly, were not convinced. The looks on their faces said, "Let's get this over with."

Down the hall, Dave Odom knew this was one night where he wouldn't need any fire-and-brimstone speeches. His concern was just the opposite: that after the five seniors and the senior managers had been introduced with their families everyone would be too emotional and too wound up to play.

"This is a special night for a lot of reasons," he told the players. "But remember we've got a job to do and if we want to have happy memories of this night, we've got to get that job done."

If there was any doubt that the night would be emotional, all anyone in the room had to do was look at the tape around Duncan's knee. Like a lot of athletes, Duncan often wrote messages on the white tape. The first thing he had written for this game was "Mom." Duncan's mother had died of cancer when he was a freshman in high school. His father and sisters were in the building. Clearly, Duncan wanted his whole family to be a part of this.

Tech was the perfect opponent for a night like this. The Yellow Jackets simply didn't have it in them to make the evening tense. Wake was up 11–2 after five minutes and 34–22 at halftime. The Deacons got careless early in the second half and let Matt Harpring, who was still playing as hard as anyone in the league, pull his teammates to within four. After a lecture from Odom in which he recommended that they remember that this was not an exhibition, the Deacons pulled away steadily. Duncan came out to a huge ovation with thirty-six seconds left and Kenny Herbst, upping his total as the second-leading Jewish scorer in Wake Forest history, got the last basket of the night. The final was 71–55.

Cremins then held the most sparsely attended postgame press conference in ACC history. There were three people in the room: Cremins, Tech sports information director Mike Finn, and *Atlanta Journal-Constitution* beat writer Norman Arey. Everyone else was on the court watching the ceremony honoring Duncan.

The biggest question — at least among the players — was how long Odom would talk. Odom is very precise when he talks, very detailed, wanting to make sure he gets his complete message across. He is perfectly capable of starting a sentence by saying, "Let me address that briefly," and then talking for ten minutes without coming up for air. The over-under for his speech was twenty-two minutes. He surprised everyone by getting off the stage in less than twenty but admitted the next day that he felt rushed. "There were just some things that I felt needed saying that I didn't get to."

He got to the highlights, though: how he first heard of Duncan; seeing him play for the first time; his remarkable transformation into a star; and how proud he was that Duncan had opted to stay four years and would graduate in the spring. He talked about Duncan's family. Then, finally, he introduced "the boy from St. Croix," and the building shook. Not a soul among the 14,407 had left.

Duncan joked that he had never been nervous on a basketball court — until this moment. Then he talked about playing at Wake Forest and about his mom. Finally, he looked around and said, "So, how about one more year?"

That got the biggest cheer of the evening.

One of the spectators during the ceremony was Matt Harpring. No one was happier to see that than Kevin Cantwell, who also walked out to watch. Harpring was a junior and he had been so discouraged by Georgia Tech's play at times that he had talked about passing up his senior year. "Maybe seeing that will help him understand what it means to stay four years," Cantwell said.

Dave Odom also noticed Harpring. The next day, he wrote him a note, thanking him and telling him what a classy move he thought it was for him to come out of a losing locker room to see Duncan honored.

There were no numbers retired the next night at Clemson, even though Rick Barnes had strong feelings about the three seniors playing their last home game — Merl Code, Bill Harder, and walk-on Brian Chester. Code and Harder had been part of the Slab Five. Harder, of course, had been the subject of Dean Smith's pointing and yelling the year before that had led to Barnes-Smith II. As Smith and his North Carolina team left the court during warm-ups just before the senior ceremony, someone jokingly asked Smith if he wasn't going to stick around to see Harder honored. (No visiting teams stay on the court during senior ceremonies). "He's a fine young man," Smith answered. "He should just learn to play without grabbing people."

He wasn't smiling when he said it.

He was smiling by the end of the evening. This was another night when Littlejohn Coliseum rocked from start to finish. But Carolina was a team that was locked in; Clemson was a team that was searching. The Tigers were still recovering from their stunning loss the previous Sunday to Florida State.

In that game they had fallen behind, then come back to lead before losing when Kerry Thompson dashed around Terrell McIntyre to rebound his own missed shot and bank it in as the buzzer sounded for a 67–65 victory. It was the third ACC game that Thompson had won for the Seminoles in the final seconds. What stunned Barnes was that the player beaten on the last play was McIntyre.

The next day, he called McIntyre in for a talk. He had been concerned for several weeks that so much of the offensive burden had fallen on McIntyre and Buckner that it was affecting their play — especially McIntyre, who had also been sick earlier that week.

"Boogie, why do you think we lost yesterday?" Barnes asked.

"Because I let Thompson beat me on the last play."

"Wrong. Because we all made mistakes. I made mistakes, the other guys made mistakes. We're all human. We all make mistakes. We're going to make some more of them this week. But you can't wallow in it. You pick yourself up and go on to the next play, the next day, the next game."

McIntyre nodded. Barnes didn't think he was getting through. "Boogie, let me ask you a question. How did you feel when your daddy died two years ago?"

"Awful."

"Why?"

"Why? Because he was my dad and I loved him and he was gone."

"Exactly. Now that was worth getting upset about. That was worth crying about. This isn't. This is just a basketball game. We work our tails off to try and win and we're disappointed if we don't, but nobody has died. Nobody died yesterday. We have another game to play Wednesday. It's all right. Everything is all right."

Barnes thought he saw a light in McIntyre's eyes. "OK, Coach. I hear you."

The standings had changed considerably since the two teams had met in the DeanDome on Super Sunday. Carolina was now a game ahead of

Clemson in the ACC standings and the Tar Heels (number nine) were the top ten team. For the first time since November, the Tigers (number twelve) were out of the top ten. Barnes wasn't concerned about that.

"There's a little bit of panic around here right now because we've lost a few games," he said, gazing at the eighteenth green behind the clubhouse of the Clemson golf course. It was a warm, overcast day and Barnes couldn't help but think about golf season — at least a little bit. "I'm not panicked. We've lost to good teams. I mean, how talented is Florida State? Are you kidding me? There's no shame in losing to them. Can we play better? Of course. But when I look at what this team has already done, heck, we're a year ahead of schedule right now. I thought we'd be doing the things we're doing now a year from now."

Maybe he was rationalizing a bit, but what he said made sense. The only important player who would graduate was Code, and Johnny Miller, a jet-quick transfer from Temple, was primed to step into his spot. That didn't mean Barnes was throwing in the towel on this season. He was just preparing himself mentally and emotionally in case things didn't work out the way he hoped.

They started out that night as well as he could possibly have hoped. With the crowd primed after the senior ceremony, the Tigers played almost perfect basketball for twelve minutes. McIntyre was out of his funk and Smith's favorite player, Iker Iturbe, also started hot. It was 28–15 after a Harold Jamison rebound basket. Like everyone else in the league in recent weeks, Barnes had geared his defense to stop Antawn Jamison and Shammond Williams. And as before that strategy left openings for Vince Carter and Ed Cota. The two of them combined to score 12 straight points in a four-minute stretch to cut the lead to 28–27. A Code three finally stopped that binge and the Tigers pushed the margin back to 36–30 just before halftime.

The last play of the half underlined the continuing tension between the two coaching staffs. With four seconds left, Clemson inbounded from under its own basket. The pass went to Tony Christie at halfcourt, who tried calling a quick time-out while catching the ball. He bobbled it, recovered, and called time. Only 0.7 seconds went off the clock. The Carolina coaches insisted more time should have run off. They began yelling at the scorer's table. Frank Scagliotta consulted with the table briefly, then left the clock where it was.

Even as Clemson was inbounding, Dave Hanners, the Carolina assistant closest to the scorer's table, was still yelling at timekeeper Bill Shane. Naturally, Shane yelled back. As soon as Clemson's last-second shot had bounded away, Hanners made a beeline for Shane. "I want your name!" he yelled. "Right now."

Before Shane could even think to reply one way or the other, Larry Shyatt, representing the Clemson bench, arrived on the scene.

"What's going on?" he demanded.

"I want his name," Hanners answered.

"Well, you can't have it!" Shyatt roared.

The two men took a step toward one another before cooler heads prevailed. They were still shouting at each other going into the tunnel.

Barnes was more concerned with tightening the defense than with taking anyone's name. He could feel Carolina getting more comfortable with the game late in the half and he wanted to put a stop to that quickly. Even down six, even not having Shane's name, Carolina had to feel good after the lead had once been 13.

The Tar Heels started the second half the way Clemson had started the first. In eight minutes, they outscored the Tigers 18–6 and took control. Clemson — most notably McIntyre who would finish with 24 points — kept trying to rally, but the Tar Heels always had an answer. The closest it got was 60–59 after a McIntyre three with 3:11 left. Cota answered that with a jumper and Williams followed that with a three, pushing the lead back to six. Carolina held on from there, 76–69.

Smith was genuinely delighted and maybe even a little bit surprised. He had known this would be a big game emotionally for Clemson and he couldn't have expected another performance as efficient as the one at Maryland. Carolina had now strung together three excellent performances — Wake Forest, at Maryland, at Clemson.

"The key," Bill Guthridge said, laughing, "has been the assistant coaches."

Coming from a member of the Carolina staff, this represented uproarious humor. But that was the mood of a team that had gone from 3–5 in the league at the halfway mark to 10–5 with one game to play. The only negative to the whole night was the trip home. By the time Carolina's bus pulled out of the runway leading to the tunnel at Littlejohn, it was almost midnight. The weather in Anderson was lousy, but it was worse back home in North Carolina. The airport would be closed until at least 7 in the morning. Smith — as always — let the seniors decide what to do. They voted to bus home. The bus pulled up to the DeanDome at 7 A.M. Everyone went to bed exhausted, but happy.

Twelve hours later, Gary Williams sat in an empty locker room directly above the one where his players were getting dressed in Cameron Indoor Stadium and worried about the way the regular season was ending for his team. Technically, the Terrapins still had a chance to tie for first place in the ACC. But to do that they would have to win at Duke and at Virginia. Two losses would mean fourth place. Certainly respectable, but not where the Terrapins had appeared headed at the end of January.

"There is something about Carolina and Duke that no matter what they always find a way to be good," he said, staring at his Duke scouting report. "I mean, look back a month and who would have figured we'd be behind both of them right now. Sometimes, they just have better players than us. OK, I understand that's gonna happen. But in a year like this when they go past you, it makes you wonder. I mean, they both have very good players, but at the beginning of the year they didn't look all that good. Then you look up and it's March and who's playing the best in the league?"

Duke had finally slipped the previous Sunday, losing at UCLA. The Blue Devils had trailed much of the game, come back to lead late, then hadn't been able to hit critical shots down the stretch. Trajan Langdon, coming off his monster game against Clemson, turned human, missing two open threes, including one in the last twenty seconds. Krzyzewski was disappointed, but not discouraged.

"The thing we learned from that game is that we can't afford to be too dependent on Trajan," he said. "I'm not so much talking in terms of points, but emotionally. In the first half, when he wasn't hitting, you could see that it bothered the other guys. Then, he hits a couple and we pick up. We can't afford to do that. In fact, if anything, it should be just the opposite: if he's missing the other guys need to pick up the slack for him."

Senior Night at Cameron is a little different than it is at the other ACC schools. These days, most schools turn the senior ceremony into a family affair. Parents, sometimes brothers and sisters, join the honored seniors as they're introduced. Krzyzewski has never included families in the ceremony. The seniors are introduced and then they stand in the center jump circle by themselves and drink in the cheers. "I think involving the parents is more for graduation," Krzyzewski said. "This is more of a farewell, student to student. When the guys go out there, the students are thanking them for four years and then after the game they thank the students." That was another part of Duke's Senior Night that was unique. At game's end, win or lose, the seniors went back on the court to address the crowd.

Senior Night or no Senior Night, this was a game that had great meaning for Duke. A victory would clinch at least a tie for the ACC regular season title. After the travails of the previous two seasons, after being 4–3 following the Maryland game this season, that would mean a lot to Krzyzewski and for these players. The only ones in the locker room who had been involved with a championship in college were the seniors: Newton, Capel, and Wallace had played on the '94 team that had won the ACC regular season championship and gone on to the national championship game. This was full circle for them: from first to last and back.

"You've earned this," Krzyzewski told them. "You've worked your butts off to get into this position. And you know what's great about it? It ain't gonna be easy. Maryland's not going to come in here afraid or intimidated by the crowd or anything. They've won at Carolina; they've won at Wake. They're a damn good basketball team. Which is what will make beating them to win this title so satisfying."

Krzyzewski's prediction that it wouldn't be easy was accurate. Duke led 32–24 late in the half, but Maryland came right back to cut the margin to 34–33 at halftime. Krzyzewski had started Newton because it was his last home game, and he had played well in the first half with six points and four rebounds. But he decided to go back to the small lineup for the second half. "Not because you've done anything wrong, Greg," he said. "But because that's been our best lineup and I think it's our best chance to win the game."

He was still searching for a lineup that could win the game when he inserted freshman Mike Chappell five minutes into the second half.

Chappell had been brilliant at times in practice, but never seemed to be able to get going in games. This time he did. He scored 10 points in the next seven minutes, including two critical threes, the first giving Duke the lead, the last coming at the end of an 8–0 spurt that pushed the lead from one to nine. Then everyone chipped in. During a five-minute stretch, five different Duke players hit threes. For almost thirty minutes, Maryland had done a great job of not giving up open threes. That had kept the Terrapins in the game. Then came the onslaught. It was too much for Williams's team. The final was 81–69.

The last minute was an extended celebration for the Blue Devils, torture for the Terrapins. First Newton came out, then Wallace, and, finally, Capel. Ten weeks after he had heard the mocking "Oh No, Not Capel" chant, Capel heard warm, ear-splitting cheers and got a huge hug from his coach. His parents were sitting a few feet away with tears in their eyes. Clearly, their son was a long way from being an outcast.

When the buzzer finally sounded, Williams congratulated Krzyzewski and walked to his locker room as the raucous postgame celebration began. As much as he respected Krzyzewski, Williams admitted to himself that night that there were moments when he was jealous of him. Williams had built a good program at Maryland; Krzyzewski had built the program Williams wanted to build. Williams was well-known and popular; Krzyzewski was an icon. All the banners hanging in Cameron, like the ones down the road in the DeanDome, represented reaching the very top in Williams's chosen profession.

"Players at Duke and North Carolina walk onto the court and they look up at all those banners and retired jerseys and they realize they're part of something special," he said. "Their goal during their four years is to win the national championship or come damn close to it. Sometimes, when I get really down, I think our guys just want to get through four years at Maryland without dying of an overdose of cocaine."

Even with all the success Williams had brought to his alma mater, the ghost of Len Bias, eleven years later, still haunted Cole Field House.

24

Forty Minutes Till Dance Time

ALL SEASON LONG, getting back to the NCAAs had been the goal for Virginia. Jeff Jones was fully aware that there were factions at Virginia who would be delighted to use two straight non-NCAA seasons as an excuse to not extend his contract. Since he only had one year left, Jones needed an extension if he was going to recruit effectively during the summer. Terry Holland knew that and had told Jones he wanted to sit down and talk about an extension when the season was over. Jones knew it would be a lot easier for Holland to deal with those in the Virginia power structure who were concerned about the breakup of his marriage and the arrests a year earlier if he had an NCAA bid — not to mention five in seven seasons — to talk about.

As Jones and his team prepared for their make-or-break regular season finale, everyone else in the ACC was virtually locked into their postseason role. Duke's victory over Maryland three days earlier had clinched a tie for first place for the Blue Devils. On Saturday, Florida State had handed the title to them outright. Having been humiliated three days earlier at NC State (67–44), the Seminoles returned home and, on their

Senior Day, reverted to their Dr. Jekyll persona and beat Wake Forest, 68–64. Dave Odom, who had hoped that his team was finally through its February funk after the Georgia Tech game, started March with a big-time headache.

Wake's victory meant that Duke's game at North Carolina the next afternoon had no meaning in terms of the final conference standings. Duke would be first regardless of the outcome, and even though Carolina would tie Wake for second place at 11–5 with a victory the Deacons would still be the second seed in the tournament because of tiebreakers. Carolina would be the number three seed win or lose because it had the tiebreaker against Maryland.

In fact, the entire ACC tournament draw was already complete on Sunday morning even before the final two games of the regular season, Duke-Carolina and Maryland-Virginia, were played that afternoon. Georgia Tech would play the Les Robinson game Thursday night against suddenly red-hot NC State, which had used the victory over Wake Forest as the catalyst to a four-wins-in-five-games string. The winner would play Duke on Friday. The other three games that day would be Maryland (four) versus Clemson (five), Wake (two) versus Florida State (seven), and Carolina (three) versus Virginia (six).

The seedings were set and Duke and Carolina would go into the DeanDome playing for pride, especially Carolina, which didn't want to have Duke finish first and sweep the season series. Two hundred miles to the northwest of Chapel Hill, Maryland-Virginia was just as meaningless in terms of the conference standings but was Armageddon to the Cavaliers.

Even though they had forced themselves not to "what if" after the Duke game nineteen days earlier, the Virginia coaches couldn't help themselves on the morning of the Maryland game, a cool, breezy day in Charlottesville. "Just think," Anthony Solomon said. "If we win that Duke game, we all might have gotten some sleep the last few nights."

Actually, they were fortunate to be where they were, having barely escaped from Virginia Tech the previous Tuesday. The Hokies had the basketball trailing 58–57 in the last ten seconds and missed a layup and a short runner in the lane. Tech's coaches screamed for fouls on both shots — "There are people doing time for less than that" was Coach Bill

Foster's postgame comment — but nothing was called and the Cavaliers got a win they had to have. A loss there might have meant that the Cavaliers had to beat Maryland and then beat Carolina in their first ACC tournament game to get an NCAA bid. Now, they all felt confident that a 7–9 ACC record and 18 victories overall would be — should be — enough. But getting that seventh ACC victory would not be easy.

Jones set the tone for the day at pregame meal. "The first time we played them, fellas, they dictated the game to us," he said. "They came right at us and we took a step backwards and never really recovered. Well today we're taking it right to *them*. Right from the start, we're the aggressor on every single goddamn play. That's the way it has to be. You all know what's at stake. It's going to be an emotional day because of these three guys" — seniors Harold Deane, Jamal Robinson, and Martin Walton — "but we have to get past all that. This is for an NCAA bid. Simple as that. We can't let anyone get in our way."

Gary Williams knew that would be Virginia's approach to the game. That was why he had rooted so hard for Virginia the previous Saturday. He had nothing like that to give his team. They had their twenty wins, they were already in the NCAAs. But he didn't want to lose three in a row going into the ACC tournament. Their record since the win at home over Duke five weeks earlier was 4–6. That hardly represented momentum heading into postseason.

"You had a chance to win at Duke on Thursday," Williams told his team, "and you didn't get it done down the stretch. It's a forty-minute game, fellas. We have to come out ready to play today for forty minutes. Thirty isn't good enough."

The first twenty had all the intensity either coach could reasonably expect. In the first minute Walton, getting the start because of Senior Day, took a charge from Sarunas Jasikevicius so eagerly that he cut the back of his head. No one led by more than five throughout the half, which ended with Virginia catching a giant break when Curtis Staples banked in a desperation 25 footer from the right side just before the buzzer. That cut Maryland's lead to 39–38. Williams stood in front of the bench for a moment with his hands on his hips after Staples's shot dropped as if to say, 'When do we catch a break.'

Jones wasn't thinking about breaks or lucky shots in the locker room.

He knew Maryland had played well. He knew his team was trying. He also knew that none of that was going to matter if they were still behind when the second half ended.

"I know you're trying, guys. I know the effort is good," he said. "But you know what? *That's not good enough!* This game isn't about any goddamn moral victories or saying, 'Well, we tried.' This is about our entire season! It's about playing in the NCAAs! Chase Metheney, Colin Ducharme, you get your hands on a rebound, *you hold on to it!* I don't care if you get pushed or shoved or whatever. You hold on to the goddamn ball! Sports is about survival of the toughest. You have got to be tougher than you have been so far today. We've got twenty minutes to go out there and lay everything on the line. I mean *everything!* I don't want to hear any bitching about referees or the other team or anything else. I want you locked in on what you have to do and that is get in their ass for twenty minutes like you've never done before. Everything we have worked on for five months comes down to this twenty minutes. Do you understand that? Now take a minute, gather yourselves, take a deep breath, think about what we have to do, and let's go do it!"

For five minutes, Maryland did all the doing. Laron Profit, who had slumped through most of February, had his shot back. He scored five straight points, including a three-point play on a drive to make it 50–40. Jones was screaming one minute; pleading the next. He was about out of ideas. He had switched to a zone at the start of the second half and Maryland seemed able to slice it apart.

But then the freshmen, Ducharme and Dersch, came up with a pair of tough baskets inside. The crowd, quiet and nervous, came to life. Maryland began to get impatient against the zone. Jasikevicius, a good shooter, had several good looks from outside the arc and couldn't get anything to drop. He had killed the Cavaliers with 24 points in the first game and had 10 at the half. But he was two for ten in the second half, many of his misses critical. Maryland was still clinging to a six-point lead with eight minutes to go when Staples and Alexander each hit from way outside. Maryland went cold, going six minutes without a field goal. Everything was a jumper over the zone; nothing dropped. Alexander and Staples took over. By the time Keith Booth made a layup to end the Maryland drought with 2:32 left, the Cavaliers were up, 70–65.

From there, it was a matter of hanging on and making their free throws. UVA was nine for 14 in the final minute, but that was good enough because Maryland still couldn't make anything from outside. Appropriately, it was Deane, the senior who had come so far to be the leader of this team and had played hurt for almost two months, who made the final two free throws with three seconds left. The final was 81–74 and Anthony Solomon was screaming, "Let's dance!" as soon as the clock hit zero. Players call the NCAA tournament "the Dance." Virginia, at long last, would be dancing.

While the Virginia seniors were being honored after the game, the two coaches had very different thoughts about what had just taken place. Williams had seen his team perform well for thirty minutes — again.

"The last ten minutes of a close ball game is about guts and courage," he said. "Good teams, great teams, teams that aspire to win championships know all about guts and courage. Right now, we don't. Right now, we're not playing with any heart. Without heart, you've got nothing. We need to figure out where our hearts have gone these last few weeks because we still have a lot of basketball to play — if we want it bad enough. That's up to you."

Naturally, Jones's feelings about the last ten minutes were quite different. As his players poured into the locker room before the senior ceremony, he called them together briefly. They formed a huddle around him and he said softly, "That was guts, guys. Guts. That was playing for everything and coming through. I'm proud of you."

While Deane, Robinson, Walton, and their families were being honored, the players and assistant coaches stood by the bench, joining in the applause. Jones stood back near the door that led from the locker room hallway to the court; close enough so he could see, far enough away that the moment belonged to the players. When the ceremony was over, he walked back to the locker room and sat in his chair to wait for his team.

Then, it all came out. All the work, all the wondering, all the pressure, all the public talk about his private life. It all crashed at once. Jones didn't want his players to see him crying, but he was crying when they came in the door. Tears of joy, relief, and exhaustion. So much had happened in the two years since the 1995 run to the final eight. So many doubts and questions. So many bad nights. He had questioned himself more than once, at least as many times as he had questioned the team. The 12–15 season had been an unending nightmare, on and off the court. This season had been better, but they had still taken a lot of hits between the injuries and the internal troubles and referees not letting subs into games. And when they absolutely had to put everything they had on the floor for forty minutes, they had done it.

Jones pushed the tears out of his eyes as his players sat in front of him. He said quietly, "Damn good job, guys. Go out and have a good time tonight. You earned it."

Of course Jones wouldn't go out that night. He didn't go out in Charlottesville anymore. But he would celebrate too. He had also earned it.

25

The Dance
Before the Dance

A LITTLE MORE than two hours after Virginia virtually clinched its trip to the Dance, the ACC regular season finally ended. North Carolina beat Duke in the DeanDome in a wild game in which Duke fell way behind, then climbed back, then fell way behind, then climbed back again. Down 13 with 4:42 left, the Blue Devils closed to within four, with the ball, in the final minute, before losing 91–85.

Some of the statistics for the game were mind-boggling. Antawn Jamison was extraordinary, with 33 points and 11 rebounds. He was completely unstoppable inside, but so was his entire team, which outrebounded the Blue Devils 49–18. Jamison and Serge Zwikker alone outrebounded Duke, 21–18. And yet, in spite of that incredible margin, Duke still had a chance to win the game because it shot an almost-as-amazing 17 of 34 from behind the three-point line. Steve Wojciechowski, the player Carolina fans most loved to hate because of his die-to-win grit, was six for seven.

The game was intense because all Duke-Carolina games are intense. But when Mike Krzyzewski said in the postgame interview room that he thought perhaps his team wasn't as emotionally into the game as he would have liked (witness the rebounding total) because it had already clinched first place, you would have thought he had said Dean Smith knew nothing about coaching.

"How dare he!" screamed the pro–Tar Heel media members for the next couple of days. Which was fine. What is Duke-Carolina without some postgame animosity?

Dean Smith could have cared less about whether Duke was emotional or whether his loyal media minions took offense at the notion that it might not have been. All he knew was that his team had now won nine straight and had gone through the second round of the ACC undefeated to finish tied for second with Wake Forest at 11–5, one game behind Duke.

For all nine teams the end of the regular season meant a brief respite, something everyone needed. Watching Wake Forest–Florida State and Clemson–Georgia Tech on the final weekend, Gary Williams had been struck by how tired everyone looked. He knew his team was tired too. "You always feel a little bit beat up at the end of the regular season," he said. "But this year, it seems to be even more true because we were all so competitive with one another. Just look at how different the second round of games was from the first round. It was almost a complete flip-flop. That's a sign of balance."

Comparing the standings for the first eight games against the second eight games backed up Williams's theory. The standings for the first eight games looked like this:

Wake Forest	7–1
Clemson	6–2
Maryland	6–2
Duke	5–3
Virginia	4–4
Florida State	3–5
Carolina	3–5
Georgia Tech	2–6
NC State	0–8

The second half looked like this:

Carolina	8–0
Duke	7–1
NC State	4–4
Wake Forest	4–4
Virginia	3–5
Florida State	3–5
Maryland	3–5
Clemson	3–5
Georgia Tech	1–7

The contrast was remarkable. Only one team had managed to play better than .500 ball in both rounds — Duke, which was why the Blue Devils had won the regular season. NC State had gone from nowhere ninth the first round to tied for third in the second. If you had been able to place a bet on February 1 that State would win as many games as Wake Forest in the second round of ACC play, you could have retired for life.

None of that mattered now that the regular season was over. For most of the teams, ACC tournament week was enjoyable. Everyone had four days off between games — even State and Tech, who had to play in the Les Robinson game Thursday night since they had finished their seasons on Saturday — and all the coaches gave their players some time off.

Once upon a time, ACC tournament week was the most intense week of the season for everyone. From 1954 through 1974 it was the tournament that determined the ACC's one NCAA tournament representative. The regular season almost didn't matter. In the very first ACC tournament, after Duke had finished 9–1 to win the regular season, it lost in the semifinals to fourth-seeded NC State, which went on to win the tournament. Six years later, Duke got even when, as the fourth seed with a 7–7 record, it won the tournament and got the only bid. The biggest injustice of the system had occurred in 1970 when South Carolina went 14–0 in the regular season but lost in a slow-down final to NC State, 42–39 in double overtime. That was the game that sent Bobby Cremins into the mountains in despair.

The last one-bid year was 1974, the year of the overtime NC State–Maryland game for the ages. The quality of the game was so high that at one point when players began jostling one another for position before an inbounds play, referee Hank Nichols jumped between them and said, "Come on, fellas, not in *this* game." Everyone understood. The jostling stopped.

In 1975, the NCAA expanded the tournament from 25 teams to 32 and began taking up to two teams per league. That meant that the ACC regular season champion was assured of a bid regardless of how it did in the tournament. It is probably not coincidence that in the 21 tournaments played in which the regular season champion had to win to advance to the NCAAs, the champion (or a cochampion) won 14 times. Since 1975, the regular season champion (or a cochampion) has won the tournament seven times in 23 tries. To carry it a step further, only three teams in the last 23 years (North Carolina in 1977 and Duke in 1986 and 1992) have won both the regular season title outright and the ACC tournament.

So, the odds against Duke, heading into the weekend in Greensboro, were pretty long.

The NCAA had expanded the tournament again in 1980, relaxing all limitations on the number of teams a conference could send. That changed the character of the ACC tournament even more. Now, anywhere from three to six teams might arrive at the tournament with bids already locked up. That meant a lot of the tournament games were played for nothing more than pride. Some coaches worried about their players getting too wound up about winning the ACC tournament because it might leave them drained emotionally the following week. The final usually matched two teams who were playing for NCAA seeding. The last ACC tournament finalist that hadn't played in the NCAA tournament had been Wake Forest in 1978. That was back in the days of the two-school limit. Duke, the tournament champion, and North Carolina, the regular season champion, got the bids that year.

For a number of years, Dean Smith intentionally held his team back ACC tournament week in order to be ready for NCAA play. Only when people began moaning that Carolina hadn't won the title for a number of years (1983–1988, horrors!) did he relent and prepare in earnest for the ACC tournament.

"We worked very hard to win it in 1988 and lost," he said. "But then we won it in '89 and I hoped that would make people happy."

It did, until they started noticing that Carolina hadn't been to the Final Four since 1982. "Now that one I worried about," Smith said. "Getting back [in 1991] was a big deal. I had started to wonder a little bit myself."

Five ACC teams came to Greensboro absolutely certain they would be receiving NCAA bids on Sunday evening: Duke, North Carolina, Wake Forest, Maryland, and Clemson. All had won twenty games or more and had winning conference records. Virginia was confident that the victory over Maryland had wrapped up a bid, but Jeff Jones was hoping for at least one more win to avoid any nervous moments on Sunday.

Only two of the nine teams arrived feeling they had something truly important at stake: Florida State, 6–10 in league play and 16–10 overall, believed that if it could beat Wake Forest in the first round, it would get a bid. "We would then have two wins over Wake Forest and wins over North Carolina, Maryland, and also Clemson on the road," Pat Kennedy said. "We will have beaten every one of the top five teams in the top conference in America except for Duke. I would hope that would get us in."

He didn't use the word hope to his players. "Win and we *will* be in the NCAA tournament," he told them.

Herb Sendek wasn't naming any tournaments or making any guarantees. He simply told his players they were playing for a postseason bid. Barring a miracle that was going to mean the NIT, but that was OK with Sendek. NC State was 13–13 going into the Les Robinson game and everyone in the State locker room knew that a victory over Georgia Tech would give the Wolfpack its first trip to postseason since 1991.

Georgia Tech wasn't going anyplace but home unless it won four games in less than seventy-two hours and that wasn't likely to happen since the Yellow Jackets hadn't won four games in the previous two months. That didn't mean Bobby Cremins didn't have one last pregame speech in him.

"Fellas, we haven't played together all season," he said. "Let's try to play one game as a team. You owe it to the seniors, you owe it to these coaches, and you owe it to yourselves. One time!"

The Thursday night atmosphere at the ACC tournament does not lend itself to taut, emotional basketball games. There has not been a public sale of tickets for the event since 1966 and, for most of the crowd, this is a social occasion, something they plan on every year for the second weekend in March. Adding an extra game in 1991 after Florida State joined the conference didn't thrill anybody associated with the league.

For the fans it meant the possibility that, if your team had a bad year, it might not even be around for the twin doubleheaders on Friday that everyone looked forward to because it was such a basketball feast. The feast didn't taste as good if the team you cared about didn't even make it to the table.

The media didn't like the extra game because it meant instead of having a leisurely day watching the pre-tournament practices and then going out to dinner on Thursday evening they had to attend the practices in the afternoon, eat in the Coliseum because there was no time to write, then go out and fight the traffic coming back for a 7 o'clock game, and then stick around until 10 or 11 o'clock to write a story about two teams who weren't likely to be around by dinnertime on Friday.

But no one loathed the Thursday game more than the coaches. They hated the stigma of playing in the game or of being in position to play in the game. When the Les Robinson Game monicker began circulating, they decided that the play-in game was helping to get coaches fired. They argued for a change in the system and, shortly before the start of the tournament, they had gotten one. The league had voted to change the format starting in 1998 so that there would now be *two* games on Thursday instead of one: the number one seed would play the nine seed and the seven seed would play the eight seed. That, they claimed, would eliminate the Thursday night stigma. It would also create an imbalance on the weekend since the winner of the one-nine game would get a bye into Saturday's semifinals while the seven-eight winner would play the second seed on Friday and the four-five and three-six games would continue as in the past. The new system meant that a nine seed had a better chance to win the tournament than a seven or eight seed since it only had to win three games, while the seven-eight winner had to win four. It was a horrible, silly change caused strictly by the paranoia of the coaches.

The Thursday game was usually played at a low level. The teams were there because they were struggling. Even their own fans weren't that enthusiastic about the game and the fans from the other seven schools really didn't care who won. It wasn't as if there was an underdog to root for. Both teams were underdogs. The 1996 game had been so poorly played and had dragged on for so long that Gene Corrigan, who had created the Thursday night debacle by taking Florida State into the league, threw his hands into the air with two minutes to go and said, "Will this game never end?"

State–Georgia Tech was a little better than that. State did have something to play for and Tech didn't want the humiliation of losing on Thursday. In the seven years that the game had been played only three schools — North Carolina, Wake Forest, and Virginia — had avoided playing in it at least once. This was Tech's first appearance. It was State's fifth. Both coaches sincerely hoped it would be their last.

The first half was less than inspiring, the Yellow Jackets leading 20–19. Things did pick up in the second half, though not that much. Tech was still leading 37–33 with under eight minutes to play when Gary Saunders fired a quick, wild three on a possession when a basket would have put his team up six or seven. Instead, Jeremy Hyatt hit a three at the other end to start a 16–2 Wolfpack run. Cremins called time twice to try and get his team under control, but it was too late. As soon as the Yellow Jackets fell a few points behind, their desire to work the game disappeared. Only Matt Harpring scored in double figures (18). Everyone else looked like they just wanted to go home.

Michael Maddox, who had looked like a budding star as a sophomore, finished an awful junior season with nine points in thirty-six minutes. Cremins had been so upset with him in the last few games that he had told him he was worried that he was heading for a senior year like Greg Newton's. It wasn't meant as a compliment. Saunders and Kevin Morris, in their final appearances for Tech (although they didn't know it yet) were two for eight and one for eight. State's margin in the last eight minutes was 27–9. The final was 60–46. It was an embarrassing end to a humiliating season.

In the quiet locker room, Cremins paced up and down in front of his players for a moment. His assistants, the team doctors and trainer, and the managers stood off to one side near a half-full garbage can. Cremins turned his back to the players and indicated that everyone should take a step away from the garbage can. Then, when they were all at a safe distance, he kicked the can over. Of course, Cremins being Cremins, he didn't do what all other coaches do after kicking something over — let the managers clean up. Instead, *he* cleaned up. Then he straightened his tie and said, "We'll start individual meetings on Monday."

That was it. He walked out of the room. "I didn't want to say something personal that I'd regret later on," he said. "I was so angry and frustrated by the whole season. I wanted to let them know I cared and I was upset, that's why I kicked over the garbage can. But I didn't want to say anything hurtful."

During the final minutes of the game, the NC State fans began chanting the three letters that many basketball fans consider a profanity in early March: "N-I-T, N-I-T." Normally, this was a mocking chant, delivered by fans of one team to an opponent that is about to lose a key game and may suffer the indignity of being relegated to the thirty-two-team National Invitation Tournament. Once, the NIT was every bit as prestigious as the NCAA Tournament. But as the NCAA has grown into a premier American sports event, the NIT has become nothing more than a consolation bracket, usually filled by big-name schools from big-name conferences who haven't done enough during the regular season to merit an NCAA bid. Most people now believe that NIT stands for Not Invited Tournament.

In 1997, the Big East, in the midst of an awful season, would suffer the indignity of sending more teams to the NIT (six) than to the NCAA (four). To long-suffering Wolfpack fans, the prospect of playing anyplace the week after the ACC tournament sounded like something just this side of nirvana. And so, they giddily chanted as State won for the sixth time in seven games to raise its record to an NIT-worthy 14–13.

The victory meant the Wolfpack would play in the second game of the Friday afternoon doubleheader against Duke after Clemson and Maryland began the proceedings with a noon game. There is no day in college basketball longer than Friday at the ACC tournament. Yes, there are eight twin doubleheaders played around the country the following week during the first round of NCAA play. But that's different. For one thing, many of those games don't sell out. The ACC is always sold out. For another, many NCAA fans only show up to see their own team play or, at most, to watch one of the doubleheaders. More than 95 percent of the ACC fans watch all four games. It is tradition. If the last game, which usually isn't over until close to midnight, is a dud, the Greensboro Coliseum will start to empty. If the last game is tight, few people leave before the final buzzer. And most of them will have pulled into the parking lot by no later than 11 o'clock that morning.

Scalpers are everywhere at the ACC tournament. Since there is no public sale of tickets, there is huge demand for them. Once a team loses, many fans will look to sell their tickets for Saturday or Sunday so they can go home. Inevitably, if any of the four North Carolina teams reaches the final, their fans will fill a large chunk of the building, having scalped tickets from out-of-state fans heading down the road.

Most years, the best Friday matchup is the first one. The number four and number five teams should be the most evenly matched, and often one or both of them is trying to cement an NCAA bid with one more victory. That wasn't the case with Clemson and Maryland, but both locker rooms had an air of desperation before the game. Both teams had limped to the finish line, going 3–5 in the second round after being 6–2 in the first. Maryland had now lost seven of ten; Clemson four of six.

Gary Williams had watched his team go south late in the season in 1996 and he wanted very much to avoid a repeat in '97. Earlier in the week, he had called his sophomore center, Obinna Ekezie, in for a one-on-one meeting. Ekezie was a project for Williams, a kid who had made giant strides since arriving as an out-of-shape 280-pound freshman. But Williams and his assistants thought Ekezie as much as anyone on the team had gotten the dreaded "big head" after the fast start. He had listened to all the people who wanted to tell him how good he was and he had stopped doing the things that had made him successful. Watching him on tape, Williams had noticed a lot of whining at the officials. Maybe, he thought, that was his fault to some degree, since he was constantly on them. Once, he had noticed Ekezie fake an eye injury after getting beaten to a rebound. He showed Ekezie the tape. "Stop looking for excuses Obinna," he said. "Just go out and play."

He had also been doing some espionage work. He knew that in March motivating players with the same bromides often didn't work. He had done an interview with Ken Rosenthal, a columnist for the *Baltimore Sun*, in which he had been critical of Terrell Stokes. Without saying it for the record, he had even implied that he was so disappointed with Stokes's play down the stretch that he wasn't absolutely certain he would be the point guard next season. He knew how publicity conscious Stokes was so he left it to Rosenthal to speculate. He wasn't planting a story, but he was pretty certain he knew what Rosenthal would write. Then, he made sure Stokes saw the column before tip-off.

"I didn't do anything intentional," he said. "I didn't try to tell Ken what to write. But when he wrote it, I didn't mind that Terrell saw it."

His pregame message was very basic: this team has beaten us twice — that's enough. His first key almost sounded silly for college players: "Catch the ball." Watching tape, Williams had noticed that his players were trying so hard to make things happen, that they were starting to make moves with the basketball before they had caught it cleanly. "Catch it cleanly and there is plenty of time to make a play," he said. "I know that doesn't sound like much, fellas, but it makes a big difference — especially in transition, when most passes aren't perfect."

His fourth key was "No holds barred." Clemson was a very physical team. They had to be equally physical to win the game.

While his players warmed up, Williams sat and looked at the names of the three officials for the game: Dick Paparo, Karl Hess, and Sam Croft. "You think Fred's mad at me?" he asked, half-joking. Paparo had tossed him for the first time in his life in January and Hess had teed him up in February. And Croft? "He worked last night. Why does he work the noon game? He's got to be tired."

Croft insisted that wasn't the case. "You go on adrenaline this time of year," he said, trotting out before tip-off.

Williams wasn't buying that argument — at least not early. The first whistle of the game came from Croft — a traveling call on Keith Booth as he made a rare outside jumper. "Sam, what in the world are you talking about?" Williams said, leaping to his feet, arms extended, palms turned upward in disbelief.

The next eight minutes were all Clemson — unless you count an Ekezie basket and Williams hollering at the officials (mostly Croft) and his players. Finally, down 9–2 with 12:59 left, Williams called a twenty-second time-out. Since Croft was the nearest official, he blew his whistle and made the time-out signal to the scorer's table. As he did, Williams clapped his hands mockingly and said, "Good call, Sam!"

Croft put his whistle in his mouth, took a step toward Williams, and then thought better of it. Barakat had given all the officials a lengthy pep talk/lecture on Wednesday night about the difficult season they had been through. He had counseled them to be extra patient with the players and coaches during the weekend since the fans and the media were looking for a reason to jump on them for past indiscretions.

Actually Maryland was lucky only to be down 9–2 at that juncture. The lead grew to 11–2 a moment later but easily could have been 20–2. The Tigers missed four free throws and several layups during that stretch. Barnes crouched in front of his bench with an uneasy feeling in spite of the early lead. "We could have knocked them out early and we didn't," he said later. "They were tight at the start because they were nervous about losing to us three times. When we missed all those free throws and layups you could see them loosen up."

And how. An Ekezie dunk started a 16–0 run for the Terrapins. Ekezie had taken Williams's lecture to heart and Stokes had read the morning newspaper. Both looked like the players who had led Maryland to the top of the league in January. What's more, Williams had made a conscious decision to deny Terrell McIntyre the ball and the lane at all costs. That left the rest of the Tigers with plenty of openings — which they couldn't convert.

Barnes rarely goes off on his team at halftime. This time, though, he did. "What pisses me off is that they're just kicking our ass inside," he said. "They are the aggressors, not you. Ekezie is just killing you guys. There is not a single excuse for this. We're down six" — 31–25 — "and we could have been up twenty if you guys had come ready to play. How the hell can we be two for eight at the foul line? Let's just go out now and see if we can't play basketball the way we know how to play it."

They couldn't. Although the game stayed close for eight minutes, Maryland was in control. Having weathered the early troubles, the Terrapins were confident that they could shut Clemson down. Williams had pointed out that the Tigers were shooting less than 40 percent from the field for the season, and if they weren't allowed to get to the foul line, they weren't nearly as dangerous. Keith Booth broke the game open midway through the half with three straight baskets — one on a drive, one on a steal, and one on a third rebound. That summed up the day and sealed the deal for the Terrapins. They won, 74–61, for their most satisfying victory since the late-January win over Duke. It was a disappointing finish to the ACC for Clemson.

"One guy in this locker room played hard today and that was Boogie [McIntyre]," Barnes told his team. "The rest of you need to understand that this time of year if you let the other team be the aggressor, you lose. You play like this next week and we'll play one game and go home. I promise you. All these months of work and we're one game away from being done if this keeps up."

Ten yards away, the mood in the Maryland locker room could not have been more different. Williams was so relieved and happy to win that he almost choked up talking to his players. "I knew you guys were tired, but I couldn't tell you that because we had to keep playing," he said. "Now, we're rested. And when we're rested, there's no one in the country — no one — I won't go play with you guys. That's really how I feel. It pisses me off that people have been taking shots at us the last couple of weeks. We went out and showed those assholes from Baltimore" — that would be *Sun* columnist Rosenthal — "what kind of team we are when we're ready to play. I can't wait to play tomorrow because whoever the hell we play, Duke or State, we're going to be the more rested team and we will be ready to play, just like today. I am damn proud of you fellas. Damn proud."

If he had been giving out game balls, he might have given one to Rosenthal. Of course he didn't mention that to the players.

As Williams was speaking, Gene Corrigan was walking into the Duke locker room. Corrigan made it a practice to go into each locker room before a team's first game in the tournament to wish the coach good luck.

Mike Krzyzewski was nowhere in sight. "Actually," Tommy Amaker told Corrigan, "he's in the shower room."

Krzyzewski was not taking a pregame shower. Instead, while his team was on the floor warming up, he was opening soap packets and arranging them in the soap dishes. Anything to kill time.

"Nervous?" Corrigan asked.

"Apprehensive," Krzyzewski answered. "I'm not sure where my team is right now."

Coaches are always uptight when they play a game in which they are heavily favored. That fear is doubled or tripled against a team you have already beaten a couple of times during the regular season. "One of the hardest things to do is beat a good team three times," Dean Smith often says. Down the hall from Krzyzewski, Rick Barnes could attest to that fact.

Almost no one in the Greensboro Coliseum expected NC State to give Duke any trouble that afternoon. The Wolfpack had won its NIT game the night before. It had now been playing without freshman center Damon Thornton for almost three weeks. Thornton had hurt his knee late in the Wake Forest game, had tried to play against Virginia, and hadn't been in uniform since. Herb Sendek had changed his offense after Thornton went down. Since he was playing five perimeter players, all of them capable of putting the ball on the floor, he spread everyone out, played no one in the low post, and turned everyone on the court into a potential driver. It was a different look, one that teams weren't used to. That was the advantage the Wolfpack had. The disadvantage was lack of size — no one starting over six seven — and lack of depth.

"The five guys they start are all good players," Krzyzewski said. "If they get the game at their pace, they're dangerous against anybody."

Which was why Krzyzewski's pregame message to his team was "sprint, sprint, sprint." He wanted to turn the Wolfpack over, get them into a running game, and wear them down. A half-court pace, he knew, was dangerous because all five State starters could score out of their half-court set.

Krzyzewski's jangly nerves had as much to do with his team as with the opponent. For four games he had felt that his team hadn't been the same as it had been when it took command of the ACC race. Not only had it become a jump-shooting team, which was entirely predictable playing the small lineup, but it had become a team whose on-court emotions were tied to how well it shot the ball. If shots were dropping, everyone played defense. If they weren't, he was convinced he saw a blank look come over their faces and their shoulders droop.

And so, after the loss to Carolina, he had given them "a collective punch in the face." For two days, he watched practice from the stands, while the assistants ran them through drills normally discarded after preseason. He reminded them that the best way to win was with defense. "Defense is the most consistent thing in basketball," he said. "Shooting isn't. It's great when you make shots, but on nights when you don't, you need something to fall back on. We haven't got that right now."

For ten minutes against the Wolfpack, they had everything. Shots were dropping, the defense was giving State fits, and the score was 21–5. On television, Billy Packer, who is almost never wrong in analyzing a game, made the comment that "Mike's job the rest of the way is to get his team ready for tomorrow."

Sendek and State weren't thinking that way. Given an opening when Duke missed back-to-back layups, they worked their way back into the game. Duke missed eight straight shots and State closed the gap to 31–25 by halftime. Leaving the court, Tommy Amaker heard the State players talking to one another. "We're a second half team," they were saying. "Duke's not making shots."

When Amaker reported those comments to Krzyzewski back in the shower room (which the coaches were using for their halftime meeting) Krzyzewski grimaced. "They're exactly right. I can't get them out of this shooting-dependency thing."

He was far more uptight now than before the game. Like Clemson, they had had a chance for an early kill and blown it. The difference, he knew, was that if State had a chance to win late, the entire Coliseum would pull for the underdog.

"Guys, you started pacing yourselves after we got the lead," Krzyzewski told the players. "You can't do that. We'll worry about tomorrow when there's a tomorrow to worry about. State isn't pacing itself. They're going to play as hard as they can for as long as they can. Go out and start this half the way you started the first and then go from there."

They did exactly that, beginning the half with an 11–2 flurry. That made the lead 42–28 with less than fifteen minutes to go, and everyone began wondering how Duke and Maryland would match up the next day.

They wouldn't. Before anyone on the Duke bench knew what had happened, Justin Gainey and C. C. Harrison combined to run off 11 straight points in less than three minutes. Gainey, who had been so awful in January, was now a confident college point guard, very much in command of his team. His presence had freed up both Harrison and Ishua Benjamin to concentrate on scoring. "Ishua Benjamin has never been a point guard and never will be a point guard," Sendek said. "When he was handling the ball for us it was like having a running back play quarterback. It didn't matter how well your line blocked, the ball wasn't going to get where it had to go. Once Justin got established, it changed our personality as a team."

State was confident, playing with nothing to lose, and — as Krzyzewski had predicted — it had the crowd behind it. Krzyzewski kept pushing different buttons to get his team going, but nothing worked. Out of the spread offense, Duke wasn't quick enough to guard Gainey or Harrison. If the defense collapsed on them, they were pitching the ball outside to Danny Strong or Jeremy Hyatt, who were confident three-point shooters. A Hyatt three with 6:07 left put State up 48–46. Amazingly, that was the game's last lead change. Duke never got even again. When Duke tried fouling late, State calmly made 12 of 14 free throws. In the final 15 minutes, they outscored the Blue Devils 38–18, playing almost perfect basketball.

"We had become a good team," Sendek said later. "All the hard work paid off for us that weekend. But it wasn't as if we just woke up to it one morning. The last few weeks of the regular season, we were getting steadily better." State's weakness was inside, but when you shoot well from the field (12 cf 22 the second half) and consistently get to the foul line, there aren't that many rebounds for the other team to get. Duke might have won if it had hit a couple more jump shots when it had the big leads. But it didn't and Krzyzewski's worst fears were realized.

"This game was coming," he told his players afterward. "I was hoping that if I acted like it had already happened during practice this week, that we might avoid it, but we couldn't. You weren't any worse today than against UCLA or Carolina. The difference was, it didn't seem like that big a deal to lose at UCLA or at Carolina because they're good. You played like pussies at Carolina. The only reason the score wasn't worse was because you shot well."

He spent a good fifteen minutes telling them that they had lost the identity that had made them the ACC's most consistent team throughout February. "Maybe this will be good for us," he said. "Maybe, by getting this out of our systems now, we'll get back to who we really are for next week. Because I still believe in you guys. I'm just not sure you believe in you. You're just too wrapped up in shooting the basketball. There's a lot more to the game than that."

He wasn't angry with them, just frustrated. The last thing he told them before the media came into the locker room was very direct: "I don't want to hear one excuse," he said. "You give that team down the hall credit. They beat us, pure and simple. They were better than us today. Period."

Down the hall, that other team was still celebrating. It was Jeremy Hyatt who voiced the impossible thought. "Two down," he said. "Two to go."

The building was still buzzing with talk about State's upset when Wake Forest and Florida State launched the evening session. One thing that had been true of both Duke and North Carolina throughout the nineties (Duke's lost '95 notwithstanding) was that they rarely fell victim to major upsets, especially in March. That's why Duke's becoming only the second number one team in league history to lose to a number eight (the other had been State losing to Maryland in 1989) was a stunner.

Neither Dave Odom nor Pat Kennedy cared all that much about what had happened in the afternoon. Neither was that shocked either. Each had lost to State in February and knew the Wolfpack had evolved into a very competitive team. "You live by the jump shot, some nights you die by the jump shot," Pat Kennedy said, sounding as if he had been listening to Krzyzewski all week.

This game was a rare rematch, in that the teams had ended the regular season playing each other and now opened the tournament playing again.

If beating a good team three times in a season is difficult, then how tough is beating a good team twice in a week? Kennedy knew that Wake would be primed and ready for his team, but he felt the confidence his players had gained by winning the game in Tallahassee could work to their advantage. "Let Wake know right away that we have come here to dominate them again!" he wrote on the board.

Wake wasn't going to be dominated again, in large part because Tim Duncan wasn't going to allow it. Odom had again gone back to the drawing board after the FSU loss. On Monday, he had told his players that only one player was assured of a starting position on Friday — Duncan. Every other spot was available. He would conduct open tryouts and find out who was playing the best basketball.

The next morning, on the weekly ACC conference call (each of the nine coaches answers questions for ten minutes apiece) Odom was asked by *Durham Herald-Sun* reporter Al Featherston about the open tryouts. Odom quickly spluttered that he didn't want to talk about that and asked for another question. When he hung up, Odom was furious. Who had leaked what was going on to Featherston? "If I find out it's one of my coaches," Odom said, "I swear to God I'll fire him."

He was genuinely angry. It wasn't until Thursday at the pretournament practice that he learned the name of the leaker: George David Odom. "You mentioned it on your radio show on Monday night," Featherston told him.

"I did?"

Featherston nodded. Odom had completely forgotten.

"Well I have no choice," he said. "I have to fire myself."

He also had a new nickname: Scoop.

All Scoop wanted from his team this weekend was to see some fire and some jump shooting. He knew Duncan would play well, but he wasn't sure about anyone else. Sean Allen had re-earned a starting spot through the tryouts along with holdovers Ricky Peral, Tony Rutland, and Jerry Braswell. That was the lineup they had started the season with. Odom hadn't expected anything different, but he had wanted to up the intensity during practice. That much had been accomplished. Even so, he knew the game would be difficult.

"They're talented and now they think they can get in" — to the

NCAAs — "by beating us," Odom said. "If we beat 'em in Tallahassee, they're goners. We gave 'em life. Now, they'll come to play."

Actually, both teams came to play. They produced the best game of the day, filled with runs and superb plays. The difference in the end was Duncan, who scored a career high 31 points, fouled out the entire FSU front line, and could have scored 40 if he had been able to convert more of his free throws. Wake's jump shooting was better than it had been. And yet, the Seminoles hung in. Down 12 with less than five minutes to go, they cut the margin to 60–56 with more than three minutes left. They even got the ball back trailing 63–59 with just under two minutes left and had three cracks at a three pointer that would have cut the margin to one. But none of them dropped and Wake hung on to win, 66–65.

Odom was relieved but happy. Kennedy was disappointed but not unhappy. His team had played well. It hadn't died when it fell behind. He went to his press conference and campaigned for a bid he knew wouldn't come. "If you look at the power ratings, we belong in the NCAAs," he said.

More realistically he had already talked to NIT chairman Jack Powers earlier in the week about his team's possible draw. Since the Leon County Civic Center was committed to another event the next week (another drawback of playing off-campus) FSU would have to go on the road for its first game. Then, it would get at least one home game if it won in the first round.

"Fellas, I know how disappointed you are because we were so close," Kennedy said. "We've made big strides this season. We've turned the program back around in the right direction. We still have a chance to win a championship before this is over. The NIT is a big event in New York City. That should be our goal, to get to New York. Let's get Kerry Thompson back to New York with all he's done for us this year. There is no reason, fellas — no reason — to throw in the towel on this season. We're playing too well right now to go home yet. Let's play five more games."

Odom was worrying at that moment only about his next game. His team had been better, but it still wasn't back to where it had been. "If we play Carolina," he said. "We'll have to be sharper than we were tonight."

They would play Carolina. The Tar Heels led Virginia for most of the final game but couldn't get the Cavaliers to go away until very late. UVA actually tied the game at 59 — after trailing by 11 — on a Courtney Alexander three with 5:37 left, but Carolina responded by scoring the next 11 points and cruised home, 78–68. Jeff Jones felt his team had let a great opportunity slip away. The game had been winnable, but they hadn't been mentally prepared to win.

Now, they had to go home and wait until Sunday evening to be sure that their Dance ticket was punched.

Gary Williams woke up with his stomach twisted in a knot the next morning. He had been as surprised as anyone by State's victory over Duke. Walking out of the Coliseum, he had caught himself thinking, "We've got a really great opportunity here." That immediately led him to a second thought: "If I'm thinking that, imagine what the players are thinking." He knew Duke's loss should give his team an opening to get to the final. He also knew that his players — like their coach — had been preparing mentally to play Duke.

"The reason State won the game is because they were better," he said that night when he met with the players. "They're playing a style that's tough to play against because you have to be patient. Duke couldn't do it. That's why they lost."

The players were in their rooms and bed-checked by 10:30. With a 1:30 tipoff, Williams wanted them up no later than 8:30 for a 9:30 pregame meal. If they were going to play three games in three days, they were going to need their rest.

The victory over Clemson had been Williams's 143d at Maryland — one more than his coach Bud Millikan — and the 350th of his college coaching career. Both milestones were significant to him. They also reminded him that in ten previous ACC tournaments — three as a player, seven as a coach — he had never been to the final. He wanted to end that string and play for an ACC title. He also knew that if his team could somehow win the tournament, they could still end up as a number three seed in one of the NCAA regionals. Right now, most people were figuring Maryland as a four or five seed. In that slot, the

Terrapins might have to face the number one seed in the round of sixteen. As a number three, they could avoid a meeting with a top seed until the regional final. That was all way down the road, but it crossed Williams's mind as Maryland's bus pulled into the Coliseum just before 11:30 in the morning.

Semifinal day at the ACC tournament always feels markedly different than Friday. More than half the teams have gone home. So have some of the out-of-town fans. The festival has now become more serious. Everyone still around has a game under their belts and can reasonably think about winning the championship. Williams was keyed up, expectant. He thought his team had cleared a major hurdle the previous day, that it had turned things back around by beating a tough, rested team. If they kept themselves together today, they should play for the championship.

Herb Sendek's only real concern was fatigue. The victory over Duke had been exhilarating for several reasons. He hadn't forgotten the pain Krzyzewski and Duke had inflicted in 1992 when Christian Laettner had hit the shot to beat Kentucky in the East Regional final. He had always admired Krzyzewski and, coaching against him for a year, was even more convinced now that he was a great coach. "He has a way of getting the most out of his personnel without doing anything too complex," he said. "He did a great job with this team. That's what made beating them so satisfying."

During the first two days, Justin Gainey had played forty minutes and forty minutes, C. C. Harrison forty and thirty-nine, Jeremy Hyatt thirty-five and forty. Given Maryland's frenetic up-tempo style, Sendek worried about his team's ability to go another forty minutes full bore. He didn't even want to think about what a win in this game would do for this team or for his program. "Day-tight compartments," he kept telling himself and his staff. "Get through today, then worry about tomorrow."

The second matchup of the day, Wake Forest and North Carolina, was entirely different. With Duke's loss, both teams now had to feel that winning the ACC tournament would clinch a number one seed. Duke had gone in with the inside track for that seed, but had almost certainly knocked itself down to a number two by losing to State. The ACC was going to get a one seed and the Wake-Carolina winner was likely to be it.

Carolina was the hot team — it had now won ten straight dating back to January 29 in Cameron. Wake felt better after the FSU victory and it was fairly clear that Tim Duncan wanted his ACC career to end with a third straight tournament title.

Gary Williams's pregame message to his team was direct: we're the better team, let's make sure State knows it right away. He told them they had to be prepared for a very physical game, and that officials tended to feel a certain sympathy toward teams that were giving away size. "I know," he said, "I benefited from it when I was at American."

His fourth key was "Respect, but . . .

"The point being, fellas, that we respect this team — just ask Duke — but we kicked their butt twice this year so let's not get carried away thinking they're better than we are. They're not. *You* are the team that should be playing tomorrow for the championship."

The only problem was, no one had yet told State that it was supposed to be long gone from Greensboro by now. As Sam Croft had said, you don't worry about being tired in March, you go on adrenaline. The Wolfpack was all adrenaline and confidence now. Falling behind wasn't a problem. They were used to that. They knew they were hard to guard in their spread offense and that teams couldn't believe it when they got to the last ten minutes and the game wasn't over yet.

The first eighteen minutes were played to a 20–20 tie, neither team able to get any kind of run going. Then Rodney Elliott hit a three for Maryland and Ekezie hit a pair of late free throws and the Terrapins had a 25–20 halftime lead. Stay patient, Williams kept preaching at halftime. He was concerned about Laron Profit and Stokes. Neither had made a basket in the first half (zero-for-one apiece) and both had three turnovers. When he caught Profit staring into space while he was talking, he went semi-ballistic.

"Jesus Christ, Laron, what is it with you?" he yelled. "I look at you right now, the look on your face, your body language, and I have zero confidence in you. Zero. I can just feel another lousy half coming on. Hey, fellas, come on, remember what we're playing for here! We have to go out and keep working, just like you did in the first half. It's not easy, I know, but goddamn it, it's not supposed to be easy!"

It only got harder in the second half. Profit woke up and started the half by dunking off a pretty pass from Booth. Then State began another of its now-patented second half clinics. It ran off nine straight points to take a 29–27 lead and extended the binge to 18–4. That put the 'Pack up 38–31. And, as had been the case the first two days, once in the lead, State never looked back. Maryland kept grinding, cutting the margin to three and four on several occasions. But every single time State came up with a basket. Harrison was dynamite once more with 24 points and Gainey, playing all forty minutes again, played a near-perfect floor game and outplayed Stokes at both ends of the floor.

One play symbolized the entire afternoon for Maryland. Trailing 55–49 with a little more than two minutes left, Williams didn't want to let State run the clock down. Ishua Benjamin had fouled out and Sendek had been forced to bring in little-used sophomore center Luke Buffum. Noting that Buffum was three for nine from the foul line all season, Williams ordered his team to foul Buffum immediately. They did. Buffum promptly stepped to the line and swished both free throws.

"That's when I knew it was their day," Williams said.

The last twist of the knife came a minute later when Profit didn't hear him screaming to foul Gainey and allowed him to dribble fifteen extra seconds off the clock before feeding Hyatt, who drilled a jumper. Final score: 65–58.

"Three lambs down and one more to go," Hyatt screamed in the hallway as he ran past the Maryland players. "Who's next? Who's the next lamb?"

Williams was more sad than angry. He was upset with himself because he believed he had failed to get his players excited about playing the game. "They would have been excited if it was Duke," he said. "But that's easy. This was hard and none of us dealt with it."

He was standing in the hallway just outside the locker room trying to decide what to say to his team. His three assistants, Billy Hahn, Dave Dickerson, and Jimmy Patsos, leaned against the wall. They all wore the same shocked look that the Duke coaches had worn twenty-four hours earlier.

"I should've played Rudy, that's what I should've done," Williams finally said, referring to senior walk-on Matt Raydo, who had been dubbed "Rudy" three years earlier in honor of the movie about the Notre

Dame football player wannabe. "Maybe Rudy would've gotten them excited."

"Gotta give State credit," Patsos said. "They played well."

"Yeah, well, screw that," Williams said. "That's still no excuse for losing. I mean, how bad were Laron and Terrell? They got their asses kicked all day long."

This was not Williams's in-game railing. This was genuine confusion over a baffling performance. Stokes had scored two points and had five turnovers against a freshman point guard playing his third game in less than forty-eight hours. Profit had shot the ball better in the second half after Williams's halftime explosion, but had clearly not been into the game mentally or emotionally.

Williams finally walked into the locker room. "The only thing I can say is I don't understand what just happened. I don't understand how we could kick away an opportunity like this. None of you have ever played on Sunday in this tournament. I've never been there on Sunday in this tournament. And we just let a golden opportunity to be there slip right through our fingers."

He walked around the locker room in a circle as if thinking about what to say next. Then he decided to say nothing. He picked up a Pepsi and a stat sheet and walked out the door to meet the media.

Wake Forest and North Carolina were already on the court by then and the Coliseum was full of sound. A lot of Wake and Carolina scalpers had picked up tickets overnight and it seemed as if 75 percent of the seats now belonged to their fans.

Both teams were flying. Duncan was again running amok, virtually unstoppable inside, and Carolina was hitting from everywhere. Every time Duncan made a move in the low post Dean Smith was up screaming: Foul! Walking! Double-dribble! Three-seconds! If his players couldn't stop Duncan, Smith figured, maybe he could. This was Smith at his most competitive. When Duncan was finally called for a charge — after scoring 13 of Wake's first 19 points, including a three and a spectacular flying dunk — Smith threw his arms into the air as if to say, "Hallelujah, my prayers have finally been answered."

That call didn't stop Smith. He kept screaming for the officials to clamp down on Duncan. Their response was to call a technical on Ademola Okulaja for swinging an elbow at Duncan. "What'd he do?" Smith demanded.

"He threw an elbow at a player's face," Karl Hess answered.

"OK," Smith said and then, ever consistent, he took Okulaja out of the game as he always did when a player received a technical. Two minutes later, Makhtar Ndiaye picked up a technical for throwing another elbow and out he came, although Smith kept arguing the call with Duke Edsall — even though it was Dick Paparo who had made it. Smith wasn't going to mess with the quickest tech in the West.

They got to halftime, jawing and shoving all the way, tied at 35. The building was electric and so was the game. The players even did a little yapping at one another in the hallway en route to the locker room. Odom was happy with the way his team had played. It was the most competitive he had seen his players in a month. The tension in the game was still evident when the two teams walked back to the floor. Odom and Smith were no more than an arm's length apart. Neither looked at the other or even made the pretense of small talk. Smith sipped a Coke — smuggled in by his managers because the ACC had a contract to supply only Pepsi inside the building — while Odom stared at the stats.

One team was able to maintain the breakneck pace in the second half: Carolina. Duncan kept his team in the hunt for the first ten minutes, hitting every shot imaginable and some that weren't. When he finally got some outside help — a Rutland three with 10:42 left — it was a two-point game, 53–51, Carolina. But Wake couldn't keep it up. The Tar Heels pulled away slowly but surely as Duncan wore down and Wake's perimeter shots refused to go down. When Ed Cota hit a three that was nothing more than a throw with the shot clock at zero to put the Tar Heels up 71–59 with 4:26 left, it was over. It ended with Serge Zwikker hitting the first three of his career and running off the court screaming. The final was 86–73.

Even Smith was impressed. "We played awfully well," he said, shaking his head as he walked to the locker room. "I didn't know we could play that well."

Neither did Odom. He knew Carolina had improved but he hadn't expected to lose a game in which Duncan scored 33 points and shot 14 for 21 from the field. The problem — again — was the lack of help. The rest of the team was 12 for 36.

"I swear," Odom said afterward, "our perimeter guys are like gunfighters who lost a fight somewhere and can't find their confidence again. The numbers backed him up: Peral zero for five; Braswell one for five; Goolsby one for six; Rutland five for 14.

"The effort was great, guys," Odom said, crouching in front of his seated players so he could make direct eye contact with them. "I'm proud of that. Very proud. Maybe we'll see these guys again down the road. They're good enough to go a long way. So are you. Remember that."

At that point, everyone in the room needed reminding.

It was halftime of the second game by the time the Maryland players boarded the bus to go back to their hotel. Everyone was tired and discouraged, no one more than Williams. He sat silently in the front seat of the bus and said nothing during the fifteen-minute ride. When the bus pulled up, he walked into the hotel lobby and found a number of Maryland alumni standing around. They hadn't stayed for the second game either.

One of them, in a red jacket, walked up before Williams could escape to an elevator. The last thing in the world he wanted to hear right now were encouraging words from his fans — or from anyone else for that matter. What he got was anything but encouraging.

"Hey, Gary," the man said, "what in the world were Stokes and Profit doing down at the Four Seasons last night?"

Williams was baffled by the comment. He had been with his players until 10:30 and they had been bed-checked by the assistants. "What are you talking about?" he answered. "We were all out here."

"Not at 12:15 in the morning you weren't," the man answered. "I saw Terrell and Laron down there a little bit after midnight. A bunch of us did."

For a minute, Williams thought he might get sick. On the night before an ACC semifinal game — an afternoon ACC semifinal — two of his starters had sneaked out after curfew to hang out in a hotel lobby with a bunch of alumni and students? Impossible. They had to care more than that.

He escaped from the red coat, went to his room, and called his assistants. He didn't want to confront the two players directly at that moment because he was so angry he didn't know what he would do or say if they confirmed they had been out. "Find out what happened," he told the assistants. A little while later, they reported back: Stokes and Profit had sneaked out of the hotel and had taken a cab to the Holiday Inn Four Seasons. They said they had been back by about 12:30.

Williams couldn't believe what he was hearing. He didn't want to believe it. Again, he decided to wait before acting. Maybe by the time they got home later that night, he would be calm enough to talk to the two players. Not now. Absolutely not now.

This was the most unlikely ACC final in history. No eighth seed had ever won the tournament or been in the final. The lowest seeded team ever to make the final had been Virginia, a number seven seed in 1977. The lowest seed to win the event was a number six. That had happened three times: Virginia in 1976, NC State in 1987, and Georgia Tech in 1993. Interestingly, each number six had beaten North Carolina in the championship game. The only difference was those Carolina teams had been top-seeded. This one was a number three.

State was now dreaming the impossible dream. In seventy-two hours it had gone from one win away from the NIT to one win away from the NCAAs. A victory would give the Wolfpack the ACC's automatic berth. No one was more frightened at the prospect of a State victory than Jeff Jones. "I figured if they won, the committee would just give them our spot," he said. "Never in my life have I rooted harder for North Carolina to win a basketball game."

As with Georgia Tech, as with Duke, as with Maryland, State made it difficult. Carolina led almost the entire game, but State simply would not go away. The Tar Heels led by 10 midway in the first half; State cut it to six at halftime. State had trailed Tech by one, Duke by six, and Maryland by five at intermission. Justin Gainey still hadn't come out of a game in four days. C. C. Harrison had been out for one minute. They had to be exhausted. But they also knew they were only twenty minutes away from pulling off one of college basketball's all-time miracles: four victories in less than seventy-two hours in the sport's most intense conference tournament.

Carolina wasn't going to let it happen. When State made its daily second-half run the Tar Heels did something no one else had done: they refused to let the Wolfpack get its nose in front. After a Gainey jumper cut the lead to 36–34, with the Coliseum going wild in anticipation of one last State miracle, Shammond Williams (the tournament MVP) buried a three. Then he buried another. And another. Suddenly, it was 45–34.

Then a Gainey three with 6:48 left brought State back to within 47–45. But Carolina was steel. Surprised as they were by State's resilience, the Tar Heels pounded the ball inside against State's exhausted, smaller players and there was nothing they could do but foul. Carolina kept making free throws (11 for 14 down the stretch) and time finally ran out on the Wolfpack. Down 58–54 with under a minute to go, they couldn't come up with one last defensive spurt. The Tar Heels scored their last 10 points at the line, six in the last minute, and won, 64–54.

While Carolina celebrated, the entire arena stood to applaud the Wolfpack for what it had done. Four games in seventy hours with four starters playing all forty minutes in the finale. They had never given up, and even though they hadn't won, they had given their fans something to feel good about again. It had been a long time since State people had felt that way.

In the locker room, there were hugs and tears; tears of pride and joy and disappointment. They would be the first ACC finalists since 1978 not to go to the NCAAs. But they knew there was absolutely no shame in what they had accomplished.

For Carolina, it was a remarkable turnaround, from 0–3 and 3–5 to 11 straight ACC victories that gave Dean Smith his thirteenth ACC tournament title and wrapped up a number one seed in the East for his team.

The win over State did one other thing. It left Smith with 875 victories — one shy of Adolph Rupp's all-time record of 876. Now, Smith would go for the record on the biggest stage there was in college basketball, the NCAA tournament.

He could not have been happier with the way his team was playing. But he could not have been unhappier with the scenario that superb play had created.

"I still haven't won a single game," he protested for at least the 875th time in his career. "Players win games, not coaches."

Smith was speaking into a very loud microphone. No one heard a word he said.

~ 26

The Dance

EACH YEAR, the second Sunday in March is college basketball's best day. For sixty-four teams, almost five months of hard work and long hours comes to fruition. For thirty-two more, there is a consolation prize and the knowledge that your season — or career — can be extended another three weeks. For everyone else, there is an understanding that something was missing from the season and, sadly, it is time to pack the uniforms away until next fall.

Most of all, it is a day of anticipation. Around the country, several conference championship games are being played. But most hearts and minds are focused on what will happen shortly after 6:30 P.M. eastern time when the NCAA tournament field will be announced. Everyone speculates. Which bubble teams are in? Who will the four number one seeds be? How many bids will the power leagues get? Will any teams from smaller conferences who won their regular season championship but failed to win the automatic bid through the conference tournament get a reprieve?

Around the country, teams gather in their locker rooms or meeting rooms to turn on CBS and watch the pairings go up, region by region, on their TV screens. In 1982, when CBS outbid NBC for the rights to the NCAA tournament, Len DeLuca, one of their programming executives, came up with the idea of announcing the pairings on TV. That simple idea has grown into a national tradition. The pairings show has become such a big deal that CBS has pushed it back from late afternoon until 6:30, making it the lead-in to *60 Minutes*. Even as the pairings are being announced, ESPN is airing an hourlong special analyzing the pairings.

For the nine ACC teams, there were no major surprises on Selection Sunday. Only Georgia Tech was going nowhere. Both NC State and Florida State were invited to the NIT. The other six teams — with Virginia huffing and puffing with jangled nerves right until the end — all had their dance cards punched.

North Carolina, which now had the best record among league teams (24–6) and a 12-game winning streak, was the top seed in the East. It would open the tournament in Winston-Salem, one of the East's two subregional sites, against sixteenth-seeded Fairfield, one of those teams that had miraculously gotten into the field by winning its conference tournament after finishing eighth in the regular season. Fairfield's record was 11–18. Carolina's potential second round game was the one that intrigued most people: the winner of Colorado-Indiana. That set up the tantalizing prospect of Dean Smith trying to break Adolph Rupp's record in a game against Bob Knight, who had just won his seven hundredth game and, being ten years younger than Smith, was positioned to someday break Smith's record if he didn't go completely off the deep end — of which there was at least a fifty-fifty possibility.

There had been some talk in Greensboro that both Duke and Wake Forest would be number two seeds. That didn't happen. Duke got a number two, going to the Southeast subregional in Charlotte to play Murray State on Friday in the first round. Wake Forest was shipped west as the three seed. It would also open on Friday against St. Mary's of California, a team that had a seven-foot-three, 345-pound center named Brad Millard. Dave Odom had no idea who Brad Millard was until Tim Duncan, seeing St. Mary's name go up on the TV screen said, "Hey, Big Continent!" That was Millard's nickname, a takeoff on "Big Country," the nickname that Oklahoma State's Bryant Reeves, a seven-foot, three-hundred-pound kid from a small country town, had acquired several years earlier.

Neither Duke nor Wake would have an easy road to Indianapolis. The Blue Devils were in the same region as Kansas, the number one seed in the tournament with a 30–1 record. That meant the committee had decided that Duke was the weakest of the four number two seeds. Wake was in the same region with its old nemesis Kentucky, the top seed in the West, and faced a possible round of sixteen game against Utah, the two seed. That was the good news — possibly facing a team they had beaten. Of course that New Year's Eve game felt like it had been played on the last day of 1896 rather than 1996 at this stage of the season.

Clemson was the fifth seed in the Midwest, opening against Herb Sendek's old school, Miami of Ohio, on Friday in the Kansas City subregional. Virginia had to hold its breath until the final bracket — the West — went up. Then, the Cavaliers popped onto the screen as the ninth seed, opening against number eight Iowa, the winner to play top-seeded Kentucky in the second round. Jeff Jones and his staff let out huge sighs of relief when they saw their name on the screen. But even as the players celebrated, Jones couldn't help but note the location of their subregional: Salt Lake City. Virginia had gone there in 1987 and lost in the first round to Wyoming and had returned in 1991 and lost a first round game to Brigham Young. "It hasn't exactly been a lucky place for us," he said. He immediately told Norwood Teague, his director of basketball operations, to make plans to get the team out there as early as possible to adjust to the altitude. The game was Thursday night. The Cavaliers would fly to Salt Lake on Tuesday.

The most surprised — and disappointed — ACC coach was Gary Williams. He had already dealt with the Profit-Stokes situation, confronting the two players at Cole on Saturday night and telling them he would decide how to discipline them by the time they practiced on Monday. He had told the other players the same thing just before the pairings were announced. When Maryland's name went on the board as a number five seed in the Southeast, that seemed to make sense. The name of the first round opponent, the twelve seed in the region, did not: the College of Charleston.

"Are you kidding me?" Williams thought when he saw the pairing go up.

The College of Charleston was an upstart program, pieced together by a very bright coach named John Kresse. It had only been in Division I for eight years, but Kresse had put together a little powerhouse. In 1994, Charleston had attracted national attention when it had gone into Atlanta and upset Georgia Tech several days after Tech had beaten then-top-ranked Duke.

That game had made scheduling very difficult for Kresse. No one wanted to play a team with no name and good players. Too much to lose; almost nothing to gain. Kresse had managed to get his team invited to the Great Alaska Shootout at the start of the season and they had beaten both Arizona State and Stanford — which was a six seed out West — before losing to Kentucky. Charleston was 28–2, it had won 22 straight games, and it was ranked 16th in the AP poll — six spots ahead of Maryland. But because it played in a weak league (the Trans-America) and because it had trouble getting games against quality opponents, it had a low power rating — since those ratings were largely based on who you played. ACC teams all had high power ratings because they played each other all the time.

The NCAA Tournament Committee had made the power ratings a major part of its decision making for about fifteen years in order to discourage power schools from piling up wins by playing weak teams. That was a good policy. The problem was, the power ratings worked against smaller schools like Charleston. The other problem was that the nine-man committee, busy with its computer printouts, apparently didn't watch basketball games. Because if it did, there was no way it could have reached the conclusion that Charleston was no better than the forty-fifth best team in field (the four number twelve seeds are the number forty-five, -six, -seven, and -eight teams).

"Sometimes a team that is beating bad teams is a good team," Williams said. "When we watched them on tape, it was obvious they were a good team. All seniors, all experienced, all trying to prove something. Not exactly an ideal first round matchup."

Essentially, it was an unfair first round matchup — for both teams. Charleston deserved a higher seed and Maryland deserved to play a real number twelve seed, not a team that should have been no worse than a sixth seed. The winner of the game would play Arizona or South Alabama in the second round of the Memphis subregional.

Williams had already decided that Stokes and Profit would not start in the first round game. Now, his team faced a difficult opening game at a time when it was coming off a disappointing loss and would have to deal with the Stokes-Profit situation all week. "Not exactly ideal," Williams said again.

Ideal that week was being North Carolina. Of course the Tar Heels had earned the right to be exactly where they were. If Wake Forest had been the number one seed in the East, it would have had to play in the Pittsburgh subregional, since teams can't play on their home court. But Carolina could play in Winston-Salem in front of a partisan crowd and Duke could play in Charlotte with a lot of its fans in the stands.

Of course there are about ten times more Carolina fans in North Carolina than there are Duke fans, so they jumped all over the 14,407 tickets. Many had bought way in advance in the hope that the Tar Heels would be in Winston-Salem, figuring they would either sell the tickets or go to watch eight other teams play if their heroes weren't there. But they were. And the entire week was rapidly evolving into a celebration of Dean Smith and Carolina basketball in anticipation of Rupp's record falling on Saturday.

That, of course, was the last thing Smith wanted to talk about. He didn't want his players talking or thinking about it either. Naturally, it was on everyone's mind. Fairfield was considered a virtual walkover. Everyone was anticipating that Indiana, even though it had limped into the tournament after a mediocre season in the Big Ten, would beat Colorado, setting up the game CBS had scheduled to open the second round on national TV early Saturday afternoon.

Smith's discomfort with all the hoopla surrounding his impending record had to do with three things: his concern that the players would get caught up in it and not be focused on the task at hand, his antipathy for the spotlight in any and all situations, and his discomfort with being connected through history with Rupp.

Smith had known Rupp, first meeting him in 1959 when Rupp accepted an invitation from Frank McGuire to speak at Carolina's post-season basketball banquet. Smith was Rupp's escort for the day. Later, Smith-coached Carolina teams faced Rupp-coached Kentucky teams seven times. The Tar Heels won five of seven, including the game in 1962 when Smith first unveiled his four corners delay offense, which would become one of the signatures of his coaching style.

The media had boiled the entire Smith-Rupp story down to an issue of race. Smith, the ardent civil rights activist against Rupp, whose all-white Kentucky team had lost the famous 1966 NCAA final to all-black Texas Western. It had been widely reported for years that Rupp asked local newspaper editors to put asterisks next to the names of black players so he would know who not to recruit. Only in 1969, kicking and screaming, did Rupp finally recruit a black player.

Rupp's defenders insisted that much of that was unfair. They liked to say that Rupp was merely a "product of his upbringing." Rupp's defenders also point out that Kentucky reached that famous final in 1966 by beating an all-white Duke team in the semifinals. That was true. In fact, only one ACC team — Maryland — was integrated that season. But Duke had two black players on its freshman team (freshmen couldn't play on the varsity in those days) and Smith had already recruited one player as a walk-on two years earlier and was recruiting Charles Scott that same year.

What most people missed was the fact that Smith's feelings about Rupp went beyond the issues of civil rights. Kentucky basketball has long been the symbol of the excess and obsession that Smith has tried not to be sucked into as the coach of a powerhouse program. Kentucky's basketball history is as much about NCAA investigations and allegations of payoffs and being shut down for an entire season for point shaving as it is about winning championships. Smith never claimed his program was perfect, and the DeanDome itself is a tribute to excess, but he has always tried to emphasize things other than winning and making money. One thing that can certainly be said about him is that he could easily have cashed in on his name far more than he has.

The inevitable mingling of Rupp/Kentucky and Smith/North Carolina as the record loomed did not thrill Smith. That was never more evident than in the moments after Carolina's shockingly difficult 82–74 victory over Fairfield in round one of the NCAA tournament. The kids from Fairfield played the game of their lives, understanding that this was a night they would always remember. They were almost perfect for the first twenty minutes, leading 35–28 at halftime. Even after the Tar Heels caught them early in the second half, they refused to go away. With a little more than seven minutes left, a three pointer by John Tice tied the game at 59. Carolina inched ahead again. Fairfield still hung in, creeping to within 72–69 with 3:33 left. By this time, all the Carolina people in the building were getting a little jumpy. It was still only 74–69 with a little more than a minute to play when Shannon Bowman missed a three for the Stags and Carolina was finally able to take command, making its last six free throws for the eight-point margin.

"I thought we played well," Smith said later. "Fairfield was just sensational."

The crowd stood to applaud Fairfield for the effort and Smith for tying the record. Smith went down the line of Fairfield players, congratulating them while they congratulated him. Even the Fairfield mascot, a kid dressed up as a Stag, got in line to congratulate Smith, grabbing the surprised coach with both paws as he went by.

"I don't often shake hands with the mascot," he said.

Then Smith went back to the locker room where his SID, Steve Kirschner, told him CBS wanted to interview him. "What's this for?" Smith asked suspiciously.

"Just the routine postgame interview, Coach," Kirschner answered, telling the truth.

Reluctantly, Smith went back onto the court, where Colorado and Indiana had started warming up. Andrea Joyce was doing the interview for CBS. Her first question — naturally — was about Rupp and the record.

"Coach, you've admired Adolph Rupp for so many years," she said. "What does it mean to you to tie this record?"

It was on the word "admired," that Smith visibly flinched. If Joyce had stuck a knife into his ribs he probably would not have reacted any more obviously. Then he gathered himself to answer the question:

"Well, I've admired a lot of coaches. I admired Henry Iba and my old coach Phog Allen and Bob Spear. [Pause.] I admire Bob Knight. [Pause, groping.] I admire all coaches who do things the right way."

Not a single mention of Adolph Rupp. Absolutely no implication that Rupp was one of those coaches he admired who did things the right way. Smith is too honest to look into a camera and say he admired someone he didn't admire. So he danced around the question as best he could. If he had been down thirty with a minute to go, he could not have looked more uncomfortable.

Indiana and Bob Knight did not do their part to make the CBS dream come true. The Hoosiers played as if their bus was double-parked against Colorado, losing convincingly in a game the Buffaloes led from the first minute until the last. On the bench, Knight looked like a man who had decided that the sooner this season was over, the better. He didn't even bother to harangue his players or call time-outs to try to get control of the game. Clearly, he had no interest in being around to see Smith crowned king of coaching victories.

He was the exception, not the rule. By the time Carolina-Colorado tipped off on Saturday, The Lawrence Joel Coliseum looked like a Carolina alumni gathering. Specifically, a gathering of those alumni who played basketball for Dean Smith. They came from everywhere, some flying through the night to be there. "I don't know where they all got tickets," Smith said later. "[LA Lakers general manager] Mitch Kupchak told me he was flying in on a red-eye and I told him that was ridiculous. But he said he wanted to come."

They all wanted to come, and even though security at most NCAA tournament games is only slightly tighter than at the White House, they all made it back to the locker room and the hallway outside the locker room after the game. Terry Holland, chairman of the basketball committee, Smith's longtime rival, had quietly left word with the security people than anyone who could prove he had played for Smith was to be allowed through.

For twenty-four minutes, Colorado tried to spoil the party. The Buffs led 31–30 at halftime and it was still 38–37 four minutes into the second half. Then the Tar Heels decided they had been through enough suspense in the Fairfield game. Taking complete control of the boards (52–31 margin for the game) they manhandled Colorado over the next nine minutes. When the carnage had cleared, the run was 30–8, the score was 68–45, and the last seven minutes were just a countdown to the record.

For all his stubbornness about not wanting to focus on the record or

Rupp, Smith was stunned when he saw all the ex-players in the hallways and locker room. The veneer disappeared. "I told them all later that I wished they had come back during the off-season so we could go play golf or something," he said.

They were all there in March, not June, because they wanted him to know how special he was to them. Smith always talks about how special his players are to him. This was their chance to turn it around. Flying in to play a buck nassau would not have been the same. Bill Guthridge, who had been by Smith's side for thirty of the thirty-six years, watched the players come and go inside the locker room and said quietly, "He'd never admit it, but having them here means the world to Dean."

That was evident in the press conference. Smith talked emotionally about all the men who had coached with him at North Carolina — naming them all of course — and then threatened to go down the list of players and name all of *them*. No one in the room doubted his ability to do that. More than fifty years earlier, he had thought it was neat that his dad's old players would come by the house when they were in Emporia to see their old coach. No doubt his dad would have thought the scene in Winston-Salem that day was neat too. Being the wise man that he was Alfred Smith would no doubt have pointed out to his son that what mattered was not the number of games he had won, but the number of lives he had so clearly touched.

It was a historic day, a warm day outside the Coliseum and inside too. Most important it was a day focused on Dean Smith, not Adolph Rupp. And on the players. From Jim Hudock, the captain in 1961, to Ed Cota, the star freshman in 1997. "They're the ones who won," Smith said. "The guys in the uniforms are the ones who got *this* Carolina team to the round of sixteen. That's what I'm happiest about."

This win. The players. For the 877th time. And counting.

Two ACC teams didn't make it out of the first round. Neither was a huge surprise, except perhaps to the teams' coaches.

Virginia again fell victim to the dreaded Salt Lake Disease, starting out flat against Iowa and never getting better. The Cavaliers never led in the game and the last tie was 6–6. The Hawkeyes were up 37–28 at the half, and after Jones blistered his players in the locker room for lack of effort, they responded by giving up the first nine points of the second half. That was for all intents and purposes the end of Virginia's season. The margin never got below 13 after that and it grew to as much as 22. The final was 73–60 and it was apparent that Iowa could pretty much have named the score.

Jones was angry and confused by what he had seen. "What I don't understand," he told his players, "is how you can work so hard to get someplace, then get there and not show up at all. I just don't understand it." He was so upset with Norman Nolan and Colin Ducharme, who had combined for a total of four rebounds and been killed by Iowa's big men inside, the he could barely look them in the eye. Nolan, in particular, who had made such strides, was a mystery.

Gary Williams was at least as shocked after Maryland was beaten, 75–66, by the College of Charleston. Williams hadn't expected an easy game, especially with Profit and Stokes starting the game on the bench. But he had expected to win. The team was rested and ready — or so he thought. Williams tried to get the players re-revved by pointing out to them how many people were picking Charleston to win the game. If he had to play a team as strong as Charleston, why not use that fact to cast his team as the underdog again? That had been the role that had worked best for them early in the season.

"They weren't buying, though," Williams said later. "Whatever I said, whatever anyone said, we were from the ACC, they were from the TAC. We were supposed to win."

The Terrapins started slowly and were down 11–4 six minutes in when Profit and Stokes came into the game. Williams had never formally told them they were benched, he had simply put Rodney Elliott and Matt Kovarik with the first team at practice on Monday. Neither player knew when he would get into the game, although Williams had made it plain that they would play. He was in a delicate position: the players had to be punished, he knew that and the other players knew that. But he didn't want to jeopardize the whole team's chances because of Profit and Stokes's mistake.

Profit came in hot, making five of eight shots — four of them threes — in the first half. He hit two deep threes in the final minute of the half to tie the game at 33. Williams felt comfortable with the game at that juncture. "We haven't even played well yet and we're tied," he told them during intermission. "If we turn up the defense a little more in the second half, we'll be fine. We *are* the better team, so let's go out and prove it."

They couldn't. Profit's shot disappeared (one of seven) and no one could pick up the slack. Charleston, solid and experienced, kept getting the ball inside and the Terrapins kept sending them to the foul line. For the game, the Hawks shot 33 free throws — making 23 — to Maryland's eight of 12. That was the difference. "That and the fact that we couldn't shoot," Williams said. "Shots we had made most of the year didn't go in."

Maryland's last lead of the season was 38–37, four minutes into the second half. A 12–2 Charleston run put them in a hole they never came close to climbing out from. Williams was devastated. A year earlier, when his team had lost in the first round to Santa Clara, he had not been surprised or even that upset. He might even have been a little relieved. Not this time. This was a team that had so much hope, had worked so hard to get to 17–2 and fifth in the country. Then, from the day the students returned to campus until the end of the season, the Terrapins had gone 4–9.

Clearly, ACC teams figured Maryland out the second time around. Carolina was better in February than January; so was Duke. But the Terrapins weren't as good. Jasikevicius lost his confidence. Stokes, Profit, and Ekezie went up and down. Only Keith Booth was solid almost every night. But he was never the kind of one-on-one scorer who could carry a team when everyone else was struggling.

Williams needed a couple of minutes to gather himself before he spoke to the team. This wasn't the ending he had wanted for this group, for Booth in particular. "There's a lesson in this last month, fellas, and it goes beyond basketball," he said. "We all set goals in life and that's good. But when you reach a goal, that doesn't mean you stop. You have to want to keep going, reach higher, get to another goal. And then another. You guys wanted to prove people wrong when they picked you eighth in the league. You did that. You proved you were a good team.

"But then you stopped. You got to your goal and stopped. You can't do that. If you're good enough to reach a goal, then there's still someplace else to go. You don't just stop. You keep trying to be better. We got satisfied too early. We won our twentieth game in mid-February and then we won once more."

He talked about the two seniors: Booth, the star, and Raydo, the nonstar. What they had in common, he said, was that they were both willing to give everything they had to make the team better. He thanked them.

"You're good kids," he said finally. "You won twenty-one games and you made it back to the NCAA tournament for a fourth straight year. You have a lot to be proud of. I really enjoyed coaching you this season." He paused. "I just wish I could have coached you for a little bit longer."

Three ACC teams in addition to North Carolina survived the first round. Wake Forest found that Big Continent was a very large obstacle, but gradually figured a way around him, pulling away from St. Mary's early in the second half to win, 71–56. Dave Odom was happy with the way the Deacons had played, but nervous about a second round game against Stanford. The Cardinal had a truly great player in five-ten guard Brevin Knight and a bevy of big men who could be expected to put their bodies on Tim Duncan and use up all their fouls trying to control him.

Clemson also played very solidly, beating Miami in what was the best all-round performance the Tigers had produced in several weeks. That sent them into a second round game against Tulsa. Duke was in control against Murray State most of the way, leading by 10 with a little more than five minutes left, but managed to play carelessly enough in the endgame to make the last seconds nerve-racking before surviving, 71–68.

Both Mike Krzyzewski and Rick Barnes had spent the week between their abrupt ACC tournament endings and the start of the NCAA tournament trying to get their teams back to where they had been earlier in the season. Since the "punch in the face" hadn't worked for Krzyzewski the previous week, he went in the opposite direction. One day the players walked in for practice and found rap music blaring from the loudspeakers in Cameron. On another day, Krzyzewski walked them out to the football stadium to sit and relax in the sun for a while so they could appreciate how much fun it was to be still playing at this time of year. He wanted them to relax, to get back their enthusiasm, to understand the challenge of the NCAA tournament so they would play the way they had when they felt challenged by the ACC.

They were tight against Murray State, but that didn't shock him. Only the three seniors — Jeff Capel, Carmen Wallace, and Greg Newton — had ever won an NCAA tournament game. That had come when they were freshmen and the 1994 team reached the championship game. Only Capel had gotten serious playing time that year. Therefore, it wasn't surprising that Capel was the one player who appeared comfortable throughout the game, scoring 25 points and making the shots Duke needed to win the game.

Krzyzewski was pleased to get through the Murray State game, but worried about playing Providence in the second round. The Friars had been a Jekyll and Hyde team all season. They had looked very good in a surprisingly easy first round win over Marquette. Krzyzewski was concerned about that, but more concerned about his own team. Trajan Langdon was clearly exhausted. His knee had bothered him more and more as the season went on and the team became more dependent on his shooting. He had shot two for eight against Murray State and appeared to be dragging his knee every time he tried to make a hard cut.

Krzyzewski had tried one last time with Greg Newton before the Murray State game. He had hoped against hope that Newton would, at some point, play so well in practice that he had to be given a lot of minutes again. But he never had. His attitude had worsened as the season went on. Some things, Krzyzewski knew, were out of his control. His back was still a problem and he had lost twenty-five pounds since the start of the season because he simply couldn't keep weight on. His fiancée had left town with their infant son and he was unsure of what was to become of that relationship or his professional career.

In short, he was a mess. Krzyzewski tried to simplify things for him. "Newt," he said, "all I ask is that you come in, play hard, rebound, and screen. You don't have to score to help us at this stage. Rebound and screen."

During the afternoon walk-through before Murray State, Krzyzewski caught Newton getting lazy on his screens, bringing his arms up, instead of keeping them at his side. Anytime officials see a player with his arms up on a screen, they call a foul. Krzyzewski reminded Newton to keep his arms down. That night, he brought Newton into the game with 9:38 left in the first half. On Duke's first possession, Newton set a screen and brought his arms up. The whistle blew. Offensive foul. Illegal screen. It had taken Newton eight seconds to do the one thing Krzyzewski had reminded him a few hours earlier not to do.

That was it. Krzyzewski was done trying with Newton. When he came out, it was for good.

The final box score of Greg Newton's career had a DNP next to his name for "did not play." That fact would be the subject of endless speculation among Duke fans in the weeks that followed. Many of them were convinced that if Newton had played, Duke would not have been outrebounded 43–24 by Providence. Of course none of them had watched Newton practice or interact with his teammates. None of them had known about the screening lesson two days earlier. None of them understood that, at that stage, Taymon Domzalski, the six-ten sophomore who had missed most of the season because of a bad knee, was ahead of Newton in the rotation even though he wasn't in playing shape and could barely run up and down the court.

Providence did pound the Blue Devils inside. The Friars also shot brilliantly, especially in the second half (64.5 percent) and out-quicked Duke for most of the game. Their best player, Austin Croshere, scored 21 points in spite of foul trouble, but that didn't matter because Derrick Brown, whose inconsistency during the season mirrored his team's, was phenomenal with 33 points and 10 rebounds.

Once again, Langdon struggled, going four for 13. Roshown McLeod played well, but fouled out with nine minutes left. Mike Chappell couldn't find his shot and neither could Ricky Price. Only Capel — nine of 13, 26 points — was able to stay with the Friars from start to finish. Trailing most of the second half, the Blue Devils managed to tie the game at 74 on a Chris Carrawell layup with 5:33 left, but then Providence ripped off the next seven points and proceeded to score an amazing 24 points in the last 5:11, pulling away to win, 98–87. They were outstanding. Duke was out of gas. "When you're tired, you lose your quickness," Krzyzewski said. "They were quicker than us when it mattered. We didn't play that badly. They just played better."

It was a sad way to end what had been a remarkable season. No one in the world would have picked Duke to win the ACC regular season title in October, November, December, or January. Krzyzewski knew that many people would judge this team on the way it had performed in March, just as some of his Final Four teams had been judged that way. That's the way college basketball is nowadays.

But he didn't want them to feel as if they had failed. "You guys helped make me love coaching again," he told them. "I wasn't sure after last year if that could happen. I wasn't certain if I liked coaching. But I loved coaching you guys. You worked hard, you gave everything you had. It's OK to feel sad right now. But don't feel sad because we lost. Only one team in this thing isn't going to lose. Feel sad because the journey's over."

A few minutes later in the press conference, Wojciechowski and Capel each broke down, talking not about losing but about each other and how sad they were that they wouldn't be playing together again. Krzyzewski walked out of the building with a smile on his face. He felt good about the future. More important, he felt good about the present.

A few hours later, Dave Odom saw tears in his locker room. It was difficult, though, to feel comforted by them. These were tears of shock and disappointment. Disbelief. Anger.

The Demon Deacons had just lost to Stanford 66–61. They had been way behind, battled back, but were never able to catch up. Odom's worst fears had been realized. Brevin Knight was every bit as good as advertised and Stanford's big men were every bit as rough and tough as Odom had expected.

"We needed someone to get in there and restore law and order," he said later. "There were times when I thought the Stanford guys were trying to hurt Tim, not just push him around; hurt him. The referees should have done something about it, but we also should have had someone do it. We just didn't have anybody like that."

Several years earlier, Wake had had a player named Scooter Banks, a six-seven tough guy who was afraid of nothing. Odom could envision him laying out one of the Stanford players early in the game to send a message that trying to knock Duncan down would not be tolerated. This year there was no Scooter Banks. Odom got so frustrated late in the second half that he jumped off the bench after one play and screamed at the officials. "If Tim Duncan's last college game ends with him being carried off, I will hold all of you responsible! Do something!"

By then it was too late. Wake tried to rally. Duncan gamely hung in to the finish, but the Cardinal didn't back down and made the shots it had to in the final minutes. As soon as the locker room door was closed, Odom was confronted with an amazing sight. Since there were no chairs in front of the players' lockers, they had a choice, to sit in the lockers or on the floor. Everyone was on the floor, many of them with their faces down. Everyone in the room was sobbing. Why now? Odom couldn't help but think. Why couldn't I have found this kind of emotion inside them earlier? Second-guessing was pointless. They had never been the same team after the Justin Gainey steal from Tony Rutland in the NC State loss.

"Something was lost that day," Odom said. "Confidence, cockiness, call it what you want. We didn't have the same attitude after that game. I tried everything I could to get it back, to find what it was that we had in January and I couldn't. Because we had Tim, we were always competitive. He wouldn't allow us not to be competitive. But we didn't control games the way we had. We didn't slice people up the way we did. We weren't a bad team, but we weren't the team I had wanted us to become in March."

And so March ended much sooner than it was supposed to end. The Deacons had gone 4–4 after the NC State game, but more important, just 1–1 in the NCAA tournament. That left them five wins short of their goal.

Dry-eyed, Odom thanked all the seniors for what they had done for the program, for the ninety-seven victories, and for all the hard work. He thanked Duncan for coming back for his senior year and for everything he had done in his four years. Then he made them all stand up and stand around him in a tight circle as he often did after painful losses.

"We still have one more job to do this season," he said. "Seniors, you'll all come with me to the interview room. No complaining about the referees, I'll deal with that later. Give all credit to Stanford. We've been gracious with the media after wins and losses all year long. We'll do that one more time, even if it's a difficult thing to do."

It was a devastating defeat for the players and for their coach. They had started out with plans to make this a championship season. Odom had known all along that this team would be judged only by what it did in March. He had planned the entire season around playing at a peak in

March. It hadn't happened. Second-guessing, he knew, was human nature. It was also a waste of time.

And so, after a regular season filled with so many brilliant games and intense performances, only two ACC teams made it to the second week of the NCAAs: North Carolina and Clemson.

Rick Barnes had hit rock bottom after the Maryland loss in Greensboro. He felt his team had been flat and lifeless at a time of the season when there was no excuse for being either. Before he left the Greensboro Coliseum that day, he told his assistants that he wanted them to set up individual meetings with each player in his room over the course of the rest of the afternoon and evening. He wanted to talk one-on-one with each member of his team and see if he could figure out exactly what had gone wrong.

At 1 o'clock that morning, when the last meeting was over, he thought he had the answers. As he suspected, the crux of the problem was the team's offensive dependence on Greg Buckner and Terrell McIntyre. He had understood for several weeks that the offense had become predictable and that the Tigers had not been hard for teams to guard.

What he hadn't understood was the effect that had on his players. Buckner and McIntyre were both pressing, feeling as if they had to make every shot they took if their team was going to win. At least as important — maybe more important — the other players felt diminished. Every play call, or so it seemed, was for Buckner and McIntyre. They had lost some of their fire because they had felt as if they had become secondary to the team's success.

"It's easy to forget when you're in close game after close game that you have to keep everyone involved," Barnes said. "You get so wrapped up with *this* possession being critical. I had fallen into that trap and all I was doing was going to Boogie and Buck all over again. It wasn't their fault; it was mine."

Not only did the all–Boogie-Buck offense make them feel pressured and the others left out, it had apparently created some hard feelings inside the locker room. Nothing blatant, no one throwing punches, but a feeling that was in its own way more dangerous because it was insidious.

"We had lost our closeness," Barnes said. "We weren't the same as we had been. We weren't one anymore. We had become a bunch of individuals trying to find playing time, trying to get shots. We had scattered. That was my fault too."

Before the pairings show on Sunday, Barnes gathered the team and told them what he had discovered. He told them it was his fault, but they needed to forget what had happened and move forward. The offense would be different, he said. That didn't mean the two best players on the team weren't going to see the ball, but things would be more spread out. There would be more chances for guys on the bench to get minutes. Any hard feelings, he said, let's get them out now. "When we come to practice on Monday," he said, "I want it to be like October. I want us to get after it like we never have before."

They responded. Ten minutes into practice on Monday, Barnes knew they had been listening to him the day before. The intensity was back. More important, as Barnes put it, "the laugh was back. I realized it had been weeks since I had heard the guys laughing at each other. Now, I heard laughter again."

They practiced so hard during that week that Barnes had to back them off a couple of times. True to his word, in the Miami game, Barnes played ten players for at least several minutes. They won the game with McIntyre only taking seven shots and scoring 10 points. Buckner had 22, but Iker Iturbe had nine points and seven rebounds; Merl Code had 12 points and seven assists; Tony Christie came off the bench to score eight. Nine players scored. The Tigers controlled the game from start to finish and won 68–56.

Sunday against Tulsa was much closer and much more tense, but more of the same. Nine players played at least 13 minutes; eight of them scored. Buckner had an awful shooting day (one of nine) but did a superb defensive job on Tulsa star Shea Seals, holding him to four points. Tulsa led by seven early in the second half, but Clemson came back, took the lead, lost it with two minutes left when Tulsa got even at 55–55, then played near perfect basketball to win, 65–59. McIntyre hit the shot that put the Tigers ahead for good; Code hit a pair of free throws; then Buckner hit a pair to build a six-point lead. That was enough.

It was Clemson's first trip to the Sweet Sixteen since 1990. For Barnes, who had gone into the Miami game with an 0–4 record in NCAA play

(0–3 at Providence; 0–1 at Clemson) the weekend was a breakthrough. His team had played its best basketball at the time of year when it was most important. It had come together when it had to. Now, they would play Minnesota, the only team they had lost to during the 16–1 start. That game had been played in Puerto Rico in front of less than a thousand people. This one would be in San Antonio, in the Alamodome. The crowd, Barnes reckoned, would be just a little bit bigger this time around.

27

The Final Days

RICK BARNES was absolutely convinced that his team was good enough to win the Midwest Regional, even though it would have to beat a Minnesota team that was 29–3 and had dominated the Big Ten, and then probably beat UCLA, which, like North Carolina, hadn't lost a game since January. He was convinced Minnesota was the big hurdle and told his team that repeatedly throughout the week. The Tigers had flown directly from Kansas City to San Antonio, since Clemson was on spring break and there was little point in flying back home late Sunday night to be on an empty campus for two days before flying all the way to southwest Texas.

"If you win this game," Barnes told his players, "you're going to the Final Four. I promise you that. Minnesota is very, very good, but so are you. And I think we're both better than the other two teams [UCLA and Iowa State] out here. This is a game we're all going to remember the rest of our lives one way or the other, so let's do everything we possibly can to make it a happy memory."

By now, the Tigers were back to where they had been in January. They were happy again (winning will do that) and enjoying their status as one of two ACC teams still playing. Barnes pointed out to them how many good teams — Duke, Wake Forest, Maryland, and Virginia among them — were no longer playing. Clemson was. That was another step forward for the program.

Minnesota and Clemson had a lot in common. Both felt as if they were treated as unwanted stepchildren in their own league. The Big Ten's glamour teams were Indiana and Michigan. Purdue was respected nationally because Gene Keady's team seemed to overachieve every year. Michigan hadn't even made the field this year, Indiana was gone in the first round, and Purdue, after winning a round, had played top-seeded Kansas tough in the second round. But the Boilermakers were home too.

Not only was Minnesota the only Big Ten team left, it was the first Big Ten team since 1994 to make the Sweet Sixteen. For a power conference, that was a remarkable drought. Clem Haskins, the Gophers coach, was a strident, outspoken man who often said he didn't get enough credit or respect. He was an old schooler, a disciplinarian who insisted his players dress neatly, not wear earrings or tattoos, and keep their caps on with the bill facing forward. They had won the first game in November fairly easily — "They manhandled us," Barnes reminded his team — and everyone from Clemson was eager for another chance to play them.

There were 29,231 fans in the Alamodome for the regional semifinal doubleheader, which was about 29,000 more than had been in attendance the first time Minnesota and Clemson had played. What they saw was an extraordinary game, one that seemed to go on all night with no one — players, coaches, officials, or fans — minding.

For 18 minutes, Clemson looked outclassed. Minnesota started the game red-hot, making almost every shot it looked at, inside or outside. The Gophers' two fabulous guards, Bobby Jackson and Sam Jacobson, were 11 of 15 in the first half. The Tigers found themselves down 33–20 after almost 13 minutes. Barnes wasn't rattled. During a TV time-out, he told his players not to panic. "Believe me, we're fine," he said. "They are not going to keep shooting like this all night, and when they start missing we'll be right back in this thing. Just keep working the game, doing what you're doing. They can't hit every shot they take."

Naturally, Jackson drilled a jumper out of the time-out to make it

35–20. It wasn't until the last two minutes that the Gophers finally cooled. Then, Mohammed Woni, the freshman who had been one of the forgotten men of February, single-handedly got the Tigers back into the game. He scored six points in the final minute of the half, then kept a missed jumper by Merl Code alive on the backboard in the final seconds so that Tom Wideman could tip it in. With 1:40 to go, it had been 40–27. At halftime, it was a very manageable 41–35.

Barnes loved where the game was. Minnesota had shot just under 60 percent and only led by six. The Gophers loved to wear teams down with their depth, but they wouldn't be able to do that in this game. Haskins had gone deep into his bench in the first half, using nine different players. Barnes had used ten.

The second half was a basketball war. Clemson took its first lead at 49–48 with 9:44 left. Minnesota took control again. The lead was 70–64 with 2:08 left after Jacobson made two free throws, but Clemson rallied again. Wideman — who would finish with 10 points and 10 rebounds, his best game in months — tipped in a McIntyre miss with eight seconds left to make it 72–70. Clemson called time. Then the Tigers fouled Quincy Lewis before the ball even came inbounds so no time would run off the clock.

They were out of time-outs. If Lewis made two, the game was over. If he made one, they would have to hustle downcourt and shoot a three. If he missed both, they would race down and take the best shot they could get. Lewis missed the first. Then, he missed the second. Buckner got the rebound and made a great play. Instead of trying to dribble through traffic and be a hero, he spotted Tony Christie on the left wing. He fed the ball ahead to Christie, who went all the way to the basket and laid the ball in as the buzzer was sounding.

The game was tied at 72. Overtime. It was Christie's first basket of the night and a perfect example of what Clemson had become after Barnes's ACC tournament meetings. Buckner didn't feel as if he had to make the play. Barnes had enough confidence in Christie to have him in the game at that vital juncture because he was a scorer.

Four months and five days after opening the season by going overtime with Kentucky, Clemson was back in overtime in the NCAA Sweet Sixteen. Barnes said exactly the same thing to his team that he had said in November: "Guys, you gotta love this. Let's just play all night if we have to."

They almost did. The first two minutes of the overtime belonged to Clemson. A three by Buckner; a three by Code; a jumper by Buckner. They were up 80–74. The Elite Eight loomed. But Minnesota hadn't won 29 games without being in tough situations. Jackson and Jacobson brought them right back. A Jackson rainbow tied it at 80–80 with forty-nine seconds left. No one scored again before the clock hit zero.

Double overtime. Barnes repeated his speech. Deep down, though, he worried that their best chance to win had come and gone. He was right. Minnesota controlled the second overtime. A Jackson three and a Jackson jumper pushed an 82–81 lead to 87–81 with 1:43 left. Buckner missed a three on the next possession and then fouled out a few seconds later. Symbolically and realistically that was the end for the Tigers. The Gophers made their free throws in the last minute and the final was 90–84.

Barnes felt drained and exhilarated at the same time. He was sad that the season was over, but proud that it had ended so dramatically, that his team had shown the guts to come back again and again and push an excellent team to the brink. He had wondered in January after the overtime victory over Duke if he would be able to step back after a loss and appreciate a great basketball game. Now, he knew the answer. "All I could think walking off the floor was, 'That was one hell of a basketball game,' " he said. "It had everything. I never felt better about a team than I did about my guys that night."

He told them how far he felt they had come since October. He had wanted them to be better in March than November and they had been. He wanted them tougher and closer to that ultimate goal: the Final Four. "Look around you before you leave tonight and remember how close we were," he said. "Then remember where we are and start working to get back to this place a year from now."

The 1998 Final Four would be in the Alamodome.

Barnes saved the most difficult part for last. Larry Shyatt had been with him for nine years — six at Providence and three at Clemson. Now, he was leaving to become the head coach at Wyoming. "You guys all know what Coach Shyatt has meant to the program, but I'm not sure you know how much he means to me as a friend," Barnes said. "Without him, we wouldn't be here and I wouldn't be here."

He hugged Shyatt and then, one by one, everyone else hugged him too. Shyatt didn't say anything. He was in no shape to give a speech.

The season was over. Barnes couldn't wait for the next one to begin.

Clemson's loss meant that North Carolina was the one ACC team still alive. Few people would have thought on January 11, the night the Tar Heels dropped to 0–3 in the ACC, that they would be the last league team standing when March rolled around.

But there they were, in frigid Syracuse, now a heavy favorite to make the Final Four since the highest seeded team they would have to face in the Carrier Dome was number five California. South Carolina, New Mexico, and Villanova, two through four in the East, were long gone.

Dean Smith was, of course, terrified. Cal was a great story, having lost its coach and most of its players the previous summer because of an impending NCAA investigation. Then, in mid-February, the Bears had lost their leading scorer, Ed Gray. Even so, they kept on winning. They had excellent size and Ben Braun had clearly done one of the best coaching jobs in the country. And, for 31 minutes, their size and toughness gave the Tar Heels fits. They were leading 45–38 with 8:56 to go when Tony Gonzales missed a pair of free throws that could have stretched the lead to nine.

That was all the opening Carolina needed. With Antawn Jamison taking over inside, they went on a 20–6 binge that gave them a seven-point cushion with three minutes to play. The Bears never quit, but they weren't going to catch the Tar Heels once they had the lead. The final was 63–57.

That left Louisville standing between Carolina and the Final Four. Once upon a time, the Cardinals had been one of the country's dominant programs, going to six Final Fours during a fifteen-year span, winning two national titles. But since their second championship in 1986, the program had fallen, not to the scrap heap, but certainly out of the elite. In fact, this was the deepest Louisville had been in the NCAAs since '86. The Cardinals would have had a difficult task under any circumstances but their chances of winning the game became almost nil when their best player, DeJuan Wheat, twisted a knee in the semifinal victory over Texas.

Wheat played, but clearly wasn't himself, standing on the perimeter and firing threes (two of 11). He couldn't cut or penetrate or play much defense. Carolina was brilliant in the first half, rolling to a 54–33 lead. Then, obviously thinking the game was over, the Tar Heels reverted to their January personality, taking quick, bad shots and handling the ball carelessly. Suddenly, Louisville had somehow cut the lead to 69–66 and there were still more than eight minutes to play. Carolina awoke and scored the next 12 points. Game over. Regional over. Win number 879 for Smith put him into his eleventh Final Four, thirty years after win number ninety-two had put him into his first one.

He was grayer and heavier, a grandfather four times, eligible for Social Security and Medicare. And not one bit less competitive.

Carolina was not the only ACC team still playing in the season's final week. NC State had beaten Southwest Missouri State in the opening round of the NIT, but then, with Reynolds Coliseum sold out and rocking like in the old days, the Wolfpack lost a taut second round game to West Virginia, 76–73. When the game was over, everyone in the building was on their feet. They were sorry the team had lost, but thrilled with the way it had competed. State had become a good team in the last month of the season, a team worth watching, worth caring about. All in all Sendek had to consider that a pretty good first year.

"The people liked our effort," he said, ever cautious. "So did I. Now, we've raised the bar for the future. That's not easy. But it's also what we want."

Florida State had done the same thing by reaching the NIT Final in New York. The Seminoles went to Syracuse and hammered the Orange-men, three days after Syracuse coach Jim Boeheim, upset about being left out of the NCAA field, had said, "why did Virginia get in? Who did they beat?" One team they had beaten was Florida State — twice. That was the same Florida State that easily beat Boeheim's team on its home floor.

From there, FSU went home and beat Michigan State before going back on the road to come from behind and win at West Virginia. That put the Seminoles in New York, in the semifinals. They went overtime to beat Connecticut for their twentieth victory of the season, before losing the final to Michigan. Pat Kennedy felt good about the way his team had competed in the NIT. It hadn't thrown in the towel the way a lot of teams from big conferences do in the second-tier event. But they too had raised the bar. With Randell Jackson, Cory Louis, Kerry Thompson, and LaMar Greer back, the Seminoles would be expected to compete in the ACC in 1998 the way they had in their first two seasons.

For Dean Smith, this Final Four represented a return to the scene of one of his worst moments in coaching. In 1991, when his team made it back to the Final Four after a nine-year drought, it had opened the semifinal doubleheader against Kansas, coached by ex–Smith assistant Roy Williams. Kansas won the game and Smith didn't see the end of it, tossed by referee Pete Pavia after getting his second technical in the final minute. Bill Guthridge was so angry that he tried to get at Pavia in the hallway when the game was over. To make matters worse, that was the day that Duke upset Nevada–Las Vegas in the second game and went on to win its first national title. Now, Smith had a chance to bury the ghost of Indy '91 forever.

The Final Four matchups were North Carolina–Arizona and Kentucky-Minnesota. Three number one seeds had made it to Indianapolis. Only Kansas, the consensus choice to win the title going into the tournament, didn't join the other number ones. The Jayhawks were stunned in the regional semifinals by Arizona, which then went on to beat Providence in overtime to become the fourth team to qualify for the last weekend.

The Wildcats were a huge surprise to everyone. They had faltered so badly down the stretch that many people were angered when they were seeded fourth in the Southeast with a 19–9 record after finishing fifth in the Pacific-10. But the Pac-10 turned out to be the league everyone had underrated. For the first time in history, four Pac-10 teams — Arizona, UCLA, Stanford, and California — reached the Sweet Sixteen. Cal and Stanford lost in that round while UCLA made it to the round of eight before losing to Minnesota.

Carolina and Arizona had already met once, in the season opener in November. But both coaches agreed that game would have little bearing on this one. Arizona's best player, Miles Simon, had been academically ineligible. Two of Carolina's keys, Ed Cota and Vince Carter, had still been searching for their games and their comfort zone in the Smith system at that stage. Both teams were better, much better, than they had been then.

One thing hadn't changed, though: Arizona's quickness. That worried Smith more than anything. In basketball, speed kills — the other team.

It didn't start out like that. The first five minutes looked like a Carolina dunking clinic. The Tar Heels kept going to the rim and Arizona looked helpless trying to stop them. Jamison dunked; Carter dunked. Jamison again. Carter on an alley-oop. It was 15–4 and Carter was running down the court sticking his chest out as if the game were over. "We did a good job of making them feel overconfident the first five minutes," Arizona coach Lute Olson said later.

He was kidding — but he was also right. For the rest of the half, Carolina played like a bunch of out-of-control kids let loose on a playground. They forced passes inside, they threw lobs with no one around to catch the ball. They took quick shots and they took bad shots. "It was too easy the first few minutes," Smith said. "We made a couple of spectacular plays and got to thinking we could do that all day. Usually against a good team, that's not the case."

The lead disappeared. It wasn't as if Arizona was lighting the place up, but Simon began to find the range as the game went along. The Wildcats scored the last eight points of the first half — holding the Tar Heels scoreless for four minutes — to take a 36–31 lead at the break.

Being behind at halftime didn't bother Smith. Carolina had been behind in its first two tournament games and only up two in the third. The most nervous he had been at intermission had been against Louisville — with a 21-point lead. Now, though, he was anxious and he was angry. Everything they had done to win sixteen straight games seemed to have been forgotten in the latter stages of the half.

Smith went through his normal halftime routine: check the statistics — shooting and points per possession in particular. Ask the coaches if they had any specific suggestions. Talk to the team, checking periodically with the manager standing in the back of the room to see how much time was left. Ask if the coaches or the seniors had anything they wanted to say. All routine. He had done it more than a thousand times. But he didn't feel comfortable with the way the game was going. "I got on them more than I normally would because I wasn't pleased with the way we had played but also because I wanted them to understand that we were going to have to play really well in the second half to get it turned around," Smith said. "They weren't going to hand it to us."

In other words: this wasn't Fairfield.

Maybe it was the strange playing conditions inside the RCA Dome — it actually felt as if there were a wind blowing through it for most of the evening — but neither team could get much going offensively. At 7:45 of the second half, the score was 47–42. In other words, two Final Four teams had played more than twelve minutes of basketball in front of 47,028 spectators — plus millions more on television — to an 11–11 standoff. Arizona hadn't scored for almost four minutes and still led by five.

Someone was going to hit a jump shot sooner or later. It was Arizona. Simon hit a three. Then Mike Bibby, the superb freshman point guard, hit one. Serge Zwikker, who had struggled all day, hit twice to keep Carolina within striking distance. But then Bibby bombed two more threes. Suddenly, it was 61–46 with less than five minutes to play.

Carolina tried to rally with seven quick points. Then Bibby hit his fourth three in a five-minute span to push the margin back to 11 and Arizona, even missing foul shots in the last minute, made it to the finish line. Carolina's last possession was symbolic of the entire game. Trailing 64–58 with 35 seconds left, there was still a chance. Carter missed a three; Ademola Okulaja missed a three; Ed Cota missed a three. That was it. The final was 66–58.

The numbers for the game were ugly. Arizona, the winning team, had shot 33 percent — 22 of 66. Carolina, after making seven of its first 11 shots, was 16 of 63 the rest of the way. Shammond Williams, the MVP of both the ACC tournament and the East Regional, hit his first shot and then missed his next 12. Only Carter — eight of 15 — shot 50 percent from the field.

In the quiet Carolina locker room, Smith made a point of consoling several players one-on-one. Williams was devastated by his shooting performance. So was Serge Zwikker. The locker rooms in the RCA Dome are football locker rooms so they are huge. Smith made a point of going to each of them to tell them that he was proud of their seasons and, in Zwikker's case, his career. He second-guessed himself for jumping them at halftime. Maybe, he thought, if he had acted like a five-point deficit was no different than the other games when they had been behind, they would have played with the same loose composure they had shown in all those other games. But that was hindsight. Maybe Arizona had just been the better team.

This was a team and a season that was difficult for Smith to walk away from. They had come as far as any team he had ever coached, improving from one that looked in January as if it might miss the NCAA tournament to one that reached the Final Four. Smith had 879 victories, 13 ACC tournament titles, 11 Final Four trips, five appearances in the championship game, and two national titles.

But he walked away from his thirty-sixth season feeling crushed. "The hardest thing about coaching is that if you're good and you make the tournament every year, the odds are you're going to end the season with a loss," he said. "You can't help but second-guess yourself a little. I told the players they'd had a great year and I meant it. They did have a great year." He smiled. "I would just like to have had the year last one more game and see what would have happened."

Even after all the years and all the games and all the wins, Dean Smith was like everyone else in his chosen profession. He wanted to coach on Monday Night.

Epilogue

SIX MONTHS later, Dean Smith decided that thirty-six years, 879 victories, 11 Final Fours, five Monday Nights, and two national championships were enough. Keeping the promise he had made years ago to keep coaching until he didn't feel the fire and the energy when October rolled around, he stopped coaching.

It was a shocking decision. It was also a predictable one. And, most of all, a sad one.

It was sad because, at sixty-six, Smith was simply worn out. And what had worn him out most — though he would never, ever admit it — was the group that had made coaching such a joy for him for most of his career: his players. There was no way that an opponent would ever drive Smith from coaching because he always figured out a way to beat an opponent. In fact, that was what he enjoyed most: challenges. But being challenged from within wore him down. Dealing with players who often didn't listen; players who had little interest in graduating; players who would trash talk opponents, referees, and fans no matter how many times Smith told them not to, made coaching less fun.

Smith didn't have to retire. The team he would have coached in 1997–98 would have gone into the season ranked in everyone's top five, perhaps as high as number two — behind Arizona — in the minds of most people. But when October rolled around, the fire just wasn't there. While he may have relished the idea of going back to Cameron and silencing the students; of singing the Maryland fight song in the locker room at Cole; of coaching in another Final Four on one more Monday Night, he just couldn't deal with all that would go with trying to accomplish those things.

And so, on October 9, 1997, in an annex of the building that bears his name, in a jam-packed press conference, Dean Smith said goodbye. He only choked up once — when he tried to talk about the loyalty he had received through the years from his players and coaches — and even then, he seemed embarrassed by that show of emotion. He handed the reins to Bill Guthridge, the loyal lieutenant for thirty years.

Most people — including Guthridge — had assumed that the two men would ride off into the sunset together; Butch and Sundance, no doubt going out in a blaze of gunfire in some gym. But Guthridge, six years younger, wasn't quite ready for that final scene. He was given a multiyear contract, but the consensus around the ACC was that he wasn't likely to stay more than two or three years. Perhaps even less than that. Then, the speculation would begin anew: Roy Williams? Phil Ford? Eddie Fogler?

Some people wondered about the timing, coming just ten days before practice began for the new season. But Smith had said for years that he would never make a decision about retirement at the end of a season when he was tired and wondering if he wanted to go through another season of practices, film work, preparation, and — worst of all — recruiting. He always said when an October rolled around and he didn't feel excited about the start of practice, he would quit. And that was exactly what he did.

Others wondered why he didn't coach one more season, take a final victory tour through the league he had dominated for so long. Of course anyone who knew Smith at all knew that was the *last* thing he would want. He even alluded to it in the farewell press conference. "Can you imagine me going into all those places and being given all those rocking chairs?" he said. "Or having people act as if they *liked* me?"

That was quintessential Smith. He would sooner sing the Duke fight song than listen to a standing ovation from the Duke students. So much of him was about *competing* that the idea of having his competitors be nice to him was anathema — even if they meant it.

Smith's decision, even to those who knew he had been thinking about it seriously since that frustrating 1966 season, was a shock, if only because most people in the ACC thought he would probably coach forever. On the day of the announcement, a newspaper reporter called Gary Williams and asked him to recount a funny Dean story. "I can't," Williams answered. "I'm in shock right now. I'm sad, I'm really sad. The ACC will never be the same without him."

Mike Krzyzewski felt the same way. The antipathy between him and Smith through the years was genuine. But they respected each other, and both agreed each made the other a better coach. "I will miss competing against him," Krzyzewski said. "Because, as hard as he was to beat, when you did beat him, there was no better feeling. It was the ultimate challenge. I think it's sad for college basketball that someone who enjoyed coaching as much as he did felt he had to get out at sixty-six. That's not old these days. I feel a loss, I really do. There's a part of me that had kind of hoped we'd go out together."

Krzyzewski was in New York the day of the press conference. When he heard the news, much of the past seemed forgotten. He called and ordered flowers for Smith and his wife, Linnea. Then he did the same for Bill Guthridge and his wife. "When things calm down in a couple of weeks, I'll call him," Krzyzewski said. "I'd like to sit down and talk to him. Maybe things will be different now that we aren't competing with one another 365 days a year."

Carolina's loss in the national semifinals to Arizona had meant that, for the third year in a row, no ACC team reached Monday Night. Arizona went on to beat Kentucky, 84–79, in overtime in a sensational game, one worthy of Monday Night.

It was both surprising and disappointing to those who follow the league that the '97 postseason turned out the way it did after a regular season that most agreed may have been the best the league had produced in forty-four years. Perhaps Gary Williams's notion on that last weekend that everyone looked tired had merit. Or perhaps the ACC in 1997 was a league of remarkable balance, filled with good and very good teams, but without a truly great one. The way the conference race turned around in the second half would be an indication that there is validity to that theory. So would the fact that six conference teams won twenty or more games but only one (North Carolina with twenty-eight) got to twenty-five. Twenty victories is college basketball's benchmark of quality. Twenty-five is an indication that a team is very good. A handful of great teams win thirty.

All ACC off-season news paled in comparison to Smith's decision to step down. But that didn't mean there wasn't a lot of it.

North Carolina was the second ACC school to lose its head coach. The first was Florida State. After the Rutgers job fell through, it appeared that Pat Kennedy and Dave Hart were stuck with each other for at least one more season. Once again, Hart refused to roll over Kennedy's contract, leaving him with three more years. The word around the league was that unless the Seminoles had an absolutely spectacular season in 1998 Hart would pay Kennedy $1 million to buy out the last two years of the contract.

Kennedy heard all that. He didn't like the idea of being what amounted to a lame-duck coach. It had been uncomfortable hearing all the rumors swirling around Tallahassee for the past year; the next year promised to be even worse. And so, when DePaul called in May after firing Joey Meyer, Kennedy was willing to listen. This time, he was the top candidate for the job. The contract was for six years, and the money was similar to Florida State: about $500,000 a year. Kennedy said yes. He was looking for security and a fresh start and DePaul offered both. The job wouldn't be easy, recruiting to a school that had virtually no campus and played its home games a solid thirty-minute ride from the school in a creaky gym right next to O'Hare Airport. To Kennedy, it looked like heaven. He would trade the murky winters of Tallahassee for the frigid winters of Chicago. At least there he wouldn't spend ten months a year hearing about football. DePaul doesn't play Division I football. Win at DePaul and you are king. Kennedy decided it was worth taking a shot.

Kennedy's replacement at Florida State was Steve Robinson, who had been very successful in two years at Tulsa and had just signed a seven-year contract extension when Hart called him. Robinson was able to get out of the contract to take a shot at coaching in the ACC. He became the second African-American head coach in the history of the ACC, taking over a team that returned four starters and would enter his first season with high expectations. Unlike Herb Sendek, of whom little if anything was expected in his first season, Robinson would be expected to produce an NCAA tournament team right away.

The off-season's coaching soap opera took place at Virginia. It began on the Wednesday before the Final Four, when Jeff Jones walked into Tom Perrin's office late in the afternoon, shut the door, sat down across from him, took a deep breath, and said, "T.P., I've decided to make a change."

It took several seconds for Perrin to understand what Jones was saying: he was fired. Perrin was flabbergasted. He and Jones had worked together for fifteen years. They were friends. Their kids played together. Perrin's two daughters looked at J.J. as an uncle.

This was strictly business. Jones had been pressured by Holland prior to the season to make a change. During his first twelve years at UVA, as a volunteer coach, a graduate assistant, and a part-time assistant, Perrin had been the master of scouting opponents, breaking down film, and preparing game plans. "I've never met anybody better at those things than T.P.," Jones said. But for the past three seasons, as the number one assistant, Perrin had been a recruiter. Although head coaches ultimately take the hit for recruiting mistakes, assistants share the burden. Holland felt Perrin was miscast as a recruiter. Jones, under pressure, finally decided to go along with him.

If Virginia had gone 12–15 again and had four players arrested, Perrin would not have been that shocked. But after the Cavaliers pieced together eighteen victories and made it back to the NCAAs, Perrin thought he was off the hook. He knew Holland had been after Jones, but he thought that would end after a successful season. "No one would say we had a great season," Perrin said. "But we got better. We had a good season."

Apparently, not good enough. Talking about the move three days later, Jones was still clearly shaken. "It was the most difficult thing I've ever done as a coach," he said.

Perrin didn't really want to hear that. He was hurt and angry. He felt betrayed by Holland, whom he had looked to as a mentor, and by Jones, a friend. Since he was still under contract, he was assigned to work for assistant athletic director Craig Littlepage, working in a tiny office down the hall from where he had worked for so many years. The hardest part of it all was sitting at the dinner table and hearing his daughters say, "Daddy, why did J.J. fire you?"

Perrin's answer was direct: "I don't know."

His replacement was almost as big a surprise as the firing: Ricky Stokes. True, Stokes was a Virginia graduate. He and Jones had been teammates. But he had been with Dave Odom since day one at Wake Forest and most people had thought his next move would be to a head coaching job. He had turned one down — Furman — in April. Then, for a big raise ($125,000 a year) he returned to his alma mater.

Was this another Holland move? Was Stokes a coach in waiting? When recruiting began in July, Jones was still without a contract extension. He had one year left. Although Holland kept telling him he wanted to give him an extension, he didn't have one. He knew that a number of wealthy UVA alums were making an issue of his divorce and the arrests, claiming the program lacked discipline. There wasn't a program in America that didn't have kids who had gotten into trouble. The winningest coach of all time had gone through a divorce. Jones felt he should be judged on his record.

Finally, late in July, Holland came up with a two-year extension. It wasn't what Jones wanted, but it was better than nothing. Still, there were those who wondered if Virginia had a bad year in '98 if the holier-than-thou alums wouldn't buy out those two years — at about $500,000 a year — Holland had gotten him. Holland was at least as unhappy with the situation as Jones. He even expressed interest in the Florida State coaching job after Kennedy left. There was more: Courtney Alexander, the talented but troubled guard, was arrested in July for allegedly assaulting the mother of his infant child. Regardless of the outcome of the court case — he was found guilty of assault and appealed — there was no way he would be back given the team's prior off-court troubles.

Clearly, the good ship Virginia was in for another turbulent winter.

One other coaching staff went through major changes: Duke. Mike Krzyzewski had been prepared to lose Tommy Amaker for a long time, knowing he was one of the hot young commodities in coaching. Amaker's dream job had been Northwestern, because he believed Northwestern could be the Big Ten's answer to Duke. But Northwestern hired Kevin O'Neil from Tennessee. Amaker ended up at Seton Hall, becoming, at thirty-one, the youngest coach in the Big East. He took part-time coach Tim O'Toole with him, giving him a full-time slot. Krzyzewski filled the two open spots by hiring two members of his first Final Four team (1986), Johnny Dawkins and David Henderson. Neither had ever coached before, meaning Krzyzewski would begin his eighteenth season at Duke with a staff that had a total of two years of college coaching experience (both belonging to Quin Snyder).

Dave Odom, less than thrilled when his friend Holland lured Stokes away, hired a former Wake Forest graduate assistant, Dave Haith, to replace Stokes. And Rick Barnes hired Brian Cousins, who had worked for him at Providence, to take Larry Shyatt's spot on his staff.

One other coach got a new contract: Herb Sendek, who was rewarded for State's fast finish with a raise (to $500,000 a year) and an extension through 2003.

For the first time in years, the ACC did not lose any underclassmen to the NBA draft. The buzz all winter had Antawn Jamison leaving North Carolina. Schoolwork was difficult for him, and if he had been guaranteed a top five slot in the draft Smith probably would have urged him to go. But some pro scouts were put off by his lack of shooting range. Most likely, he would have been picked somewhere between eighth and twelfth, so he opted to deal with school for at least one more year. So did Matt Harpring, who after asking Bobby Cremins to check on his draft status, decided to return to Georgia Tech when he found out he was unlikely to go in the top twenty picks. That knowledge and Cremins's signing of two highly touted guards in the spring, swung Harpring back to college for his senior year. None of the other ACC underclassmen were rated highly enough to seriously consider going. Vince Carter improved immeasurably as the season went on, but still clearly needed at least one more year at North Carolina. Wake's seven-one freshman Loren Woods has tremendous potential, but struggled greatly during his freshman year.

What all that means is that the ACC should be very strong again in

1998. With Jamison back, North Carolina returns five of the six key players who took it to the Final Four and has a strong recruiting class coming in to bolster that group. Duke lost one key player off a team that won the ACC regular season title and has scheduled to be in uniform this season one of the most highly touted recruiting classes ever. Clemson lost only Merl Code from its top ten players and had Temple transfer Johnny Miller eagerly waiting after sitting out last season.

Maryland will be without NBA first round pick Keith Booth but returns four starters and has two redshirts and two freshmen ready to play. Florida State loses James Collins, a hugely underrated player, and Kirk Luchman, but has five of its first seven back and a solid recruiting class. NC State loses two very good players in Danny Strong and Jeremy Hyatt but has a six-player recruiting class and all the experience and confidence it gained this season. Virginia has three starters back, although Harold Deane's departure will be critical, since a freshman will probably have to play point guard and Alexander's departure will make scoring very difficult. Wake Forest took perhaps the biggest hit of any team in the country, losing the national player of the year in Tim Duncan and two other starters, Ricky Peral and Sean Allen. But Odom will have two senior guards and a talented class coming in, not to mention Woods, who is bound to make giant strides now that he is out of Duncan's shadow. And Georgia Tech will return Harpring and Mike Maddox, two four-year starters, and have a very talented though inexperienced backcourt.

What does all this mean? That once again there will be no walkover nights in the ACC. Who will stay healthy and whose young players will develop the fastest, no one knows. Every team has possibilities, every team has question marks. Most winter nights in the ACC will again be tense and unpredictable. About the only thing that *is* guaranteed is that the referees will have their hands full once again.

Whether the ACC will have a team playing in San Antonio next year is nothing more than a wild guess. History says it will. Regardless of what happens in March, each coach will have nights when he hates his job. Dean Smith admits that almost every time he loses a game, he flashes back to that first loss in 1961 and thinks the same thing he thought that night: "The heck with this coaching."

They all think that after losses. Gary Williams says every year when he flies home after his team's last loss, he almost wonders if the plane going down would be such a bad thing. Then he thinks about playing golf and getting ready for next season and prays for a safe landing.

Each of them is where he is because of the past. They are paid big money to take on big responsibility in a pressure-filled, big-time league because they have won a lot of games. Nowhere is the bar set higher than in the ACC. Until you have made the Final Four, until you have coached on Monday Night, you aren't truly fulfilled as an ACC coach. And, even after you have done those things, you still want more. Ask Dean Smith. Ask Mike Krzyzewski.

If it is the past that gives them their identity, it is the future that gives them their drive. Regardless of how or when this season ends, there is always next season. Next season is what keeps them going, keeps them working. If this season ends in the Les Robinson game, next season will be different. If this season ends on Monday Night, nothing would be better than ending next season the same way. And the season after that, and after that, and . . .

Afterword

AS THE NINE ACC basketball teams gathered in October of 1998 to begin their preseason preparations, the landscape of the league had undergone a remarkable transformation in less than two years.

At the start of the 1996–97 season, Herb Sendek was the league's only rookie coach. In fact, Sendek and Clemson's Rick Barnes — entering his third year — were the only ACC coaches who had not been on the job for at least six seasons. Two years later, Sendek, entering his third year at North Carolina State, ranked *fifth* in the league in seniority. Gone during that two-year stretch were Dean Smith after thirty-six years at North Carolina; Pat Kennedy after eleven years at Florida State; Jeff Jones after eight years at Virginia and, perhaps most surprisingly, Barnes, after just four years at Clemson.

Each had left under an entirely different set of circumstances: Kennedy had fled to DePaul after two years of whispers that his athletic director wanted him gone. Smith, in what may have been as dramatic a retirement scene as college basketball had ever witnessed, had decided he didn't have the fire to go through any more winters of coaxing kids to act like adults.

The two coaching changes that occurred after the '97–98 season had nothing in common except this: each provided a textbook example of the kinds of pressure that exists within the ACC.

Jeff Jones received a contract extension at Virginia in July of 1997 after the Cavaliers had made it back to the NCAA tournament the previous spring, reaching the tournament for the fifth time in Jones's seven seasons at the school. But the extension was for just two years and rumors were rife as the season began that Jones was still in trouble.

The rumors were true. The Cavaliers began the season by losing in overtime to in-state rival Richmond. ACC teams are not supposed to lose to teams from the Colonial Athletic Association anywhere, anytime. Things got worse before they got better. A humiliating loss at home to Liberty in front of an embarrassing crowd announced at 3,405 that looked like a lot less than that, turned the whispers into howls.

From that moment forward, things went skidding out of control for Jones and UVA. Jones had known the winter would not be easy. He had known that he was going to lose seniors Harold Deane and Jamal Robinson from the '97 team, although he hadn't counted on losing Courtney Alexander, his best scorer. But after Alexander's arrest in August, Jones was left with a team that had two reliable scorers — three-point specialist Curtis Staples and power forward Norman Nolan.

Both had superb seasons, yet they weren't nearly enough to make Virginia competitive in the ACC. Often, the Cavaliers stayed in games for thirty or thirty-five minutes because they still played hard and made opponents work to score. But when games were on the line, they couldn't come up with the key baskets they had to have to win. As the losses mounted, the stories in the Virginia media about Jones's impending doom increased.

Through it all, Jones kept his emotions to himself as always, even though he was hurting inside. He felt betrayed by Terry Holland, his old coach, who was now his boss. The facts were these: based strictly on his eight-year record, Jones would not have been in jeopardy. But he *was* in jeopardy because he had had an extramarital relationship with a woman four years earlier and had gone through a highly publicized divorce in a small town. Jones had never defended what he had done either publicly or privately. He did feel that if he was going to be fired for botching his marriage, he should have been fired then. But then had been 1995, when Virginia had been to four NCAA Tournaments in five years and had reached the final eight, winning twenty-five games.

The complaints about his personal life within the UVA community hadn't really started until the Cavaliers had gone 14–15 in 1996. They ebbed the following winter when Virginia was 18–13 but came roaring back as the losses mounted. Jones couldn't understand why Holland wasn't standing up for him, wasn't pointing out that all the rumors had hurt recruiting and that Jones had paid for his mistake in his personal life and should now be given a fair shot to succeed professionally.

Holland didn't see it that way. He saw a shattered program. He saw empty seats in a building that seated fewer than 10,000 people. Even the Duke and North Carolina games weren't sellouts. Holland knew recruiting had been damaged by the rumors about Jones's job security, but that didn't matter anymore. The team was going to finish last in the ACC (3–13) and the two best players were graduating. Jones's relationships with most of the in-state media had soured. What's more, Holland was getting pressure from above to make a change. He felt he had no choice.

An hour before what he knew would be his last game in University Hall as Virginia's coach, Jones sat in his locker room, just as he had done so many times during the past eight seasons. His mood was melancholy, reflective.

"In some ways, it's hard to believe it ever got to this point," he said quietly. "I know I made a mistake and I'll have to live with it the rest of my life. I'm not even sure I want to coach again after this experience. Maybe I do because it's what I've always done. But maybe not. Almost surely, not next year."

The buyout of the last two years of his contract — at $300,000 a year — gave Jones flexibility. He didn't want to leave Charlottesville because he lived ten minutes away from his three children. He had two years to ponder his future. No doubt he would spend at least part of that time wondering about his past.

Rick Barnes also experienced a disappointing season. But there wasn't anyone at Clemson calling for his head. In fact, when he announced in mid-April that he was leaving to become the head coach at Texas, almost everyone connected with the school was shocked.

It was Barnes who had brought a new attitude to Clemson; Barnes who had said over and over that the time for Clemson to take a backseat to the traditional powers of the ACC had passed. It was Barnes who had talked about how happy his family was being back in the South and Barnes who had driven to every corner of the state drumming up support for Clemson basketball.

Then, in what seemed like an instant, he was gone.

Texas paid him a lot of money to make the move — $700,000 a year for seven years — but it wasn't money that pushed Barnes out of the ACC. His concern about the education his children were getting in the South Carolina public schools might have been a factor, yet it wasn't the reason he left Clemson.

Actually, there were two reasons he left Clemson: North Carolina and Duke. In 1998, the Tigers played Duke and Carolina five times. They lost five times, with a very good team, one that Barnes and his staff had worked hard to put together. For all the talk about the intensity Barnes brought to the Carolina-Clemson rivalry (and he had indeed done that) Clemson had a 1–9 record in four seasons against the Tar Heels. And after beating Duke twice in his inaugural season (the year of Krzyzewski's illness), Barnes had gone 2–5 against the Blue Devils during the next three seasons. That meant in three years in which Clemson was good enough to make the NCAA Tournament, the combined record against Duke and Carolina was 3–12.

It wasn't going to get any easier in the future. Dean Smith had retired and Vince Carter and Antawn Jamison had turned pro a year early, so Carolina had gone out and reloaded, signing three of the top high school seniors in the country. Duke would lose two senior starters, Steve Wojciechowski and Roshown McLeod, to graduation and a talented sophomore backup, Mike Chappell, to transfer, and would still begin the '98–99 season ranked in everyone's national top three.

Barnes had yelled at Dean Smith about not respecting his players. He had yelled at Fred Barakat about referees not respecting his program. He had yelled at his players about not respecting themselves enough when they played the ACC powerhouses. But he saw no end in sight.

Of course being third in the best league in the country isn't exactly shabby, but Barnes hadn't even gotten there yet. Despite its 16–1 start in 1997, Clemson had finished the season tied for fourth in the ACC with a 9–7 record. A year later, having lost just one starter to graduation, the Tigers began the season ranked fifth in the country. By the end of the season, they had gone 7–9 in league play to again finish tied for fourth in the conference. Unlike 1997, when they were able to regroup in the NCAA tournament and come within one play of the final eight, they didn't make it out of the first round, losing to Western Michigan.

Barnes was bitterly disappointed by his team's season. He had expected continued progress and instead had seen the program slip backward a step. What's more, Greg Buckner, who had been the heart and soul of his team almost from his first day on campus, was graduating. A solid nucleus would be back, but Barnes wasn't sure the team could get better the next year or even be as good. Duke would be as good or better. Carolina would be very good. So would Maryland. Realistically, Clemson would be no better than fourth in the ACC. And the next year might be tougher.

Along came Texas. Like Clemson, it is a football school first, but it has superb basketball facilities. The Austin campus is beautiful, and money for recruiting expenses is virtually unlimited. Most important, Texas is in the Big Twelve. In the Big Twelve, Kansas is a perennial powerhouse. Oklahoma and Oklahoma State have had good teams in recent years. But there are breathers in the Big Twelve for a good team: Baylor, Texas A&M, Texas Tech, and Colorado. They may have an occasional good team, but year in, year out, a program like Texas should dominate them. Clemson dominates no one in the ACC because very rarely are ACC teams dominated — except perhaps by Duke and Carolina.

With a couple of good recruiting classes, Barnes could see Texas quickly jumping to no worse than second most years in the Big Twelve. It wasn't as if the job would be easy; there was some serious rebuilding to be done. But once the house was built, there would be no brick walls to run through. Roy Williams was beloved at Kansas, but he wasn't an icon the way Smith had been or the way Krzyzewski still is.

Barnes had never really expected to leave Clemson when he arrived. But four years later, when he sat down and thought about the past and, more important, the future, leaving seemed like the only sensible thing to do.

On the night of January 14th, 1998, North Carolina arrived at Cole Field House to play Maryland. When Bill Guthridge walked onto the floor, he found Gary Williams waiting for him, hands on hips, an angry look on his face.

"Every coach in the league is pissed off at you," Williams said. "We keep telling our bosses how hard this job is, how much we need to be paid to keep winning, and then you show up and make it look easy."

Guthridge smiled. "Believe me, Gary," he said, "it isn't as easy as it's looked."

Williams had been joking. Guthridge was not.

Guthridge *had* made it look easy during the season's first two months. Carolina arrived at Cole Field House ranked number one in the country, having won the first seventeen games of the Guthridge era. The Tar Heels weren't a deep team — Guthridge usually used only six players most of the game — but they had two of the best players in the country in Antawn Jamison and Vince Carter, and they were loaded with experience: Shammond Williams and Makhtar Ndiaye were seniors and Ademola Okulaja and Ed Cota, though both underclassmen, were twenty-three years old. That made Carolina about as mature as a college basketball team could be.

At least in a basketball sense.

Real life was another story. One of the things that had disturbed Dean Smith near the end of his career was the tendency to taunt and preen that had become a part of college basketball. Smith had always prided himself on the notion that his teams were above things like that. As far back as 1984 he had chided Michael Jordan for a spectacular backwards dunk at the end of an already decided game in Cole Field House. "Just take the two points and get out," Smith had counseled. "No need to rub it in when you're going to play them again."

Now, like a lot of other teams, Carolina tended to rub it in. Carter was a chest-pounder and a trash-talker and Jamison, quiet and polite by nature, had picked up on some of that. The biggest problem, though, was

Ndiaye, the fifth-year senior who had bounced from Wake Forest to Michigan to Carolina during a very mediocre career. Strictly from a playing point of view, Ndiaye was perfect for this team: he was a big body who could give Jamison and Okulaja a chance to rest while he went in to rebound, play physically, and hit an occasional inside shot. His statistics for the season were a reflection of the kind of player he was: twenty-four minutes a game that produced 5.4 points, 4.1 rebounds, and 3.5 personal fouls. His 133 fouls were 39 more than anyone else on the team had, even though he played between eight and ten fewer minutes per game than the other five regulars.

But that was only part of the problem. Ndiaye was a primo trash-talker, a constant whiner who complained almost every time a call went against him, and a bad example for his teammates, most of whom looked at him (for some reason) as a respected elder. He picked up a foolish technical foul in the Duke game in Chapel Hill that almost opened the door to a belated Duke rally.

Smith had been unable to deal with the new Carolina "attitude," and had walked away. Guthridge dealt with it, for the most part, by taking a boys-will-be-boys approach. But as the season wore on, even as the Tar Heels continued to play superbly, the situation grew worse. After Carolina won an overtime game at Georgia and several Carolina players jumped on their bench at game's end and waved towels at the Georgia fans, Fred Barakat called Guthridge to ask him to please insist that his players cease and desist in ACC games. Barakat remembered the near-riot at NC State a year earlier and was afraid things could get even uglier if the taunting continued. Guthridge did talk to his players, and for a while, things got better.

Carolina and Duke emerged as the league's dominant teams and their two regular season games were among the most overhyped events in the history of sports. Mark McGwire's sixty-second home run — which deserved every bit of hype it received — didn't receive any more ink than Carolina-Duke I and Carolina-Duke II in 1998. The Tar Heels easily won the game in Chapel Hill, but Duke rallied to squeeze out the game in Durham, coming from 12 points down in the second half to win, 77–75.

That game made Duke the regular season champion for a second straight year, since the Blue Devils' only league loss had been the game in Chapel Hill. Carolina had lost at Maryland in overtime and, remarkably, at home to a hot-shooting NC State team. A week later, Carolina bounced back in the ACC tournament final to beat Duke in the rubber match, 83–68.

All three games were marked by bad feelings on both sides. The worst moment came at the end when Ndiaye jumped on the scorer's table during the post-tournament celebration and taunted the Duke fans, pointing to his heart as if to say, "We tore your hearts out." Furious, Mike Krzyzewski ripped Ndiaye publicly the next day, leading to an eruption of ire throughout the state between Duke and North Carolina fans. Basketball's best rivalry had truly turned ugly.

If Guthridge could be criticized for being lax with Ndiaye and friends in terms of conduct, there was absolutely no questioning the job he had done coaching his team. Most people had expected Guthridge to be a mirror image of Smith. He wasn't. Just watching a Carolina huddle during a time-out was evidence of how different things were. With Smith in command, no one spoke during a time-out unless asked a specific question. Guthridge was far more democratic. He encouraged his assistants to be vocal. Players often spoke up, either to each other or the coaches. The very fact that a reporter could sit next to the bench and look into the Carolina huddle was a radical change. Smith would have stationed at least three managers between himself and any outsiders.

The best thing Guthridge did was not take himself too seriously. He took the games seriously and his job seriously, but not himself. He made a point of accepting responsibility on the rare occasions when the team didn't play well. He didn't appear the least bit uncomfortable being thrust into the spotlight after thirty years in the shadows. He didn't revel in it, but he didn't shrink from it either.

The true surprise at Carolina was the way Smith handled his retirement. Most longtime Smith observers figured he would slip quietly away, perhaps do some teaching, play a lot of golf, maybe spend some time observing some of his ex-assistants around the country.

But Smith wasn't going gently into the night. Shortly after his retirement press conference, he showed up in an ESPN college basketball commercial. The bit was actually very touching and funny all at once. It began with Smith walking across the court in an empty DeanDome, hearing crowd noises in his head, looking up at all the championship banners as he paused by the bench. The next shot was of Smith sitting near the top of the stands, wearing one of those head masks that fanatic fans wear and standing to wave a number one hand pom-pom. The last thing you heard was Smith saying, "I think I liked my old seat better." Of course the shot from the top of the stands wasn't really Smith. It was shot from behind and a double was used. Even so, the ad surprised people because it was so un-Smithlike.

Still more surprising was his continued presence in the DeanDome on a day-to-day basis. He didn't even turn his office over to Guthridge until January, and then he moved in down the hall. His stationery continued to say "Carolina men's basketball." He even began to work on future schedules for the basketball team and he agreed to work as an in-studio commentator for CBS during the NCAA tournament. Seeing Smith sitting stiffly behind a desk, clearly ill at ease as he tried to talk in sound bites was disconcerting. On the night the draw came out, anchor Greg Gumble asked Smith about the possibility of a North Carolina–Charlotte second-round matchup.

Smith couldn't deal with the notion of his old team looking past *any* opponent. "Well, of course North Carolina will have to beat Navy in the first round," he pointed out.

Smith knew that TV wasn't made for him. "I'm a lot more comfortable in front of a blackboard than in front of a camera," he said.

Naturally, he tried as best he could to defend Ndiaye, whom he had brought to Carolina, even as the evidence against him mounted. "Makhtar isn't a bad kid at all," he said after the ACC Tournament. "He just gets overly enthusiastic."

Sadly, the worst for Ndiaye was yet to come.

For the second straight season, the best regular season in the ACC was pieced together by Duke. Once again, there was an element of surprise to the Blue Devils' performance.

From the outset, it was clear that all the hype surrounding the freshmen was legitimate, especially where six-eight, 250-pound Elton Brand was concerned. He was a dominant player in practice from the start and led the team in both scoring and rebounding throughout the month of December.

But shortly after the team returned to campus from Christmas break, Brand broke a foot in practice. Initially, it appeared that Brand was through for the season. Krzyzewski was devastated. He had started to believe that this group had a chance to be a Final Four team by March. But not without Brand.

Remarkably, the Blue Devils didn't appear to miss Brand. Senior Roshown McLeod, who had lost a good deal of playing time to Brand, stepped into his role and played superbly. Only against Carolina — and Jamison — did Brand's absence cause a problem. When he surprised everyone by coming back during the last week of the regular season, few expected Brand to be the presence he had been before the injury. But down the stretch in the win over Carolina in Cameron, he was the key man, coming up with several critical baskets during Duke's rally.

Krzyzewski had enjoyed coaching the '97 team because it had overachieved for much of the season. But coaching this team was more what he had in mind. He was beyond the point in his career where coaching gutsy overachievers was going to be enough to satisfy him. He wanted to coach teams that could win national championships; reach Final Fours. This team had a chance to do those things.

And with ten minutes left in the South Regional Final against Kentucky, it appeared that Duke was heading back to the Final Four for the first time since 1994. The Blue Devils led by 14 and looked in control of the game. But they couldn't make it to the finish line. Kentucky's pressure defense and three-point shooting broke Duke down. The players lost their poise, calling time-outs they should not have called, rushing shots, and missing free throws. Kentucky rallied to win, 86–84. Krzyzewski was gracious after the game, saying all the right things about Kentucky. But it was a devastating loss. Under Krzyzewski, Duke had been 7–0 in regional finals; it had always been a team that kept its poise in the clutch and made the big shots. That hadn't happened this time. Even though his team finished 32–4, Krzyzewski would have to wait at least another year to feel as if his comeback from the back surgery and the lost season of '95 was truly complete.

Gary Williams would also have to wait another year for the chance to fulfill his mission — a Final Four trip — but he was able to walk away from the '98 season feeling a lot better than he had at the end of '97.

Maryland played well throughout the season, beating Kansas in December, North Carolina in January, Temple in February, and Illinois in March — all quality wins against quality opponents. The Terrapins were solid throughout the ACC season, finishing third in the league behind Duke and Carolina.

The only team Maryland couldn't compete with was Duke. The Blue Devils beat them twice, by a combined margin of 59 points, both games blowouts long before halftime. Williams didn't see much of the game in Cameron because he was ejected early for arguing about a taunting technical called on Laron Profit. Although he was furious with Larry Rose for tossing him, Williams made a point of going to the Duke locker room after the game to apologize to Krzyzewski. He felt it was unfair for people to focus on his ejection instead of Duke's play and he knew that, inevitably, that would be the case.

Williams's other source of continuing frustration was his point guard, Terrell Stokes. Try as he might, there was a part of Williams that had trouble putting the Stokes-Profit curfew-breaking at the ACC Tournament the previous year completely behind him. When either player had a poor night, Williams couldn't help wondering why. Were they tired? Did they not care enough? Williams even went so far as to bench Stokes for a while in favor of another senior, Matt Kovarik, even though he knew Stokes would have to play the bulk of the key minutes before the season was over.

Stokes did just that and, at times, he was very effective. But he was still inconsistent. He would have an excellent night against North Carolina, then get eaten alive by Steve Wojciechowski when Duke was the opponent. In an early-season loss to George Washington, Stokes was outplayed at both ends of the floor by five-foot-four Shanta Rogers.

Maryland reached the Sweet Sixteen in March for the third time in five years before losing to defending national champion Arizona. Williams was pleased with that performance and, with five of the seven players who had received the bulk of the playing time returning, he had good reason to believe his team could go even farther in '99. But he wasn't convinced it could happen with Stokes running the team. So he went out and recruited a highly touted junior college point guard, Steve Francis. Throughout the summer, Francis received rave reviews everywhere he played, and it seemed likely that he would be the starter when November rolled around.

That possibility excited Maryland fans. But Williams knew he had to handle the situation delicately. Benching a senior who had started for most of three years would not be easy, especially if his classmates, Profit and starting center Obinna Ekezie, saw the change as some sort of betrayal. Williams knew that the fall would begin at Maryland with great anticipation. He also knew that he would have to be both a coach and a politician before a single game had been played.

Changing point guards was not a problem for Bobby Cremins. In fact, it had become something of an annual ritual. He had gone from Travis Best in '95 to Stephon Marbury in '96 to Kevin Morris in '97 to Travis Spivey in '98. Spivey had been an improvement on Morris, who had struggled from the very beginning at Georgia Tech both academically and athletically, but when the '98 season ended, Cremins was point-guard hunting again. This time he came up with Tony Akins, a six-foot jet from Lilburn, Georgia. Spivey, who could take a hint, transferred to Iowa State, meaning that Cremins would have his fifth point guard in five years and his fourth freshman point guard in four years, dating back to Marbury's lone season at Tech.

Cremins felt better at the end of the '98 season than he had at the end of '97, but he was a long way from being satisfied. His rebuilt team — with two seniors and three freshmen as starters — played much better than the team had a year earlier. The Yellow Jackets rebounded from a 2–6 start in the league to be 6–7 with three games to play. At that stage, they had a reasonable chance to make the NCAA Tournament field. But they finished the regular season with four straight double-digit losses, including an embarrassing 83–65 loss to Maryland in the ACC tournament quarterfinals, a game that included a shoving match on the bench between Matt Harpring and freshman star Dion Glover.

Those four losses consigned Tech to the NIT. There, the Jackets managed to win two home games before losing — again at home — to Penn State in the quarterfinals. The final record was 19–14, certainly an improvement on 9–19, but a far cry from the glory days. It was the fourth time in five years that Tech failed to make the NCAA's and, for a second straight year, there were a lot more non-sellouts than sellouts in what had once been called the Thrillerdome.

Harpring and Michael Maddox would be gone in '99 (along with Spivey), but Cremins was convinced that Glover — who averaged 18.4 points per game as a freshman — center Alvin Jones, and six-eleven Indiana transfer Jason Collier gave him a nucleus he could build around. Even so, the Yellow Jackets would start the new season picked somewhere between fifth and seventh in the ACC, a team likely once again to be on the NCAA Tournament bubble come March. Cremins's hair was already gray, he had been through his midlife crisis and through his career nadir. It was time, he knew, for something good to happen to him and to his team.

Or so he hoped.

Herb Sendek and Steve Robinson saw both the good and the bad during the '98 season.

Sendek's second season at NC State began with high hopes, due in part to the way the Wolfpack had finished the '97 season, and perhaps even more so because of the recruiting class Sendek had assembled. At times, the Wolfpack lived up to those high hopes. They began ACC play with an impressive win at Georgia Tech and went into January with a 9–2 record. But injuries were a problem, specifically the one that forced sophomore center Damon Thornton, who had shown so much potential as a freshman, to sit out the season after just three games.

State still had moments — most notably the stunning 86–72 win at Carolina in February — but when the regular season ended, the Wolfpack was in eighth place once again with one more ACC victory than it had accumulated a year earlier. The good news — sort of — was that the coaches, in their wisdom, had eliminated the ACC tournament's Les Robinson Game. Under the new No Les Is More system, the top seed (Duke) played the ninth seed (Virginia) on Thursday night after the seventh seed (Florida State) played the eighth seed (NC State).

The fact that the new system was completely unfair didn't seem to bother the coaches. Since the winner of the 1–9 game was given a bye into the semifinals while the 7–8 winner had to play the number two seed in the quarterfinals, a number nine seed could theoretically win the tournament by playing only three games. For a seventh or eighth seed to win, it had to survive four games. The fact that State had reached the final in

1997 as the eighth seed made the notion that a number nine could take advantage of the new format not so farfetched.

State didn't reach the final in '98, though it did pull a mild upset of Florida State on opening night. The following afternoon, still tired from the night before, the Wolfpack faced a North Carolina team that wanted badly to make up for the embarrassing loss two weeks earlier in Chapel Hill. The final, not surprisingly, was 73–46, Tar Heels.

That left State with a 16–14 record, identical to the record it had left the ACC tournament with a year earlier. There were two differences: the euphoria of the run to the final wasn't there, but the notion that State was a better team than it had been then was there. Sendek had produced another solid recruiting class and, combined with the three freshmen who had played extensively, a healthy Thornton, and a now-veteran Justin Gainey, there was good reason to believe that State was headed in the right direction, especially when one considered that the 1999 team would not have a single senior on the roster.

The same was true at Florida State, in spite of a rather strange ending to the season. With four starters back from Pat Kennedy's last team and junior college transfer Terrell Baker stepping in at the shooting guard spot, the Seminoles started very fast under Steve Robinson. They upset Connecticut in the semifinals of the preseason NIT, lost a tight game to Kansas the next night, and then stunned defending national champion Arizona two weeks later. They were 12–2 and ranked thirteenth nationally when they arrived at Cole Field House in early January to play a game against a Maryland team reeling from an embarrassing 32-point loss to Duke a few days earlier.

That turned out to be poor timing. The fired-up Terrapins won the game 81–74 and, as had happened so often in Kennedy's last years, FSU hit the skids in ACC play. They played with manic intensity at home against Duke, closing to within one midway through the second half before losing by 12. There were some good wins but some embarrassing losses: 103–55 to Carolina in Chapel Hill; 78–49 *at home* to Clemson. By the time March rolled around, the Seminoles were banged up and, having lost six of their last seven to finish 17–13, clearly headed for another NIT bid.

But fate and the NCAA tournament committee intervened. Feeling it had to give the country's top-rated conference at least five tournament bids, the committee had to choose among FSU, Georgia Tech, and Wake Forest for the final bid. The Deacons appeared to have the best case. They had finished the strongest — a major criterion according to the committee — and were 7–9 in league play. FSU and Georgia Tech were 6–10, though they had more overall wins (17) than Wake (14) in large part because they had played extra games in preseason events. All three teams had 13 losses.

The committee decided to abandon its "finish strong" notion and the idea that all other things being equal, if two teams from the same league are contending for one spot, you take the team with the better league record. Florida State got in, largely on the basis of its early-season wins over Connecticut and Arizona. The 'Noles then made the committee look good by upsetting TCU in the first round before losing to the tournament's Cinderella team, Valparaiso, in the second round.

In all, it was a good first year for Robinson, although he could not have been thrilled when his leading scorer, junior Randell Jackson, opted to turn pro a year early. That meant Baker would be his only returning starter, even though seven-two center Karim Shabazz had played more and more as his freshman year progressed. Nonetheless, FSU would be the ACC's least-experienced team in '98–99, and that almost always makes for a long winter — even a winter spent in Florida.

Dave Odom was disappointed when the NCAA tournament bids were announced on the evening of March 8, but not shocked. He knew the committee could never be trusted to stick to its criteria and he had believed deep in his heart that his team had needed to beat Clemson in its ACC tournament game to have a serious chance to get a bid.

"If we had won that one, we'd have been in," he said. "We had a chance at it [leading by 8 midway through the second half], but they closed strong. I felt all year we would be right on the bubble when all was said and done and that's exactly where we were."

That they were that close was amazing considering the rocky road they had taken to that point. The plan had been for seven-foot-one Loren Woods, now a sophomore, to step into the center spot that Tim Duncan had occupied for four years. No one expected Woods to be Duncan, but he had flashed star potential during his freshman year. However, it never came to be. Woods continued to struggle with his emotions as a sophomore. Odom had worried often about his tendency to beat himself up, never to be satisfied with himself, and, faced with the pressures of being a starter, those problems only got worse. Midway through the season, Odom sat Woods down for seven games, telling him to take time off and to get his head together. Woods came back for the last seven games of the regular season but played a relatively minor role. He went scoreless in Wake's opening-round NIT victory over North Carolina–Wilmington, then didn't play at all in the loss to Vanderbilt that ended the season.

That game proved to be his last in a Wake Forest uniform. He and Odom agreed that it would be best for him to go someplace where he could sit out a year and start fresh. That place proved to be Arizona.

While Woods did almost nothing and the senior class — Tony Rutland, Jerry Braswell, and Steve Goolsby — played with the same kind of inconsistency that had plagued them as juniors, Wake's freshmen were superb, most notably ACC rookie of the year Robert O'Kelly, who was the team's leading scorer at 16.6 points per game. With O'Kelly and three other sophomores projected to come back, along with a strong freshman class (again), Odom was convinced that Wake's NCAA tournament absence — its first since 1990 — would be only temporary.

For the ACC as a whole, 1998 was almost eerily similar to 1997. Once again, North Carolina was the only league team to reach the Final Four. Duke got to the final eight, Maryland to the round of sixteen, Florida State to the second round, and Clemson lost in the first round. But once again the Final Four proved lethal to the Tar Heels. In fact, their loss to Utah in 1998 was a lot worse than their loss to Arizona in 1997.

In losing to Arizona, Carolina simply lost a basketball game. In falling to Utah, the Tar Heels lost a large chunk of their integrity.

The culprit — not surprisingly — was Mahktar Ndiaye. Ndiaye fouled out of the game, his fourth foul a technical for flagrantly swinging an elbow. That was the least of his crimes. During the first half, frustrated because he was being outplayed, Ndiaye spit on Utah freshman Brett Johnsen. After the game, when asked about the incident, Ndiaye denied spitting on Johnsen and then claimed that Johnsen had called him a nigger.

The next day, at Utah's prechampionship press conference, Utah coach Rick Majerus angrily denied the charge (as did Johnsen) and said he would be willing to fly Johnsen to North Carolina to take a lie detector test. "If he's lying," Majerus said, "I will resign on the spot."

The gauntlet had been laid down. The next day, back in Chapel Hill, Guthridge met with Ndiaye. When the meeting was over, North Carolina issued a statement from Ndiaye in which he apologized to Johnsen and admitted that he had lied about the racial epithet. No apology or admission was going to be enough in this situation. Ndiaye had humiliated himself, his team, and his school. If it was possible to make matters worse, he did. After being accused of assault later in the spring, Ndiaye was asked during his trial about the fact that he had publicly admitted to lying in the wake of the Johnsen incident. Ndiaye then claimed he had nothing to do with the statement that had been put out under his name, that the athletic department had issued it without ever consulting with him.

Ndiaye had now done the impossible: he had even turned Carolina people against him. Sports information director Steve Kirschner was outraged when he heard what Ndiaye had said and didn't hesitate to say he was outraged publicly. "He was calling into question my integrity, Coach Guthridge's integrity, and the entire athletic department's integrity," he said.

The saddest part of the whole ugly incident was that it sullied a magical year for Guthridge and Carolina. With the winningest coach of all time watching from the sidelines, Guthridge took his team to a 34–4 record, an ACC tournament title, and the Final Four. He proved emphatically that life as a head coach can begin at sixty. But he walked away from what should have been a wonderful season with the spectre of Ndiaye and his inexcusable behavior hanging over his head.

Thankfully for Carolina, Ndiaye was finally out of eligibility. The Tar Heels would start anew in October with a brilliant freshman class and bright hopes for what was to come next. But Duke also had a lot to look forward to, as did Maryland. And Wake Forest and Georgia Tech and NC State and Clemson and Florida State and even rebuilding Virginia.

In the ACC, the end of a season is never an ending. It is merely an intermission. A new act begins every October.

Acknowledgments

ONCE, ACCORDING TO LEGEND, when Ernest Hemingway was struggling to finish a book, he was lamenting his choice of profession to a friend. The friend expressed shock that he could say such things about his craft. "But, Ernest," he cried in protest, "you love writing!"

"Wrong," Hemingway answered. "I love having written."

So, as it turns out, Hemingway and I have one thing in common.

But I do love writing acknowledgments. They give me a chance to remember people I spent time with on a project, and to become nostalgic about a book that isn't even in bookstores yet.

These are the people who made this book possible and, if truth be told, a lot of fun.

I have to start, of course, with the nine ACC coaches. Without their cooperation, this book never would have gotten past the idea stage. Rick Barnes, Bobby Cremins, Jeff Jones, Pat Kennedy, Mike Krzyzewski, Dave Odom, and Gary Williams all gave me extraordinary access to themselves and their teams and countless hours of interview time. Herb Sendek and Dean Smith gave me all the interview time I requested, though neither felt comfortable giving me the access I had from the other seven. That was, of course, their prerogative, and explains why my descriptions of their teams and games are not as detailed as they are of the other seven. But I believe they were open enough with me that I was able to give a fairly complete portrait of each of them.

One other note on the coaches. You have heard most of them use profanity in this book. I know there are some people who find these words offensive. But almost every coach alive, especially at the college and pro level, uses these words in varying degrees. Dean Smith is an exception. I have quoted coaches using profanity only when I believe it is important to the telling of a particular story or when they were using the word or words to make a point. Understand one other thing: most college athletes use a lot of profanity, especially in the heat of competition. For most coaches, using it is a way of speaking to the players in their own language. Perhaps in a utopian society that wouldn't be true. In this society, it is a fact of life.

While the coaches are the linchpin to this book, there were people at all nine schools who aided me immeasurably: *all* the assistant coaches, who are too numerous to name here, were patient and, for the most part, forthcoming. The sports information staffs — Chuck Walsh at Maryland; Rich Murray, Doyle Smith, and Mike Colley at Virginia; Mark Bockelman and Joan von Thron at NC State; Rick Brewer and Steve Kirschner at North Carolina; Mike Cragg, Tom Kosempa, and Lori Winters at Duke; John Justis and Dan Zacharias at Wake Forest; Tim Bourret at Clemson; Mike Finn, Allison George, and Mike Stamus at Georgia Tech; and Rob Wilson and Chris Walker at Florida State — all bent over backwards (and in some cases beyond) to help me throughout the season and after the season was over. The same is true for the office staffs in each of the nine basketball offices, all of whom no doubt got sick and tired of hearing from me by the time April rolled around.

The people who run the ACC had no idea what to make of this book, but they could not have been more helpful. Gene Corrigan was supportive; Fred Barakat not only took my phone calls in the toughest of times, he always answered my questions honestly. Tom Mickle was merely Tom Mickle, which means he was (and is) a great friend and the brightest and most creative athletic administrator I know. Brian Morrison took care of all my needs, especially during the grueling ACC tournament week.

Every author rambles on about how wonderful his editor and agent are. What's funny is when you pick up the author's next book and they are going on at length about his editor and his agent — and they're different than the great guys he worked with on the last book. I've only had one agent in my life, Esther Newberg, and, unless she drops me someday for saying the wrong thing about her beloved UConn Huskies (which I'm too smart even to consider doing) that will never change. I've said it before, but it bears repeating: she is the best agent there is and a better friend. Her assistant at ICM, Jack Horner, is a very patient (not to mention efficient) man.

Michael Pietsch is also very patient. To be my editor, you must be that — in spades — extremely flexible and able to calm a frazzled writer at any and all hours of the day. Michael does all of that and more. He even laughs at my jokes and is always willing to eat Chinese food. He also had the good sense to hire Nora Krug as his assistant at Little, Brown and Company. That was his gain and my good fortune, although not always so great for Nora.

I gave up the notion of listing all my friends several books ago because invariably I would leave somebody out and that person's distress always seemed to be the one thing I remembered about the book. For this book, a few friends have to be mentioned because they were directly involved in its creation: Bill Brill, Keith Drum, Jill Mickle, Doug Doughty, David Teel, Terry Hanson, Ken Rosenthal, Dave Kindred, Tony Kornheiser, and David Maraniss all contributed advice and support throughout the process. Norbert Doyle was willing to contribute every last bit of his college basketball expertise. Wes Seeley was Wes Seeley. Enough said.

And, of course, my family. Mary, Danny, and Brigid are the ones who keep me going when I'm exhausted or convinced I'll never get to the finish line on a project. Dad, Margaret, and Bobby have put up with me for forever, and all my in-laws — Jennifer, Kacky, Annie, Jimmy, Brendan, Stan, and Gregg — have become good friends. My parents-in-law, Jim and Arlene, are the best and my brother-in-law, David Sattler, helped me buy my first real computer and then spent countless hours counseling me not to smash the thing to smithereens when I couldn't make it work.

This book involved a lot of travel and a lot of work. There were some long nights on the highway and in airports and hotels. But there were also some remarkable nights, a lot of superb games, and many moments I will never forget.

One stands out. Late in the North Carolina–Duke game in Cameron Indoor Stadium, there was a time-out. Duke led by one. As I stood at the edge of the Duke huddle listening to Mike Krzyzewski calmly describe the play he wanted his players to run, I looked around the building. Everyone was standing, even the fans upstairs. The students were chanting and cheering all at once. The place was absolutely electric.

I felt a chill run through me. There wasn't going to be a better college basketball game played this season in a better atmosphere than this one. And I was smack in the middle of it, as inside as anyone not playing or coaching could possibly hope to be. Right then and there, I realized how lucky I am. To be inside the ACC for an entire season, to get the view from the floor — and the locker room — night after night and get paid to do it. What more could someone who loves basketball possibly ask for?

Mike Krzyzewski likes to describe every basketball season as a journey. This was my journey. I can say without hesitation, it was one hell of a ride.

John Feinstein
Bethesda, Maryland

Index

Look for these other books by John Feinstein

A Good Walk Spoiled
Days and Nights on the PGA Tour

"The best-ever account of life on the PGA tour.... A good read rewarded."
— *Golf*

"The golf tour's true heart.... Feinstein gets it right."
— *New York Times Book Review*

"*A Good Walk Spoiled* is as close as most people will get to understanding the guys they watch on TV each week hitting magnificent shots and missing meaningful putts. . . . Feinstein, as always, is observant, insightful, and amusing."
— *Golfweek*

"A winner.... The action never drags. It's fascinating inside stuff and, best of all, it's fun."
— *GolfWorld*

NOW IN PAPERBACK • BACK BAY BOOKS

A Civil War
Army vs. Navy — A Year Inside College Football's Purest Rivalry

"The best college football story of the year."
— *Chicago Sun-Times*

"Highly readable. . . . Feinstein is an outstanding chronicler of the game as a game."
— *Houston Chronicle*

"An excellent book.... With Army-Navy, you always get your money's worth."
— *Wall Street Journal*

NOW IN PAPERBACK • BACK BAY BOOKS

The Majors
In Pursuit of Golf's Holy Grail

Feinstein returns to the world of his #1 bestseller *A Good Walk Spoiled* in this behind-the-scenes look at the most competitive events in golf — the four tournaments known as "the majors."

ARRIVING AT BOOKSTORES IN APRIL 1999

 Little, Brown and Company   AVAILABLE WHEREVER BOOKS ARE SOLD